LLEWELLYN'S SUN SIGN BOOK

Forecasts by
Gloria Star

Book Editing and Design: K. M. Brielmaier
Cover Art: Kristi Schaeppi/RKB Studios
Cover Design: William Merlin Cannon
Copyright 2000

Llewellyn Publications
A Division of Llewellyn Worldwide, Ltd.
P.O. Box 64383 Dept. K965-2 St. Paul, MN 55164-0383

2000

JANUARY
S	M	T	W	T	F	S
						1
2	3	4	5	6	7	8
9	10	11	12	13	14	15
16	17	18	19	20	21	22
23	24	25	26	27	28	29
30	31					

FEBRUARY
S	M	T	W	T	F	S
		1	2	3	4	5
6	7	8	9	10	11	12
13	14	15	16	17	18	19
20	21	22	23	24	25	26
27	28	29				

MARCH
S	M	T	W	T	F	S
			1	2	3	4
5	6	7	8	9	10	11
12	13	14	15	16	17	18
19	20	21	22	23	24	25
26	27	28	29	30	31	

APRIL
S	M	T	W	T	F	S
						1
2	3	4	5	6	7	8
9	10	11	12	13	14	15
16	17	18	19	20	21	22
23	24	25	26	27	28	29
30						

MAY
S	M	T	W	T	F	S
	1	2	3	4	5	6
7	8	9	10	11	12	13
14	15	16	17	18	19	20
21	22	23	24	25	26	27
28	29	30	31			

JUNE
S	M	T	W	T	F	S
				1	2	3
4	5	6	7	8	9	10
11	12	13	14	15	16	17
18	19	20	21	22	23	24
25	26	27	28	29	30	

JULY
S	M	T	W	T	F	S
						1
2	3	4	5	6	7	8
9	10	11	12	13	14	15
16	17	18	19	20	21	22
23	24	25	26	27	28	29
30	31					

AUGUST
S	M	T	W	T	F	S
		1	2	3	4	5
6	7	8	9	10	11	12
13	14	15	16	17	18	19
20	21	22	23	24	25	26
27	28	29	30	31		

SEPTEMBER
S	M	T	W	T	F	S
					1	2
3	4	5	6	7	8	9
10	11	12	13	14	15	16
17	18	19	20	21	22	23
24	25	26	27	28	29	30

OCTOBER
S	M	T	W	T	F	S
1	2	3	4	5	6	7
8	9	10	11	12	13	14
15	16	17	18	19	20	21
22	23	24	25	26	27	28
29	30	31				

NOVEMBER
S	M	T	W	T	F	S
			1	2	3	4
5	6	7	8	9	10	11
12	13	14	15	16	17	18
19	20	21	22	23	24	25
26	27	28	29	30		

DECEMBER
S	M	T	W	T	F	S
					1	2
3	4	5	6	7	8	9
10	11	12	13	14	15	16
17	18	19	20	21	22	23
24	25	26	27	28	29	30
31						

2001

JANUARY
S	M	T	W	T	F	S
	1	2	3	4	5	6
7	8	9	10	11	12	13
14	15	16	17	18	19	20
21	22	23	24	25	26	27
28	29	30	31			

FEBRUARY
S	M	T	W	T	F	S
				1	2	3
4	5	6	7	8	9	10
11	12	13	14	15	16	17
18	19	20	21	22	23	24
25	26	27	28			

MARCH
S	M	T	W	T	F	S
				1	2	3
4	5	6	7	8	9	10
11	12	13	14	15	16	17
18	19	20	21	22	23	24
25	26	27	28	29	30	31

APRIL
S	M	T	W	T	F	S
1	2	3	4	5	6	7
8	9	10	11	12	13	14
15	16	17	18	19	20	21
22	23	24	25	26	27	28
29	30					

MAY
S	M	T	W	T	F	S
		1	2	3	4	5
6	7	8	9	10	11	12
13	14	15	16	17	18	19
20	21	22	23	24	25	26
27	28	29	30	31		

JUNE
S	M	T	W	T	F	S
					1	2
3	4	5	6	7	8	9
10	11	12	13	14	15	16
17	18	19	20	21	22	23
24	25	26	27	28	29	30

JULY
S	M	T	W	T	F	S
1	2	3	4	5	6	7
8	9	10	11	12	13	14
15	16	17	18	19	20	21
22	23	24	25	26	27	28
29	30	31				

AUGUST
S	M	T	W	T	F	S
			1	2	3	4
5	6	7	8	9	10	11
12	13	14	15	16	17	18
19	20	21	22	23	24	25
26	27	28	29	30	31	

SEPTEMBER
S	M	T	W	T	F	S
						1
2	3	4	5	6	7	8
9	10	11	12	13	14	15
16	17	18	19	20	21	22
23	24	25	26	27	28	29
30						

OCTOBER
S	M	T	W	T	F	S
	1	2	3	4	5	6
7	8	9	10	11	12	13
14	15	16	17	18	19	20
21	22	23	24	25	26	27
28	29	30	31			

NOVEMBER
S	M	T	W	T	F	S
				1	2	3
4	5	6	7	8	9	10
11	12	13	14	15	16	17
18	19	20	21	22	23	24
25	26	27	28	29	30	

DECEMBER
S	M	T	W	T	F	S
						1
2	3	4	5	6	7	8
9	10	11	12	13	14	15
16	17	18	19	20	21	22
23	24	25	26	27	28	29
30	31					

2002

JANUARY
S	M	T	W	T	F	S
		1	2	3	4	5
6	7	8	9	10	11	12
13	14	15	16	17	18	19
20	21	22	23	24	25	26
27	28	29	30	31		

FEBRUARY
S	M	T	W	T	F	S
					1	2
3	4	5	6	7	8	9
10	11	12	13	14	15	16
17	18	19	20	21	22	23
24	25	26	27	28		

MARCH
S	M	T	W	T	F	S
					1	2
3	4	5	6	7	8	9
10	11	12	13	14	15	16
17	18	19	20	21	22	23
24	25	26	27	28	29	30
31						

APRIL
S	M	T	W	T	F	S
	1	2	3	4	5	6
7	8	9	10	11	12	13
14	15	16	17	18	19	20
21	22	23	24	25	26	27
28	29	30				

MAY
S	M	T	W	T	F	S
			1	2	3	4
5	6	7	8	9	10	11
12	13	14	15	16	17	18
19	20	21	22	23	24	25
26	27	28	29	30	31	

JUNE
S	M	T	W	T	F	S
						1
2	3	4	5	6	7	8
9	10	11	12	13	14	15
16	17	18	19	20	21	22
23	24	25	26	27	28	29
30						

JULY
S	M	T	W	T	F	S
	1	2	3	4	5	6
7	8	9	10	11	12	13
14	15	16	17	18	19	20
21	22	23	24	25	26	27
28	29	30	31			

AUGUST
S	M	T	W	T	F	S
				1	2	3
4	5	6	7	8	9	10
11	12	13	14	15	16	17
18	19	20	21	22	23	24
25	26	27	28	29	30	31

SEPTEMBER
S	M	T	W	T	F	S
1	2	3	4	5	6	7
8	9	10	11	12	13	14
15	16	17	18	19	20	21
22	23	24	25	26	27	28
29	30					

OCTOBER
S	M	T	W	T	F	S
		1	2	3	4	5
6	7	8	9	10	11	12
13	14	15	16	17	18	19
20	21	22	23	24	25	26
27	28	29	30	31		

NOVEMBER
S	M	T	W	T	F	S
					1	2
3	4	5	6	7	8	9
10	11	12	13	14	15	16
17	18	19	20	21	22	23
24	25	26	27	28	29	30

DECEMBER
S	M	T	W	T	F	S
1	2	3	4	5	6	7
8	9	10	11	12	13	14
15	16	17	18	19	20	21
22	23	24	25	26	27	28
29	30	31				

Table of Contents

Meet Gloria Star 5
New Concepts for Signs of the Zodiac 6
Understanding the Basics of Astrology 8
Signs of the Zodiac 9
The Planets 10
Using this Book 11
2001 at a Glance 12
Ascendant Table 14
Astrological Glossary 16
Meanings of the Planets 22

2001 Sun Sign Forecasts

Aries 28
Taurus 51
Gemini 74
Cancer 97
Leo 120
Virgo 143
Libra 166
Scorpio 189
Sagittarius 212
Capricorn 235
Aquarius 258
Pisces 281

2001 Sun Sign Articles

The Twelve Houses of the Zodiac 304

Rising Signs
  by Sasha Fenton 306

New Age Love: Romance and Your Sun Sign
  by Marguerite Elsbeth 318

The Sun in Relationships:
Your Path to Vitality and Happiness in Love
  by David Pond 328

House Hunting and Your Sun Sign
  by Alice DeVille 344

How Your Sun Sign Affects Your Career
  by Stephanie Clement 360

The Sun, the Moon, and Compatibility
  by Dorothy Oja 374

Solar Returns
  by Joanne Wickenburg 391

When the Atman Meets the Dragon:
How the Sun and Lunar Nodes Interact
  by Therese Francis 399

Economic Forecasts for 2001
  by Kaye Shinker 414

Coming of Age: World Predictions for 2001
  by Leeda Alleyn Pacotti 432

Activities Ruled by the Planets 445

Planetary Business Guide 446

Planetary Associations 447

About the Authors 448

Meet Gloria Star

All horoscopes and sign descriptions for this book were written by Gloria Star. An internationally renowned astrologer, author, and teacher, Gloria has been a professional astrologer for over two decades. She has written for the *Sun Sign Book* for Llewellyn since 1990, and has been a contributing author of the *Moon Sign Book* since 1995. Her most recent work, *Astrology: Woman to Woman*, was released by Llewellyn in April 1999. Her feature column, "Hortiscope," appears in *Rebecca's Garden Magazine*. She is the author of *Optimum Child: Developing Your Child's Fullest Potential through Astrology*, now translated into four languages. She also edited and coauthored the book *Astrology for Women: Roles and Relationships* (Llewellyn 1997). Her astrological computer software, *Woman to Woman*, was released by Matrix Software in 1997. Ms. Star has also contributed to the anthologies *Houses: Power Places in the Horoscope* (Llewellyn 1990), and *How to Manage the Astrology of Crisis* (Llewellyn 1993).

Listed in *Who's Who of American Women*, and *Who's Who in the East*, Gloria has been honored as a nominee for the prestigious Regulus Award. She has served on the faculty of the United Astrology Congress (UAC) since its inception in 1986, and has lectured for groups and conferences throughout the U.S. and abroad. A member of the Advisory Board for the National Council for Geocosmic Research (NCGR), she also served on the Steering Committee for the Association for Astrological Networking (AFAN), was editor of the *AFAN Newsletter* from 1992-1997, and is now on the AFAN Advisory Board. She currently resides in the shoreline township of Clinton, Connecticut.

New Concepts for Signs of the Zodiac

The signs of the zodiac represent characteristics and traits that indicate how energy operates within our lives. The signs tell the story of human evolution and development, and all are necessary to form the continuum of whole life experience. In fact, all twelve signs are represented within your astrological chart.

Although the traditional metaphors for the twelve signs (such as Aries, the Ram) are always functional, these alternative concepts for each of the twelve signs also describe the gradual unfolding of the human spirit.

Aries: The Initiator is the first sign of the zodiac and encompasses the primary concept of getting things started. This fiery ignition and bright beginning can prove to be the thrust necessary for new life, but the Initiator also can appear before a situation is ready for change and create disruption.

Taurus: The Maintainer sustains what Aries has begun and brings stability and focus into the picture, yet there also can be a tendency to try to maintain something in its current state without allowing for new growth.

Gemini: The Questioner seeks to determine whether alternatives are possible and offers diversity to the processes Taurus has brought into stability. Yet questioning can also lead to distraction, subsequently scattering energy and diffusing focus.

Cancer: The Nurturer provides the qualities necessary for growth and security, and encourages a deepening awareness of emotional needs. Yet this same nurturing can stifle individuation if it becomes smothering.

Leo: The Loyalist directs and centralizes the experiences Cancer feeds. This quality is powerfully targeted toward self-awareness, but can be shortsighted. Hence, the Loyalist can hold steadfastly to viewpoints or feelings that inhibit new experiences.

Virgo: The Modifier analyzes the situations Leo brings to light and determines possibilities for change. Even though this change may be in the name of improvement, it can lead to dissatisfaction with the self if not directed in harmony with higher needs.

Libra: The Judge is constantly comparing everything to be sure that a certain level of rightness and perfection is presented. However, the Judge can also present possibilities that are harsh and seem to be cold or without feeling.

Scorpio: The Catalyst steps into the play of life to provide the quality of alchemical transformation. The Catalyst can stir the brew just enough to create a healing potion, or may get things going to such a powerful extent that they boil out of control.

Sagittarius: The Adventurer moves away from Scorpio's dimension to seek what lies beyond the horizon. The Adventurer continually looks for possibilities that answer the ultimate questions, but may forget the pathway back home.

Capricorn: The Pragmatist attempts to put everything into its rightful place and find ways to make life work out right. The Pragmatist can teach lessons of practicality and determination, but can become highly self-righteous when shortsighted.

Aquarius: The Reformer looks for ways to take what Capricorn has built and bring it up to date. Yet there is also a tendency to scrap the original in favor of a new plan that may not have the stable foundation necessary to operate effectively.

Pisces: The Visionary brings mysticism and imagination, and challenges the soul to move beyond the physical plane, into the realm of what might be. The Visionary can pierce the veil, returning enlightened to the physical world. The challenge is to avoid getting lost within the illusion of an alternate reality.

Understanding the Basics of Astrology

Astrology is an ancient and continually evolving system used to clarify your identity and your needs. An astrological chart—which is calculated using the date, time, and place of birth—contains many factors which symbolically represent the needs, expressions, and experiences that make up the whole person. A professional astrologer interprets this symbolic picture, offering you an accurate portrait of your personality.

The chart itself—the horoscope—is a portrait of an individual. Generally, a natal (or birth) horoscope is drawn on a circular wheel. The wheel is divided into twelve segments, called houses. Each of the twelve houses represents a different aspect of the individual, much like the facets of a brilliantly cut stone. The houses depict different environments, such as home, school, and work. The houses also represent roles and relationships: parents, friends, lovers, children, partners. In each environment, individuals show a different side of their personality. At home, you may represent yourself quite differently than you do on the job. Additionally, in each relationship you will project a different image of yourself. Your parents rarely see the side you show to intimate friends.

Symbols for the planets, the Sun, and the Moon are drawn inside the houses. Each planet represents a separate kind of energy. You experience and express that energy in specific ways. (For a complete list, refer to the table on the next page.) The way you use each of these energies is up to you. The planets in your chart do not make you do anything!

The twelve signs of the zodiac indicate characteristics and traits that further define your personality. Each sign can be expressed in positive and negative ways. (The basic meaning of each of the signs is explained in the corresponding sections ahead.) What's more, you have all twelve signs somewhere in your chart. Signs that are strongly emphasized by the planets have greater force. The Sun, Moon, and planets are placed on the chart according to their position at the time of birth. The qualities of a sign, combined with the

Signs of the Zodiac

Aries	♈	The Initiator
Taurus	♉	The Maintainer
Gemini	♊	The Questioner
Cancer	♋	The Nurturer
Leo	♌	The Loyalist
Virgo	♍	The Modifier
Libra	♎	The Judge
Scorpio	♏	The Catalyst
Sagittarius	♐	The Adventurer
Capricorn	♑	The Pragmatist
Aquarius	♒	The Reformer
Pisces	♓	The Visionary

energy of a planet, indicate how you might be most likely to use that energy and the best ways to develop that energy. The signs add color, emphasis, and dimension to the personality.

Signs are also placed at the cusps, or dividing lines, of each of the houses. The influence of the signs on the houses is much the same as their influence on the Sun, Moon, and planets. Each house is shaped by the sign on its cusp.

When you view a horoscope, you will notice that there appear to be four distinctive angles dividing the wheel of the chart. The line that divides the chart into a top and bottom half represents the horizon. In most cases, the left side of the horizon is called the Ascendant. The zodiac sign on the Ascendant is your rising sign. The Ascendant indicates the way others are likely to view you.

The Sun, Moon, or planet can be compared to an actor in a play. The sign shows how the energy works, like the role the actor plays in a drama. The house indicates where the energy operates, like the setting of a play. On a psychological level, the Sun represents who

The Planets

Sun	☉	The ego, self, willpower
Moon	☽	The subconscious self, habits
Mercury	☿	Communication, the intellect
Venus	♀	Emotional expression, love, appreciation, artistry
Mars	♂	Physical drive, assertiveness, anger
Jupiter	♃	Philosophy, ethics, generosity
Saturn	♄	Discipline, focus, responsibility
Uranus	♅	Individuality, rebelliousness
Neptune	♆	Imagination, sensitivity, compassion
Pluto	♇	Transformation, healing, regeneration

you think you are. The Ascendant describes who others think you are, and the Moon reflects your inner self.

Astrologers also study the geometric relationships between the Sun, Moon, and planets. These geometric angles are called aspects. Aspects further define the strengths, weaknesses, and challenges within your physical, mental, emotional, and spiritual self. Sometimes, patterns also appear in an astrological chart. These patterns have meaning.

To understand cycles for any given point in time, astrologers study several factors. Many use transits, which refer to the movement and positions of the planets. When astrologers compare those positions to the birth horoscope, the transits indicate activity in particular areas of the chart. The *Sun Sign Book* uses transits.

As you can see, your Sun sign is just one of many factors that describes who you are—but it is a powerful one! As the symbol of the ego, the Sun in your chart reflects your drive to be noticed. Most people can easily relate to the concepts associated with their Sun sign, since it is tied to their sense of personal identity.

Using this Book

Although we can examine a number of your needs and life situations from this information, working one-on-one with a professional astrologer would let you explore many other factors to help guide you. If you would like more information, you might appreciate the personalized insights you'll receive from a professional astrologer.

I've described the year's major challenges and opportunities for every Sun sign in the "Year Ahead" section. The first part of each section applies to all individuals born under the sign. I've also included information for specific birth dates that will help you understand the inner changes you'll experience during 2001. The section illustrates your fundamental themes for the year ahead. They will be the underlying principles present throughout the year. These cycles comprise your major challenges and opportunities relating to your personal identity. Blend these ideas with the information you find in the monthly forecast section for your Sun sign and Ascendant.

To best use the information in the monthly forecasts, you'll want to determine your Ascendant or rising sign. If you don't know your Ascendant, the tables following this description will help you determine your rising sign. They are most accurate for those born in the continental United States. They're only an approximation, but they can be used as a good rule of thumb. Your exact Ascendant may vary from the tables according to your time and place of birth. Once you've approximated your ascending sign using the tables or determined your Ascendant by having your chart calculated, you'll know two significant factors in your chart. Read the monthly forecast sections for both your Sun and Ascendant to gain the most useful information.

Your "Rewarding and Challenging Days" sections indicate times when you'll feel either more centered or more out of balance. The rewarding days are not the only times you can perform well, but the times you're likely to feel better integrated! During challenging days, take extra time to center yourself by meditating or using other techniques that help you feel more objective.

These guidelines, although highly useful, cannot incorporate all the factors influencing your current life situation. However, you can use this information for an objective awareness about the way the current cycles are affecting you. Realize that the power of astrology is even more useful when you have a complete chart and professional guidance.

2001 at a Glance

Now that we've entered the doorway of a new century, it's important to take a look at what we want to create. The year 2001 is a year of ideas, and we as the human race will have ample opportunities to witness the workings of the Law of Mind: what you think, you become. Social responsibility is an important feature of this year, and it's time to embrace our common threads, interweaving them with the delights of our wide variations in cultural and individual expression. "Human rights" is more than a term now—it's the challenge for the year.

Globally and economically, the Information Age is becoming quite powerful, and the cycles this year indicate wide-ranging advances in technology which will enhance our ability to obtain and share information. Travel and transportation industries are also key players in the cycles for 2001, and that includes the space industry. Signs of intelligent life beyond planet Earth may become more noteworthy. Additionally, media influence will grow even stronger during these cycles. Although the Internet seems more commonplace, the extensions of this development have a much stronger impact during 2001, adding a more stable feature to the economy and becoming especially influential in education. In fact, education may become a chief issue politically, with businesses and communities recognizing that educational innovations are now absolutely necessary in order to prepare children for the world of tomorrow. The voices of youth become prominent during 2001 and 2002, and the choices and directions pursued by young adults will likely have a great impact on the roles of educational institutions.

On a more personal level, family and community are challenged to evolve, too. The eclipse cycles of 2001 signify challenges to outworn traditions, but also indicate a need for connection and support—based upon trust and shared ideals. Shared ideals can provide a powerful and positive link in a world which provides more and more isolation. Yet, it's the illusion of connection that can become a problem itself. After all, a person can sit at a computer and "chat" with someone on the other side of the world, but there may or may not be an honest interchange happening. Seeking out friends who share your ideals and aspirations, making contact, becoming involved in common goals—these are the experiences most likely to drive each of us to embrace something beyond information alone.

The planetary cycles suggest that our needs for contact are growing stronger. Yet there is the danger of polarization, too. What began during the last quarter of 2000 with an opposition from Jupiter to Pluto continues into 2001: alterations in the justice system, the laws, and the educational processes are all being driven by our need to make positive transformational changes. Where greed and abuses of power have eroded some of our values, we, as a collective, now have a chance to reclaim values based upon honesty, truth, and wisdom. What remains to be seen is whether or not we're up to the task!

My warmest wishes to you and your loved ones for a truly prosperous and joy-filled year.

Ascendant Table

Your Time of Birth

Your Sun Sign	6–8 am	8–10 am	10 am–Noon	Noon–2 pm	2–4 pm	4–6 pm
Aries	Taurus	Gemini	Cancer	Leo	Virgo	Libra
Taurus	Gemini	Cancer	Leo	Virgo	Libra	Scorpio
Gemini	Cancer	Leo	Virgo	Libra	Scorpio	Sagittarius
Cancer	Leo	Virgo	Libra	Scorpio	Sagittarius	Capricorn
Leo	Virgo	Libra	Scorpio	Sagittarius	Capricorn	Aquarius
Virgo	Libra	Scorpio	Sagittarius	Capricorn	Aquarius	Pisces
Libra	Scorpio	Sagittarius	Capricorn	Aquarius	Pisces	Aries
Scorpio	Sagittarius	Capricorn	Aquarius	Pisces	Aries	Taurus
Sagittarius	Capricorn	Aquarius	Pisces	Aries	Taurus	Gemini
Capricorn	Aquarius	Pisces	Aries	Taurus	Gemini	Cancer
Aquarius	Pisces	Aries	Taurus	Gemini	Cancer	Leo
Pisces	Aries	Taurus	Gemini	Cancer	Leo	Virgo

Ascendant Table

Your Time of Birth

Your Sun Sign	6–8 pm	8–10 pm	10 pm–Midnight	Midnight–2 am	2–4 am	4–6 am
Aries	Scorpio	Sagittarius	Capricorn	Aquarius	Pisces	Aries
Taurus	Sagittarius	Capricorn	Aquarius	Pisces	Aries	Taurus
Gemini	Capricorn	Aquarius	Pisces	Aries	Taurus	Gemini
Cancer	Aquarius	Pisces	Aries	Taurus	Gemini	Cancer
Leo	Pisces	Aries	Taurus	Gemini	Cancer	Leo
Virgo	Aries	Taurus	Gemini	Cancer	Leo	Virgo
Libra	Taurus	Gemini	Cancer	Leo	Virgo	Libra
Scorpio	Gemini	Cancer	Leo	Virgo	Libra	Scorpio
Sagittarius	Cancer	Leo	Virgo	Libra	Scorpio	Sagittarius
Capricorn	Leo	Virgo	Libra	Scorpio	Sagittarius	Capricorn
Aquarius	Virgo	Libra	Scorpio	Sagittarius	Capricorn	Aquarius
Pisces	Libra	Scorpio	Sagittarius	Capricorn	Aquarius	Pisces

How to use this table:
1. Find your Sun sign in the left column.
2. Find your approximate birth time in a vertical column.
3. Line up your Sun sign and birth time to find your Ascendant.

This table will give you an approximation of your Ascendant. If you feel that the sign listed as your Ascendant is incorrect, try the one either before or after the listed sign. It is difficult to determine your exact Ascendant without a complete natal chart.

Astrological Glossary

Air—One of the four basic elements. The air signs are Gemini, Libra, and Aquarius.

Angles—The four points of the chart that divide it into quadrants. The angles are sensitive areas that lend emphasis to planets located near them. These points are located on the cusps of the First, Fourth, Seventh, and Tenth Houses in a chart.

Ascendant—Rising sign. The degree of the zodiac on the eastern horizon at the time and place for which the horoscope is calculated. It can indicate the image or physical appearance you project to the world. The cusp of the First House.

Aspect—The angular relationship between planets, sensitive points, or house cusps in a horoscope. Lines drawn between the two points and the center of the chart, representing the Earth, form the angle of the aspect. Astrological aspects include conjunction (two points that are 0 degrees apart), opposition (two points, 180 degrees apart), square (two points, 90 degrees apart), sextile (two points, 60 degrees apart), and trine (two points, 120 degrees apart). Aspects can indicate harmony or challenge.

Cardinal Sign—One of the three qualities, or categories, that describe how a sign expresses itself. Aries, Cancer, Libra, and Capricorn are the cardinal signs, believed to initiate activity.

Chiron—Chiron is a comet traveling in orbit between Saturn and Uranus. Although research on its effect on natal charts is not yet complete, it is believed to represent a key or doorway, healing, ecology, and a bridge between traditional and modern methods.

Conjunction—An aspect or angle between two points in a chart where the two points are close enough so that the energies join. Can be considered either harmonious or challenging, depending on the planets involved and their placement.

Cusp—A dividing line between signs or houses in a chart.

Degree—Degree of arc. One of 360 divisions of a circle. The circle of the zodiac is divided into twelve astrological signs of 30 degrees each. Each degree is made up of 60 minutes, and each minute is made up of 60 seconds of zodiacal longitude.

Earth—One of the four basic elements. The earth signs are Taurus, Virgo, and Capricorn.

Eclipse—A solar eclipse is the full or partial covering of the Sun by the Moon (as viewed from Earth), and a lunar eclipse is the full or partial covering of the Moon by the Earth's own shadow.

Ecliptic—The Sun's apparent path around the Earth, which is actually the plane of the Earth's orbit extended out into space. The ecliptic forms the center of the zodiac.

Electional Astrology—A branch of astrology concerned with choosing the best time to initiate an activity.

Elements—The signs of the zodiac are divided into four groups of three zodiacal signs, each symbolized by one of the four elements of the ancients: fire, earth, air, and water. The element of a sign is said to express its essential nature.

Ephemeris—A listing of the Sun, Moon, and planets' positions and related information for astrological purposes.

Equinox—Equal night. The point in the Earth's orbit around the Sun at which the day and night are equal in length.

Feminine Signs—Each zodiac sign is either masculine or feminine. Earth signs (Taurus, Virgo, and Capricorn) and water signs (Cancer, Scorpio, and Pisces) are feminine.

Fire—One of the four basic elements. The fire signs are Aries, Leo, and Sagittarius.

Fixed Signs—Fixed is one of the three qualities, or categories, that describe how a sign expresses itself. The fixed signs are Taurus, Leo, Scorpio, and Aquarius. Fixed signs are said to be predisposed to existing patterns and somewhat resistant to change.

Hard Aspects—Hard aspects are those aspects in a chart that astrologers believe to represent difficulty or challenges. Among the hard aspects are the square, the opposition, and the conjunction (depending on which planets are conjunct).

Horizon—The word horizon is used in astrology in a manner similar to its common usage, except that only the eastern and western horizons are considered useful. The eastern horizon at the point of birth is the Ascendant, or First House cusp, of a natal chart, and the western horizon at the point of birth is the Descendant, or Seventh House cusp.

Houses—Division of the horoscope into twelve segments, beginning with the Ascendant. The dividing line between the houses are called house cusps. Each house corresponds to certain aspects of daily living, and is ruled by the astrological sign that governs the cusp, or dividing line between the house and the one previous.

Ingress—The point of entry of a planet into a sign.

Lagna—A term used in Hindu or Vedic astrology for Ascendant, the degree of the zodiac on the eastern horizon at the time of birth.

Masculine Signs—Each of the twelve signs of the zodiac is either "masculine" or "feminine." The fire signs (Aries, Leo, and Sagittarius) and the air signs (Gemini, Libra, and Aquarius) are masculine.

Midheaven—The highest point on the ecliptic, where it intersects the meridian that passes directly above the place for which the horoscope is cast; the southern point of the horoscope.

Midpoint—A point equally distant to two planets or house cusps. Midpoints are considered by some astrologers to be sensitive points in a person's chart.

Mundane Astrology—Mundane astrology is the branch of astrology generally concerned with political and economic events, and the nations involved in these events.

Mutable Signs—Mutable is one of the three qualities, or categories, that describe how a sign expresses itself. Mutable signs are Gemini, Virgo, Sagittarius, and Pisces. Mutable signs are said to be very adaptable and sometimes changeable.

Natal Chart—A person's birth chart. A natal chart is essentially a "snapshot" showing the placement of each of the planets at the exact time of a person's birth.

Node—The point where the planets cross the ecliptic, or the Earth's apparent path around the Sun. The North Node is the point where a planet moves northward, from the Earth's perspective, as it crosses the ecliptic; the South Node is where it moves south.

Opposition—Two points in a chart that are 180 degrees apart.

Orb—A small degree of margin used when calculating aspects in a chart. For example, although 180 degrees form an exact opposition, an astrologer might consider an aspect within 3 or 4 degrees on either side of 180 degrees to be an opposition, as the impact of the aspect can still be felt within this range. The less orb on an aspect, the stronger the aspect. Astrologers' opinions vary on how many degrees of orb to allow for each aspect.

Outer Planets—Uranus, Neptune, and Pluto are known as the outer planets. Because of their distance from the Sun, they take a long time to complete a single rotation. Everyone born within a few years on either side of a given date will have similar placements of these planets.

Planets—The planets used in astrology are Mercury, Venus, Mars, Jupiter, Saturn, Uranus, Neptune, and Pluto. For astrological purposes, the Sun and Moon are also considered planets. A natal or birth chart lists planetary placement at the moment of birth.

Planetary Rulership—The sign in which a planet is most harmoniously placed. Examples are the Sun in Leo, and the Moon in Cancer.

Precession of Equinoxes—The gradual movement of the point of the Spring Equinox, located at 0 degrees Aries. This point marks the beginning of the tropical zodiac. The point moves slowly backward through the constellations of the zodiac, so that about every 2,000 years the Equinox begins in an earlier constellation

Qualities—In addition to categorizing the signs by element, astrologers place the twelve signs of the zodiac into three additional categories, or qualities: cardinal, mutable, or fixed. Each sign is considered to be a combination of its element and quality. Where the element of a sign describes its basic nature, the quality describes its mode of expression.

Retrograde Motion—Apparent backward motion of a planet. This is an illusion caused by the relative motion of the Earth and other planets in their elliptical orbits.

Sextile—Two points in a chart that are 60 degrees apart.

Sidereal Zodiac—Used by Hindu or Vedic astrologers. The sidereal zodiac is located where the constellations are actually positioned in the sky.

Soft Aspects—Soft aspects indicate good fortune or an easy relationship in the chart. Among the soft aspects are the trine, the sextile, and the conjunction (depending on which planets are conjunct).

Square—Two points in a chart that are 90 degrees apart.

Sun Sign—The sign of the zodiac in which the Sun is located at any given time.

Synodic Cycle—The time between conjunctions of two planets.

Trine—Two points in a chart that are 120 degrees apart.

Tropical Zodiac—The tropical zodiac begins at 0 degrees Aries, where the Sun is located during the Spring Equinox. This system is used by most Western astrologers and throughout this book.

Void-of-Course—A planet is void-of-course after it has made its last aspect within a sign, but before it has entered a new sign.

Water—One of the four basic elements. Water signs are Cancer, Scorpio, and Pisces.

Meanings of the Planets

The Sun
The Sun indicates the psychological bias that will dominate your actions. What you see, and why, is told in the reading for your Sun. The Sun also shows the basic energy patterns of your body and psyche. In many ways, the Sun is the dominant force in your horoscope and your life. Other influences, especially that of the Moon, may modify the Sun's influence, but nothing will cause you to depart very far from the basic solar pattern. Always keep in mind the basic influence of the Sun and remember all other influences must be interpreted in terms of it, especially insofar as they play a visible role in your life. You may think, dream, imagine, and hope a thousand things, according to your Moon and your other planets, but the Sun is what you are. To be your best self in terms of your Sun is to cause your energies to work along the path in which they will have maximum help from planetary vibrations.

The Moon
The Moon tells the desire of your life. When you know what you mean but can't verbalize it, it is your Moon that knows it and your Sun that can't say it. The wordless ecstasy, the mute sorrow, the secret dream, the esoteric picture of yourself that you can't get across to the world, or that the world doesn't comprehend or value—these are the products of the Moon. When you are misunderstood, it is your Moon nature, expressed imperfectly through the Sun sign, that feels betrayed. Things you know without thought—intuitions, hunches, instincts—are the products of the Moon. Modes of expression that you feel truly reflect your deepest self belong to the Moon: art, letters, creative work of any kind; sometimes love; sometimes business. Whatever you feel to be most deeply yourself is the product of your Moon and of the sign your Moon occupies at birth.

Mercury
Mercury is the sensory antenna of your horoscope. Its position by sign indicates your reactions to sights, sounds, odors, tastes, and

touch impressions, affording a key to the attitude you have toward the physical world around you. Mercury is the messenger through which your physical body and brain (ruled by the Sun) and your inner nature (ruled by the Moon) are kept in contact with the outer world, which will appear to you according to the index of Mercury's position by sign in the horoscope. Mercury rules your rational mind.

Venus

Venus is the emotional antenna of your horoscope. Through Venus, impressions come to you from the outer world, to which you react emotionally. The position of Venus by sign at the time of your birth determines your attitude toward these experiences. As Mercury is the messenger linking sense impressions (sight, smell, etc.) to the basic nature of your Sun and Moon, so Venus is the messenger linking emotional impressions. If Venus is found in the same sign as the Sun, emotions gain importance in your life, and have a direct bearing on your actions. If Venus is in the same sign as the Moon, emotions bear directly on your inner nature, add self-confidence, make you sensitive to emotional impressions, and frequently indicate that you have more love in your heart than you are able to express. If Venus is in the same sign as Mercury, emotional impressions and sense impressions work together; you tend to idealize the world of the senses and sensualize the world of the emotions to interpret emotionally what you see and hear.

Mars

Mars is the energy principle in the horoscope. Its position indicates the channels into which energy will most easily be directed. It is the planet through which the activities of the Sun and the desires of the Moon express themselves in action. In the same sign as the Sun, Mars gives abundant energy, sometimes misdirected in temper, temperament, and quarrels. In the same sign as the Moon, it gives a great capacity to make use of the innermost aims, and to make the inner desires articulate and practical. In the same sign as Venus, it quickens emotional reactions and causes you to act on them, makes for ardor and passion in love, and fosters an earthly awareness of emotional realities.

Jupiter

Jupiter is the feeler for opportunity that you have out in the world. It passes along chances of a lifetime for consideration according to the basic nature of your Sun and Moon. Jupiter's sign position indicates the places where you will look for opportunity, the uses to which you wish to put it, and the capacity you have to react and profit by it. Jupiter is ordinarily, and erroneously, called the planet of luck. It is "luck" insofar as it is the index of opportunity, but your luck depends less on what comes to you than on what you do with what comes to you. In the same sign as the Sun or Moon, Jupiter gives a direct, and generally effective, response to opportunity and is likely to show forth at its "luckiest." If Jupiter is in the same sign as Mercury, sense impressions are interpreted opportunistically. If Jupiter is in the same sign as Venus, you interpret emotions in such a way as to turn them to your advantage; your feelings work harmoniously with the chances for progress that the world has to offer. If Jupiter is in the same sign as Mars, you follow opportunity with energy, dash, enthusiasm, and courage, take long chances, and play your cards wide open.

Saturn

Saturn indicates the direction that will be taken in life by the self-preservative principle which, in its highest manifestation, ceases to be purely defensive and becomes ambitious and aspiring. Your defense or attack against the world is shown by the sign position of Saturn in the horoscope of birth. If Saturn is in the same sign as the Sun or Moon, defense predominates, and there is danger of introversion. The farther Saturn is from the Sun, Moon, and Ascendant, the better for objectivity and extroversion. If Saturn is in the same sign as Mercury, there is a profound and serious reaction to sense impressions; this position generally accompanies a deep and efficient mind. If Saturn is in the same sign as Venus, a defensive attitude toward emotional experience makes for apparent coolness in love and difficulty with the emotions and human relations. If Saturn is in the same sign as Mars, confusion between defensive and aggressive urges can make an indecisive person—or, if the Sun and Moon are strong and the total personality well developed, a balanced, peaceful, and calm individual of sober judgment and moderate actions may be indicated. If Saturn is in the same sign as Jupiter, the reaction to opportunity is sober and balanced.

Uranus

Uranus in a general way relates to creativity, originality, or individuality, and its position by sign in the horoscope tells the direction in which you will seek to express yourself. In the same sign as Mercury or the Moon, Uranus suggests acute awareness, a quick reaction to sense impressions and experiences, or a hair-trigger mind. In the same sign as the Sun, it points to great nervous activity, a high-strung nature, and an original, creative, or eccentric personality. In the same sign as Mars, Uranus indicates high-speed activity, love of swift motion, and perhaps love of danger. In the same sign as Venus, it suggests an unusual reaction to emotional experience, idealism, sensuality, and original ideas about love and human relations. In the same sign as Saturn, Uranus points to good sense; this can be a practical, creative position, but, more often than not, it sets up a destructive conflict between practicality and originality that can result in a stalemate. In the same sign as Jupiter, Uranus makes opportunity, creates wealth and the means of getting it, and is conducive to the inventive, executive, and daring.

Neptune

Neptune relates to the deepest wells of the subconscious, inherited mentality, and spirituality, indicating what you take for granted in life. Neptune in the same sign as the Sun or Moon indicates that intuitions and hunches—or delusions—dominate; there is a need for rigidly holding to reality. In the same sign as Mercury, Neptune indicates sharp sensory perceptions, a sensitive and perhaps creative mind, and a quivering intensity of reaction to sensory experience. In the same sign as Venus, it reveals idealistic and romantic (or sentimental) reaction to emotional experience, as well as the danger of sensationalism and a love of strange pleasures. In the same sign as Mars, Neptune indicates energy and intuition that work together to make mastery of life—one of the signs of having angels (or devils) on your side. In the same sign as Jupiter, Neptune describes intuitive response to opportunity generally along practical and money-making lines; one of the signs of security if not indeed of wealth. In the same sign as Saturn, Neptune indicates intuitive defense and attack on the world, generally successful unless Saturn is polarized on the negative side; then there is danger of delusion and unhappiness.

Pluto

Pluto is a planet of extremes—from the lowest criminal and violent level of our society to the heights people can attain when they realize their significance in the collectivity of humanity. Pluto also rules three important mysteries of life—sex, death, and rebirth—and links them to each other. One level of death symbolized by Pluto is the physical death of an individual, which occurs so that a person can be reborn into another body to further his or her spiritual development. On another level, individuals can experience a "death" of their old self when they realize the deeper significance of life; thus they become one of the "second born." In a natal horoscope, Pluto signifies our perspective on the world, our conscious and subconscious. Since so many of Pluto's qualities are centered on the deeper mysteries of life, the house position of Pluto, and aspects to it, can show you how to attain a deeper understanding of the importance of the spiritual in your life.

2001 Sun Sign Book Forecasts

By Gloria Star

Aries . . . . Page 28
Taurus . . . . Page 51
Gemini . . . . Page 74
Cancer . . . . Page 97
Leo . . . . Page 120
Virgo . . . . Page 143
Libra . . . . Page 166
Scorpio . . . . Page 189
Sagittarius . . . . . Page 212
Capricorn . . . . . Page 235
Aquarius . . . . . . Page 258
Pisces . . . . Page 281

Aries

The Ram
March 20 to April 19

♈

Element:	Fire
Quality:	Cardinal
Polarity:	Yang/Masculine
Planetary Ruler:	Mars
Meditation:	I actively pursue the fulfillment of my destiny.
Gemstone:	Diamond
Power Stones:	Bloodstone, carnelian, ruby
Key Phrase:	I am
Glyph:	Ram's head
Anatomy:	Head, face
Color:	Red, white
Animal:	Ram
Myths/Legends:	Artemis, Jason and the Golden Fleece
House:	First
Opposite Sign:	Libra
Flower:	Geranium
Key Word:	Initiative

Positive Expression:
Daring
Innovative
Assertive
Intrepid
Energetic
Independent

Misuse of Energy:
Impatient
Blunt
Abrasive
Rash
Belligerent
Careless

Aries

Your Ego's Strengths and Shortcomings

Free-spirited and ready to take action, you're courageous when it counts. When your enthusiasm glows, others naturally follow your leadership and trust you to blaze the trail when new pathways are necessary. When life seems to be at a standstill, activating your role as "The Initiator" of the zodiac can be what gets things back up to speed again.

You're in the forefront—a contrast to what can seem to be a world of apathetic observers waiting for someone else to get the job done! Sometimes, you may feel that you're rushing ahead too quickly, although you are quite capable of focusing on the power of the moment. Directing your assertiveness and drive toward the most viable options and goals helps you make the best use of Mars, your ruling planet. However, your exuberance and daring can feel abrasive to others if left unchecked. Remember to consider the effects of your words and actions. It can save you the trouble and time of apologizing to those reeling from the shock waves of your need to forge ahead.

Your passion for life helps you remain ever young, and you relish the emergence of new horizons to keep you uplifted, feeding your creativity and drive. Developing patience can help you learn to quell your desires for immediate gratification, although there's little that can diminish your appetite for joy. This is your special light, inspiring others to believe in possibility!

Shining Your Love Light

Just the idea of falling in love can quicken your pulse. Your spirit is fed by the rush of energy, the flirtation and play of the chase, and the exhilaration of the conquest. Waiting for the other person to make the first move can leave you feeling frustrated, and you'll be happier with a partner who can stand the heat of your desires, since the shy types may be overwhelmed by your spirited disposition. Sustaining passion can be difficult, and you may wonder if you're still in love during the times when pressures of daily life suppress the flames of love. Your partner needs to welcome your independence, since your love has the best chance of staying alive when you feel free and without bounds.

You feel powerfully attracted to your zodiac opposite, Libra, since her/his polished charm can be captivating, although you can feel pressured by her/his standards of perfection. Honesty helps you develop a complementary relationship. However, you may find that fire signs—Aries, Leo, and Sagittarius—will be most likely to empower your adventurous needs!

Love can burn brightly with another Aries, although your fire may rush out of control when tempers flare or rivalry arises. You're prompted to slow down to enjoy the sensuality of a Taurus, but the pace can get on your nerves. Gemini can provoke an exhilarating battle of wits, fanning the flames of your desire and stirring your attraction. You enjoy the soul-soothing tenderness of Cancer, but can feel thwarted if you're scolded for not returning the same attentiveness. The lover in your personality is ignited by Leo, prompting you to pour out your heartfelt desires, although your loyalty will be required if you are to sustain a relationship. With Virgo, you can feel an immediate connection of friendship, although you may be uncomfortable if you have to fulfill too many expectations.

The wild intensity you feel with Scorpio can be soul-stirring, but if control games arise you may do a quick disappearing act. The humor of a Sagittarius is invigorating, and sharing your dreams with someone who seems bent on a quest for adventure will keep your love alive. Capricorn's promise of security can be enticing, but it may come with too many rules, which squelch your passion. You're at ease with Aquarius, and the ability to open to unconditional acceptance can feed your needs for free self-expression. With Pisces, you can feel a strong bond and fall right into a mystical connection, although you may never know exactly where you stand.

Making Your Place in the World

Driven to find a life path which helps you develop your self-respect, you will appreciate a career and other experiences that provide mental and physical challenges. Working independently can be appealing, and occupations in sales, politics, or tourism and travel can be exciting. The endless challenges of medicine or surgery can capture your interest, but you might also feel called to answer your mechanical aptitudes in auto design or mechanics, or even may have a yen for racing!

To answer your creative drives, work in the beauty industry. Jewelry, fashion design, or metal-working can be interesting challenges. The physical demands of a job in physical or occupational therapy, athletics, dancing, coaching, police work, firefighting, or the military can be rewarding. Any job will need to provide room to exercise your leadership and offer a chance for you to try fresh ideas.

Power Plays

Although the primary purpose of power in your life is to underscore your feelings of personal autonomy, you feel most alive when you're facing a challenge head-on. Beginning something new keeps you feeling invogorated, and whenever you feel your enthusiasm dwindling, taking a fresh path or creating an enticing, growth-oriented goal can be empowering to you. You always enjoy situations which offer a chance for you to take the lead, although you may have to make an effort to avoid becoming domineering or selfish.

What appear to be insurmountable obstacles to some are merely fresh challenges to you, although scrutinizing your motivations can help you determine if the provocation will be worthwhile. Defeats can diminish your sense of self-respect, and it is in this frame of mind that you can become reckless or frustrated and subsequently undermine your power. Spiritually, you may be seeking a path of penetrating self-knowledge, yearning to uncover the courage which stems from your connection to the Source through your higher self.

Famous Aries

Kareem Abdul-Jabbar, Margot Adler, Johann Sebastian Bach, Bela Bartok, Joseph Campbell, Oleg Cassini, Cesar Chavez, Robert Frost, Tama Janowitz, Ashley Judd, Conan O'Brien, Steven Tyler, Vincent Van Gogh, Robin Wright Penn

The Year Ahead for Aries

You're eager to forge ahead into the century with all options open, although you do have your eye on your priorities and responsibilities. The year 2001 promises to be one of high enthusiasm and clear insight into the things that will keep your spirit soaring. The rhythm of the year can be a bit uneven, but your usually good reaction time should keep you in step so that you can take advantage of exceptional growth opportunities.

Jupiter's cycle in Gemini from January through July 11th provides the perfect stimulus for fresh ideas, coupled with high enthusiasm for the things you want to accomplish. You may also feel especially empowered by the growing network of support for your ideas, and are likely to be highly confident about your choices. Travel may be on your agenda, and if you can coordinate travel and work, you can also increase your influence while building your contacts and reliable resources. However, this is also a wonderful time to travel for pleasure, leaving your obligations behind while you experience the joys of unfettered freedom to explore your favorite adventure! For the remainder of the year, Jupiter's energy highlights your need to expand your home base, and you may be more drawn to family activities or to fulfilling personal needs. If you feel you need more room at home, you may be prompted to get rid of clutter in order to create a sense of space, or even decide to pack up and move into new digs. One thing's certain: you're ready to rebel against anything that instills a feeling that you're "penned in."

The focusing influence of Saturn's energy continues to evoke attention to finances and material concerns through April, and you may feel that it's time to set up an entirely different budget or to strengthen the way you handle your resources. Irresponsible spending can lead to large problems during this cycle, but clear, focused efforts on your part can also help you turn around an uncomfortable financial situation. Beginning in May, Saturn's influence shifts, and you feel a great sense of relief as you turn your attention toward strengthening your work skills, building better communication, and developing your understanding through educational pursuits. This planetary influence in your solar Third House marks a significant two-year period when learning fills important needs. You may also have ample opportunities to teach or guide others, discovering that this will provide the ultimate learning experience in the process!

The slower-moving planets—Uranus, Neptune, and Pluto—are providing some amazing creative motivation, and you are likely to feel strong reassurance as you make changes which eliminate many of the obstacles from your path toward success and fulfillment. Whether you're in classrooms, traveling, or simply exploring fascinating ideas with others who share your interests, your connections through common ideals helps you feel more integrated into the fabric of life.

The eclipses and nodal transits for 2001 emphasize your need to balance the personal and professional elements of your life, and you may be more inclined toward limiting your involvement in situations which inhibit your freedom. The solar eclipse on June 21st can call forth memories of the past, and you may feel that you're finally ready to reintegrate into your life the people and values which you've learned to appreciate. By contrast, the December 14 solar eclipse stimulates your need to expand your view of the world, and you may find yourself expending more energy on your spirituality and strengthening your sense of universality. It's crucial that you establish a strong connection to your ethical and moral views, since you may find yourself needing the platform they provide when dealing with decisions like contracts or political matters.

If you were born from March 20 to April 5, you're feeling the support drawn from your hard work and experience while Saturn transits in sextile aspect to your Sun from April through December of this year. It's the perfect time to align your priorities with your goals, so that you're actually focusing your energy on the things that matter most. You're also seeing the value of taking a stand for yourself and your ideas, since others are forming well-defined concepts of your identity. If you've been looking for the best time to polish your self-image, this is a great year to do just that—ranging from reworking your wardrobe and appearance to refining your communication skills and strengthening your knowledge in your chosen field. Your health may also stabilize this year, and getting into habits which strengthen your endurance can provide the kind of base that allows you to accomplish more in your daily life. If you're reasonably happy with your life choices, then this year may be a time when you feel you can establish a more consistent foundation. However, if you want to make changes, your experience and expertise may be sufficiently established so that you can move into a position which allows you to take responsibilities leading to the kind of advancement you crave.

If you were born from March 25 to 30, you're experiencing an enhanced sense of imagination while Neptune transits in sextile aspect to your Sun, in addition to feeling the effects of the Saturn transit described above. As you apply your spiritual awareness and creativity to your daily life, you may feel you're more in the flow, and surrendering your selfish desires to a higher cause can also prompt you to take on an entirely different view of your priorities. It's easier now to let go of the things you no longer need (forgiving old hurts and releasing disappointments can be part of easing your burden). You may feel you can trust your intuition or psychic impressions more readily, and are likely to experience insights into people and circumstances which instill a deeper awareness and understanding. However, since Uranus is transiting in semisquare to your Sun, you need to be especially careful about jumping into new situations with inadequate preparation. Looking before you leap might be a helpful motto to keep in the back of your mind, just to keep you out of dangerously hot water!

If you were born from April 2 to 7, Pluto is transiting in trine aspect to your Sun for the entire year. This cycle represents a period of healing and uplifting transformational change. You're finding it easier to determine and understand your motivations, and are likely to grow comfortable taking on the things which are empowering while you continue to slough off attitudes and situations that rob you of your sense of personal power. While you may experience a number of endings this year, they're the kinds of things you can celebrate, since the endings now are representative of accomplishment and stepping onto a more fulfilling path. You're also more comfortable with people in positions of influence, and may, yourself, find that others are seeking your advice and guidance. The manner in which you use your own influence will determine whether or not this cycle opens the way for constructive or destructive change in the future.

If you were born from April 8 to 15, you're feeling the stimulus of Uranus traveling in sextile aspect to your Sun. This transit is frequently accompanied by a period of exciting change—a time when it's easier to feel good about simply being yourself and allowing your individuality to shine brightly. Your natural needs for free self-expression are enhanced by the freeing qualities of Uranian motivation, and you're more likely to take the risks necessary to propel yourself into the situations you desire. It's the best year in a long time to alter your goals or to become involved in projects and activities which allow your special talents to shine and which can advance your career or improve your reputation. You may have more ideas than you can accomplish in the brief period of a year, and if that's the case, consider making a file or notebook of your inspirations, since you're likely to be able to use them in the future!

If you were born from April 16 to 19, you may feel most challenged from January through April 2001, when Saturn completes its transit in semisextile to your Sun (this began last year). Taking careful steps during this period can help to assure your long-range success, but giving in to fears or taking on responsibilities that are beyond your capabilities can saddle you with unpleasant burdens. Think of this as a time to finish what you've started so that you'll be free to move onto other things as the year progresses. By the latter half of the year, you're likely to find opportunities to uncover your special abilities or to refine them in some way, since Pluto will remain in a sesquiquadrate aspect to your Sun for the remainder of 2001. Be wary of circumstances which appear too good to be true, or in which you feel that others would use your power simply to enhance their own, since you could end up feeling used and left behind in the long run.

Tools to Make a Difference

You may feel hungry to learn, since the planetary cycles most strongly influencing you this year indicate a time when you're open to ideas which expand your awareness. This is the perfect year to enjoy the adventure of opening ever-increasing doorways of your consciousness. Whether you're reading more, joining in an active discussion group, traveling, or back in school, your desire to expand your knowledge, expertise, and understanding can lead you onto an illuminating path. In the process, you might also benefit from keeping a personal journal or diary, since your reflections and inner exploration can have exceptional value now. Sometimes, journal-writing also serves as a way to uncover your deepest desires as well as your fears about making those desires a reality! Take advantage of any opportunity to teach or train others, since sharing your knowledge now can be the best way to actually learn more.

Physical regeneration remains a powerful possibility, since the cycles which affect your overall vitality indicate that this can be an excellent period for health and improved fitness. Acupuncture, reiki, and chi gung can help you bring your chi, or physical/spiritual energy flow, back into harmony. You're eager to change the energy within and around you, and learning techniques like feng shui to help you alter and strengthen your environment can make a difference in your sense of stability. You might also respond to devices that help you alter your electromagnetic energies, and the shape of a tri-septigon fashioned of copper can be a good conductor to wear as jewelry, or to keep on a nearby desk or nightstand.

Your spirituality can be greatly enhanced this year. Working closely with your spiritual teachers or a personal shaman can help to guide you along your spiritual path, but you might also feel an awakening which seems like rekindling ancient memories. Whether you're connecting to The Source or recalling lessons your soul has experienced in the past, this is your year to surrender to Higher Knowledge as a means of illuminating your life path and feeling more in sync with your soul's purpose.

♈
Affirmation for the Year

I am open to the Truth of myself and cooperate with my Highest Needs through every thought and action.

Aries/January

In the Spotlight
Your reputation and profile within the community can open the door to greater success. The lunar eclipse on January 9 emphasizes your need to establish stability before you make changes. Delve into thorough background searches before investing time or energy.

Wellness and Keeping Fit
Your overall vitality may suffer due to the stress of emotionally charged situations early in the month. After January 20 your desire to increase your activity level is stronger, although avoiding high risk sports helps keep you injury-free.

Love and Life Connections
An undercurrent of unrest in your intimate relationship may stem from your changing needs. If you're still committed to the relationship, Jupiter's supportive cycle encourages open communication, and after January 10 you may feel a new quality of understanding if you're willing to look at your true feelings. The New Moon on January 24 stimulates your need to make connections with friends based upon your shared ideals.

Finance and Success
Career is likely to be front and center, and the strides you're making can lead to advancement in your position or salary before month's end. If you're feeling uncertain about contracts or business deals, taking the time necessary to explore your questions will yield positive results. From January 21-31 you're more ready to stabilize your options and move forward with confidence.

Cosmic Insider Tip
The days surrounding the New Moon on January 24 are filled with imaginative possibilities, and your ability to take the initiative to take advantage of fresh directions works to your advantage.

Rewarding Days: 2, 3, 6, 10, 19, 20, 24, 25, 29, 30

Challenging Days: 8, 9, 14, 15, 21, 22, 23

Affirmation for the Month
I believe in myself and have faith in my dreams.

Aries/February

In the Spotlight
Through communications and connections with others who share your interests and ideals you gain progress. The admiration others show for your leadership and willingness to take a stand increases your courage to continue toward your goals.

Wellness and Keeping Fit
After a low-energy beginning, you're feeling more alive and your vitality improves after February 15. Explore your health concerns with a professional who appreciates your desire to take an active part in your own health care.

Love and Life Connections
Love's in the air, and with Venus moving into your sign for the next four months, you couldn't ask for a better time to pursue romance. From February 1-13, your need to reach closure with some old emotional issues can bring an ending to situations which have kept you from experiencing what you need from intimacy and true love. A strong attraction grows during the Full Moon on February 8. Take the initiative after February 25.

Finance and Success
Financial matters concerning taxes and indebtedness need special attention, and you may even uncover a hidden financial drain from February 1-16. Mercury retrogrades from February 4-25, marking a time when contracts require extra care, but final signatures should be postponed until February 26-28.

Cosmic Insider Tip
Patience has never been your strong suit, and if you're rushing headlong into a new situation you may find yourself in over your head. Send signals, but first do your homework!

Rewarding Days: 3, 7, 8, 15, 16, 20, 25, 26, 27

Challenging Days: 1, 5, 6, 11, 12, 18, 19

Affirmation for the Month
I gladly release the things from my past which I no longer need.

Aries/March

In the Spotlight
Venus and Mars energies enhance your self-confidence, creativity, and drive. Fresh ideas are as close as the blink of an eye, and your courage and enthusiasm can open doorways that may previously have been closed.

Wellness and Keeping Fit
Eliminating things from your life which drain your energy has an amazing effect. Whether you're dropping a destructive habit, delving into psychological issues, or simply clearing out your closets and cupboard—it's time to free up some breathing room!

Love and Life Connections
You're reconsidering a heart-centered connection, searching your soul for the deeper meanings of your relationship. This cycle can bring an improvement to an existing relationship, but if you're free to pursue someone else, you may discover that you're ready for an entirely new approach to loving. Passions run high from March 15-31, and during the Aries New Moon on March 25 you're ready to let your feelings show, but only if you get the right signals.

Finance and Success
Snags in the details of a financial agreement can be frustrating early in the month, and cooperation from others may seem inadequate during the Full Moon on March 9. Work toward resolutions of old issues early, then set your sights on initiating an important project with the Aries New Moon on March 25.

Cosmic Insider Tip
Even if you're not getting the "all clear" to proceed, you can plant seeds in fertile soil which will take root later. Be especially attentive to new undertakings if you want to ensure success.

Rewarding Days: 2, 3, 6, 7, 15, 16, 24, 25, 26, 29

Challenging Days: 4, 5, 10, 11, 12, 17, 18, 31

Affirmation for the Month
My heart surrenders to the voice of true love.

Aries/April

In the Spotlight
Getting your ideas out there is easier, and you have a greater ability to attract the support and attention you deserve. Your reputation and career can advance in remarkable ways.

Wellness and Keeping Fit
Strengthen your vitality by getting back to nature or spending more time in natural surroundings, where you may also discover a new level of creative inspiration. Even if you can't take a vacation, time away for a day or long weekend can recharge your batteries.

Love and Life Connections
A romance gains momentum when you share your dreams and ideals from April 6-20. During the Full Moon on April 8 progress in establishing a powerful link in a love relationship can give you hope that the future does hold promise after all. New directions emerge in an existing partnership, but if you're seeking love, you may want to wait until you're feeling less vulnerable.

Finance and Success
Business travel, educational pursuits, advertising, or publishing can provide the kind of outreach which allows you to expand your options. You may feel more confident about the value of your professional offerings after April 21. You're especially well received from April 7-24, when you're also in a great position to negotiate contracts which favor your needs.

Cosmic Insider Tip
Take inventory of your belongings, since Venus retrograde in your sign through April 20 is the perfect time to get rid of anything just taking up space. Yes, that can include people!

Rewarding Days: 3, 11, 12, 16, 17, 21, 22, 26, 30

Challenging Days: 1, 7, 8, 13, 14, 15, 27, 28, 29

Affirmation for the Month
My words and actions provoke kindness and understanding.

Aries/May

In the Spotlight
You may finally feel more self-assured financially, although the manner in which you manage your resources plays a crucial role. It's easy to yield to self-indulgence before thinking through the long term consequences.

Wellness and Keeping Fit
High-spirited competition can be great for your health and a marvelous way to meet your fitness goals. You might also enjoy a challenging fitness class or an active outdoors vacation. You gain energy by staying active this month.

Love and Life Connections
Now that Venus has turned direct in Aries, your certainty about your feelings is easier to identify, and you may also be more open with your communication, encouraging a love relationship to grow by leaps and bounds! Exotic travel can add a romantic flair, but if you're looking for love, you may discover an overwhelming attraction while away on a journey from May 6–31.

Finance and Success
You're eager to let others know what you have to offer, and whether you're promoting yourself or your products and ideas, this is the perfect time to spread the word. Conferences provide the perfect links for success, but your career can also gain momentum through publications or broadcasting. Contracts and legal matters fare beautifully after May 6, although you need to be attentive to any loopholes that could leave you vulnerable.

Cosmic Insider Tip
Be watchful of your promises, since it's easy to commit to more than you can fulfill. Leaving others under the crush of unfulfilled expectations can be ultimately disastrous.

Rewarding Days: 1, 8, 9, 13, 18, 19, 23, 27, 28

Challenging Days: 4, 5, 11, 12, 25, 26, 31

Affirmation for the Month
I enjoy taking the lead when I know what I want!

Aries/June

In the Spotlight
Taking people at their word can be difficult, especially if things seem to get blown out of proportion too easily. You may feel tempted to rush headlong into something unprepared, creating a need to backtrack or begin again. Think twice before taking action!

Wellness and Keeping Fit
With Mars in retrograde this month, you may be feeling a lag in your energy, although it's unlikely that you'll be willing to slow down. Measuring risks is a good idea, though, since you may push past your limits before you realize it.

Love and Life Connections
While you're pursuing the person you desire, you may overlook some important needs from the folks close to home. The solar eclipse on June 21 marks the potential for critical changes on the home front, and you are likely to feel a shift in the balance of power. Nothing is set in stone, and remaining flexible will always give you the best options.

Finance and Success
Things are changing, and the economic fluctuations in the world around you can leave you feeling a bit unsettled. Communication breakdowns or equipment failures can complicate matters during Mercury's retrograde from June 4-28, and the resulting frustrations can lead to argumentative circumstances. You're eager to try out some innovations or make changes, but this is not the best time for them to run smoothly!

Cosmic Insider Tip
Marshaling sufficient energy to do all the things you want can be tricky. Keeping your priorities straight will help steer you safely through the stormy planetary cycles after June 16.

Rewarding Days: 5, 6, 10, 14, 15, 16, 19, 23, 24

Challenging Days: 1, 7, 8, 21, 22, 27, 28, 29

Affirmation for the Month
In all matters I seek the guidance of my Higher Self.

Aries/July

In the Spotlight
The lunar eclipse emphasizes your need to assess the balance between your personal and professional obligations. You may feel it's time to open alternate lines of communication in order to reach a better understanding of what others need from you.

Wellness and Keeping Fit
Your sense of adventure is peaking, and staying active will help satisfy your restlessness. Failing to funnel your drive into physical activities can result in a lack of energy—and you have places to go and people to see!

Love and Life Connections
The lunar eclipse on July 5 provokes your need to address family matters, and you may feel that you're caught in the midst of situations which should have been resolved long ago. Your ability to take an assertive role can lead others toward resolutions, but your interests may be better served by observing from a distance. Your love life improves after July 4, and your spiritual connections are strengthened as you share ideals and dreams from July 23-31.

Finance and Success
Contracts require careful negotiation, since legal maneuvering can either cripple your possibilities or give you a solid platform for long term growth. Keep your eye on your important goals, and let your ideas open doors from July 2-11 and again after July 22 to set in motion your most significant options. Learn about your competition, too, since later you may be on the same side!

Cosmic Insider Tip
Emotional appeals can throw you off balance during the Moon's eclipse on July 5, and the same strains echo again with the New Moon on July 20. Remember your own priorities.

Rewarding Days: 2, 3, 7, 12, 13, 17, 21, 29, 30

Challenging Days: 4, 5, 6, 19, 20, 25, 26, 31

Affirmation for the Month
My confidence glows with Truth as my shield!

Aries/August

In the Spotlight
Structures are changing, priorities shifting, and business is definitely unusual with Saturn and Pluto in opposition this month. It's good for you that you're ready to take advantage of the changing climate, and your leadership can direct real progress.

Wellness and Keeping Fit
Although you may feel physically up to the challenge, falling short of your own expectations can take the wind out of your sails. Keep a careful watch on your strengths and limitations and you can set a pace that's easier to maintain.

Love and Life Connections
Maintaining clear communication can help you avoid the pitfalls of getting in over your head, especially where others are concerned. Fortunately, your love relationships continue to improve, and near the Full Moon on August 4 you may feel on top of the world. Your excitement and desire to share what's in your heart can be almost overwhelming near the New Moon on August 19, but have a little patience for pretense.

Finance and Success
Business conferences and communications fare best from August 1-13, although your ideas and actions are influential throughout the month. Be attentive to details from August 2-5 and then August 20-23. Moving or improvements at home can result in cost overruns, so it's a good idea to keep an eye on your "cushion" to avoid running short of resources.

Cosmic Insider Tip
The need for optimism strongly imprints the collective, and you may have just what it takes to keep confidence high. Honesty is required, but that's perfectly fine with you!

Rewarding Days: 3, 4, 8, 9, 17, 18, 26, 27, 31

Challenging Days: 1, 2, 15, 16, 21, 22, 23, 28, 29

Affirmation for the Month
The path to my success is clear.

Aries/September

In the Spotlight
Although you may not always show it, your romantic side is ready to play. Bringing your creativity into your daily life keeps you smiling, and will inspire others to feel better about themselves.

Wellness and Keeping Fit
Extra attention to your health regimen is important, and if you've been overindulging in things that sap your vitality you're likely to feel the sting this month. Ceasing habits which undermine your health is a top priority.

Love and Life Connections
With romance in the air, you're more confident about sharing what's in your heart. Add excitement by sharing unforgettable moments and favorite pleasures from September 7-19. If you're looking for new love, circumstances can be just right to open the door from September 1-15, although jumping in too quickly can lead to disappointments if you're in unfamiliar territory. Send out your scouts first!

Finance and Success
Convening with others in your profession can give your career a boost from September 1-8, although others may show appreciation for your talents and insights through September 21. Tensions in the workplace can escalate near and during the Full Moon on September 2, when taking sides may get you into trouble. Choose your battles wisely! Clarify expectations from others, since assumptions can be a thorn in your side after September 22.

Cosmic Insider Tip
Fine-tuning business deals and agreements before Saturn turns retrograde on September 26 can help to assure a stronger position for you in the long run.

Rewarding Days: 1, 4, 5, 6, 9, 14, 22, 23, 27

Challenging Days: 2, 11, 12, 17, 18, 19, 24, 25

Affirmation for the Month
I am clearly aware of the impact of my actions and words.

Aries/October

In the Spotlight
Mercury retrogrades the first 23 days of the month, marking a time when retracing your steps and taking back your words may be necessary, especially since the planetary pictures indicate that you may be in a bit of a fix due to impatience.

Wellness and Keeping Fit
You're feeling competitive and are unlikely to back away from a contest. However, take a careful look at your challenger and then examine what you have invested. It may not be worth the trouble in the long run.

Love and Life Connections
Sometimes it's a good idea to determine whom you're trying to please. Partnerships take center stage during the Aries Full Moon on October 2, and if you're unhappy with a situation you may decide to break away. If you're committed and want to continue, it's time to cut off any destructive habits and set the stage for healthier interaction and support. After October 16, it's your partner's turn to take the lead.

Finance and Success
If you simply could not come to an agreement last month, then it's now time to go back to the drawing board and fine-tune your list of wants. Fresh ideas can stir your imagination from October 13-31, but expect delays, misfires, and breakdowns. Use this time to learn from those mistakes.

Cosmic Insider Tip
With Mercury, Mars and Jupiter setting up a series of frustrating options, you need plenty of room to let off steam. After October 14, watch for foot-in-mouth syndrome.

Rewarding Days: 1, 2, 3, 7, 11, 12, 19, 20, 29, 30
Challenging Days: 9, 10, 14, 15, 21, 22, 23

Affirmation for the Month
I am an attentive listener.

Aries/November

In the Spotlight
You're filled with inspiration and ready to take action to make your dreams and goals a reality. Careful assessment of your resources—including time and money—will play a large part in determining whether or not you are satisfied with the results.

Wellness and Keeping Fit
Getting to the core of physical distress and uncovering the relationship between your emotions and sense of well-being helps you feel more in control of your health. You may decide to abandon an unsuccessful therapy if it fails to nourish you as a whole person.

Love and Life Connections
Underlying issues in an intimate relationship need careful exploration, and since the month begins with a Full Moon, you may be getting to the core of problems right away. Love can blossom from November 1-7 and again after November 22. Take care to avoid jumping to conclusions from November 9-24, since you could quickly be up the proverbial creek with no paddle!

Finance and Success
Negotiate a sweet deal on the 1st under the influence of the Full Moon, when you're ready to make the most of the situation at hand. Presentations and proposals fare best from November 1-5, but you're also in a good place to get into the details of financial agreements from November 7-26. Launch your pet projects from November 25-30, when you're feeling virtually unstoppable!

Cosmic Insider Tip
With Saturn once again in exact opposition to Pluto, structures are transforming. You may be able take advantage of changes and move into positions previously unavailable or blocked.

Rewarding Days: 3, 7, 8, 15, 16, 20, 21, 25, 26, 27, 30

Challenging Days: 5, 6, 11, 12, 13, 18, 19

Affirmation for the Month
I am sensitive to the needs and feelings of others.

Aries/December

In the Spotlight
The eclipses of Sun and Moon draw your attention to career growth and reputation enhancement. It's time to move away from circumstances which inhibit your ability to shine.

Wellness and Keeping Fit
Although you may be feeling your life is more high-profile now, you do need down time. Allowing ample time for rest, introspection, and rejuvenation keeps you strong through a very active month.

Love and Life Connections
If you're searching for love, travel and cultural pursuits may be the prime opportunities to meet the right person. Your ideals are high, and the solar eclipse on December 14 marks a time when you're aware that you are now unwilling to compromise on the things that mean in the most when it comes to intimacy and connection with another person. During the lunar eclipse on December 30 you're feeling highly introspective regarding your needs and feelings where parents are concerned.

Finance and Success
Promotional activities and advertising efforts fare best from December 14-30, although you can make some powerful connections with others in your field during the first 14 days of the month. Business travel works to your advantage, too, but you'll want to give yourself time away from career concerns after December 22, when you're ready to re-evaluate your goals.

Cosmic Insider Tip
Getting in touch with your expectations, hopes, and wishes is amplified during the Moon's eclipse on December 30—just in time for your New Year's Resolutions!

Rewarding Days:
1, 4, 5, 13, 14, 18, 22, 23, 24, 28

Challenging Days: 2, 3, 8, 9, 10, 21, 29, 30

Affirmation for the Month
I am open to fresh ideas and ready to set new goals.

Aries Action Table

These dates reflect the best—but not the only—times for success and ease in these activities, according to your Sun sign.

	JAN	FEB	MAR	APR	MAY	JUN	JUL	AUG	SEPT	OCT	NOV	DEC
Move							12-29					
Start a class					6-31	23, 24	1-13					14, 15
Join a club	24, 25											
Ask for a raise				24-26								
Look for work	1-9							14-31				15-31
Get pro advice	14, 15	11, 12	10, 11	7, 8	4, 5, 31	1, 27, 28	25, 26	21, 22	17, 18	15, 16	11, 12	8-10
Get a loan	16-18	13, 14	12, 13	9, 10	6, 7	2, 3, 30	1, 27, 28	23, 24	19-21	17, 18	13, 14	11, 12
See a doctor		1-5	17-31	1-5				14-31				
Start a diet	12, 13	9, 10	8, 9	4-6	2-3, 29-30	25, 26	23, 24	19, 20	15, 16	13, 14	9, 10	6, 7
End relationship				7, 8								
Buy clothes						1-5	30, 31	1-13				
Get a makeover			24, 25	21-30	1-31							
New romance								18, 28-31	1-20			
Vacation	19, 20	14, 15	14-16	11, 12	8, 9	5, 6	2-3, 29-30	25-27	22, 23	19, 20	15-17	13, 14

50 • Llewellyn's 2001 Sun Sign Book

Taurus

The Bull
April 19 to May 20

Element:	Earth
Quality:	Fixed
Polarity:	Yin/Feminine
Planetary Ruler:	Venus
Meditation:	I cherish and safeguard my environment.
Gemstone:	Emerald
Power Stones:	Diamond, blue lace agate, rose quartz
Key Phrase:	I have
Glyph:	Bull's head
Anatomy:	Throat, neck
Color:	Green
Animal:	Cattle
Myths/Legends:	Isis and Osiris, Cerridwen, Bull of Minos
House:	Second
Opposite Sign:	Scorpio
Flower:	Violet
Key Word:	Conservation

Positive Expression:	Misuse of Energy:
Prosperous	Avaricious
Loving	Covetous
Steadfast	Unyielding
Enduring	Rigid
Calm	Lethargic
Sensible	Resistant

Taurus

Your Ego's Strengths and Shortcomings

Consistency, focus, and reliability are all woven into your drive to build a secure life filled with creativity and love. Once your heart is committed, you're there for the duration and prefer the steady course in all your life experiences—from career options to relationships to building a home. Your role in the zodiac is that of "The Maintainer"—the dependable person radiating steadfastness and aiding in attracting and accumulating the resources necessary to happiness in life.

You do not like change, especially if it threatens your stability, and if you do feel threatened your stubborn resistance is the first defense you muster! Yet it is that same quality which, positively directed, allows you to sustain and comfort others through life's ups and downs. Through your natural connection to the energy of Venus, your planetary ruler, your loving energy embraces those who have your heart—radiating and attracting beauty and artistry. It's quite possible that you excel in music and the arts, and at the very least you generally prefer to fill your life with beautiful people and beautiful things.

Whether you're a dedicated patron of the arts or working to preserve the Earth's resources, you're keenly aware that some things simply cannot be duplicated or replaced. Your life lessons help you understand that you are more than what you have. As you release what you no longer need in favor of growth, you open your connection to the continuing spiral of never-ending love from the Source, and it flows directly into your own heart.

Shining Your Love Light

You're looking for the kind of love that feels total and complete and can endure the tests of time. As a lover, you can express tenderness and strength, and you may enjoy the most sensual qualities of sharing all that love has to offer. Losing someone you love can deal a crushing blow to your heart, and if your self-worth is threatened or inadequately supported by a relationship you may feel unwelcome jealousy. Keeping your heart open to the transformational processes of love will allow you to accept the evolutionary changes which occur in all relationships.

Since you're an earth sign, you'll appreciate the stabilizing and practical qualities of the other earth signs—Capricorn, Virgo, and Taurus. Aries can be extremely attractive, although he or she may be ready to move on before you get settled into the connection. The right match with another Taurus can be difficult, but if you're in sync you can feel completely at home with a long term commitment. You're challenged by Gemini to be more flexible, since he or she relishes variety and change. Contentment with Cancer can be easy, especially if you have shared values about home and family. Watch for ego conflicts with Leo, although you may be completely taken in by her or his drama and constancy. You may feel that Virgo is your ultimate lover: hungry for the sensual experiences of love, but also sensible about priorities.

You can be enticed by Libra's grace and sense of class, but his or her indecisiveness can drive you crazy. Watch out for your attraction to Scorpio, your opposite, since the passion may be wild but you're both equally possessive! If you don't mind the periods of separation, you can enjoy the playfulness and generosity of Sagittarius. Capricorn can enhance your ideals and may be your perfect match in your drive toward financial and emotional stability. You may feel that Aquarius never gives you the personal attention you crave. Yet, with Pisces, you can drift into fanciful romance while creating a place to bring your dreams to life.

Making Your Place in the World

Finding the perfect niche—one which allows your special abilities to shine while strengthening your security base—requires your trademark patience and focus. In the arts you may feel comfortable expressing your talents as a musician, sculptor, or gallery/museum owner. Or you might prefer to filter your sense of structure and design into architecture, building, or carpentry. Other creative outlets such as gardening, the floral industry, farming, ranching, forestry, or landscaping can provide ample opportunities for growth and fulfillment.

Your natural business sense can be applied to situations from restaurants to retail outlets, or to the world of finance, banking, real estate, or investment. An encouraging counselor, you might also excel at helping others make the most of their strengths.

Power Plays

Your fascination with power stems from your deep need to assure and preserve your comfort and emotional security. You feel most secure when surrounded by ample resources and loyal friends and family. Exercising your ability to create a strong foothold and to persevere through adversity reinforces your ability to cooperate with and direct your destiny and confers a sense of power. You respect others who make the most of their resources, since you know that waste and abuse diminishes power. In fact, your ultimate compliment is to acknowledge the value of others by sharing your time and resources with them.

You can feel powerless when faced with endings and loss, and if you're forced to choose between having something or someone and letting go of your attachments, you can become extremely upset. Anything you perceive as yours is difficult to release, but learning how to graciously say good-bye when the situation requires it will ultimately fortify your power. Nature teaches the most profound lessons, showing the cycles of renewal and rebirth. It is your attunement to and honor of nature's resources and the true abundance and grace of the Universe which ultimately provides the power that sustains you, and will secure a positive future for the generations which carry your legacy.

Famous Taureans

Charlotte Bronte, Pierce Brosnan, Salvadore Dali, Martha Graham, Andie MacDowell, Karl Marx, Michael Palin, Evita Peron, Heloise Reese, William Shakespeare, Talia Shire, Aaron Spelling, George Strait, Barbra Streisand, Uma Thurman, Mike Wallace

The Year Ahead for Taurus

As the year 2001 progresses, you may feel an increasing sense that your burdens are growing lighter, although the challenge to keep pace with the changes in the world around you may still leave you occasionally winded. Fortunately, your optimism grows this year, and you may actually feel eager to embrace a life filled with the prospects of exceptional growth.

By late April, Saturn finally completes its transit in Taurus, which began in 1998, and has presented a test of your values and priorities during the last two years. Since you've probably been steadily working toward your goals you will most likely have experienced a greater appreciation for responsible action. During the spring, Saturn moves into the Second House of your solar chart, initiating a two-year cycle focused on evaluation and positive use of your resources. This is the time to set out a reasonable plan for getting your finances in order, and to be thinking long-term when making decisions about your expenditures and investments. Immediate gratification can get you into trouble!

Fortunately, Jupiter's expansive influence from the summer of last year through July 12, 2001 is stimulating an increase in your expendable resources, although you may have been tempted to spend beyond your means. If that's the case, you're likely to put on the brakes by the second quarter of this year! Beginning in July, when Jupiter moves into the sign of Cancer, you'll likely feel you have a better understanding of how to apply your resources, and can take advantage of some important connections, which may lead to career advancement and helpful support in your personal growth. This cycle is also a confidence-booster and marks an important time to enhance or develop the skills and knowledge that can advance your career.

The slower-moving planets Uranus, Neptune, and Pluto activate change on a deeper level. Uranus and Neptune continue to provide a challenge focused on your life path or career, and you may feel that you're still struggling to adapt to changes beyond your control. Fortunately, you're experiencing enhanced stability and may have a better handle on your priorities, so responding to things like a changing economy or job market may seem more normal than in the past. However, if this is the year when either planet is transiting in square aspect to your Sun (see sections below), you may feel especially unsettled. Pluto's cycle continues to bring your inhibitions and the nature of your emotional attachments to the forefront so that you can take a better look at them. Sometimes these are the things you'd just as soon leave hidden in the depths of your psyche, and nothing says you have to tell the world your secrets. You simply need to acknowledge them to yourself, and may discover hidden strengths while improving your ability to understand your needs for intimacy and self-knowledge.

The three lunar eclipses and two solar eclipses draw your attention to what and how you're communicating to the world. Not only do you need to feel that others understand what you have to say, but you may feel some urgency about expressing very clearly what you need from them. Just as important is your need to open your mind to the ideas of others, and you may be challenged to integrate concepts from others whose philosophical or cultural backgrounds contrast with your own. The solar eclipses on June 21 and December 14 underscore the significance of exploring your values and clarifying for yourself why you value certain things, ideas, and people. While some of your connections will grow stronger, others will break free. Your job is to determine when and how to let go or hold on to the things in your life.

If you were born from April 19 to May 4, you're feeling the influence of Saturn transiting in semisextile to your Sun this year. It's time to fortify the structures you've been building during the last two years and to eliminate unnecessary expenditures of energy and resources. Think of this year as a time to take the next logical steps which help you maintain your momentum and progress. There may be some responsibilities associated with your life that you'd just as soon ignore, but embracing them and working with true commitment to fulfill them can actually help you move forward faster. Your practical sensibilities have been strengthened over the last couple of years, and now you have a chance to advance to a more influential level in your career and path toward personal growth. While this cycle is not necessarily energizing, it does confer an ability to bring more order to your life and can be the time when you feel more capable of initiating the kinds of habits and routines which strengthen your productivity and overall physical vitality. So, if you've been waiting for the right time to get serious about that exercise program or to enroll in a class you need to take, this is it!

If you were born from April 25 to 29, you're feeling Neptune's energy traveling in square aspect to your Sun. The most profoundly noticeable element of this cycle is an increase in your sensitivity—across the board. You may feel more physically susceptible to your environment, experiencing symptoms such as allergic reactions, or having greater sensitivity to other environmental changes or toxic elements such as pollutants. It's also likely that you'll feel more emotional, and you may discover that you're more aware of the feelings and needs of others, whether you want to be or not! Maintaining your personal boundaries—knowing when to get involved and when to remain distant—can be a challenge, especially with those you love. Even in relationships with those you do not know well you can become the victim of unscrupulous or deceptive dealings, and for this reason it's a good idea to wait until you have greater clarity before making long-term commitments or getting involved financially. Although this is an excellent time to devote the energy and resources to make a difference in your quality of life, knowing when, how, and where can be difficult. For this reason, determining the most reliable outlets for charitable efforts or donations will be helpful. To maintain your physical strength, use the releasing qualities of this cycle to let go of habits that undermine your vitality, and take advantage of your desire to rest more. You may actually require more sleep now, and failing to give your body time for the rejuvenation it requires can undermine your overall health. If you do have health concerns, it's crucial that you investigate them, since you can worry over the worst potential outcomes or tend to deny what you know you need to do. Remember: knowledge is power! Look for the answers, and if you feel uncertain, give yourself permission to ask the hard questions.

If you were born from May 3 to 8, Pluto is transiting in quincunx aspect to your Sun. The qualities of this cycle evoke your need to carve out a path that allows you to feel more self-expressive and satisfied. In many ways, this is a time of fine-tuning—making adjustments which allow you to eliminate some things while inviting new elements or experiences into your life. The difficulty resides in knowing when to open up and when to withdraw. Physically, your body is also changing, and your physical weak links are more noticeable. Now is the time to make any necessary changes to improve the quality of your life, but if you fight against those changes you can actually undermine your ability to heal. Relationships, especially those of an intimate nature, are also evolving, and if you're stuck in your old patterns you may feel dissatisfied with yourself or with your partner. You'll feel more confident if you're taking smaller steps and remembering to stay focused in the moment instead of getting stuck in the past or projecting too much into the future. Keep telling yourself that your power is in the "now," and use your increasing awareness to embrace the day!

If you were born from May 9 to 16, you're feeling the frustrations of unexpected change while Uranus transits in square aspect to your Sun. Circumstances changing beyond your control can be especially frustrating, until you realize that you have the ability to choose responses that allow you to experience the positive qualities of change, instead of simply lamenting that some things are no longer part of your life. If you've been ignoring your own need to break away from situations that inhibit your growth or that you've outgrown, you're likely to discover that while you no longer feel comfortable, you are still be uncertain about which way to turn. Simply burning bridges is not the answer, although saying good-bye to the people and things you no longer need may seem necessary. Think of this as a time when the real you is ready to emerge. At first, others may not recognize you, but if you're in touch with your motivations and needs, they and you will accept the "new and improved" model!

If you were born from May 16 to 20, you're capable of accomplishing more this year, since Saturn is transiting in conjunction to your Sun, although this influence will be gone after this May. This cycle will not occur again for another twenty-nine years, so it's a good idea to make the most of it! It's time to create a stable platform for long-term growth, and set up the structures which will support your efforts and advancement personally and professionally. The manner in which you handle your responsibilities is important, but that does not mean that you're supposed to take on more than you can carry. True responsible action includes knowing when to say, "No." To that end, you're also seeing things reaching a conclusion, especially circumstances that belong in the past and are not part of your vision for the future.

Tools to Make a Difference

You'll appreciate the overall benefits of experiences and tools that help you relieve stress, relax, and get into a comfortable pace, especially since you do not enjoy feeling pushed! Creating a tranquil environment at home and at work can be accomplished by adding comforts that soothe away tension. The right ergonomic chair at work and the addition of colors which evoke the spirit of nature can help you maintain your focus more easily. At home, create a space that is balanced and harmonious, adding music and aromatherapy to stimulate the kind of mood you desire. For passion, infuse the air with cinnamon or floral scents like ylang ylang and lavender with your favorite rich, sensual background music. For quiet reflection use sandalwood or frankincense, and enjoy the tones of ancient chants, the timeless music of Brahms, or contemporaries such as Will Ackerman. Filling your home with freshly cut flowers can also lift your spirits, since colors are a feast to your eyes; fragrant roses may be your favorites, though!

You might also benefit by working to consciously balance your physical, emotional, mental, and spiritual bodies through such methods as chi gung, tai chi, or hatha yoga, or you might find exercises using toning and chanting techniques helpful. Singing can be a healing experience for you, since it opens the heart and throat chakras, allowing your spiritual and emotional energy to flow more easily through your physical form. Taking an active role in letting go of physical tension is important, but you'll also gain tremendous benefit from massage therapy with a special focus on neck, shoulders, and back.

♉

Affirmation for the Year

In all things, love guides my actions and desires.

Taurus/January

In the Spotlight
Getting on track can be difficult, since you may feel agitated if things are not coming together the way you want. You're likely to complain that everything is simply taking too long. It's not the waiting, it's the interruptions! Strive for flexibility.

Wellness and Keeping Fit
With Mars transiting in opposition to your sign, you can become easily exhausted, since it's difficult to recognize your limitations. It's also conceivable that the effects of stress are wearing on you more than you realize. A few time-out periods during each day will help.

Love and Life Connections
Your friends are a positive source of joy and inspiration, although you're also discovering distinctive differences in your value systems midmonth. Spending time with your loved ones during the Moon's eclipse on January 9 seems natural, but you may be reluctant to offer details about your aspirations unless you're certain about trust issues. Unexpected conflicts between family and partner can be upsetting after January 19, and it's possible that you'll only be safe as an observer!

Finance and Success
Competitive situations can bring out your best efforts, unless you're blind-sided by undermining or deceptive actions from January 1-6. Even then, your recovery is aided by peers or friends whose support can keep you in the game. Dreams of better circumstances beckon during the New Moon on January 24.

Cosmic Insider Tip
If you're resisting change, you may end up on the bottom of the pile of rubble that remains when situations change beyond your control. Use changes from January 16-24 to your best advantage!

Rewarding Days: 4, 5, 9, 12, 13, 21, 22, 23, 27, 31

Challenging Days: 10, 11, 16, 17, 18, 19, 24, 25

Affirmation for the Month
I am sensitive to the needs and desires of others.

Taurus/February

In the Spotlight
Mercury retrogrades from February 4-25, reminding you that some things need a second look, and some people deserve a second chance! You may also reach the end of your rope with those situations that no longer fulfill your needs. Cross the bridge, but avoid burning it for now.

Wellness and Keeping Fit
Probing into the root causes of physical distress can unearth what you need to know. Holistic approaches offer the best solutions, and you're more aware of the psychological elements of your problems.

Love and Life Connections
You may have an absolute fascination with someone who is unavailable or unsuitable, but your fantasies can be quite real. Although you may be able to act on your attraction, hesitating in order to determine the potential risks or pitfalls can serve you well. Misunderstandings can complicate affairs of the heart, but try again during the New Moon on February 23.

Finance and Success
Knowing precisely what's expected of you can help you avoid eventual problems with superiors, although you may not like what you discover in the process! Try to keep things in perspective. Address debt issues, since you're eager to get out from under financial restraints. You may be concerned about a partner's spending, especially if you have different approaches to handling money.

Cosmic Insider Tip
Unanticipated breakdowns in equipment, or flukes which create delays in your progress, can be disconcerting from February 12-16. Accepting what you cannot change is helpful.

Rewarding Days: 1, 5, 6, 9, 10, 18, 19, 23, 28

Challenging Days: 7, 8, 13, 14, 15, 20, 21, 22

Affirmation for the Month
I can control my own actions and attitudes.

Taurus/March

In the Spotlight
Getting the background work done on a creative project now can be like money in the bank, especially if you're making headway on a situation that was previously blocked. Emotionally, you may be distracted by the reappearance of an old love.

Wellness and Keeping Fit
Exploring your psyche can give you insights into your overall health, especially if you've been resisting making changes that you know would be good for you. It's time to dance with your resistance and loosen its grip on your ability to heal old emotional wounds.

Love and Life Connections
Unresolved relationships have a way of returning—either in memory or real form. Feelings are likely to resurface under the influence of the current Venus transit. You may also discover that you want to achieve greater intimacy in your current relationship, but that your old problems have gotten in the way. Explore your feelings during the Full Moon on March 9, and plan a romantic getaway after March 25.

Finance and Success
You may feel that you're just not making the right connections to improve your career until after March 18. Review contracts and agreements to determine changes that will benefit your long term financial picture, since altering the balance of your investments and rewriting your budget can ease monetary strain

Cosmic Insider Tip
With Venus in retrograde from March 8-April 19 you're in the perfect position to clear out merchandise that's not moving or anything adding clutter or taking up space.

Rewarding Days: 1, 4, 5, 8, 9, 17, 18, 22, 27, 28, 31

Challenging Days: 6, 7, 12, 13, 14, 19, 20, 21

Affirmation for the Month:
I am open to the voice of love.

Taurus/April

In the Spotlight
Little by little, most of the obstacles which have stood in the way of your progress are dropping away. You're completing some obligations and need to think before making new commitments, since it might be a nice change to breathe more freely for a while!

Wellness and Keeping Fit
Stress relief may be job one, since the manner in which you're handling tension determines your energy level and influences your productivity. Incorporating activities that enhance your physical flexibility helps on all fronts.

Love and Life Connections
Conflicts with your partner can arise if you feel that you're getting shortchanged when it comes to the balance between give and take. If you're repressing your anxiety or feeling guilty about taking over your needs, then the situation only gets worse. A friend or counselor can offer objectivity, and then by the Taurus New Moon on April 23 you may feel that you're ready to bring issues into the open with your partner. Examine your motivations first!

Finance and Success
You may be feeling paranoid if you're getting signals that your situation at work is not what it needs to be. Background research and quiet exploration of the actual circumstances can reveal the culprit—and it may simply be a change in command. Concentrate on your obligations and priorities, but do be watchful of your investments. Plan a "discovery" meeting after April 22.

Cosmic Insider Tip
Initiating important changes after Saturn moves out of your sign on April 20 can feel like trying your wings. A test flight might be a good idea before you invite the press!

Rewarding Days: 1, 5, 6, 13, 14, 23, 24, 28, 29

Challenging Days: 2, 3, 9, 10, 16, 17, 30

Affirmation for the Month:
My desires are in harmony with my highest needs.

Taurus/May

In the Spotlight
Dilemmas about the best way to handle your finances can arise, particularly if your resources are tangled with someone else's. There may not be quick and easy solutions, but you're getting to the core and determining where you stand.

Wellness and Keeping Fit
A chronic physical complaint can become an issue, especially if you've failed to honor the limitations it suggests. If you've lost patience with the process, you may feel ready to try a more aggressive approach to healing.

Love and Life Connections
Relationships can, indeed, be an issue, and ongoing problems can escalate to a peak during the Full Moon on May 7. The question may be one of control, which is rarely easy to resolve. Explore the power struggle objectively to determine your own triggers. Accomplishing intimacy if trust has been broken requires surrender, honesty, and a desire to let go of the past.

Finance and Success
Squabbles over joint resources, inheritance, or contractual issues can try your patience. You may decide that your advisors are costing more than they're worth, but before you make an alternate choice, determine the long-term cost. A mentor can illustrate a positive solution. This may be a time to ride through the storm, expending as few resources as possible. Just remember that resistance for its own sake can undermine your position in the long run.

Cosmic Insider Tip
Jupiter and Pluto are in opposition, testing your resilience in the face of power struggles over money and property. Choose your battles, since not all disputes are your own!

Rewarding Days: 2, 3, 11, 12, 16, 20, 21, 22, 29, 30

Challenging Days: 1, 6, 7, 13, 14, 27, 28

Affirmation for the Month:
I know what I can afford to risk.

Taurus/June

In the Spotlight
Your worries about finances may escalate if others are not fulfilling their end of the bargain. Fortunately, your ability to attract the resources necessary to fix the problem is operating quite nicely, although you may end some associations as a result of this crisis.

Wellness and Keeping Fit
Increasing your activity levels diminishes stress. It's not about breaking records, but finding ways to enjoy yourself, laugh, and build your stamina at the same time. Nature provides a positive healing balance; reintroduce yourself!

Love and Life Connections
You need positive confirmation in your love relationship, and if you're feeling that your partner is not meeting your needs, you may indulge in a flirtation. But you can quickly get in over your head and find that you're flirting with disaster from June 6-17. Listen to your heart. If you're available, the path to new love opens after the solar eclipse on June 21.

Finance and Success
Money matters can be the source of battles. Rash actions can be extremely costly, and situations can escalate out of control near the Full Moon on June 6. You don't like feeling that your resources are being wasted, and may have to defend your position with logic instead of pure stubbornness. In career matters, you may be fighting for what you know you're worth.

Cosmic Insider Tip
Mercury retrogrades from June 4-28, compounded by a connection to Mars and Jupiter. This is definitely not a good time to sign contracts, since situations can change overnight.

Rewarding Days: 7, 8, 12, 17, 18, 21, 22, 25

Challenging Days: 2, 3, 9, 10, 11, 23, 24, 30

Affirmation for the Month
I carefully consider my words before I speak, and listen just as carefully to what others have to say.

Taurus/July

In the Spotlight
You're getting rid of unproductive situations, focusing instead on the actions and projects that have greater value. Good news arrives to spur your confidence, and your support network provides positive reinforcement for your self-esteem.

Wellness and Keeping Fit
Taking a break from your routine boosts your vitality. For now, mini-vacations or a few free afternoons can help you breathe more easily. Take time to connect with friends and family, since you'll feel better if you can confirm your emotional lifelines.

Love and Life Connections
Expressing your thoughts and feelings is much easier, since many of the open conflicts are at least identified, even if they're not yet completely resolved. Take a break during the lunar eclipse on the 5th to connect on a spiritual level. A getaway with your sweetheart can turn the tide after July 13. If you're seeking a new love, your paths are likely to cross in the course of your daily routine or communications. At least the flirtation can be enjoyable!

Finance and Success
Unexpected expenditures can throw your finances into a tailspin from July 1-4, although your resources do improve as you go through the month. Ironing out a new budget after July 6 can put you on firmer footing, or at least improve your confidence in the future. Rework the details of financial agreements after July 12, but wait until the New Moon on July 20 to launch new projects.

Cosmic Insider Tip
Identify weak points from July 5-18 in order to determine your liability in a situation, or even if you want to renew your commitment to it.

Rewarding Days: 4, 14, 15, 19, 20, 23, 24, 31

Challenging Days: 1, 7, 8, 21, 22, 27, 28, 29

Affirmation for the Month
I am open to new ideas and innovative, healthy change.

Taurus/August

In the Spotlight
Making improvements can take your time and resources, although you may enjoy putting your energy behind changes that brighten your personal space or strengthen your sense of security. Family activities may take center stage.

Wellness and Keeping Fit
Spending time in nature is rejuvenating, even if you're simply relaxing in your own backyard, or taking walks through the park. Bring nature inside with freshly cut flowers, or make alterations in your environment by using feng shui to balance the energy of your home or office.

Love and Life Connections
Confirm your emotional commitments by expressing your feelings and needs. Home and family are highlighted during the Full Moon on August 4, when good news dominates the conversation. Get in touch with siblings from August 1-26, when you may feel more like putting old problems behind you. Children can be a special source of joy after August 13.

Finance and Success
Business meetings, conferences, or seminars which provide enhancement of your skills can boost your career. You're filled with great ideas to improve your options. Feeling more confident about speculative investments, you're more comfortable investigating now and keeping your risk at a minimum. Eliminating debts and reworking partnership contracts can free your resources.

Cosmic Insider Tip
With Saturn and Pluto in opposition, structures like government and big business are transforming and can affect your pocketbook. Openings to your advantage occur after August 15.

Rewarding Days: 1, 2, 6, 10, 11, 12, 15, 16, 19, 28, 29

Challenging Days: 3, 4, 17, 18, 23, 24, 25, 30, 31

Affirmation for the Month
I am a trustworthy provider.

Taurus/September

In the Spotlight
Expanding your outreach professionally and educationally promotes your feelings of success. Making alterations in your schedule or work arrangements to increase your productivity can also give you more free time, bringing greater satisfaction into your life.

Wellness and Keeping Fit
You'll enjoy fitness classes which integrate philosophical concepts of energy with activity—like yoga, chi gung, or martial arts. This is a time to bring body, mind, and spirit into harmony through conscious effort and experience.

Love and Life Connections
The flow of love is amplified during the Full Moon on September 2, when you're trusting your own feelings more completely and may have a better communication with your partner, too. Romantic relationships are emphasized, and you may sense that you're more in touch with the spiritual qualities of your partner than in the past. Take steps to strengthen your commitment during the New Moon on September 17, when the wounds of the past are finally healing.

Finance and Success
Building better communications at work is important, especially if you're anticipating making some organizational changes during the next few months. Clarify expectations from September 6-12, when you may be caught playing catch-up if someone falls short. Business meetings and legal matters fare best after September 9, although your ideas may differ from those of your counterparts.

Cosmic Insider Tip
An unusual financial opportunity may arise from September 7-20 and it could be beneficial if it fits with your goals and plans. However, altering your path will feel uncomfortably risky.

Rewarding Days: 3, 7, 8, 11, 15, 16, 24, 25, 29, 30

Challenging Days: 1, 13, 14, 19, 20, 21, 26, 27, 28

Affirmation for the Month
The path of Truth is safe.

Taurus/October

In the Spotlight
Progress on the career front and positive reviews of your performance keep you hopeful about a prosperous future. Schedule changes and miscommunication can be frustrating, however, so you'll need to maintain your sense of humor!

Wellness and Keeping Fit
A vacation early in the month could be just what you need. Your energy levels are up, and staying active while building your endurance adds marvelous productivity to your days.

Love and Life Connections
Your travels are likely to lead toward the path to love, purely wonderful and uplifting. Do with it what you will: yield to creative inspiration, improve an existing relationship, or nurture your kids. But use this energy to open your heart and fuel the bright vitality of loving. It's time to release self-doubt and trust your feelings, since you probably have good evidence of what's really happening. Extending yourself to others simply feels good now.

Finance and Success
Mercury retrogrades from October 1-22, strongly influencing work-related interactions. It's a good time to review your performance and the performances of others, making positive critiques which can lead to better productivity and job satisfaction. Ethical differences may arise near the Full Moon on October 2, testing your tolerance. Finances appear strong throughout the month, with an infusion of new opportunities after October 21. Tread carefully with partners after that time.

Cosmic Insider Tip
Your ability to influence others can be enhanced from October 1-14, although if your motives are purely selfish they could backfire.

Rewarding Days: 4, 5, 9, 10, 13, 14, 21, 22, 26, 31

Challenging Days: 2, 11, 12, 17, 18, 24, 25

Affirmation for the Month
My principles are based upon Higher Truth.

Taurus/November

In the Spotlight
You're driven to accomplish your ambitions, and may be unusually competitive if you feel that your position is threatened. Harnessing your drive and directing it toward your goals without undermining anyone else can be quite a feat!

Wellness and Keeping Fit
You need a playful outlet for your tensions, and a fitness class or regular exercise routine may be your key to remaining sane and viable during this stressful period. If emotional issues have you in a knot, seek support from an understanding counselor.

Love and Life Connections
Partnerships and social relationships have their definite ups and downs. If you're happy with a relationship you may feel that you're seriously committed to enjoying the benefits; however, if you're in a situation which does not fulfill your needs, all the shortcomings will glare back at you during the Taurus Full Moon on November 1. Building a different pattern is promising after the New Moon on November 15, but old habits sometimes die a painful death.

Finance and Success
Deception from competitors or those who see you as a threat can be problematic from November 1-13. Finding the right way to bring things into the open can be a delicate maneuver. If negotiations break down early in the month, try again from November 18-24. Unexpected changes at work or with your superiors can be disruptive, but may ultimately lead to a better position.

Cosmic Insider Tip
Human relations provide the ultimate tests, and becoming aware of a hidden agenda will place you in a position of strength from November 1-15.

Rewarding Days: 1, 2, 5, 6, 9, 10, 18, 19, 23, 28, 29

Challenging Days: 7, 8, 13, 14, 20, 21, 22

Affirmation for the Month
I accept the differences between myself and others.

Taurus/December

In the Spotlight
Making adjustments to keep everyone else happy can seem too costly, and although you're willing to bend a little, you do have your priorities! Friends keep your heart singing this month.

Wellness and Keeping Fit
Team sports can be a great alternative if you want a change in your fitness routine—especially if it's a seasonal commitment. Otherwise, use the support you gain from a fitness class or working out with a buddy to keep you on track with your goals.

Love and Life Connections
Tensions with family can escalate early in the month, but you're ready to call a cease-fire by December 8. Unfortunately, if you've been ignoring important issues in an intimate relationship, they may reach a climax during the solar eclipse on December 14. At least you're in a great place to air your grievances, which is the first step toward healing. Finding common ground is easier after December 16, and by the lunar eclipse on December 30 you're ready to embrace what (and whom) you love.

Finance and Success
Power struggles over money can be the bottom-line problem, and this can raise its head in your personal and professional relationships. Year-end budgets may fall short, but a solution which will not require compromise is possible after December 15. Meetings with others who can help you promote yourself or advance your career prove beneficial from December 23-31.

Cosmic Insider Tip
Be especially attentive to the benefits of your relationship, since taking someone for granted can get you into trouble near the Sun's eclipse on December 14! Gratitude works wonders.

Rewarding Days: 2, 3, 7, 15, 16, 20, 21, 25, 26, 30

Challenging Days: 4, 5, 11, 12, 17, 18, 19, 31

Affirmation for the Month
With grace and in perfect ways, the Universe always provides.

Taurus Action Table

These dates reflect the best—but not the only—times for success and ease in these activities, according to your Sun sign.

	JAN	FEB	MAR	APR	MAY	JUN	JUL	AUG	SEPT	OCT	NOV	DEC
Move							30, 31	1-13				
Start a class						21, 22	13-29					
Join a club		23, 24										
Ask for a raise				23, 24								
Look for work		6-28	1-16						1-30	24-31	1-6	
Get pro advice	16-18	13, 14	12, 13	9, 10	6, 7	2-4, 30	1, 27-28	23, 24	19-21	17, 18	13, 14	11, 12
Get a loan	19, 20	14, 15, 17	14-16	11, 12	8, 9	5, 6	2-3, 29-30	24, 25, 27	22, 23	19, 20	15-17	13, 14
See a doctor				6-20					1-30	1-31	1-6	
Start a diet	14, 15	11, 12	10, 11	7, 8	4, 5, 31	1, 27-28	25, 26	21, 22	17, 18	14, 15	11, 12	8-10
End relationship					6, 7							
Buy clothes								14-31				
Get a makeover				23, 24		6-30	1-4					
New romance									17, 21-30	1-14		
Vacation	21-23	18, 19	17, 18	13-15	11, 12	7, 8	4-6, 31	1-2, 28-29	24, 25	21-23	18, 19	15, 16

Taurus • 73

Gemini

The Twins
May 20 to June 21

♊

Element:	Air
Quality:	Mutable
Polarity:	Yang/Masculine
Planetary Ruler:	Mercury
Meditation:	My mind is linked to the Source.
Gemstone:	Tourmaline
Power Stones:	Ametrine, citrine, emerald, spectrolite, agate
Key Phrase:	I think
Glyph:	Pillars of duality, the Twins
Anatomy:	Hands, arms, shoulders, lungs, nervous system
Color:	Bright colors, orange, yellow, magenta
Animal:	Monkeys, talking birds, flying insects
Myths/Legends:	Peter Pan, Castor and Pollux
House:	Third
Opposite Sign:	Sagittarius
Flower:	Lily of the valley
Key Word:	Versatility

Positive Expression:
Curious
Clever
Flexible
Articulate
Perceptive
Rational

Misuse of Energy:
Distracted
Prankish
Duplicitous
Gossipy
Fickle
Uncertain

Gemini

Your Ego's Strengths and Shortcomings

Your youthful aura is a reflection of your ardent desire to explore and experience the multidimensional qualities of life. With an active mind, you play the role in the zodiac of "The Questioner," leading you to meet fascinating people and explore a variety of situations. You respect clear intelligence and may strive throughout your life to develop your mind.

You're a natural in situations that call for discovery of common purpose, and can link individuals and groups from dissimilar backgrounds through identifying and communicating their mutual ties. As a result, you're frequently playing the diplomat, and have more than once been in the position of talking your way out of tight spots, especially if someone thinks you're playing both sides against the middle! Your own curiosity and love of travel may lead you to explore academic goals and relationships with people from many walks of life. Those who need consistency may be frustrated by your continual juggling of several projects at once, since this could be seen by some as indicative of a lack of focus or commitment.

The mental, communicative energy of Mercury, your planetary ruler, stimulates your need to develop a multifaceted nature. It is this same energy of rationale and logic which, when linked with your keen intuitive insights, can become your ingenuity. Ultimately, your life leads you onto the path of universality, since your true nature rests in your connection to the Source of All Knowledge, where you uncover the answers to your insatiable questions.

Shining Your Love Light

You may prefer playing the field in relationships for a while, since it can seem impossible to find one individual to fulfill your needs. Realizing that you can commit to a relationship only when you share a true meeting of the minds, you need a partner who appreciates your ever-changing nature and will support your need for independence and variety. While you can be an excellent partner, you may feel uncomfortable sorting through the complexities of deep emotional issues, since they don't always make sense! Accepting that emotions operate on a level which occasionally defies logic, you can gradually submit to the alchemy of love.

Since you're an air sign, you live in the world of the intellect, and may be most comfortable around other air signs—Libra, Aquarius, and Gemini—who also enjoy communication and ideas. You'll enjoy the freewheeling exuberance for life that Aries has. Taurus appeals to your sensual nature, but may move too slowly for you. Another Gemini may be exciting at first, but you can run into problems if your personal boundaries are not well-defined. Cancer's comfort and care feel good, although your differences in handling money can be a source for concern. With Leo, you'll love the warmth and can develop a deep bond of understanding. Virgo's analytical mind is thought-provoking and you feel at home together, although you may be frustrated if she or he overdoes it with the little details.

Libra's easy for you to love, and you'll adore her or his exceptional grace and taste. You're engaged by Scorpio's intensity but can lose patience with her/his enigmatic nature. Your natural attraction to adventurous Sagittarius, your opposite, is strong, although you'll have to cope with that wanderlust if the relationship is to work out. It's possible to become connected to Capricorn, although you may always feel that you've fallen short of the mark where they're concerned. Aquarius can be a soulful connection, sharing your philosophies while stimulating your need to reach beyond limitations. The key to enjoying Pisces is yielding to fantasy-filled nights, but you can get confused easily by what he or she wants during normal waking hours!

Making Your Place in the World

Developing your mind is a key ingredient to finding a career path with long-term appeal, although you may pursue several career directions over the course of this lifetime. Honing your communication skills builds your confidence in your abilities, as sharpening your intellect opens the way for a variety of choices.

Public speaking, writing, teaching, working in advertising, politics, counseling, or broadcasting—all can be excellent choices and good outlets for your imaginative ideas. Exercise your manual dexterity through design, dentistry, drafting, musical pursuits, or working at a keyboard. Careers in highly technical areas, such as the computer industry, can offer a chance to work with your hands while using your brain. In performing arts, consider pantomime, clowning, juggling, comedy, storytelling, and acting.

Power Plays

Abuses of power can put you off the idea entirely, although you have always been keenly aware of the power of the mind and the tremendous influence of ideas on the course of human life. You understand the value and power of keeping your mind open to fresh perceptions, and are aware of the possibilities inherent in the use of media and other communication systems. You feel most personally empowered when you have a good grasp of a concept and can clearly and concisely illustrate it to others.

Continually supporting the importance of education of youth and assuring the availability of information and technology can be a lifelong quest. You're the bridge-builder, creating the path linking what has gone before with what is yet to come. By coupling your contagious enthusiasm with brilliant ideas, rooted in wisdom, you'll have the greatest influence. You can sometimes be content with allowing your wit to get you out of a jam, but desire to be known for something more than superficial quips. Bridging your mind with higher consciousness, you're challenged to share your understanding as a means of lifting the spirit of humanity to heights that empower us as a whole.

Famous Geminis

Don Ameche, Art Bell, Boy George, Kurt Browning, Joan Collins, Jacques Cousteau, Johnny Depp, Arthur Conan Doyle, Ian Fleming, Judy Garland, Newt Gingrinch, Bob Hope, Elizabeth Hurley, Wynonna Judd, Joe Montana, Mark Wahlberg, Noah Wylie

The Year Ahead for Gemini

You're making significant progress this year, taking strides that may alter your life course and meeting the challenge of dealing with transformational changes in the world around you. Your flexibility is a definite asset during 2001, since anyone trying to hold onto anything too intensely or resisting progress will suffer disappointments. Your ability to visualize the directions these changes are taking and to share your visions will be highly sought after by others needing guidance and inspiration.

Fortune smiles from January through July 12 while Jupiter continues its transit in Gemini, invigorating your confidence and visionary capabilities. Since Jupiter travels through your sign only once every twelve years, the strides you're making now can set the stage for long-term growth. It helps to know your limits, however, since it's easy to overdo it, particularly by making promises which later are difficult to honor. By using this time to launch significant changes or reach further toward your long-term goals, you may feel you're going further, faster. From July 12 through the end of the year, Jupiter's expansive energy highlights the Second House of your solar chart, indicating a period of increasing resources. Just remember that while you may have more to spend, you can also be tempted to buy on impulse or to exceed the capacity of your resources: time and money.

Saturn moves into Gemini on April 22, initiating a cycle which will last a little over two years. Your grasp of reality improves, placing you firmly in touch with your priorities, responsibilities, and obligations. This cycle tends to add a feeling of heaviness, and your awareness that you're making meaningful choices that can and will have a long-term impact helps you weigh your decisions more carefully. You will either experience the conjunction of Saturn to your Sun this year or next year (see below to check your birth date), although you'll feel the influence of Saturn until it leaves your sign in 2003. You may also run into your fears, or can be confronted by the fears of others—who will protest if you determine that it's time for them to stand on their own two feet. After all, responsible action sometimes entails letting go of burdens that are no longer yours to carry!

The outer planets—Uranus, Neptune, and Pluto—continue their slow course, influencing your social connections and opening the way to a more independent level of self-expression. Uranus and Neptune transit through the Ninth House of your solar chart, energizing your connection to Spirit and increasing your desire to open your mind to truth. Pluto's cycle continues in your opposite sign, challenging you to unravel your commitments and to explore the nature of your partnerships. Unhealthy bonds can create problems on multiple levels, especially if you've outgrown the need for an existing partnership or if it is destructive to your well-being.

The solar and lunar eclipses add an increasing emphasis to the balance between your needs and the demands of a partnership or marriage. Your awareness of what you want and expect from such connections is increasing, and a crisis in these circumstances can lead to either a breakup or a new or different relationship. Specific challenges will be explained in the monthly forecasts section.

If you were born from May 20 to June 6, you're feeling the stabilizing, but delaying, influence of Saturn transiting in conjunction to your Sun. This cycle happens every twenty-eight to thirty years, and marks a significant period of reality testing. You cannot hide from your real self or your deeper needs, which are crying out for some level of recognition and fulfillment, but you can manifest some long-held desires for self-expression. Spiritually, this is a time when karmic ties are ripe for release, and if you're no longer tied to a situation or a person (your heart will let you know!) then it's time to begin the dissolution or ending. Keeping yourself in situations that no longer fit can become a very tight squeeze. It may require most of this year to complete your obligations, and the manner in which you accomplish this task will determine how far you can go toward a new focus next year. This is an excellent period to evaluate your career and your close relationships, since you will know if you're in a circumstance that will allow you to grow toward the true promise of your most soulful needs. It's also a year of destiny, when some endings may happen which you cannot control, but your manner of response will tell the tale! This is an important time for making commitments, and those you promise now can be lasting if they are in harmony with your needs. Physically, you may respond to stress more intensely, and consciously making an effort to let go of tension and maintain your flexibility will greatly aid your sense of well-being. An old problem can reappear, although it does not have to be debilitating. Sometimes you get to take another look at something in order to find a better way to deal with it—once and for all!

If you were born from May 26 to 31, you're experiencing enhanced spirituality while Neptune transits in trine aspect to your Sun, in addition to the influence of Saturn's cycle described above. Your intuitive awareness can be intensified during this time, and blending your intuitive sensibilities with logical processes will be easier than in the past. Creatively, you're filled with yearning and may find that you can surrender to the flow of your creative expression—dancing with the muse on a regular basis! It's time to forgive and release the things in your life that stand in the way of your sense of peace and inner harmony, including old disappointments in yourself which may have driven your guilt in the past. Although you may be more physically sensitive, you're also more aware of the mind-body-spirit connection, and can move through healing processes with grace. Your desire to make a difference in the world can spark your philanthropic spirit, and giving of your time, energy and resources can be especially rewarding now. Your actions can set a new precedent in your life, and also change the lives of others at the same time.

If you were born from June 3 to 8, it's time to surrender to transformational changes while Pluto transits in opposition to your Sun. Since this cycle is occurring at the same time that Saturn transits in conjunction to your Sun, you may be experiencing an uncommon number of endings, with many things seeming to reach their logical and inevitable conclusions. This does not have to be thought of as a "bad" thing, since nature teaches us that one cycle must end for another to begin. However, you may feel that some endings are simply beyond your control, and you may be faced with the need to cope with power struggles or large-scale alterations in the structures of your life. These influences can be much like remodeling an old house: worn-out wallpaper and coats of paint are stripped away, old plumbing and wiring gutted, and the structure is restored to its utmost quality. Instead, it's time to remodel your life, taking a careful look at your attachments and security base to determine whether or not they need to be transformed. Your sense of self is changing, too, and you may finally be ready to complete some things that have been hanging on for what seems to be an eternity. Through your creative impulse and ability to see options, you can use this time to literally recreate yourself and your life. However, you may not be able to hold onto the things you no longer need, and to do that you may have to surrender to a higher nature than your own, trusting that you will emerge as a more complete expression of all that you are and all you want to become.

If you were born from June 9 to 17, you're feeling the energy of Uranus transiting in trine aspect to your Sun. This is an exciting time—you may finally be ready to try those wings! Changes made now can be more natural, and it's simply easier to be yourself under this influence. Alterations in your relationships can lift you to a different level of understanding, and you may finally be ready to take the leap professionally into areas that foster your growth and success. Educational pursuits, including nontraditional approaches to learning, can lead toward amazing recognition and opportunities to join forces with others whose talents and expertise are on the leading edge of progress. Travel, global communications, and expanded outreach all play a part in your growth this year.

If you were born from June 18 to 21, it's time to take steps which will help you move from one situation to another. Saturn is transiting in semisextile to your Sun from January through April, marking a time when you're making steady progress toward your goals. Dealing honestly with your responsibilities during the first four months of the year can be the key to experiencing the kind of success you've hoped to achieve. You're also learning the value of acknowledging existing structures, even if you have every intention of ultimately changing them! Then, during June, you're ready to move ahead full-steam while Mercury, Mars, and Jupiter are all transiting in strong aspect to your Sun. During this time, you may feel that you're unstoppable, although you'll do yourself the favor of moving deliberately and taking actions with clarity and purpose. For the remainder of the year, there should be fewer obstacles in your path.

Tools to Make a Difference

Clutter has no place in your life now, since anything that's weighing you down will become entirely too heavy. Whether your mind is filled with worrisome thoughts or your closet is full of junk, it's time to clear out anything that's just taking up space. Putting your energy behind such simple tasks as reorganizing your office or wardrobe can be a perfect complement to the fact that you're eager to reorganize your life and to restructure your priorities.

Finding effective methods of reducing tension is important now that Saturn's in your sign, and you might even want to learn how to do massage (share with your partner!) and will do yourself a favor by keeping an eye out for effective massage tools. If you enjoy drawing or doodling, you might find study of Asian calligraphy an effective means of calming your mind and focusing your energy while learning these brush strokes. Breathing techniques are always helpful to you, but you might want to extend these to playing a bamboo flute for relaxation and enjoyment. Keep your hands and wrists supple and strong by taking the time to learn hand stretches, especially if you spend much time at a keyboard.

Reading for enjoyment and relaxation is a great idea, but you might also find that listening to books on tape during long commutes helps you pass the time, and you get a story in the process! Travel itself can be an exceptional tool for personal growth this year. If you cannot visit exotic places, consider taking a class that explores the culture and arts of an area you've always wanted to investigate. And if space is your penchant, maybe it's time to set up that telescope on the back deck and study the stars!

♊

Affirmation for the Year

I cheerfully release the things I no longer need.

Gemini/January

In the Spotlight
Patience (the virtue!) may be in short supply, especially if you're eager to implement your visionary concepts or plans. Convincing others to let go of their resistance may require you to produce practical reasons why they should follow your ideas.

Wellness and Keeping Fit
Making time for fitness activities is important now. Not only will you feel better physically, but taking the break from daily hassles gives you a chance to let go of mounting tension. However, avoid high-risk situations, especially from January 13-31.

Love and Life Connections
Your professional obligations can be a source of conflict with your partner, or you may feel that you're caught in the sticky situation of trying to keep everyone happy. Explore your deeper motivations during the lunar eclipse on January 9, when your attachments are more readily identified. By the New Moon on January 24 you're ready to release some of those connections, especially if they are going against your deeper emotional needs.

Finance and Success
Tensions at work may simply be the result of different styles of doing things. But if you're feeling unappreciated, your tolerance for all those demands grows shorter by the minute. Unresolved financial dealings require extra attention through January 20. Business meetings, presentations, and advertising can all have great results after January 19.

Cosmic Insider Tip
Clear away unfinished business early, since you'll need the time and room to explore your visionary ideas and may be ready to put them into motion with the New Moon on January 24.

Rewarding Days: 2, 6, 7, 11, 14, 15, 24, 25, 29, 30

Challenging Days: 1, 12, 13, 19, 20, 21, 26, 27

Affirmation for the Month
I respect and honor the differences between myself and others.

Gemini/February

In the Spotlight
Mercury's retrograde can work to your advantage, since you have a chance to revisit a situation and make essential alterations. New projects may be postponed, but there is progress with things that are already underway.

Wellness and Keeping Fit
Finding an enjoyable outlet for an emerging competitiveness gives you what you need: a healthy challenge. Whether you're setting personal fitness goals or involved in sports, aiming toward a goal keeps you charged and ready to go.

Love and Life Connections
Old ties can be renewed, or you may finally drop your resistance and allow the love you're feeling to guide your actions and decisions during the Full Moon on February 8. Avoiding the urging of your heart can lead to misery, although you may think you have good reasons. Rash action is not the answer, but careful exploration of your motivations can be illuminating to all concerned.

Finance and Success
You may finally feel happier with your career or community-involved activities, and the support you're receiving from peers gives your reputation and confidence a boost. Educational pursuits or convening with others in your field opens the way for progress, and you're ready to take on a major challenge. Learn about competitors to avoid being blind-sided after February 22.

Cosmic Insider Tip
Equipment breakdowns or missed appointments can waylay progress from February 7-12, but you can use this time to regroup. Fortunately, you usually think fast in a crisis!

Rewarding Days: 3, 4, 7, 8, 11, 12, 20, 21, 25, 26

Challenging Days: 1, 9, 10, 15, 16, 17, 23, 24

Affirmation for the Month
My goals reflect the yearnings of my heart and support my highest needs.

Gemini/March

In the Spotlight
Prosperity on several fronts allows you to make choices which add a sense of accomplishment and satisfaction. It's time to explore your values and hopes.

Wellness and Keeping Fit
Chronic problems can flare or old psychological issues may percolate to the surface. Either way, it's time to look at underlying causes for any discontent. A holistic approach can help turn things around during the Full Moon on March 9.

Love and Life Connections
Watch your expectations, and take special care to assure that others are not receiving mixed signals from you. Power struggles can arise over unresolved hurts from the past, and it may not take much to throw off your sense of balance from March 7-21. The New Moon on March 25 marks a time to establish better communication about what you hope to accomplish in your personal relationships.

Finance and Success
A contract or partnership needs another look, especially if you're managing your resources differently or if you feel that the brunt of the responsibility has fallen on your shoulders. Explore your investment portfolio once Venus turns retrograde on March 8, since you may need to sell options that are not performing up to your hopes or needs. Make room for innovations from March 5-31.

Cosmic Insider Tip
With Mercury and Uranus joining forces from March 4-11 and Mars and Pluto conjunct on March 18, you have powerful ammunition if you need it. Just make sure that you know the price before you agree to pay it!

Rewarding Days: 2, 3, 6, 7, 12, 19, 20, 21, 29, 30

Challenging Days: 8, 9, 13, 14, 15, 16, 22, 23

Affirmation for the Month
I am making the best use of all my resources.

Gemini/April

In the Spotlight
You're thinking about the future, but may feel very firmly centered in the present—just exactly the position you need to actualize your hopes and dreams! Establish a clear concept of your goals now and take initial steps toward them. Remember: one day at a time.

Wellness and Keeping Fit
Failing to allowing adequate time for rest and rejuvenation takes its toll, and making the adjustments to your schedule may seem futile since your time is at a premium.

Love and Life Connections
Friction with your partner can send you into withdrawal. Your attempts to bring a healthy balance into your relationship can make a difference, but you're also studying the situation to determine if your partnership is up to the task. An alternative may emerge during the Full Moon on April 8, when you have an experience of unconditional acceptance. Use your time of introspection after April 20 to explore your honest needs and feelings.

Finance and Success
Whether you're eliminating debt, products that aren't selling, or finally putting a project to rest which is simply not progressing at all—you're ready to maximize your potential. Contractual agreements fare best from April 6-20, although you may have to make compromises. Put your best spin on the situation from April 1-13, then give it a rest if nothing's moving along.

Cosmic Insider Tip
The New Moon on April 23 marks a time of intense vision, when your dreams can lead the way. It's your job to build the foundation to make them real.

Rewarding Days: 3, 7, 8, 16, 17, 21, 22, 25, 26, 30

Challenging Days: 4, 5, 6, 11, 12, 18, 19, 20

Affirmation for the Month
I am confident in the face of new possibilities.

Gemini/May

In the Spotlight
You're making definite progress where it matters most, although you may feel a slowdown due to the emergence of others who see you as competition. Careful planning and well-considered actions on your part keep you in the game.

Wellness and Keeping Fit
Setting the right pace can be a challenge, especially once Mars turns retrograde on May 11. Getting involved in social fitness or recreation can be a great idea, but nobody said you have to be captain of the team!

Love and Life Connections
Your heart is filled to the brim with good feelings, and while you may be tearing down some old structures in your life, you're open to experiencing the healing quality of pure love. It's easy to get involved with another person's agenda, and if you feel a bit overwhelmed with expectations pull back and talk about them. By the Gemini New Moon on May 23 you're ready to set the pace and clarify precisely where you want a relationship to go.

Finance and Success
Community activities or professional associations with others who share your ideas and principles provide a chance for you to actualize your ideas and take the lead where it matters most. It's crucial that you remain aware of potential undermining during the Full Moon on May 7, but you can quickly bring this situation to the surface if necessary.

Cosmic Insider Tip
The opposition from Jupiter to Pluto on May 6 continues its influence all month. You can set the pace and define the parameters, but watch for the hidden agenda of power mongers.

Rewarding Days: 1, 4, 5, 13, 14, 18, 19, 23, 24, 27, 31

Challenging Days: 2, 3, 6, 7, 8, 9, 16, 17, 29, 30

Affirmation for the Month
I am clear about my intentions and honest about my motivations.

Gemini/June

In the Spotlight
You are in the spotlight! It's time to take your place and get your ideas out there. The main problem is identifying your limitations, since this is a period of powerful opportunity, and you may not want to say "no" to any of them.

Wellness and Keeping Fit
Although you may not like to admit it, you do have to watch your tendency to run on nervous energy alone. Rest helps! Increase intake of foods high in B-vitamins, and nourish your mind with supplements like gingko biloba. Trouble relaxing? Try valerian and chamomile tea at night.

Love and Life Connections
Your exuberance can be very attractive, and if you're seeking to confirm or begin a love relationship, then around the Full Moon on June 6 you'll have just the right stimuli to help you say what's in your heart and on your mind. A situation you thought was over may return, especially if you had not reached closure. Maybe it deserves a second chance!

Finance and Success
Mercury retrogrades in your sign from June 4-27, which can be a good thing if you need to revise or complete an ongoing or existing project. Taking on new ventures is not advised, since you have plenty on your plate already. However, do take full advantage of the doors opening to you, and show interest, even if you cannot commit just yet.

Cosmic Insider Tip
The planetary pictures bring high energy your way, although you may feel very overcommitted. Mercury and Jupiter in Gemini oppose Mars: choose your battles with great care.

Rewarding Days: 1, 9, 10, 11, 15, 16, 19, 20, 24, 27, 28

Challenging Days: 5, 6, 7, 12, 13, 25, 26

Affirmation for the Month
I am fully actualizing my potentials—with great joy!

Gemini/July

In the Spotlight
You can send the right signals—but at the wrong time. By being more attentive to the responses of others and the overall climate you can better determine when a situation is ripe for you or your ideas. Then, making a commitment works for everyone concerned.

Wellness and Keeping Fit
Outside pressures can take their toll physically, and near the Moon's eclipse (July 5) you may need to take it easy. Slowing the pace, and taking time for tension-relieving massage, reflexology treatments, or a soak in the hot tub might be just what you need.

Love and Life Connections
Venus travels in your sign from July 5-31, stimulating your most attractive qualities, but also energizing your need to open your heart to those you love. Romance is emphasized, but you're serious about making sure that your sweetheart knows where you stand, especially from July 12-28, when your need to experience a melding of hearts and minds only works if you feel trust and understanding from the other side.

Finance and Success
Contract negotiations can be nerve-racking, although you're not willing to compromise on important issues. Budgetary matters can be troubling early in the month, but setting out a clear plan with long-range implications helps you determine if you can commit your energy and time to an agreement. If you're satisfied with the fine print, moving forward from July 1-4 or after July 20 can assure steady progress toward your ultimate goals.

Cosmic Insider Tip
Mars turns direct on July 19, and afterward you'll see things that were stalled start moving again. Including you.

Rewarding Days: 7, 8, 12, 13, 16, 17, 18, 21, 25, 26

Challenging Days: 2, 3, 9, 10, 11, 23, 24, 29, 30

Affirmation for the Month
I am clearly aware of my strengths when faced with challenges.

Gemini/August

In the Spotlight
Strengthening your support network may require that you juggle your priorities in order to create a better balance between what you need from others and what you have to offer in return. You may meet with ethical challenges, and need to know who's in your camp.

Wellness and Keeping Fit
Dealing with stress continues to be an important consideration in terms of your sense of well-being. Destructive habits and attitudes need careful assessment. Explore your submerged feelings.

Love and Life Connections
Resentment has a way of destroying joy, and you're seeing the interplay of emotional manipulation, which creates negative feelings and responses. Talking about your concerns with a trusted advisor during the Full Moon on August 4 can help, but the person you need to address may not be open to changing anything. Psychological tension can drain you, but you can also confront the situation honestly, even though it may hurt initially. Try open discussion on August 19.

Finance and Success
If you or your partner has failed to manage finances appropriately, problems can escalate and rapidly undermine your sense of financial stability. Revise your budget, and set up different procedures after August 17. A contract may fall apart due to circumstances beyond your control, but in the end things can work to your benefit. Make a careful reassessment, and then move ahead on August 21.

Cosmic Insider Tip
Saturn opposes Pluto, indicating that old structures are crumbling or undergoing revision. Shoulder your responsibilities, but avoid carrying burdens which others need to carry for themselves.

Rewarding Days: 3, 4, 8, 9, 13, 14, 18, 21, 22, 30, 31

Challenging Days: 5, 6, 7, 11, 19, 20, 25, 26, 27

Affirmation for the Month
I am flexible when it counts!

Gemini/September

In the Spotlight
Joint resources and family finances can be a source of dispute, although the real problems may go much deeper. You have to decide how far you're willing to probe, since you could get into risky territory if you expose those skeletons in the closet!

Wellness and Keeping Fit
You need a rest after all the high-intensity experiences of the last few months, but may feel that your obligations preclude anything like a vacation. It's still a good idea to get away, if only for a few days. You're more likely to relax between September 1-8.

Love and Life Connections
A close relationship with one who shares your ideals strengthens your emotional union. You're ready to share your dreams with a nurturing supporter, and may find that you're offering a positive reciprocity in the process. You're also confronting old inhibitions, which may be more noticeable if you're in the midst of difficulties with family during the Full Moon on September 2.

Finance and Success
Your ideas and the ability to communicate them gives your career a boost. Others are inspired by your enthusiasm, and an influential individual can offer surprising support, which opens the way toward fulfilling a long-held hope. Travel, writing, and teaching play important roles in career advancement, with new technologies adding a spin from September 12-22. Make a special effort to solicit clear communication to avoid stepping on sensitive toes.

Cosmic Insider Tip
Impulsive actions can be costly after September 15, even if you have the best of intentions, and this tendency multiplies at the end of the month!

Rewarding Days: 1, 4, 5, 9, 10, 14, 18, 26, 27

Challenging Days: 2, 3, 15, 16, 22, 23, 29, 30

Affirmation for the Month
In all things I seek Truth and clarity.

Gemini/October

In the Spotlight
Expressions of the heart take center stage. Whether you're gaining pure enjoyment from your interactions with your kids, opening more fully to a passionate relationship, or spending more time developing your creative talents, love is flowing through your life.

Wellness and Keeping Fit
Delving into root causes of physical or emotional problems leads to solutions. You're in a cycle of purification, when the body is ready to clear out toxic materials, and you can help the process by eliminating destructive habits and improving nutrition.

Love and Life Connections
On some levels you're letting go of the inhibitions which have blocked your ability to experience love at its utmost. The Full Moon on October 2 helps open the flow of love, and you may have an opportunity to rekindle the fires of passion with your sweetheart by expressing what's in your heart. You can start anew on October 16, breaking an old cycle and initiating fresh possibilities.

Finance and Success
Mercury's retrograde from October 1-22 prompts a second look at your investments. Review your portfolio and plan new strategies. Begin projects after October 23, but watch for competitors and power plays, since there may be someone in the wings who does not really want you to succeed! Fortunately, you have a diplomatic way of calling attention to the problems and issues, and you should emerge relatively unscathed.

Cosmic Insider Tip
A change of priorities or sudden alteration in the structure of your life opens the way for progress from October 1-9. Negotiate, but postpone final agreements until October 23.

Rewarding Days: 2, 3, 6, 7, 8, 12, 15, 16, 24, 25, 29, 30

Challenging Days: 13, 14, 18, 19, 20, 22, 26, 27

Affirmation for the Month
I promise only what I can reasonably expect to accomplish.

Gemini/November

In the Spotlight
Increasing activity stemming from career and community involvements keeps you on the go. Travel and political interaction can place you in the position of negotiator, although this is also a great time to promote your own agenda and advance your reputation.

Wellness and Keeping Fit
Your physical vitality improves, although you're also looking for effective ways to pamper yourself just a little. You deserve it! Consider a spa visit or retreat on November 1 or at the New Moon on November 15. At the very least, schedule a massage.

Love and Life Connections
Romance is in the air from the Full Moon from November 1-6, when a vacation or travel with your lover can provide the perfect setting to solidify your commitment. You may be pulled into work situations immediately afterward, which seems to create a wall between you and your sweetheart, but clear communication can help keep potential problems to a minimum. After November 20 you're ready to play again, and you'll enjoy taking more risks.

Finance and Success
Promotional activities are emphasized all month, although you may need to hold back just a little to determine where everyone stands. Personnel problems can arise from November 8-25 secondary to a weak link, and you may uncover deceptive practices which need to be resolved. Make a fresh start after the New Moon on November 15: the situation is ripe for reorganization.

Cosmic Insider Tip
Saturn in your sign opposing Pluto unravels tightly wound problems, and you may feel that you're finally close to resolving difficult issues. Your open mind gives you more options.

Rewarding Days: 3, 4, 7, 8, 11, 12, 20, 21, 25, 26, 30

Challenging Days: 1, 2, 9, 10, 15, 16, 17, 23, 24

Affirmation for the Month
Higher Truth inspires my thoughts, words, and actions.

Gemini/December

In the Spotlight
Social activities give your reputation a boost, and you're also experiencing gains through your partner. This is an excellent period to negotiate and finalize agreements that can set the pace for the months ahead.

Wellness and Keeping Fit
Keep up with your fitness routine by enlisting a buddy or getting into an unusual fitness class. You need a change of pace, and will enjoy exploring innovative ways to improve your physique. Stress levels are on the increase midmonth, and regular workouts can keep tension at bay.

Love and Life Connections
What you need from a partnership is changing, and if your partner is also making changes or expressing different needs you may begin to question the effects on your relationship. In some ways, these alterations can be exciting, and during the solar eclipse on December 14 your anxieties can peak, exposing the situation for what it is. From there, you can make alterations which enliven your relationship and your life experience.

Finance and Success
Publications, business meetings, or conferences fare best from December 1-10, and you may determine that you need to form different associations in order to advance your career. Clarify expectations, keeping your concerns and needs clearly in focus, and finalize agreements on or after December 14.

Cosmic Insider Tip
You may feel driven to succeed with Mars transiting through the Tenth House of your solar chart. This also indicates the emergence of competitors, so be on the alert!

Rewarding Days: 1, 5, 9, 10, 18, 19, 22, 23, 27, 28

Challenging Days: 6, 7, 13, 14, 15, 20, 21, 30

Affirmation for the Month
I am clearly aware of my motivations and intentions.

Gemini Action Table

These dates reflect the best—but not the only—times for success and ease in these activities, according to your Sun sign.

	JAN	FEB	MAR	APR	MAY	JUN	JUL	AUG	SEPT	OCT	NOV	DEC
Move								14-31				
Start a class	24, 25						30, 31	1-13, 19				
Join a club			25, 26									
Ask for a raise					23, 24							
Look for work		1-3	17-31	1-5							8-26	
Get pro advice	19, 20	15-17	14-16	1, 12	8-10	5, 6	2-3, 29-30	25-27	22, 23	19, 20	15-17	13, 14
Get a loan	21-23	18, 19	17, 18	13-15	11, 12	7, 8	4-6, 31	1-2, 28-29	24, 25	21-23	18, 19	14, 15
See a doctor				22-30	1-5						7-25	
Start a diet	16-18	13, 14	12, 13	9, 10	6, 7	2-4, 30	1, 27, 28	23, 24	19-21	17, 18	13, 14	11, 12
End relationship						6						
Buy clothes									1-30	24-31	1-6	
Get a makeover					23, 24		5-31					
New romance										15-31	1-7	
Vacation	24, 25	20-22	19-21	26, 27	13, 14	9-11	7, 8	3-4, 30-31	1, 26-28	24, 25	20-22	17-19

Cancer

The Crab
June 21 to July 22

Element:	Water
Quality:	Cardinal
Polarity:	Yin/Feminine
Ruler:	The Moon
Meditation:	I am in touch with my inner feelings.
Gemstone:	Pearl
Power Stones:	Moonstone, chrysocolla
Key Phrase:	I feel
Glyph:	Breast, crab claws
Anatomy:	Stomach, breasts
Color:	Silver, pearl white
Animal:	Crustaceans, cows, chickens
Myths/Legends:	Hercules and the Crab, Asherah, Hecate
House:	Fourth
Opposite Sign:	Capricorn
Flower:	Larkspur
Key Word:	Receptivity

Positive Expression:
Intuitive
Fertile
Nurturing
Domestic
Responsive
Patriotic
Understanding

Misuse of Energy:
Distrustful
Smothering
Defensive
Manipulative
Isolationist
Brooding
Evasive

Cancer

Your Ego's Strengths and Shortcomings
Receptive to life's cycles of ebb and flow, you also possess a keen sensibility to the feelings of others. Before you do anything, you're likely to test your "feel" for it. You also seem to innately know what someone needs in order to develop and prosper, and you readily extend your nurturing abilities to family and friends alike. You embody the qualities of "The Nurturer" of the zodiac, projecting genuine concern and an ability to provide comfort and care where it's needed most.

Your desire to establish a nest includes not only a place you can call home, but connections to a family of your own. Even if you don't have children, you may have a "brood" of friends, and may be the first person others turn to when they need solace or support. Your affinity with the nourishing energy of the Moon is illustrated through your enjoyment of cooking, crafts, gardening, or an involvement with anything which fosters growth. Your receptivity is an extension of this same connection, although maintaining your emotional boundaries can be tough—especially when you care about someone. Knowing when to pull back and let your fledglings fly from the nest can be difficult, but they'll appreciate your tenderness more if you avoid becoming overbearing or smothering.

Establishing a sense of continuity between past, present, and future is also important, although when you release your emotional attachments it can feel like you're cutting off a part of yourself. To protect your vulnerability, you may go too far and create a barrier which keeps others away, instead of inviting them to get closer. Your intuitive sensibilities will tell you when it's time to open your arms with love or to gracefully back away to give someone space. Ultimately, it is the flow from your soul to the energy of the Divine Feminine which imparts the true knowledge, "for everything, there is a season."

Shining Your Love Light
An ardent yet tender lover, you yearn for the kind of relationship that will sustain itself through time. You know what it means to be

transformed through love, since unless you open your heart to someone you may feel that your life is incomplete. Unfortunately, knowing whom and when to trust is not the easiest thing to ascertain, especially if you're barricading a previously broken heart. It is the prompting of your intuitive voice that helps signal when it's time to lower those walls. After all, in the right situation, your passion and devotion can lead to a truly fulfilling relationship that forms the core of your need to "belong."

As a water sign, you'll appreciate the emotional affinity you feel with others who share your element: Scorpio, Pisces, and other Cancers. The engaging draw to Capricorn, your opposite sign, can lead to a relationship that feels secure, and you'll be comfortable establishing a family.

You're attracted to Aries, but may become impatient with her or his apparent immaturity or selfishness. Taurus radiates earthy delight, and if you can see eye to eye there's a good chance of building a lasting tie. Gemini reminds you to play, and you'll enjoy the banter, but you may push him or her away if you hold on too tightly. Another Cancer can share your priorities and may be an enduring partner, but you can drown in emotions if you're both upset! Leo loves your attention, but you may wonder when you'll garner reciprocal care. You're comfortable with Virgo and can communicate in ways that foster true understanding and acceptance.

Libra's certainly attractive, but you may always feel uncertain if he or she does not demonstrate sufficient dedication to the relationship. Shared sensuality and passion fuel a breathless relationship with Scorpio, and you could be eternal lovers. Sagittarius is fun, but the unpredictability can make you nervous. Aquarius can be your confidant, although you may never get really comfortable together. Pisces can seem like a soulmate, and you'll mutually feed your imaginations and find it easy to share what's in the depths of your hearts.

Making Your Place in the World

To build your security base, you'll seek a career that gives you room to grow. Emotional fulfillment is important, too, and you may find great satisfaction from teaching, counseling, social work, human resources, midwifery, or medicine. You might also enjoy having your own B & B or be rewarded by work in the restaurant, hotel, home furnishings, or real estate industries.

Political positions offer a chance to influence change in areas of concern. Your love of the past can be fulfilled through careers in archaeology, history, anthropology, or antiques. Or you might prefer to use your green thumb and work in floral, gardening, or landscaping design businesses.

Power Plays

When you know you're prepared for most contingencies, you feel powerful. It's the attainment of security and safety in the world which allows you to wear your power with confidence, and when you can take an influential role protecting future generations you add a sense of satisfaction to the mix. Yet nothing seems to compare with the connection you have with your family, and it is through this relationship that you experience the power of linking what has gone before with what is yet to come.

Surrendering an existing framework to modifications that allow progressive change is not easy, and if outside forces threaten that secure base you'll abhor the feeling of vulnerability. It's learning how to build a healthy sense of shelter from the storms of life that is your challenge and also your ultimate strength—and something you impart to all who follow your lead. While you may feel most empowered when surrounded by those you love, it is your connection to the Source which reminds you that everything and everyone comes and goes through the currents of time and ever-changing seasons of life.

Famous Cancerians

John Quincy Adams, Lamar Alexander, Albert Brooks, Marc Chagall, Tom Cruise, Donna Dixon, Mary Baker Eddy, Courtney Love, Imelda Marcos, Chris O'Donnell, George Orwell, Victor Petrenko, Henry David Thoreau, Mike Tyson, James Whistler

The Year Ahead for Cancer

While changes in the world have continued at their rapid speed, you've been building a solid foundation for your dreams to manifest. This year, you may feel that you have the confidence to take your hopes to a new level, although you're still moving with reasonable caution. Self-awareness is emphasized for you during 2001, and with a more marked perception of your deeper motivations and drives you can carve out a more stable and secure place for yourself.

The year begins with a strong emphasis on the balance of power in your relationships, stimulated by the lunar eclipse in January and underscored by the transit of the Moon's North Node in Cancer for most of the year. Although it can be difficult to get out of your shell, finding better ways to ask for your needs will ultimately strengthen your connections with others, especially your partner and family members. The solar eclipse in June is also in your sign, along with the last lunar eclipse of the year on December 30th. Then the eclipse cycles move away from your sign, and you may feel less exposed (at least on an emotional level) as you head into next year.

The good news for 2001 is that Jupiter moves into Cancer on July 12, where it will stay through midsummer of 2002! It's been twelve years since Jupiter was in your sign, and now it's your turn to embrace life with greater confidence and to feel truly optimistic about your future possibilities. From January through July, Jupiter transits through the Twelfth House of your solar chart, indicating a time when your connection to your spiritual needs is positive and powerful, and it is from this space that you will launch the essence of your creative imaginings during the last half of the year. In some respects these cycles are suggestive of a strong sense that you are protected, and that sensibility may be tested if you need to call forth your courage for any reason.

Saturn's transit this year draws your attention to an examination of the past, and you are very likely to see a series of transitions manifesting in your life. It's much like passing through stages, with the vestiges of old things that are no longer part of your life falling away. If you enter this cycle with an element of fear, then it's more difficult to let go of the things you no longer need. Your dreams may seem like a replay of old movies as you quietly release the crutches you've relied upon for stability. You don't have to toss them all away at once, though. Think of this as a time when you're test-driving your visions! Another key feature of this time is learning to make room for experiences which simply nourish your spirit. That alone can take some doing.

The planets Uranus, Neptune, and Pluto continue their slowly-paced cycles. Uranus and Neptune transit through the Eighth House of your solar chart, helping you release your inhibitions and uncover insights into the workings of your psyche. Pluto's transit emphasizes your need to address your physical health requirements and your daily routine. This is an excellent time to make improvements that will strengthen your physical health, and also marks a period of embracing the power you have for true healing.

If you were born from June 21 to 25, your imagination and creativity can be enhanced while Neptune transits in biquintile to your Sun. Unless you make an effort to explore your personal expression, you may simply experience the effects of this particular cycle as an easier connection to your intuitive awareness. However, you can take full advantage of this stimulus by making extra time to exercise your special talents or work in concert with others to develop their own. Fortunately, during April and May you may feel that you're more stabilized while Saturn transits in semisextile to your Sun, and if you're seeking a mentor to aid you in your quest to strengthen your talents or understanding, you're likely to be in the right place at the right time. Since there are fewer obstacles in your path this year, it's a good time to examine your priorities and find the best ways to assure that they are met. The Sun's eclipse on June 21 conjuncts your Sun, marking a time of potential crisis and strong awareness of your needs. Some individuals choose to make significant changes under such an influence, with learning, travel, and the inclusion of fascinating people and ideas playing a meaningful role. Remember: crisis is not a bad thing—it's simply when energy peaks or situations reach their apex!

If you were born from June 26 to July 2, you may feel that your timing is off under the influence of Uranus transiting in sesquiquadrate to your Sun. One of the manifestations of this cycle can be the challenge to adapt to unexpected changes that require you to alter your priorities or step into unfamiliar territory. You're likely to feel an undercurrent of impatience, too, since the changes you may want to happen can seem to take forever, or you may get within a hairsbreadth only to find yourself waiting for things you cannot control to be settled. Saturn's influence helps bring some stability and clarity from June through December while transiting in semisextile to your Sun, and this influence, combined with the stimulus of Uranus, can be indicative of a time when you'll trust your choices more readily. These cycles indicate a positive period of personal growth, when you're ready to take the steps that can lead to greater independence and self-actualization. If you're concerned about health, you fears may be unfounded, but it's still important to seek the advice of a trusted professional to allay your worries.

If you were born from June 27 to 30, Neptune's transit in quincunx to your Sun can leave you feeling a bit confused. This influence is particularly noteworthy in regard to personal relationships, since you may feel stymied about how to satisfy the needs or demands of your partner. If you're open to working with a therapist to help you uncover and explore your concerns, you can make significant progress under this influence. It's also a great time to let go of unhealthy inhibitions concerning your sexual needs. On a material level, be cautious in dealing with finances and take special care if you're joining your resources with others. Reading the fine print is absolutely necessary. The primary problem with this cycle in regard to money matters is that your judgment can be swayed by the pretty picture, and you may not want to look behind the façade. To avoid future problems, though, you need to take at least one peek behind the curtain!

If you were born from July 3 to 7, you may feel that you're constantly making adjustments to accommodate change. Pluto is transiting in quincunx aspect to your Sun, marking a time when you simply cannot continue to carry all the burdens you've been shouldering. During the first four months of this year, Saturn is transiting in semisquare to your Sun, and it is during this time that you may feel most frustrated and discouraged. Even though you'll want to make changes, some circumstances may simply require that you continue until you've satisfied your obligation. Looking inside to uncover your drives and your fears will help you determine whether your motivations are healthy, or if you're giving in to an old internal message which can be self-sabotaging. If that's the case, then your awareness of your own attempts to defeat yourself can be the primary key to altering that old unconscious pattern. But take heart: from June onward you're making sure progress. You're moving forward toward the realization of your goals under the influence of Saturn transiting in semisextile to your Sun, a cycle that's strongest during the second half of 2001. Addressing health issues now is also a good idea, since you're in a good position to eliminate routines, habits, or attitudes which are counterproductive to your sense of well-being.

If you were born from July 8 to 18, you're feeling the unsettling influence of Uranus transiting in quincunx to your Sun. You may feel that everything's just getting on your nerves. People can be irritating. Work may seem to be filled with lots of grumbling and unnecessary change. Your relationship can be perplexing. Interesting thing though—you're learning better ways to respond, and may finally be ready to give up on the idea that you can keep everybody happy! Be on the alert for changes which seem to come out of the blue. This cycle tests your adaptability, and while you may see a shakeup in your priorities, you'll ultimately discover that you appreciate the positive qualities of the innovations brought into your life. You may need to be more attentive to nourishing your nervous system, and assuring that foods high in B-vitamins and minerals like calcium and magnesium are in ample supply will be helpful to your overall sense of well-being.

If you were born from July 18 to 22, you are experiencing the influence of two major cycles. First, Pluto is transiting in sesquiquadrate to your Sun throughout the year. Then, from January through April, Saturn completes its cycle in sextile to your Sun.

Pluto's cycle brings the most significant effects, especially if you feel you're in a circumstance that does not allow you to fully exert your influence or undermines your power in some way. The potential problems associated with this cycle involve being drawn into a situation for the wrong reasons. If your motivations are unclear or if you're operating with a hidden agenda which could run counter to a situation, then you're likely to experience things turning inside out: your inner drives can work against you! For that reason, it's important that you make choices which are healthy for all concerned, or at least that you be attentive to why you really want to do something. Saturn's influence early in the year can be helpful, since you can see the reality and may be able to confront someone who has taken unfair advantage of you in the past. Think of this as a year of rebuilding and personal renovation.

Tools to Make a Difference

To be able to funnel your best energy into your desire to expand your options, you may need to do some psychological housecleaning—eliminating self-defeating attitudes and releasing fears which have been in the way of achieving a true sense of success. Although you may not think of it this way, it's possible that you've been on a starvation diet as far as satisfaction with yourself and your life is concerned. This year, you have a chance to turn around that pattern and to move toward a more gratifying life.

Uncovering what may have been a well-hidden secret requires introspection and personal honesty. Tools such as meditation and journal-writing can be helpful. If you're resistant to the idea of keeping a diary, then working with the imagery of cards like a tarot deck, dream oracle, tatwa cards, or other decks can give you a good start. Explore several decks before you decide, and when you have quiet time, exercise your visionary sensibilities by formulating questions and using the cards to help guide you through the process of inner exploration. Meditation exercises, including moving meditations like tai chi or hatha yoga, can also help you gain insights into your inner being. Exploring other metaphysical subjects, including astrology, can also give you insights into your underlying motivations, and this may be the best time to study metaphysics and other disciplines that examine the spiritual side of the universe.

Another excellent tool for you can be the creation of your personal "medicine bag." Collect stones, crystals, small pine cones, seashells, bird feathers, and other objects you can place in a small pouch to go with you wherever you journey. Think of these items as providing all that you need to create a focal point which connects your mind to the four elements—fire, earth, air, water—reminding you of your unity with the natural processes of life itself. You can create your own rituals in harmony with the change of season, or simply celebrate the essence of each New Moon and the ever-shifting cycles of the year.

♋
Affirmation for the Year

I joyfully release my fears of change and welcome a world of fresh possibilities!

Cancer/January

In the Spotlight
Close relationships may reach a new plateau, although you may have to clarify your roles in order to get what you want from the situation. Speculative interests—financial and emotional—can have a big payoff.

Wellness and Keeping Fit
Seek out activities that seem more like play than a "work"-out, keeping in mind that you do need a fitness schedule you'll be able to sustain for a while. This is the perfect time to initiate a daily routine that allows room for your physical needs.

Love and Life Connections
The Moon's eclipse in Cancer on January 9 emphasizes family, marriage, and partnership, although any close relationship which requires a commitment will benefit from the exploration of your changing feelings and needs. Loving relationships, including your connection to children, can be more gratifying now. Changes can be unsettling after January 23, although you may simply be experiencing a test of your tolerance and ability to accept differences.

Finance and Success
Convening with others in your field gives you the perfect opportunity to showcase your talents, products, or ideas after January 3. From January 14-19, watch for competitive challenges arising from others whose ideals or ethics may not mesh with your own. You may also feel that the value you had agreed upon is being undermined in some way, and can renegotiate if necessary after January 25.

Cosmic Insider Tip
Appealing to the imagination and a desire to escape the ordinary can give you the leading edge in a career venture, or may be the perfect enticement for a romantic interest from January 6-14.

Rewarding Days: 1, 5, 8, 9, 12, 13, 17, 18, 26, 27, 28

Challenging Days: 2, 3, 14, 15, 21, 22, 23, 24, 29, 30

Affirmation for the Month
I know what I need from others who share my life.

Cancer/February

In the Spotlight
Mercury is in retrograde, but it can work to your advantage if you need to take a second look at a financial agreement or perform necessary research before signing important contracts. You may be breaking agreements, but new promises can seem too uncertain.

Wellness and Keeping Fit
Gradually building physical endurance can give you the energy to sustain the daily grind. Be aware of your limitations from February 15-21: you can become overcommitted before you know it!

Love and Life Connections
A romantic interest can get serious from February 1-14, and if you're feeling that the connection is right you may want to take the relationship to another level. But if you're uncertain or if your affections have cooled, then you may decide that it's time to bid farewell. During your explorations after the New Moon on February 23 you may take an interest in someone new, but the situation is ripe for complications, so tread carefully.

Finance and Success
You can gain favor with your superiors, especially if you're putting forth extra effort, although you may feel that your creative potential is hampered by conservative factions or outmoded regulations. There's room for experimentation later. Right now, you're laying the groundwork for advancement. Watch expenditures near the Full Moon on February 8, and take special care with new budget proposals made after Mercury goes direct on February 25.

Cosmic Insider Tip
Expectations can fall short of the mark from February 1-5, and during Mercury's retrograde from February 4-25 you have a chance to redefine your roles and the roles others will play.

Rewarding Days: 5, 6, 9, 13, 14, 23, 24

Challenging Days: 11, 12, 16, 18, 19, 25, 26, 27

Affirmation for the Month
I am making the best use of all my resources.

Cancer/March

In the Spotlight
Cutting through barriers that are counterproductive to your success on the job may require that you put your personal feelings for others aside in order to be more objective about their performance. You may also need to look at your own work in a different light.

Wellness and Keeping Fit
Allowing stress to build now quickly diminishes your creativity and drive, but finding an active way to release tension has tremendous dividends. The efforts you put forth in fitness will increase your energy throughout the day.

Love and Life Connections
Your motivations may be clear to you, but your partner could have problems understanding your priorities or needs. A romantic getaway near the Full Moon on March 9 can provide the perfect chance to demonstrate your affections and solidify a commitment. But intimacy could seem a little too close for comfort unless you're on the same wavelength. Talk over your concerns after March 18.

Finance and Success
Cultivating a positive professional image is easier if you have an idea of what's expected from your superiors or prospective employer, so work toward that end prior to March 7. Revamp your priorities at work from March 10-23, when you're ready to get rid of excess and make the most of your time and creativity. Convene with others in your field after March 18, but keep your fresh ideas closely protected until you're more certain of the competition.

Cosmic Insider Tip
Use the Venus retrograde cycle from March 9 to April 20 to explore the full range of options offered by your life path choices. Are you putting your efforts into somebody else's goals or your own?

Rewarding Days: 4, 5, 8, 9, 12, 13, 22, 23, 28, 31

Challenging Days: 10, 11, 17, 18, 19, 24, 25, 26

Affirmation for the Month
My actions and attitudes reflect love and self-assurance.

Cancer/April

In the Spotlight
To accomplish your goals you may have to push aside some of the things you want to do in favor of what you "must" do. Keep your priorities in mind, since staying on target now can ultimately lead to greater freedom.

Wellness and Keeping Fit
Your resistance to altering your daily routine diminishes, creating an opening to try something different. Whether you're changing your diet, altering your fitness activities, or rearranging your schedule, the changes you make now can have long-lasting effects.

Love and Life Connections
Are you having second thoughts about a love relationship? It may just be that your needs are changing, but you can feel uncertain as to "how." Give yourself time to reflect on the differences in your life and how they are affecting your close relationships and family life. After the New Moon on April 23 your confidence improves, stimulating your desire to let others know what you need and to reach out to them in more appropriate ways.

Finance and Success
Philosophical differences draw the lines between what you can and cannot do to advance your career from April 1-6. It's quite a balancing act before and during the Full Moon on April 8 to have enough time to enjoy the fruits of your labors. Target better-defined goals during the New Moon on April 23, when you may also feel more confident about community support.

Cosmic Insider Tip
After April 20 your outlook is likely to be quite different, since several planetary cycles shift on that day. Evaluate your long range options and the best way to accomplish them.

Rewarding Days: 1, 5, 9, 10, 18, 19, 23, 24, 28, 29

Challenging Days: 7, 8, 13, 14, 15, 21, 22

Affirmation for the Month
I am ready to establish goals which reflect my hopes and dreams.

Cancer/May

In the Spotlight
It's time to lay the groundwork for changes which will lead to greater satisfaction with your work. Your superiors or other authorities can now see what you have to offer, although you may feel that you're repeating yourself. Sometimes it just takes others a while to fully appreciate you!

Wellness and Keeping Fit
An old injury or physical weakness can come back to haunt you, although your insights into dealing with it are likely to be better than they were in the past. Explore underlying causes of health problems, since surface answers will be unsatisfactory.

Love and Life Connections
Time with friends from May 1-7 helps reaffirm your connections. In the romance department, you may be feeling less than amorous, since your focus is deeply internalized. You're searching within yourself to strengthen your connection to the spiritual elements of your life. A quiet retreat around the New Moon on May 23 can be very illuminating.

Finance and Success
Restructuring or renovation at work can be unsettling, although you'll be greatly reassured if you see positive acknowledgment from your boss. Keep your expectations to a minimum, and take care with commitments from May 7-16, since you may underestimate time or resources required to wrap up a job and could be left in the lurch as a result.

Cosmic Insider Tip
With Jupiter and Pluto in opposition you may feel that you're caught in changes far beyond your control, but you can control your responses to them!

Rewarding Days: 3, 6, 7, 16, 17, 21, 25, 26

Challenging Days: 4, 5, 11, 12, 13, 18, 19, 31

Affirmation for the Month
My dreams mirror my secret desires and I welcome them.

Cancer/June

In the Spotlight
There's a reason to reconsider your plans, since unexpected developments and changes offer previously unknown options. It's time to explore and negotiate. Final decisions will be much more satisfactory next month.

Wellness and Keeping Fit
You need ample time for rejuvenation and rest. Whether you're vacationing or just taking regular power naps, the breaks in routine give you a chance to regroup. Pushing yourself beyond your limits now can quickly exhaust your vitality.

Love and Life Connections
Before including your partner or sweetheart in the plans you've been dreaming about, think twice. You may not be ready to make changes or can be unaware of the impact your still unformed speculations can have on others. The Sun's eclipse in Cancer on June 21 marks a time when unresolved issues can be brought to the surface, and you'll want to clear up any misunderstandings or disappointments so that you can move forward with greater confidence.

Finance and Success
Mercury and Mars are in retrograde, and getting new projects off the ground can be virtually impossible. This is the time to finish what you've already started, or to accomplish any research necessary to be more confident about the outcome of future endeavors. Support from peers is helpful, but be on the alert for those who might take advantage of your goodwill from June 13-17.

Cosmic Insider Tip
It's a perfect setup for overinflation: Mercury, Mars, and Jupiter cycles definitely indicate the potential for ill effects from taking unnecessary or excessive risk. Moderation is the best remedy.

Rewarding Days: 3, 12, 13, 17, 18, 21, 22, 25, 26, 30

Challenging Days: 1, 7, 8, 14, 15, 16, 27, 28, 29

Affirmation for the Month
I am patient in the midst of delays or unexpected changes.

Cancer/July

In the Spotlight
You're on the brink of confidence-reinforcing changes. Envisioning what you want helps prepare you to make the best use of this growth-oriented period.

Wellness and Keeping Fit
You may feel you deserve a much-needed vacation, and getting away after July 12 to a place where you can indulge your favorite pleasures can be just what you need to get that second wind! Even a long weekend might suffice.

Love and Life Connections
Partnership is emphasized during the lunar eclipse on July 5, when your partner's needs can take precedence over your own. Talk about future plans together. Making time to celebrate being together can be especially affirming to your commitment this month. You're ready to turn over a new leaf during the Cancer New Moon on July 20, when sharing your fantasies with your sweetheart can lead to all sorts of fun.

Finance and Success
Soliciting support from colleagues from July 1-4 provides you with a good basis to launch plans once Mercury and Jupiter enter your sign on July 12. If you're not ready, then wait for July 20-21, when progress will move more quickly. Resistance from more conservative factions can stand in the way from July 6-18, although you'll make headway by addressing their fears (and budget concerns) before you proceed.

Cosmic Insider Tip
The eclipse suggests a turning point, and is likely to indicate that you're finding the best ways to get past your own resistance so you can move ahead with the things you really want.

Rewarding Days: 1, 9, 10, 14, 15, 19, 20, 23, 27, 28

Challenging Days: 4, 5, 12, 13, 22, 25, 26, 31

Affirmation for the Month
I joyfully express my gratitude toward others.

Cancer/August

In the Spotlight
You have every reason to feel good about yourself, and this can be an exceptional time of improvement in your work and your love life! There are definitely power struggles afoot, but you're able to steer clear of dangerous territory.

Wellness and Keeping Fit
While you may not be an excessively competitive individual, you do like to win. Set fitness challenges which build on your natural abilities. Strengthening muscles physically prepares you for times ahead, when you'll be flexing creative muscle!

Love and Life Connections
With Venus joining Jupiter in your sign, your self-esteem grows by graceful leaps and bounds. Your heart may be filled with love, and sharing these feelings with others serves to increase your passion and devotion. Consider a romantic getaway from August 15-19, arrange a special rendezvous for August 15, or indulge in your favorite entertainment with your sweetheart on August 23-24.

Finance and Success
Power plays in the workplace may be the result of technological innovations which modify the functions of different people at work. However, you can take advantage of any alterations, and you may have excellent ideas about the best ways to utilize the changes to suit everyone's interests. Watch finances during the Full Moon on August 4, and consider setting up a budget during the New Moon on August 19 based upon the effects of recent alterations.

Cosmic Insider Tip
Saturn opposes Pluto, suggesting challenges to existing structures. While these changes may be beyond your control, they can affect the quality of your work environment.

Rewarding Days: 5, 6, 11, 12, 15, 16, 23, 24

Challenging Days: 1, 2, 8, 9, 21, 22, 28, 29

Affirmation for the Month
I have abundance enough to share!

Cancer/September

In the Spotlight
Career challenges can place you in a competitive position, although you're capable of clearly sizing-up the contenders. You're definitely not eager to drop your defenses, but may need to evaluate whether or not they're in the way of your progress.

Wellness and Keeping Fit
It's easy to get in over your head if you indulge in activities beyond your capacities from September 19-30. Don't let that stop you from enjoying your favorite sports; just check conditions and get into shape before you step onto the court or playing field!

Love and Life Connections
Turmoil in your relationship after September 8 can be the result of simply spending more time together, but what's happening beneath the surface may be the emergence of competitiveness within your partnership. Before you issue a challenge, decide if there's really something to fight about. Choose your battles wisely, since you may just need more lovin'!

Finance and Success
Finances improve, and your spending may also increase. If you're uncertain, wait until after the Full Moon on September 2 before making large expenditures, since details may come to light which steer you in a different direction. Schedule meetings or presentations from September 15-23, when your ideas may be more readily accepted and understood. However, quiet conferences with your supporters can be to your advantage after September 23.

Cosmic Insider Tip
Your manner of handling difficult situations can be the perfect solution or approach from September 15-25, when others may simply feel displaced by adjustments in the power structure.

Rewarding Days: 2, 3, 11, 12, 15, 16, 20, 29, 30

Challenging Days: 4, 5, 14, 17, 18, 19, 24, 25

Affirmation for the Month
I am safe in the face of challenge.

Cancer/October

In the Spotlight
Continuing a project that's already gaining momentum works well, although you may run into a few stops and delays which try your patience. The manner in which you handle outbursts or challenges from others can also affect your reputation.

Wellness and Keeping Fit
Judging your limitations requires a bit of insight, and if you're not certain about whether you're up to the challenge of a competitive event or should engage in a particular fitness program, consult with an objective expert, like a physician or personal trainer.

Love and Life Connections
If you feel that you're being swept off your feet, maybe you are! Take special care with emotionally charged situations during the Full Moon on October 2, since you may be pulled into squabbles. Fortunately, you can also use the energy of this time to move along when dealing with personal issues in your relationship, although you may quickly discover that you cannot satisfy everyone at the same time. Perhaps you need to have them take a number!

Finance and Success
Mercury is in retrograde from October 1-22. Fortunately, ongoing projects fare well, although you may be disappointed if you discover that someone else is working on a similar endeavor. Situations turn around during the New Moon on October 16, but you may need to explore budget details more carefully. Wait until October 27-31 to sign papers.

Cosmic Insider Tip
Even though Mercury turns direct on October 22, dealing with the problems which arise during the retrograde continues into early next month. Expect complications.

Rewarding Days: 4, 5, 9, 10, 13, 14, 18, 26, 27, 31

Challenging Days: 1, 2, 12, 15, 16, 21, 22, 23, 29, 30

Affirmation for the Month
I am an attentive listener and keen observer.

Cancer/November

In the Spotlight
Your investments are paying off, but your ideas about the best ways to use your resources may differ from those of your associates. Turning your attention to creative endeavors alleviates tension.

Wellness and Keeping Fit
Exploring underlying causes of physical or psychological distress brings successful results, although you may not like the remedies! Avoidance is not the answer, so check your anxiety at the door and consult with a professional for guidance when necessary.

Love and Life Connections
Family and home require extra attention from November 1-7, although your mind is on romance during the Full Moon on November 1. Your affections are most readily returned after November 8, when your fantasies can come to life. To assure that you're not under the spell of infatuation, take a careful, but experimental, path during the New Moon on November 15. Even if the relationship is not realistic, your connection could open doors to your heart which have been closed far too long.

Finance and Success
Disputes over joint resources, taxes, or debts can be a hassle, and can wreak havoc with your investments (or may be a result of them!). Tread carefully from November 3-6, and then from November 12-25, when a lack of clarity or unexpected changes can be costly. A window of opportunity does arise from November 17-21, when you can take advantage of growth potentials if you can afford the risk. Artistic ventures fare best after November 15.

Cosmic Insider Tip
Children can be especially enjoyable now, and you may have every reason to celebrate their successes midmonth. Don't miss it!

Rewarding Days: 1, 5, 6, 9, 10, 13, 14, 23, 24, 29

Challenging Days: 11, 12, 18, 19, 20, 25, 26

Affirmation for the Month
My creative impulses are inspired by pure love and joy!

Cancer/December

In the Spotlight
Satisfying the demands and expectations of others adds extra stress, but it's something you can do if you keep your priorities straight. Your ultimate goal may be working in true partnership in a cooperative manner, and it does appear promising. Keep the faith!

Wellness and Keeping Fit
Be especially attentive to your health, since the solar eclipse on December 14 accentuates your need to maintain a balance in your daily routine, and also indicates the potential for problems to surface. You have to put forth the effort to stay strong.

Love and Life Connections
After December 8 you may feel inspired to travel with the one you love, or at least to spend time exploring your visions for the future. Nothing revitalizes a relationship like a shared vision! Partnership is emphasized after December 16, when shared endeavors can bring you closer together. However, during the lunar eclipse on December 30 you may run into a dispute over that shared vision, discovering that your ideals do have variations.

Finance and Success
Alterations in your working environment can improve productivity, but there are potential pitfalls if someone feels unappreciated. If it's your job to assure that things run smoothly, then seeking the best options for each person to utilize his or her potentials can, in itself, be rewarding. However, egos can be a problem, and you may have to make decisions which are not popular for everyone.

Cosmic Insider Tip
The focus of the solar eclipse (December 14) centers upon the need to redefine values, and ethical matters can play a large part. Your convictions can be inspirational to others in need of direction.

Rewarding Days: 2, 3, 6, 7, 11, 20, 21, 25, 29, 30, 31

Challenging Days: 8, 9, 10, 15, 16, 22, 23, 24

Affirmation for the Month
I seek Truth as my ultimate guide in my actions and decisions.

Cancer Action Table

These dates reflect the best—but not the only—times for success and ease in these activities, according to your Sun sign.

	JAN	FEB	MAR	APR	MAY	JUN	JUL	AUG	SEPT	OCT	NOV	DEC
Move									1-30	24-31	1-6	
Start a class		23, 24						14-31	17			
Join a club				23, 24								
Ask for a raise				6-20		21, 22	20					
Look for work											27-30	1-15
Get pro advice	21-23	18, 19	17, 18	13-15	11, 12	7, 8	4-6, 31	1-2, 28-29	24, 25	21-23	18, 19	15, 16
Get a loan	24, 25	20-22	19-21	16, 17	13-15	9-11	7, 8	3-4, 30-31	1, 26-28	24, 25	20-22	17-19
See a doctor					6-31	1-3, 28-30	1-12				27-30	1-14
Start a diet	19, 20	15-17	14-16	1, 12	8, 9	5, 6	2-3, 29-30	25-27	22, 23	19, 20	15, 16	13, 14
End relationship							5, 6					
Buy clothes											8-25	
Get a makeover						21, 22	20	1-26				
New romance											8-30	1
Vacation	1, 26-28	23, 24	22, 23	18-20	16, 17	12, 13	9-11	6, 7	2-3, 29-30	26-28	23, 24	20, 21

Leo

The Lion
July 22 to August 22

Element:	Fire
Quality:	Fixed
Polarity:	Yang/Masculine
Ruler:	The Sun
Meditation:	My energy glows with light from the Source.
Gemstone:	Ruby
Power Stones:	Topaz, sardonyx
Key Phrase:	I will
Glyph:	Lion's tail
Anatomy:	Heart, sides, upper back
Color:	Gold, scarlet
Animal:	Lions, large cats
Myths/Legends:	Apollo, Isis, Helius
House:	Fifth
Opposite Sign:	Aquarius
Flower:	Sunflower, marigold
Key Word:	Magnetism

Positive Expression:
Powerful
Benevolent
Vigorous
Honorable
Dramatic
Regal
Loyal

Misuse of Energy:
Egocentric
Pompous
Insolent
Domineering
Pretentious
Dictatorial
Selfish

Leo

Your Ego's Strengths and Shortcomings

With your characteristic flair for the dramatic, you can light up a room or easily take center stage. Others remember your warmth radiating from a heart of gold, since you can provide leadership, encouragement, and focus to those needing guidance or direction. It's ultimately your creativity that draws positive attention and is the source of your confidence and personal magnetism. Your role is "The Loyalist" of the zodiac, standing firm in your convictions and radiating true support for the people who form your inner circle. In your heart, you're eternally playful, feeling that life is meant to be a celebration of the spirit.

With ample room to exercise your talents, you're ablaze with passion in the right situations. Like your ruler, the Sun, you have an easy ability to bring light into the darkness, inspiring devotion from others; although you won't easily forget those who fail to honor their promises to you. When you're the object of adoration and praise, you can purr in appreciation; but your claws show when you feel unappreciated and you can be impertinent or demanding if you're not getting the attention you feel you deserve.

Betrayal is simply not tolerable for you—you take it personally, and may close your heart if your pride is wounded. Yet you can be unbelievably courageous when you take a stand. By melding your will with that of a higher power, your life becomes a testimony to a vitality illuminated by the power of divine love.

Shining Your Love Light

One thing's certain: when you love someone, there's no doubting it. Your ardent enthusiasm can sweep another off his or her feet, and your lavish affections leave an indelible mark. In stark contrast, you can close your heart if you are hurt, although it takes a lot to extinguish the flames of love. You're not likely to give up easily, and once you've found your match, you can create love everlasting.

It's easiest for you to be yourself around the other fire signs—Aries, Leo, and Sagittarius—who share your playfulness and sense of adventure. But other signs can also be intriguing. With Aries, you can have an instant attraction, yet if there's no devotion, you'll quickly lose interest. Taurus is engaging, but you can be uncomfortable if you're given the impression that you've become a possession. Your confidence and sense of hope are stimulated by Gemini, who can become your lifelong friend. Cancer can feel reassuring, although you may not be romantically inclined. Another Leo inspires exceptional flares of passion, but ego conflicts can arise if you are each not given a chance to shine. Virgo has definite appeal, and you can be successful working partners even if you do not become lovers.

Libra's grace and refined sensibilities can set your heart afire. Scorpio's sensuality can, at first, be completely enticing, although you may become engulfed by his or her emotional intensity. Sagittarius ignites your feelings of love and can fan the flames of passion more powerfully than you may realize at first. With Capricorn, sustaining a relationship can simply be too much work. Aquarius, your zodiac opposite, lifts your heart to a new level of freedom, but you may have to learn how to let go of controls before you're happy together. Pisces enchants you, but you may end up in really deep water before you know it!

Making Your Place in the World

To be dedicated to a career, you need to receive adequate recognition for your efforts, and can crave a position which commands authority or gives you a chance to exert leadership. If you do attain a position of leadership—as foreman, CEO, president, or general—you can influence lasting changes and be quite adept at delegating and organizing the work that needs to be done. In politics, you can be an attention-getting candidate or successful campaign manager, or you might prefer the entertainment fields where you can work as a performer, musician, actor, model, producer, or director.

Whether you're a teacher, attorney, or agent, you can inspire and bring a sense of self-importance to others. Businesses which cater to recreation and entertainment can be good outlets, ranging from amusement centers and nightclubs to restaurants and theaters. You'll be happiest where you feel most creative.

Power Plays

You may be fascinated by the idea of becoming powerful, but shrink away from situations filled with empty promises. You're looking for substantial opportunities to strengthen your ability to wield a positive influence, inspired by love and the joy of exercising your originality. You seem to attract power, since you possess a natural ability to take charge. It's crucial that you maintain a clear awareness of your motivations, since selfish desires can lead you to misuse your power over other people.

If your motivations are pure and your sense of self-worth is intact, you can develop the ability to illustrate truly benevolent leadership and influence. Yet if your personal esteem has been damaged or if you're feeling defensive, you can become domineering and dictatorial, tempted to displace the power of others out of your own frustration at losing your own. You shine most brightly when working in concert with others who are meeting the challenge of exercising their own talents to the fullest. At these times, you feel true joy as all your spirits are uplifted.

In your mind, fleeting power can seem useless—since you think in terms of permanence. To keep the eternal flames of hope burning, you'll be most empowered as you merge your will with that of your higher self, allowing your life to become a symbol of timeless love and devotion.

Famous Leos

Ben Affleck, Loni Anderson, Napoleon Bonaparte, Kate Bush, Fidel Castro, Elizabeth Dole, David Duchovny, Jerry Falwell, Henry Ford, Iman, Karl Jung, Madonna, Mary Matalin, Helen Mirren, Arnold Schwarzenegger, Orville Wright

The Year Ahead for Leo

Your life is heading toward positive new directions this year, as many of the blocks that have impeded your progress lift and fresh avenues for growth open to you. While some unanticipated changes can add an element of surprise, you may also welcome the possibility of trying something completely different. One thing's certain: you're seeing yourself differently!

Jupiter's transit adds a high level of stimulus to your hopes for the future from January through mid-July. During this time, your goals are expanding and you may also feel a tremendous surge of support from your friends and professional peers. Beginning July 12 and continuing through the remainder of the year, Jupiter's cycle highlights your inner life—this is a time when your dreams take on more significant meaning and your spiritual connection becomes more profound. Some elements of this cycle suggest a period of preparation, although other cycles influencing your Sun indicate that you may simply be spending more time trying to balance your public life against your very private needs.

Through the first quarter of 2001, Saturn is completing its cycle, which has been testing your resolve to complete the things you've started. But beginning in April, Saturn starts a phase which lasts over two years and emphasizes positive confirmation of your personal goals while providing strong affirmation of your success and advancement in the world. You may be more focused on accomplishing the things which will finally satisfy your most heartfelt hopes and wishes.

The outer planets Uranus and Neptune are continuing their transit in Aquarius, emphasizing your need to evaluate your relationships according to different qualities, making room for greater autonomy and supporting your ability to exercise your individuality in the most positive ways. While your perceptions of yourself and the world are altered during these cycles, you may also find yourself more willing to let go of your inhibitions in favor of surrendering to your true needs. Additionally, your needs in partnership are changing, and you may find that others are relating and responding to you differently than they have in the past. Pluto's cycle strengthens your creative expression and can be helpful as you forge bonds of love with a sweetheart or with children, aiding your personal transformation while you allow love to heal your life and those of others.

The eclipses of the Sun and Moon introduce challenges that help you become more acutely aware of your body's needs, and the finely tuned connection of mind, body, and spirit. It is your awareness of your feelings about yourself which can become an illuminating clue to some of your physical ailments, and your ability to nurture your needs on every level is becoming important. Your deeper feelings about the past are now likely to surface in your dreams, and if you're lucky enough to recall those dreams, you can use them as a guide to your progress on the inner planes of awareness and realization.

If you were born from July 22 to August 7, you're experiencing the stabilizing influence of Saturn transiting in sextile aspect to your Sun this year. You will not feel the effects of this cycle until late April, but can start planning early in the year to rearrange your priorities. By using the first quarter of 2001 to finish obligations you already have underway, you'll position yourself so that you can take on new responsibilities which will advance your reputation or career as you move through the remainder of the year. This is an excellent year for educational pursuits, and whether you're in a formal learning situation, studying independently, or in a training program at work, you're ready to enhance your skills and understanding in ways that will allow you to advance. You may also be in situations which give you a chance to teach or train others, and that in itself provides an excellent occasion to learn! Much of your success this year will depend upon your ability to master self-discipline, since it can be easy to find yourself in a situation which is guided or determined by outside parameters. However, you may also be experiencing other planetary cycles that stimulate your desire to put your own mark on something. It's time to set your goals and take advantage of advancements which will amplify your ability to answer your most cherished desires by putting forth your best efforts.

If you were born from July 27 to August 2, you're feeling the sensitizing influence of Neptune transiting in opposition to your Sun. This influence can be rather confusing, and during the early part of the year you may find it difficult to establish your personal boundaries or to determine the best course of action. Fortunately, during the summer months, Saturn's influence (described above) is strongest for you, helping you gain a sense of stability as you acclimate yourself to a changing state of awareness. Neptune's cycle presents a challenge, but not in the direct sense. What you're feeling is a deep desire to connect to something beyond yourself. This influence allows you to surrender your will to that of a higher power, but you can also be more easily swayed by others (something you may later regret if you make choices which weaken your personal power!). This is an excellent time to further your artistic talents, and it's also important that you explore your spiritual needs and yearnings. However, in mundane matters like finances you can overlook important details, and you could become involved in something that simply does not manifest as you had hoped. For this reason, it's a good idea to consult with a trusted expert if you're making plans which can significantly affect your reputation or livelihood. In health matters, you may also become more physically sensitive, and can have unusual reactions to environments or foods. You're most susceptible to things you cannot see, such as gases or toxins. If you're worried about a physical problem, your tendency under this influence can be to fall into denial or to pretend that you're okay. Check it out. You'll have more peace of mind when you know what's going on!

If you were born from August 4 to 9, Pluto is transiting in trine aspect to your Sun. This is a cycle of empowerment and positive transformational change, and affords a unique opportunity for you to release many of the inhibitions, attitudes, or circumstances which stand in the way of your self-expression. You may also discover that others are looking to you for insights, and you may value your own perspective, too. However, this is also an excellent time to align yourself with others in positions of power or influence who can work harmoniously with you toward mutual goals. The people entering (or re-entering) your life now can have a phenomenal effect and may act as a catalyst for change; similarly, you have the capacity now to introduce positive and life-altering changes in the world around you! The key to experiencing the ultimate from this period involves the extent to which you are willing to apply yourself, since you can either cruise along with fewer obstructions or forge your own pathway on your own terms. However, you may have to let go of things you thought would always be part of your life. The interesting thing about personal evolution is that the more willing you are to cooperate with the process of fulfilling your destiny, the greater your choices become concerning the manner by which you accomplish the task!

If you were born from August 10 to 19, you're feeling the challenge of Uranus transiting in opposition to your Sun. This can be a very unsettling time period, although there are elements of this cycle which can be extremely exciting! One of the primary things to remember about Uranus oppositions is that the unexpected becomes a strong feature of your life during this time period (which can last up to two years). You can bristle and bolt in resistance against changes which are beyond your control, or you can step back, evaluate the situation, and try something you've never done before. Your relationships are also likely to undergo significant changes. In existing relationships, you may discover that what originally drew you together no longer seems to be relevant or important, or that you need something quite different. This does not mean that you must abandon existing relationships, but that it is time to make way for alterations which will afford greater autonomy for all concerned. In your self-expression, you may try drastic changes, like a new hair color or a completely different wardrobe, in your attempts to express the internal revolution you're experiencing. If you're resisting changes, then you may find that people and situations around you are changing instead, or that things happen despite your attempts to keep them the same. In many ways, this is the perfect cycle for the beginning of a century: a new time for a new you to emerge!

If you were born from August 18 to 22, you're feeling Saturn's restrictive influence as it transits in square aspect to your Sun. Fortunately, the brunt of this cycle will be over by early May, after which time you're likely to feel a sense of relief as some of the heaviness secondary to your responsibilities is finally dropping away.

This is the completion of a cycle which began in June of last year, testing your priorities and giving you a chance to carefully examine your motivations. If you've felt that your progress has been blocked, be especially attentive to the things you need to accomplish in order to open your pathways to success. The care and commitment which you give to your obligations now will pay off as a more solid foundation for growth. Take advantage of the creative opportunities and cooperative support which emerge from July through October, which are rewards for your patience in the first quarter of the year.

Tools to Make a Difference

Finding time to strike a balance between your inner needs and the demands of the outside world can be a challenge, although you'll relish the chance to let go of the mundane in favor of a more sublime experience whenever you can. Your creativity remains powerful, and the inspirations you're feeling can give you just the boost you need to take a few risks. This is the year to become involved with others who share your ideals and values, or to further cultivate professional associations and close friendships which can form a strong link between your hopes and the manifestation of your dreams. Also, political associations close to home will benefit from your guidance and ability to bring things into focus. Working in concert with others can afford everyone a chance to shine. If you've ever wanted to produce or direct something, this is a great time to develop and utilize those skills. Give yourself time to have more fun, and if you still have a yen to get on stage, look into your local community theater to determine if there's a production or a part you might enjoy, or consider joining a chorus or band. Follow the desires of your heart!

Keep your vitality strong by staying active (or finally keeping your commitment to get into a regular fitness routine). Your physical target zone is your heart and circulatory system, and increasing activities which build endurance can enhance your heart function while strengthening your overall vitality and energy. A shower gel or bath oil infused with rosemary may actually serve to stimulate your circulation. But you can also add rosemary to your cooking —

it tastes great, especially with poultry dishes, and does help keep circulation strong. Consider adding foods high in Omega-3 fatty acids—like fish—to nourish your circulatory system.

To stabilize your energy, you'll benefit from the use of tools that help you fine-tune yourself. Strategically placed chimes can be enjoyable and also alter feng shui in an area that needs to be energized. You might also enjoy vibrational tools like Tibetan singing bowls or tuning forks, or you might want to keep a personal chime on your desk! Working with your dreams can also be helpful, and tools like lucid dreaming kits, keeping a dream diary, or working with dream cards can bring illumination to the messages from your dreams. To increase your peak performance, consider learning about neurolinguistic programming (NLP), or work with mind-body therapists to help you feel more integrated and powerful.

♌

Affirmation for the Year

My personal goals reflect the yearnings of a pure heart.

Leo/January

In the Spotlight
Unrest at home coupled with potential disagreements over the best way to handle joint resources can leave you in the lurch if you're trying to be the nice guy. Partnerships and legal agreements are undergoing major changes.

Wellness and Keeping Fit
Tension runs high, but you can keep it at bay by staying reasonably active—as long as you avoid unnecessary risks. Be especially careful in your daily activities, keeping a sharp lookout for construction, detours, or other potentially hazardous disruptions.

Love and Life Connections
Whether you're misreading signals or life is just in a state of unrest, tension on the home front can keep things in a bit of an uproar and you may be short-tempered as a result. The Moon's eclipse on January 9 can stimulate your desire to spend time alone. You're likely to feel ready to try a new approach to relationships after the New Moon on January 24, when it's easier to move past old issues.

Finance and Success
Delve into tax or inheritance matters with a trusted advisor, since you may uncover resources you have previously overlooked. Careful research illuminates the best avenues for long-term success. Background work supporting creative or artistic ventures prepares you for an upcoming period of outreach.

Cosmic Insider Tip
Innovative technologies and connections to unusual or exceptionally talented people can introduce you to a new world of possibilities after January 21, when keeping an open mind helps!

Rewarding Days: 2, 3, 7, 10, 11, 15, 19, 20, 29, 30

Challenging Days: 4, 5, 16, 17, 18, 24, 25, 31

Affirmation for the Month
I happily show my appreciation for and gratitude toward others who make a difference in my life.

Leo/February

In the Spotlight
Contracts and agreements may require a second look, or you could be searching for a way to back out of a promise that's no longer working out as it should. Research and negotiation are favored; final decisions can wait until after Mercury turns direct on February 25.

Wellness and Keeping Fit
Stress continues to mount and can drag you down from February 1-14 unless you're serious about dealing with it. Getting involved in fitness-related recreational activities after February 15 can immediately boost your vitality, but remember to have fun in the process!

Love and Life Connections
Watching the chain of events involving family hierarchy can seem like a soap opera, and if you're trying too hard to maintain control of everything from February 1-14 you could end up under a pile of emotional rubble! The Leo Full Moon on February 8 is your sensitive time, when unexpected changes can push your buttons before you know it. Repairing damage is easiest when you look at the big picture. Love lifts your spirits after February 10.

Finance and Success
Mercury is definitely in retrograde, and you may be stuck with the details of an agreement that leaves you holding the bag while others want to back out of their responsibilities. Searching for legal supports or seeking experienced counsel can turn around a worrisome situation. You're on safer ground after February 23.

Cosmic Insider Tip
Your confidence increases after February 15, although you'll feel more assured if you wait to reach final agreements until after Mercury turns direct on February 25.

Rewarding Days: 3, 7, 8, 11, 15, 16, 17, 25, 26

Challenging Days: 1, 2, 13, 14, 20, 21, 22, 28

Affirmation for the Month
I carefully consider options before making a decision.

Leo/March

In the Spotlight
Your vision of future possibilities inspires fresh creative endeavors, although you may also discover that there's finally a use for some of the ideas or projects you've left waiting on the back burner. Sometimes you simply have to wait for the world to be ready!

Wellness and Keeping Fit
Your vitality is strengthened, and the benefits you're gaining from gradually increasing your activity levels can become noticeable. It's a time of rejuvenation and healing on every level, and you'll feel a greater appreciation for a true holistic approach to health.

Love and Life Connections
Showing your affections is much easier, and if you've been waiting for the right time to take the initiative, it has arrived! This is a good time to repair a rift or to reconsider a relationship that's been in distress. Travel can lead to romantic possibilities, although you might not enjoy travel with your partner from March 10-17 if you have different preferences. Taking a relationship to a higher level rests on identifying common ideals after the New Moon on March 25.

Finance and Success
Promotional activities, including advertising or business conferences, help strengthen your reputation, although competitors can frustrate your plans from March 1-17. Conservative factions demand answers, and you have a way of illustrating options that can win them over if you take a patient and thorough approach. Showcase your outstanding products or talents from March 1-25.

Cosmic Insider Tip
Venus turns retrograde on March 8, marking a time to carefully evaluate everything. In business, use this month to liquidate assets which are not performing well.

Rewarding Days: 3, 6, 7, 11, 15, 16, 25, 26, 30

Challenging Days: 1, 12, 13, 19, 20, 21, 27, 28

Affirmation for the Month
In all things I make the best use of my assets.

Leo/April

In the Spotlight
There's plenty of excitement, especially in the territories of love—where your passions run high and your creative expression is on fire! Travel and cultural pursuits can also provide exceptional pleasure and may, in turn, advance your status.

Wellness and Keeping Fit
Seeking innovative or unusual fitness options keeps your enthusiasm strong, but if you're bored, you'll lose your sense of commitment. You'll benefit from a trainer or coach who can help you assess your particular needs.

Love and Life Connections
Fulfilling the desires of your heart has its own rewards, particularly if you're closely in tune with the needs of your lover. Revitalizing an existing relationship leads to a deeper understanding, and a rendezvous during the Full Moon on April 8 ignites the sparks of love. Educational pursuits and travel can favorably enhance love, and if you're ready for a new romance, you may find yourself highly attracted to someone you meet while traveling from April 7-21.

Finance and Success
Publishing, advertising, and other means of getting your ideas into the public forum fare beautifully through April 20, although convening with others in your field works to your advantage all month. During the last part of the month you may feel ready to take on a leadership position in your career. Partnership tensions ease, making room for new and more palatable agreements.

Cosmic Insider Tip
Put the finishing touches on long-standing projects or commitments, since it's time to reach closure as you prepare to step onto a new professional platform.

Rewarding Days: 2, 3, 7, 11, 12, 21, 22, 26, 30

Challenging Days: 9, 10, 16, 17, 23, 24

Affirmation for the Month
My capacity to love is boundless!

Leo/May

In the Spotlight
You're stepping into new terrain, ready to broaden your horizons. Although progress may seem slow, the connections you're making now will keep you busy for a long time to come.

Wellness and Keeping Fit
Getting into nature can be immediately rejuvenating, and you might enjoy an adventurous vacation or taking time to be out-of-doors on a regular basis. Team sports or working out with a buddy are good ways to maintain your commitment to fitness.

Love and Life Connections
Most of the doubts you've had about a relationship are satisfied, although family matters can be worrisome or may even intrude on the time you have for your intimate relationship. After the Full Moon on May 7, when a family crisis peaks, you'll have more time to enjoy playful relationships. Instead of looking for love, it may find you, and the potential of meeting someone is strongest from May 1-12 and then after the New Moon on May 23.

Finance and Success
Professional associations, political action, and community activities all serve to advance your reputation and may be in need of your leadership capacities. Writing and public speaking can be rewarding, and your ideas can spark positive changes. Schedule meetings with new contacts after May 23, but take advantage of the best opportunities to maintain or strengthen your connection with enthusiastic supporters of your efforts throughout the month.

Cosmic Insider Tip
With Jupiter in opposition to Pluto on May 6 you may be able to take advantage of changes in the hierarchy, especially if you can see positive ways to transform the situation.

Rewarding Days: 1, 4, 5, 8, 9, 10, 18, 19, 23, 27, 28, 31

Challenging Days: 6, 7, 13, 14, 20, 21, 22

Affirmation for the Month
I welcome changes which give me a chance to grow.

Leo/June

In the Spotlight
While you're still making progress, you may be reviewing or repeating things that you thought were already settled. It's actually a good time to slow down and take a second look, especially in matters of investment—and let's not forget the investments of time and love!

Wellness and Keeping Fit
The temptation to move too quickly, whether you're speeding along in your car or running through the house, can set you up for potential accidents. Burning the candle at both ends also has its price.

Love and Life Connections
Your friends and others you love may have great expectations of you, and you of them. Regroup and consider whether or not you're trying to do too much too soon. Although friends are an excellent source of inspiration and support, reciprocity is required to avoid depleting the relationship. Love blossoms during the Full Moon on June 6, when you may also be ready to voice your commitment. Allow time for introspection during the solar eclipse on June 21.

Finance and Success
Mercury and Mars are both in retrograde, and Jupiter's expansive energy adds to the potential of experiencing lengthy stops and starts—and restarts! Leave plenty of room for unexpected changes, and if you're traveling for business or pleasure, keep a close watch on your belongings. Community efforts and artistically expressive ventures enhance your reputation, although you may have to fill in the gaps created by others who fail to meet their obligations.

Cosmic Insider Tip
Situations can change quickly, but by using moderation and remembering to stay focused on the moment, you may see how to solve problems when things are moving too fast.

Rewarding Days: 1, 5, 6, 14, 15, 16, 19, 23, 24, 27, 28

Challenging Days: 2, 3, 9, 10, 11, 17, 18, 30

Affirmation for the Month
My creativity is inspired by Divine love and wisdom.

Leo/July

In the Spotlight
Your satisfaction with career increases, although by month's end you may be anticipating taking time to reflect on where you want to go from here. Dedicated training prepares you for an excellent period of peak performance.

Wellness and Keeping Fit
If you're feeling a bit draggy it could be because you've been overdoing it. The Moon's eclipse on July 5 draws your attention to health concerns. Allow ample time for rejuvenation; you'll experience a resurgence of energy after Mars turns direct on July 19.

Love and Life Connections
Social interactions are most pressing through July 11, when time spent with friends can be enjoyable, although you may feel a bit saturated. The give-and-take in all your relationships can seem to be out of balance; you may resent situations which require more than they give. A change of heart can be a reason for concern from July 15-22. However, romance appears promising after July 23, although you may keep some distance if you're feeling vulnerable.

Finance and Success
Although you may have limited resources from the July 1-5, you're still making progress on important projects or goals. Power struggles over budget concerns waylay improvements, but after July 20 most obstacles are out of the way and you're ready to move forward. The solid support of a colleague lends courage to all concerned, and unifying divergent factions prepares you for the tasks ahead.

Cosmic Insider Tip
The craziness surrounding Jupiter's last few days in Gemini calms when Jupiter moves into Cancer on July 12, although values seem to change around the same time. Watch and learn.

Rewarding Days: 2, 3, 12, 13, 17, 21, 22, 25, 26, 29, 30

Challenging Days: 1, 7, 8, 9, 14, 15, 27, 28

Affirmation for the Month
I welcome new goals which reflect my optimism for the future.

Leo/August

In the Spotlight
You're moving full steam ahead, but may run into resistance from others whose philosophical ideals are different from your own. Your persuasive abilities are in overdrive, and if your ideas make sense, others are likely to follow your lead.

Wellness and Keeping Fit
If you're feeling a bit lazy this month it could be that you need a vacation. Finding ways to ease the pressure of daily hassles keeps you sane and healthy, and you'll appreciate the benefits of inner fitness. Contemplation and meditation help balance your energy.

Love and Life Connections
If you find yourself face to face with a divergent agenda from your partner or a good friend during the Full Moon on August 4, you may have to determine whether or not your differences are sufficient reason for worry. Sometimes it's the distinctions that keep the spice in a relationship! Seek out time to enjoy the things that make your heart sing, and if you're dissatisfied, consider a different approach during the Leo New Moon on August 19.

Finance and Success
Speculative ventures can undergo a turnaround from August 1-11, giving you cause to re-evaluate and determine whether or not you want to make a change. You may simply need to make room for innovation within the current structures. Revamp your budget after August 19, but avoid taking on unnecessary debt, since it could last longer than you assume it will.

Cosmic Insider Tip
The Full Moon on August 4 is accompanied by a Saturn-Pluto opposition. That means everything gets pretty intense, especially power issues. Try not to be among the abusers!

Rewarding Days: 8, 9, 13, 17, 18, 21, 25, 26

Challenging Days: 3, 4, 5, 10, 11, 12, 23, 24, 30, 31

Affirmation for the Month
I am safe in the midst of change.

Leo/September

In the Spotlight
Although there's work to be done, you'll enjoy the connections to others who support your efforts and ideas. It's a good time to highlight your best qualities—personally and professionally.

Wellness and Keeping Fit
The pace at work quickens, and if you're traveling more you could fall under the illusion that there's not enough time to keep fit. Staying active increases your energy; inactivity leads to burnout—but you do need to rest, too. Daily adjustments may be required.

Love and Life Connections
Venus transits in your sign through September 20, bringing her energy of attraction your way. The temptation to be self-absorbed can get you into trouble, but turning your love light onto someone else can have the effect you're after: mutual adoration! Romance fares best from September 1-9 and then after September 22. Communication is positive all month, so even if you can't spend as much time together as you'd like, maintaining contact works wonders.

Finance and Success
Meetings and presentations keep the avenues open for progress in career. However, monetary matters can be a source of dispute near the Full Moon on September 2, and unless your ideas are practical, your proposals may be shot down by conservative factions. Try again after September 8, but do your research! Unanticipated actions throw a monkey wrench in the works from September 15-19, but in all the excitement you're likely to be the one who comes out on top.

Cosmic Insider Tip
Take advantage of technologically enhanced communication from September 13-23 to reach into unusual areas of support. Others will be impressed by your imaginative resourcefulness.

Rewarding Days: 4, 5, 6, 13, 14, 18, 19, 22, 23

Challenging Days: 1, 7, 8, 20, 21, 27, 28

Affirmation for the Month
My words and actions are motivated by love and compassion.

Leo/October

In the Spotlight
If you're on the go a lot this month you may run into unavoidable detours. Negotiations can meet the same fate, requiring you to maintain a cool-headed attitude, even if you're not in the mood to be cooperative!

Wellness and Keeping Fit
Extra care is needed from October 1-6, when it's easy to move too quickly for conditions, or when stress and tension can lower your resistance. Your sense of humor can be a great relief!

Love and Life Connections
Despite your best efforts you may say or do things that set off a series of misunderstandings. It's not just Mercury's retrograde cycle, but frustrations from Mars and Jupiter adding to the strain. Circumstances can escalate before you have a chance to take control. During the New Moon on October 16 you may feel that you simply cannot wait to let your intended know how you feel. Watch the signals to be sure it's not a one-way attraction!

Finance and Success
Frictions at work or in your daily routine can be unnerving, and eliciting cooperative attitudes from others can leave you at your wits' end. Mercury retrogrades from October 1-23, and although you may anticipate that things will be better when the retrograde ends, it's likely that problems which surfaced will still be functioning until the end of the month. Take care with finances from October 1-6 and again after October 27 to avoid overspending.

Cosmic Insider Tip
Mixed signals abound, indicating that moderation with investments and special care with negotiations is the only way to avoid getting into a sticky situation.

Rewarding Days: 3, 7, 11, 12, 15, 19, 20, 29, 30

Challenging Days: 4, 5, 14, 17, 18, 24, 25, 31

Affirmation for the Month
I am clear about my motivations and speak honest words.

Leo/November

In the Spotlight
Competitive situations challenge you to honor your limitations while putting forth your best efforts. But the real problem is what you can't see! Whether it's deception or things changing without your knowledge, it's easy to feel confused.

Wellness and Keeping Fit
Environmental pollutants can be especially irritating, since you can be especially sensitive during these cycles. Consider working with a mind-body therapist to help balance your energies.

Love and Life Connections
You may be more sensitive to family matters than you thought, especially if you're left out of the loop in important discussions. Your connection to siblings is helpful during the Full Moon on the 1st, although you may wonder if your partner understands what's really going on. Satisfying the demands of family and partner may seem to require a fully functional clone of yourself, although situations calm a bit after November 22.

Finance and Success
Progress in negotiations is heartening from November 1-6, although you may wonder if you're seeing the whole picture. If you do feel uncertain, consider postponing final decisions until after November 15 when the fog clears. Avoid precarious financial dealings until you're more stabilized. You may also decide to break your ties in situations which no longer support your best interests.

Cosmic Insider Tip
Saturn and Pluto are once again in opposition, but this time other factors indicate that somebody's not playing fair. Deal yourself out of that game!

Rewarding Days: 4, 7, 8, 16, 17, 25, 26, 30

Challenging Days: 1, 2, 13, 14, 15, 20, 21, 28, 29

Affirmation for the Month
I am safe and secure.

Leo/December

In the Spotlight
Concentration on expressing or developing your talents opens the way for personal satisfaction, and can lead to career advancement, too. Besides that, those who love you will be overjoyed by the experience of seeing you shine!

Wellness and Keeping Fit
Delving into the core of any physical concerns can be illuminating. Your mind, heart, and body connection may be in need of balance, and by exploring psychological issues you may find the best way to handle your physical distress.

Love and Life Connections
Love can take a positive turn during the solar eclipse on December 14. However, if you're needing to break free of a situation in order to allow your heart to heal, you may find that letting go is easier from December 1-8. A healthy love connection presents its own challenge, since you may want to explore deeper levels of intimacy and can run into your own inhibitions! Before you bolt and run, ask yourself what you really fear, since the past has already happened.

Finance and Success
You may still be pushing through a competitive challenge until December 8, although you're feeling better equipped to handle it and can see the best ways to take advantage of your victory. Speculative interests can positively alter your financial picture, but before you spend your money, consider your long-range plans and explore tax liabilities. Rash action works against your best interests after December 9, even if you think you have a good motivation!

Cosmic Insider Tip
Spending extra time with the people you love warms your heart this month. Tangible assets can only take you so far.

Rewarding Days: 1, 4, 5, 9, 10, 13, 14, 23, 28

Challenging Days: 11, 12, 17, 18, 19, 25, 26, 30

Affirmation for the Month
Sharing love makes my heart sing and sets my spirit soaring!

Leo Action Table

These dates reflect the best—but not the only—times for success and ease in these activities, according to your Sun sign.

	JAN	FEB	MAR	APR	MAY	JUN	JUL	AUG	SEPT	OCT	NOV	DEC
Move											8-25	
Start a class			24-26						2-30	24-31	1-6	
Join a club					23, 24							
Ask for a raise								18, 19				
Look for work	1-9			22-30	1-5							16-31
Get pro advice	24, 25	20-22	19-21	16, 17	13-15	9-11	7, 8	3-4, 30-31	26-28	24, 25	20-22	17-19
Get a loan	26-28	23, 24	22, 23	18-20	16, 17	12, 13	9-11	5-7	2-3, 29-30	26-28	23, 24	20, 21
See a doctor	1-9						13-29					15-31
Start a diet	21-23	18, 19	17, 18	13-15	11, 12	7, 8	4-6, 31	1-2, 28-29	24, 25	21-23	18, 19	15, 16
End relationship								3, 4				
Buy clothes											26-30	1-14
Get a makeover								18, 19,	1-20			
New romance												2-25
Vacation	2-3, 29-30	25, 26	24-26	21, 22	18, 19	14-16	12, 13	8, 9	4-6	1-3, 29-30	25-27	22-24

Virgo
The Virgin
August 22 to September 22

♍

Element:	Earth
Quality:	Mutable
Polarity:	Yin/Feminine
Planetary Ruler:	Mercury
Meditation:	I experience love through service.
Gemstone:	Sapphire
Power Stones:	Peridot, amazonite, rhodochrosite
Key Phrase:	I analyze
Glyph:	Greek symbol for containment
Anatomy:	Abdomen, intestines, gall bladder
Color:	Taupe, gray, navy blue
Animal:	Domesticated animals
Myths/Legends:	Astraea, Demeter, Hygeia
House:	Sixth
Opposite Sign:	Pisces
Flower:	Pansy
Key Word:	Discriminating

Positive Expression:
Precise
Efficient
Perspicacious
Meticulous
Helpful
Practical
Conscientious

Misuse of Energy:
Intolerant
Skeptical
Hypercritical
Tedious
Hypochondriac
Fretful
Persnickety

Virgo

Your Ego's Strengths and Shortcomings
You're always delving into the meaning and workings of everything, your analytical mind and keen observational skills providing valuable insights into the very nature of life itself. Your efficient abilities and practical approach to life keep you busy, and you rarely turn down a chance to teach or guide others requesting your assistance or skillfulness. Whether you're working with others to bring out the best of themselves or in a situation which requires proficiency or improvement, your effectiveness as "The Modifier" of the zodiac definitely keeps you in demand.

Learning is a high priority, and you relish the idea of an absorbing conversation with others whose expertise and intelligence stimulate your mind. This influence is an extension of your connection to the energy of Mercury, the planet of communication and discernment. With your knack for bringing complex information into a workable format, you're the person to call when anything (or anyone) needs to be put in order. But that should not fool people into thinking that you're perfectly organized, since you may not be the neatness freak in every area of your life. After all, you do have your priorities! Yet you are continually scrutinizing everything, and can become excessively critical when it comes to your diet and your relationships. It's learning how to express your criticisms in a palatable manner that can be one of your great lessons.

Your spiritual quest for excellence has its mark in your psyche, since you may feel that your soul cannot rest until you are sufficiently pure to pass through the gates of higher consciousness. Your quest is to become more tolerant of your imperfections and other's flaws; then your efforts can shine more brightly upon a finely tuned life path reflecting true insight and understanding.

Shining Your Love Light
Your sensuality may be one of your best-kept secrets, since you don't let just anyone get close enough to discover your tender and powerfully expressive nature. There's quite a list of qualifications for your perfect partner, and you have a definite process of elimination.

The reason for this is that you have a deep yearning for a love that holds a quality of eternal endurance, an ability to grow through the tests of time. When your dreams of love are answered, you can be a devoted partner, surrendering body, mind, and soul to the alchemy of love nourished in an atmosphere of acceptance and trust.

As an earth sign, you'll appreciate the stable energy and comfortable pace you feel with the other earth signs—Taurus, Virgo, and Capricorn. There's a strong attraction to your opposite, Pisces, whose idealism mesmerizes you, but the Pisces dreaminess can frustrate your practicality.

Excited by Aries, you can feel sexually comfortable but may find the day-to-day relationship irritating. The endurance and sensuality of Taurus are simply delicious, and you'll appreciate her or his conservative stability. Gemini's mentality, levity, and intellectualism can be fun, although you may be frustrated by the number of times you simply cannot connect. Cancer provides a comfortable mix of friendship and sensuality. Leo's warm embrace can seem to be the answer to your dreams, but you'll be uneasy unless there's a strong sense of acceptance from each of you. Another Virgo can be a cozy partner, but it's entirely too easy for either of you to quibble over the endless details of your existence.

Libra helps support your self-esteem, but you will each need to work on objectivity if you want to stay together. Passion and deep love are your natural connection to Scorpio, who seems to know all your secrets. Sagittarius can be fun, but the times you're apart can leave you uneasy. Capricorn stimulates something very primal and may be your ultimate lover and lifelong companion. Aquarius confirms your spiritual strength and can be a stimulating ally, except you may never be entirely at ease together.

Making Your Place in the World

At the end of the day, you like to feel that you've accomplished something, and you'll appreciate a career which challenges your mind. The independence of running your own business can suit you well, although you'll tend to overwork! You may be a talented musician or artist. Writing, editing, public speaking, and teaching can be especially rewarding. Or, put your manual dexterity to work in drafting, design, art, crafts, or detail work in the building industry.

Service fields such as counseling, social services, or the health professions and healing arts can be perfect. Or your abilities in scientific research, administration, office managements, desktop publishing, accounting, systems analysis, or secretarial services may be in great demand. Over the course of your lifetime, you may develop skills in several areas and may even have more than one job at a time. Always, though, you'll do your reliable best.

Power Plays

Although seeking power for its own sake seems wasteful, you can see the advantages of rising to a position from which you can positively influence healthy change. The power of the mind is something you readily embrace, and in shaping the course of your own life or the lives of others, you strive to make wise and honest use of information. Education is an important issue for you, and whether you're accomplishing your own quest for knowledge or involved in shaping educational opportunities for youth, you're insightful about the best ways to facilitate learning.

Your list of accomplishments can be rather impressive, amazing others with the scope of what you've done—since you make it look so easy! For this reason, you may feel that others are not fully appreciative of your efforts; promise to appreciate yourself more fully! Also keep in mind that in your desire to serve others you can be drawn into the quagmire of codependency. The proper use of your power will be seen after you've learned when to take charge and when to pull back and let someone fail or succeed on their own.

Famous Virgos

Jane Addams, Fiona Apple, Yasser Arafat, Lauren Bacall, Eldridge Cleaver, Rudy Galindo, O. Henry, Damon Hill, Gustav Holst, Julie Kavner, LeAnn Rimes, John Ritter, Leo Tolstoy, Louden Wainwright III, Barry White

The Year Ahead for Virgo

The platform you've been creating during the past two years serves you well during 2001, when you're ready to broaden your goals. You're definitely facing a year of growth which is likely to test your adaptability. Yet it is through such cycles that you tend to perform at your best, incorporating possibilities which reinforce your skills and strengthen your understanding.

Your reputation is enhanced during Jupiter's cycles this year, and the manner in which you handle this increased influence will determine exactly how far you climb up the ladder of success. While this period of opportunity is certainly a plus, it's easy to become overcommitted from January through July, and this can be stressful if you feel it's undermining your ability to do your best work. On July 12, Jupiter moves into Cancer, and throughout the remainder of the year you may feel that you have a better grasp on the way to handle the growth options which continue to knock at your door. However, your goals are changing, and one of the key features of this cycle is learning how to maintain supports from others in your field whose expertise can be utilized in harmony with your own. On an emotional level, you're finding better ways to receive, which may be an unusual concept for you. Giving is the easy part; accepting what others (and the universe) offer to you means you have to let down your barriers and fill your heart with joy. Oddly enough, this means you'll have a lot more to give—so try it and see you how you like the change!

Saturn's qualities of discipline and focus are yielding a period of concentrated learning during the first quarter of the year, and through this time you may be working toward important objectives that strengthen your status. Then, after April, Saturn will be transiting through the Tenth House of your solar chart, marking a time of increasing responsibilities in your career. This can be a good thing if you're ready for it, but if you enter this cycle unprepared you can be held back until you've met your obligations or finished necessary training or testing. Slowing your pace a bit can help, but just as important is a re-evaluation of your obligations, since if you're carrying unnecessary burdens you'll be frustrated and discouraged by their heaviness.

Uranus and Neptune continue their journey through your solar Sixth House, altering the way you approach your daily routine. Whether you're incorporating different technologies or tools into your work or simply changing the order of your priorities, you can enjoy the new freedom which accompanies these cycles. Pluto's cycle can be a challenge, especially if your family structure is changing and you're resisting. Fortunately, you usually welcome change that leads to growth, but your emotional attachments to old circumstances may be stronger than you realized. Probing into your deeper feelings will help you make the best use of this transformational cycle.

The solar and lunar eclipses during 2001 emphasize your connections to community, friends, and environment. You may decide that this is the year to make alterations in your home environment to accommodate your varying needs, or your immediate family can be changing. The indications from the transit of the Moon's Nodes are that you are becoming more aware of your deeper feelings about your dreams and hopes, and the changes in the world around you need to reflect your awareness of how you can best fulfill these wants and desires.

If you were born from August 22 to September 7, you're experiencing Saturn's transit in square aspect to your Sun. While this can be a frustrating cycle, it's also a time when you're ready to eliminate the things from your life which are counterproductive—including attitudes which have inhibited your ability to build a real sense of personal strength and security. This cycle does not begin until May, and will last about a year. It is most intensive for those born from August 31 to September 7. Since the key feature of Saturn's square is a time of testing, you may be more critical of yourself and your life circumstances, and need to realize that if you're feeling stuck you'll be even more stressed during this cycle. Perhaps the most positive use of this influence is through your outreach in teaching or training others, although you can also become more fully involved in a large-scale project which simply demands more of your time and energy. Your responsibilities will definitely increase, but that does not mean that you also have to carry burdens for everyone else. Sometimes the opposite is true: it's time to let go of things that others finally need to do for themselves! You can better prepare for this period by using the first quarter of 2001 to complete obligations you no longer wish to carry or which are not leading you toward your goals. Taking better care of your health is important too, although you are usually fairly attentive to your body's needs. However, if you've been procrastinating about dealing with a physical issue, you may have to address it now. Fortunately, you're also experiencing the supportive confidence of Jupiter transiting in sextile to your Sun from September through December, and even though you're feeling the tests of Saturn, you will have potential for help. You simply have to take advantage of it. Ask!

If you were born from August 28 to September 2, you may be feeling a bit out of sorts while Neptune transits in quincunx to your Sun. The challenge of this cycle is learning to let go of the things you cannot control, and through surrender you are discovering a different way of looking at things. This is a spiritualizing influence, and alters the way you see yourself and your life. However, it's not exactly clarifying, and the stimulus can be similar to that of getting used to a new environment after a move. It's just that the "environment" is you and your sense of self. You're more physically sensitive now and can also be more sensitive to the energy and influence of others. Eliminating potential toxins from your diet and environment can help you stay physically stronger, although you may discover that you have reactions to things that have not bothered you in the past. Also, you may have less tolerance for people who get on your nerves or drain your energy. Channeling some of your time and energy into creative or artistic pursuits will add strength and confidence during this cycle.

If you were born from September 4 to 10, you're feeling the tension of Pluto transiting in square aspect to your Sun. This cycle adds an undercurrent of deep tension resulting in powerful transformational change. You can experience physical changes, moves, alterations in family structure and relationships and a different perspective on your life work. Some changes you'll want to make, while you'll resist others. It all depends upon your emotional attachment to the particular situations (or people). You do have an advantage in that Jupiter will be offering an uplifting and supportive energy from September through December, and if you're eliminating some of the things that drain your vitality, you may actually find this to be a period of exceptional growth. It's just that some progress may take longer than you want it to take! It's much like restoring a historic building. First, you have to assess the structure to determine which elements need elimination or repair, but you're also looking for the things which can be revitalized. Meanwhile, everything's a mess until the project is done—and that's how you might feel about your life. You have the vision, you're tearing down the rotten parts, and you are adding elements which strengthen and renew your very being. This is the essence of transformation: some things have to fall away so that your wings can unfold and you finally fly!

If you were born from September 11 to 18, Uranus is transiting in quincunx aspect to your Sun. This influence can be unsettling, since there are changes happening within and around you that seem beyond your control. However, it's also a time when you're ready to take advantage of fresh technological advancements or when you can create a few of your own. While this particular cycle can indicate the emergence of health issues, it's also a time when you may be able to make alterations in your lifestyle which not only resolve the health problems but improve your life in the process. Incorporating alternative healing concepts and techniques can give you an advantage, too. It's important to remember that many of the changes happening now are transitional, and therefore trying to build something stable may be too frustrating. It's remaining open to possibility that makes all the difference, and realizing that sometimes you're either on a detour or crossing a bridge. This period is about the journey, not the destination. Your attitudes and viewpoints determine whether that journey is pleasant and exciting or just one frustration after another!

If you were born from September 19 to 22, you're experiencing the support of Saturn transiting in trine aspect to your Sun. While this influence only lasts through April, the structures and relationships you build now can be part of your basic support for a long time to come. Educational pursuits, publishing efforts, and teaching opportunities are all advantageous to your growth during this time. Also, you're experiencing a transit of Uranus moving in biquintile aspect to your Sun, indicating that this can be a year of powerful creative and spiritual development. The extent of that development is dependent upon how much energy and time you choose to direct toward your talents and special abilities.

Tools to Make a Difference

Although you're usually fairly conscientious about your health, you may be looking for fresh alternatives and tools which complement your desire to stay as healthy as possible. Improving the quality of your environment can be inspirational, and may also provide the kind of comfort zone which allows you the perfect space for rejuvenation from life in a hectic world. If you've not yet learned about feng shui, then look into it! You may be able to make some very minor alterations employing basic principles of this ancient oriental art that will allow the energy in your home or work environments to flow more harmoniously and advantageously. If you're moving or remodeling, consider having a feng shui master explore the home you're considering to determine which changes will need to be made. You need to clear any blocks to energy flow, and will also appreciate anything which allows you to feel more comfortable during your limited "downtime." And remember that "downtime" is a truly valuable tool all by itself!

Your target zone for health is the digestive system, and you may need to make some adjustments in your diet or dietary routine to make the most of the foods you're eating. If you feel you're not assimilating your food properly, consider the addition of digestive enzymes, like bromelain or papain, to your diet. You may also need to be particularly aware of nourishing your nervous system and brain, so try adding supplements like gotu kola, ginkgo biloba, B-vitamins, or Omega-3 fatty acids (which contain helpful DHA) to your diet.

To lift your spirits this year, make time for contemplation and meditation. Since you may be more comfortable with moving meditations, you might enjoy adding a yoga class (even if you're an old pro) or a retreat. To complement your exercise routines, look into props which can enhance the effectiveness of your movements. Counteract the tension-producing qualities of Saturn's cycle by maintaining your flexibility. From simple stretching exercises to more elaborate routines involving Pilates equipment, you'll enjoy the benefits of staying resilient.

♍

Affirmation for the Year

My priorities reflect my true needs,
which originate from pure love of myself and others.

Virgo/January

In the Spotlight
Relationships take center stage, and your special talents garner the attentions that make your heart sing with delight. Sharing such times with those you love makes memories which become the highlights of your life.

Wellness and Keeping Fit
Your physical vitality grows stronger, although you may also be feeling a bit indulgent and might not have the motivation to stick with your fitness routine. Incorporating different elements gives you a boost after January 24.

Love and Life Connections
Surrendering to love can be easy, and during the lunar eclipse on January 9 you may feel that you're finally ready to open your heart and trust love to guide your way. Your romantic nature is likely to take precedence over family matters, although children may also give you ample reasons to feel joyful. Your passionate nature is enhanced under the influence of Venus and Mars, although you may be impatient if your sweetheart seems to be hesitant.

Finance and Success
Contract negotiations fare best after January 3, but you can run into budget constraints from January 12-20. A creative project or speculative venture gains momentum from January 1-10; then it's possible that you'll need to find additional help to finish what's been started. You might have better luck after the New Moon on January 24, when interest and effort both seem to be present.

Cosmic Insider Tip
Although you can benefit from your partner's good fortune, you also need to safeguard your mutual resources to assure that they are not too quickly depleted.

Rewarding Days: 4, 5, 9, 12, 13, 17, 18, 21, 22, 23, 31

Challenging Days: 6, 7, 19, 20, 24, 26, 27, 28

Affirmation for the Month
I show gratitude for life's many blessings.

Virgo/February

In the Spotlight
Interruptions in your schedule can frustrate your ability to keep things operating at a smooth pace, although some changes may actually shift your focus to a more creative viewpoint.

Wellness and Keeping Fit
Staying on track with your fitness routine can be difficult, although your ingenuity can find a way! In fact, alternating your routine may actually result in more reliable energy levels. Schedule body work near the Full Moon on February 8.

Love and Life Connections
A strong relationship moves toward deeper levels of intimacy, or if you're having problems you may be able to bring issues to the surface to determine whether or not the two of you are strong enough to deal with them. A fresh approach to your needs in partnership works best after the New Moon on February 23, although you may still feel uncertain about your commitment. If you're single, you may decide to stay that way for a while!

Finance and Success
Progress may seem more like an illusion than a possibility. During Mercury's retrograde from February 3-25 you're in a good position to make changes that leave room for innovation or experimentation. In fact, trying to finalize things can seem futile. Joint finances can be a headache, and contractual agreements, costly. Let your practicality work to your advantage, since it can also be a great argument for researching options or exploring your concerns.

Cosmic Insider Tip
Be alert to the tendency for people and situations to move too quickly from February 14-24. Remind yourself to slow down so that you can be more alert to potential risks.

Rewarding Days: 1, 5, 6, 9, 10, 18, 19, 28

Challenging Days: 3, 4, 15, 16, 17, 23, 24, 25

Affirmation for the Month
I am flexible in the face of change.

Virgo/March

In the Spotlight
Increasing family activity or turmoil at home can be unsettling and stressful. Although this can be a time of much-needed change, your objectivity may seem limited. Turn your concentration to the things you can do something about!

Wellness and Keeping Fit
Impatience can be your enemy, and if you're pushing beyond your physical or emotional limits you can run into painful problems. It's a good time to break destructive habits or to finally let go of anything working against your best interests.

Love and Life Connections
Highly charged issues can lead to angry outbursts, but if you can funnel your anger toward positive solutions you may actually make a breakthrough. If you're feeling extrasensitive near and during the Virgo Full Moon on March 9 you might tend to withdraw, although broaching important issues can lead to progress. Indignant attitudes from others can create a barrier which you'll have trouble breaking through; perhaps you're seeing people as they are.

Finance and Success
While others may be offering support, it does come with a price—one which you may unwilling to pay! To determine if an agreement is worth the price of the paper on which it's written, explore the true value of what's being presented and clarify what will be expected of you in return. You're of no mind to give away your talents, time, or resources. More palatable arrangements can emerge after March 26.

Cosmic Insider Tip
Venus is in retrograde from March 8 to April 19, and during this time you're questioning love relationships and commitments. Explore what you need now, not how you felt years ago!

Rewarding Days: 1, 4, 5, 8, 9, 13, 17, 18, 27, 28, 31

Challenging Days: 2, 3, 14, 15, 16, 22, 23, 29, 30

Affirmation for the Month
I honor the true value of myself and others.

Virgo/April

In the Spotlight
Most of the loose ends that have frustrated your progress seem to be coming together as the month moves along. Your success may depend upon how well you can coordinate your efforts with the talents and resources of others. This can be a win-win situation!

Wellness and Keeping Fit
Delving into your deeper feelings can uncover the links between physical complaints and your emotions, especially those which have been repressed. It's time to forgive so you can move on. Forgive yourself first.

Love and Life Connections
Disagreements over the best ways to handle family issues can escalate from April 1-6, when you may need to step away from conflicts in order to ultimately resolve them. It's about knowing which are your battles to fight, and which belong to somebody else. Everything looks different after April 20, when a more optimistic attitude allows love to flow more freely. Travel can open romantic pathways after the New Moon on April 23.

Finance and Success
Defining expectations from superiors helps you pinpoint your target for your best efforts. Look into budget questions before the Full Moon on April 8 to avoid being caught in a bind financially (or contractually). Schedule promotional activities, business conferences, or important meetings after April 20. You can be especially persuasive, and your talents, ideas, or efforts gain the most favorable responses from April 23-29.

Cosmic Insider Tip
Some of the weightiness begins to lift after April 21. Open your eyes: the horizon is much more promising now!

Rewarding Days: 1, 4, 5, 6, 13, 14, 15, 23, 24, 28, 29

Challenging Days: 11, 12, 18, 19, 20, 25, 26

Affirmation for the Month
Truth and integrity always work to my benefit!

Virgo/May

In the Spotlight
Changes beyond your control can push you into a situation which at first seems threatening to your plans. However, as the power base is altered it will make room for fast-paced opportunities which can advance your position to one of increasing influence.

Wellness and Keeping Fit
You need a positive challenge, and setting fitness goals which increase your endurance and flexibility will have positive ramifications in other parts of your life. Unexpressed emotional tension can undermine your vitality, but regular activity has a balancing effect.

Love and Life Connections
With Mars entering its retrograde in the Fourth House of your solar chart, you may feel a shakeup in the very foundations of your life. If you're making changes of your own accord, others may not be responding as you had hoped; or a move can be especially stressful. Until the Full Moon on May 8 you can experience a strengthening of a powerful love bond. After May 12, distance or obligations can create a physical separation which tests your association.

Finance and Success
If alterations in the hierarchy or the economy have an unsettling influence, you may react too defensively. Determine your motivations and goals. You may be ready to move on to a different situation and can use these changes to your advantage. Your confident leadership and clarity can be inspirational to others, especially if you help determine the nature of the emerging structure.

Cosmic Insider Tip
The opposition of Jupiter and Pluto hearkens back to changes which happened last September, but now there's a different power base. As a result, your goals may be changing.

Rewarding Days: 2, 3, 7, 11, 12, 21, 22, 25, 29, 30

Challenging Days: 6, 8, 9, 16, 17, 23, 24

Affirmation for the Month
I know what others need from me and what I can accomplish.

Virgo/June

In the Spotlight
The demands on your time seem to be coming from all directions, and you may have to let a few things slide if you're going to do your best to satisfy your top priorities. Your ethical and moral imperatives place you in an advantageous position.

Wellness and Keeping Fit
Since you're likely to be burning the candle at both ends, nourishing your nervous system is especially important. A diet rich in B-vitamins can be helpful, but you'll also benefit from catnaps to recharge your energy during the day.

Love and Life Connections
Argumentative situations within the family can be unnerving and seem to escalate out of control over the smallest things near the Full Moon on June 6. While work can be a blessing, you'll welcome a respite of time spent with friends during and after the solar eclipse on June 21. They may also come to your aid if you need anyone to help you support the true needs of your family and loved ones.

Finance and Success
With Mercury retrograding from June 4-27 in opposition to Mars, you may feel that time is not only flying, but that it's on fire! Getting everything done can be quite an assignment, and while some situations fall apart, other positive options emerge which keep your hopes alive. Be on the alert for potential deception from June 9-16, when exploring ideas or negotiating can be safer than making any final decisions.

Cosmic Insider Tip
Think of this as a time of undoing or reshaping, when working with a prototype or experimentation yields better results than pouring the final mold.

Rewarding Days: 3, 7, 8, 17, 18, 21, 22, 25, 26, 30

Challenging Days: 5, 6, 12, 13, 14, 19, 20, 28

Affirmation for the Month
I am open to the Truth in all matters.

Virgo/July

In the Spotlight
The manner in which you handle criticism can determine the level of your advancement. Although your ideas may differ from those of your superiors, you may have to put their priorities ahead of your own before you can finally do things your way!

Wellness and Keeping Fit
It's the perfect time to get rid of habits that are robbing you of your energy. You'll also feel better if you take the time to eliminate clutter from your life—ranging from a cluttered and worried mind to clearing out the junk piled up in your closets!

Love and Life Connections
A love relationship grows stronger, and during the lunar eclipse on July 5 you may forge a deeper understanding of what you need from one another. The fallout from a family crisis still lingers and may create some sadness midmonth, but by the New Moon on July 20 you are seeing your way past the most troubling problems. You're leaving behind the situations you no longer need and moving toward a more fulfilling future.

Finance and Success
Outreach advances your reputation from July 1-5, but then you need to move with caution, taking into account the obligations others expect to have fulfilled. Conservative attitudes win out over innovation from July 10-18, and if you can satisfy these concerns, then you have breathing room after July 20. Forge positive connections to those who share your interests after July 12, since you will all benefit from unified efforts.

Cosmic Insider Tip
The pace of change can seem very slow; getting new things started is thwarted until after Mars turns direct on July 20.

Rewarding Days: 4, 5, 6, 14, 15, 19, 23, 24, 27, 31

Challenging Days: 2, 3, 9, 10, 11, 16, 17, 18, 29, 30

Affirmation for the Month
I am open to the ideas of others.

Virgo/August

In the Spotlight
You may feel that you're in the calm after the storm, although the way your life is organized is still changing. Use this as a period of rebuilding and restoration; use changes to inspire your creativity.

Wellness and Keeping Fit
Maintaining a strong energy level can be difficult; you'll do better if you allow more downtime to avoid running on empty. Seek out enjoyable recreational activities which are mildly challenging physically. And seek out joy—laughter can be your best medicine.

Love and Life Connections
The love flowing through an intimate relationship grows, or, if you're seeking a new love, you may feel that you're finally ready to open your heart. While a very private affair warms your affections during the Full Moon on August 4, you'll also enjoy sharing your future hopes with your sweetheart, and if she or he shows enthusiastic support, your trust can take root. You're likely to remain cautious regarding long-term promises, however.

Finance and Success
To further your career you may have to move, or at least shift your office space! The more profound changes can be beyond your control, as old leadership or tradition falls away. To accomplish the job at hand, you may be making things up as you go, but you're creative under pressure and can pull in favors from others in influential positions when necessary. Your ability to outline long-term benefits stems from your clearly emerging goals.

Cosmic Insider Tip
The powerful influence of Saturn in opposition to Pluto can result in a changing of the guard. You may even decide that it's time to explore new options for yourself.

Rewarding Days: 1, 2, 10, 11, 12, 15, 16, 19, 20, 28, 29

Challenging Days: 5, 6, 7, 13, 14, 25, 26, 27

Affirmation for the Month
I welcome the support of friends and offer assistance of my own.

Virgo/September

In the Spotlight
Your creative vitality lifts your spirits and opens the way for positive recognition and advancement. It's time to accept a fresh challenge which calls your talents into action. The more you give of yourself now, the further you go toward fulfilling your most cherished hopes.

Wellness and Keeping Fit
Disciplined dedication to your fitness routine pays off, and you're seeing the results you've hoped to achieve. Remember that what you're seeking most is balance.

Love and Life Connections
Romantic whims can overtake your rational judgment during the Full Moon on September 2, and you might be tempted to overdo it—which could work to your advantage if your sweetheart enjoys drama! While you're likely to keep your private affections under wraps (no prying eyes in those special moments), you're still feeling quite demonstrative. After September 9, your passions grow even stronger. If you've been hesitating, take advantage of the Virgo New Moon on September 17 to initiate contact or express your mind.

Finance and Success
Work out details behind the scenes from September 1-8, and then seek opportunities to showcase your talents or make important presentations. Research investment options, and consult with expert sources regarding potential changes in your portfolio after September 17. Take care in unfamiliar territory or with new people at work, since you can be misunderstood if you're moving too quickly.

Cosmic Insider Tip
Working in concert with others requires attention to egos, especially if some people are prone to upstaging you. Your talents shine brightly on their own after September 22.

Rewarding Days: 7, 8, 12, 15, 16, 20, 24, 25

Challenging Days: 2, 3, 9, 10, 22, 23, 29, 30

Affirmation for the Month
Love guides my thoughts, words, and actions.

Virgo/October

In the Spotlight
Your artistic sensibilities are working overtime, and you're enjoying added success as a result of your ingenuity. However, Mercury's retrograde can add an element of frustration if your schedule has too many requirements. Try to keep a few openings for the unexpected.

Wellness and Keeping Fit
You're in the pink, and to stay that way indulge in beneficial activities like massage therapy, or a manicure. In fitness, continue to emphasize building your endurance and strength.

Love and Life Connections
With a little help from Venus and Mars you're feeling good about yourself and more trusting of your feelings, although you may question a relationship on October 1 if facts come to the surface which trigger your own issues. Allow time for romance, and plan a special event or amusement to share with your true love from October 2-15. A quiet getaway can be memorable after October 23, but you'll be happier if plans are kept on the simple side.

Finance and Success
The Mercury retrograde cycle from October 1-22 indicates potential trouble with budgets and financial arrangements, especially if you're not paying adequate attention to your expenditures. Take special care from October 15-23, and if you're still in negotiations on a contract, you might decide to wait until next month to finalize the deal. Business meetings from October 4-14 show promise if you're adequately prepared.

Cosmic Insider Tip
Getting caught in the wave of enthusiasm from October 2-8 can be inspiring, although it's not the best time to abandon a positive course of action in favor of a distraction. Think twice.

Rewarding Days: 4, 5, 9, 10, 13, 14, 18, 21, 22, 23, 31

Challenging Days: 6, 7, 8, 19, 20, 26, 27, 28

Affirmation for the Month
I gladly share my abundance!

Virgo/November

In the Spotlight
Work can be high pressure, especially if you're straddling two different worlds. The potential of having strong commitments to more than one project is very high, although you're efficient enough to manage it and make it look almost easy.

Wellness and Keeping Fit
To fulfill the long list that is your agenda, you're going to require plenty of energy. Staying active is one key, although you could benefit from restful days from November 3-6. Energetic healing techniques can also be especially revitalizing this month.

Love and Life Connections
A soulful love gains momentum during the Full Moon on November 1, when your words have a significant impact. Travel has romantic implications after November 8, but you may find yourself in the midst of a profound infatuation with either a place or a person—and distinguishing between the two can be difficult! Renew your connection to siblings after the New Moon on November 15, but avoid those "hot" buttons if you want to maintain the peace!

Finance and Success
Deception from others in the workplace can be a problem through November 8, and you may also run into protocol or politically correct disputes after November 12. For these reasons, careful maneuvering with an eye on the responses of others helps you continue in a productive manner. Saturn and Pluto repeat their opposition, marking further changes in the hierarchy.

Cosmic Insider Tip
Rash actions after the November 12 can create disruptions with long-term implications. Minding your own impulsiveness places you in a position of greater objectivity.

Rewarding Days: 1, 2, 9, 10, 14, 18, 19, 28, 29

Challenging Days: 3, 4, 15, 16, 17, 23, 24, 30

Affirmation for the Month
My words, spoken with love, can heal and restore the peace.

Virgo/December

In the Spotlight
Family and social obligations seem to get in the way of your productivity. Combative situations can also emerge at work, undermining your sense of stability. However, by month's end you're back on track.

Wellness and Keeping Fit
Rash actions can lead to accidents, and if you're caught in situations beyond your control, erring on the side of caution may slow your progress but can keep you safe. A little healthy sports competition can suit your needs quite nicely after December 9.

Love and Life Connections
Conflicts over priorities ruffle your feathers and can create a distance with your partner. Your greatest concerns may arise near the solar eclipse on December 14 when a family crisis can emerge. Knowing when to be supportive and when to let others carry their own burdens requires great finesse. After December 16, romance underscores the positive qualities in your life, and during the Moon's eclipse on December 30 you experience tremendous joy from sharing love.

Finance and Success
With people jockeying for position from December 1-8, you feel like pulling up a chair to watch the frenzy. Unfortunately, you have your own fish to fry, and may not get much help doing it, either. Consider reopening contractual agreements. Shrinking from supporting your own position works against your best interests.

Cosmic Insider Tip
Breaking away from traditions can put a distance between you and your family, although it may be just what you need in order to establish more meaningful traditions of your own.

Rewarding Days: 2, 3, 6, 7, 11, 15, 16, 25, 26, 30

Challenging Days: 1, 13, 14, 20, 21, 27, 28

Affirmation for the Month
I cherish the gifts of the heart.

Virgo Action Table

These dates reflect the best—but not the only—times for success and ease in these activities, according to your Sun sign.

	JAN	FEB	MAR	APR	MAY	JUN	JUL	AUG	SEPT	OCT	NOV	DEC
Move											26-30	1-14
Start a class				23, 24							8-25	
Join a club						21, 22	20					
Ask for a raise			1-16						17			
Look for work	10-31	1, 28			6-31	1-2, 29-30	1-11					
Get pro advice	26-28	23, 24	24-26	18-20	16, 17	12, 13	9-11	5-7	2-3, 29-30	26-28	23, 24	20, 21
Get a loan	2-3, 29-30	25, 26	24-26	21, 22	18, 19	14-16	12, 13	8, 9	4-6	1-2, 29-30	25, 26	22-24
See a doctor	10-31	26-28	1-17				30, 31	1-13				
Start a diet	24, 25	20-22	19-21	16, 17	13-15	9-11	7, 8	3-4, 30-31	1, 26-28	24, 25	20, 21	18, 19
End relationship									2, 3			
Buy clothes	1-9											16-31
Get a makeover								14-31	1, 16, 17			
New romance												26-31
Vacation	4, 5, 31	1, 2, 28	1, 27, 28	23, 24	20-22	17, 18	14, 15	10-12	7, 8	4, 5, 31	28, 29	25, 26

Libra

The Balance Scales
September 22 to October 23

Element:	Air
Quality:	Cardinal
Polarity:	Yang/Masculine
Planetary Ruler:	Venus
Meditation:	I am creating harmony and beauty.
Gemstone:	Opal
Power Stones:	Tourmaline, kunzite, blue lace agate
Key Phrase:	I balance
Glyph:	Scales of justice, setting sun
Anatomy:	Kidneys, lower back, appendix
Color:	Blue, rose, pink
Animal:	Brightly plumed birds
Myths/Legends:	Hera, Venus, Cinderella
House:	Seventh
Opposite Sign:	Aries
Flower:	Rose
Key Word:	Harmony

Positive Expression:	Misuse of Energy:
Impartial	Inconsiderate
Affable	Remote
Gracious	Conceited
Fair-minded	Indecisive
Diplomatic	Unreliable
Artistic	Argumentative
Refined	Hypercritical

Libra

Your Ego's Strengths and Shortcomings
Your love of life's most beautiful qualities is easy to spot. Surrounding yourself with pleasant and creative people and adding your flair for the artistic to your personal image or immediate environment, you're in tune with Venus—the expression of love and beauty. You're a natural in social situations, and can be perfectly diplomatic when symmetry, logic, or harmony are required.

While you can be objective where others are concerned, sometimes you lose your ability to be objective about yourself—especially if you're comparing your life, accomplishments, or circumstances to that of another. Ideally, you prefer to please others, and may go out of your way to assure that your own actions and manners are palatable to them or perfect for the situation. This quality can be helpful, but sometimes gets you into trouble if you're acting against your own needs just to keep somebody else happy! Acting as "The Judge" of the zodiac, you're happiest when your choices reflect a perspective that's in balance with your deeper and truest values.

Everything is relative for you, and you prefer to think in logical, objective terms. Making decisions can be difficult, although you do strive to reach conclusions that will have the best possible outcome and effect. It's your attempt to balance the scales between the world surrounding you and your inner self that is your greatest challenge, and it is your profound desire to radiate a palpable quality of peaceful, loving energy and to see it reflected around you.

Shining Your Love Light
If life were like the old fairy tales, love would lead you to living happily ever after; but in your search for this ideal you may feel that you are, instead, writing tales of everything from broken hearts to victorious conquests! Any heartbreak is unlikely to quell your desire to find the ideal mate, since you hope for a relationship with true equality. Learning to allow yourself to experience the creation of that ideal requires a bit of patience with the evolutionary process of love itself and a tolerance for differences, which, ultimately, you're

realizing may be the thing that keeps your love life the most interesting and energetic.

It is with the air signs—Gemini, Libra, and Aquarius—that you'll feel the most at ease, since you share and appreciate the joy of socialization, communication, and a fascination with ideas. Your attraction to your zodiac opposite, Aries, has the potential for delightful fireworks, although you may be frustrated if the relationship seems too one-sided. Taurus shares your love for the aesthetic; however, monetary control issues can be a problem. Gemini keeps you on your toes mentally, tickling your interest and sharing your love of travel and learning. With Cancer you'll enjoy the nurturing until you've had enough, and you may not know how to kindly say, "Back off!" A love connection with Leo can be unforgettable, since it's easy to open your heart to her or his supportive warmth and passionate sensibilities. Virgo feels comfortable and you'll treasure her or his attention to quality and detail, although you may not necessarily be romantically inclined.

Your love of beauty and culture may be shared by another Libra, and while you can see eye-to-eye on important matters, maintaining stability can be a challenge. Scorpio can overtake you with an intense tidal wave of energy, and you can lose track of your personal boundaries if you've been swept off your feet! The exciting adventure and fun you share with Sagittarius can fill your diary for years. Capricorn can stimulate a powerful connection, but you'll have to deal with control issues. Aquarius stirs your desire to experiment with the joys of love and you may share a truly remarkable bond of understanding and acceptance. While Pisces' mystery can carry you into fanciful escape, you may feel overwhelmed if the tide of emotions is too unsettling.

Making Your Place in the World

You can be a tireless worker when your creativity is engaged and you love what you're doing. You may find success and joy in fields falling under the canopy of "human relations"—ranging from diplomatic service or politics to personnel management, public relations, advertising, or sales. Your love of academics and social sensibilities may lead you into a career in law, literature, the arts, or teaching or promoting the arts through conservatories, galleries, or museums.

You might also prefer a fully engaged artistic career as a designer, artist, costumer, interior designer, set designer, or as an arts writer. You also know how to help others enhance their own strengths and might decide to help others as a counselor, image consultant, or agent. In any career choice, you'll bring a touch of class!

Power Plays

At first response you may think you really don't care much for power, but when you step back to take a look, you'll realize that the idea of holding a position which could positively influence change is rather attractive! In fact, you can be a marvelous figurehead when your sense of fairness and refined sensibilities are working to their fullest. The mere thought of unfairness leaves you cold, and you may find it almost impossible to witness a misuse of power, since you probably have highly developed ideals of justice and humanitarian treatment for all. You have the right balance of logic and diplomacy to help spearhead revolutionary change, but will prefer to work in concert with others who share your ideals.

If you're driven by emotionally prejudicial choices you can lose track of your balanced perspective, and can even appear impossibly perfectionistic or aloof in your attitudes. To avoid undermining your personal power base, apply realistic ideals to a person or situation, including yourself—especially if your self-esteem is faltering. Learning how to establish positive personal boundaries while valuing your own abilities and strengths will allow you to build a life which reflects your true values shared with those you love. Connecting to the light of the Source, your life can illustrate an unmatched beauty whispering the truth of love on the winds of eternity.

Famous Librans

Jason Alexander, Chris Carter, Tiffany Chin, Matt Damon, Phil Hartman, Rita Hayworth, Jesse Helms, Donna Karan, Elmore Leonard, Heather Locklear, Peter Max, Ed Sullivan, Oscar Wilde, Kate Winslet, Catherine Zeta-Jones

The Year Ahead for Libra

As the tasks you've been accomplishing are completed, you're entering a more fun-filled and creatively inspiring year. While some cycles prompt you to take greater risks with your self-expression, others signify positive support and feedback from the world that can be helpful in your determination of just how far you can safely go. You're not likely to feel particularly patient with anyone or anything that might suggest waiting for gratification of your desires, and, fortunately, you may not have to wait that long. The universe seems to have issued you a "speed pass!"

From January through July 2001, Jupiter is transiting through the Ninth House of your solar chart, signifying an exhilarating sense that the future is *now*! Travel, publishing, advertising, and educational pursuits can open the doors that lead to advancement and satisfaction. Then, from July 12 through the end of the year, Jupiter's influence emphasizes career and public recognition. Although this can be an exceptional period of growth, some of the opportunities presented to you may push you beyond your limitations. Exploring precisely what is being offered in return for your efforts before you commit can help you avoid getting involved in situations that are more trouble than they're worth.

Saturn's travels move into a more supportive space in your life, and after April you are likely to feel an emergence of focus and clarity, which help you determine the best paths for your long-term success. If you've needed to complete educational requirements, certification, or testing, the next two years can be the perfect time to take such steps. It's also a good time to teach or become involved in publishing or other pursuits which add credibility to your work.

Uranus and Neptune continue their transits through the Fifth House of your solar chart, stimulating a powerful urge to express your unique artistic sensibilities. These transits are also exceptional influences in the love department, since the stimulus is to open your heart and let the love flow through. Whether you're finally experiencing the kind of love you've hoped to find in an intimate relationship or feeling the excitement and change wrought by children, you're ready to smile, and the light in your eyes helps to assure that others will be smiling back. Pluto's cycle continues to influence alterations in the way you communicate, and adds a quality of penetrating insight to your communicative abilities.

The solar and lunar eclipses and the transit of the Moon's Nodes draw your attention to your need to balance your personal and public lives, making ample time for each. The influence of each eclipse will be identified in the monthly forecasts. However, the transit of the Moon's Nodes is the underlying influence you'll feel most. The repercussions of the nodal transit strike a chord in your belief systems and ideologies, and you may feel that regardless of the implications of your choices and actions you simply cannot ignore what you feel to be right or wrong. Circumstances that challenge your ethics are likely to place you on the high road, which is precisely where you prefer to be!

If you were born from September 22 to 27, you're experiencing a cycle that stimulates an initiative to develop your special talents and abilities. Pluto is transiting in quintile aspect to your Sun, marking a period in which it's easier to let go of your inhibitions or self-imposed judgments about your talents, allowing you to simply exercise them. If you are an artist or musician, this cycle can bring amazing results if you're working to perfect your abilities, and you may also find that your ability to influence evolutionary changes in your field of endeavor is strong. Regardless of your expertise, by consciously accessing your talents you'll feel more satisfied with your life. Also, from April through June, you're feeling the supportive and important transit of Saturn in trine aspect to your Sun. This influence is one you can use on any levels. Your ability to accomplish your aims is stronger during these months, and if you're making commitments they're likely to withstand the tests of time. Much depends upon the strength of your desires.

If you were born from September 28 to October 9, you're feeling the support of Saturn transiting in trine aspect to your Sun. This influence is strongest from May onward. During this cycle, you'll find it easier to stick to your plans, but most importantly, you'll gain clarity about yourself, your life, and your aims. Professionally, this cycle marks a period in which you're attracting the types of responsibilities which allow you to develop your skills and build your reputation. It's a great time to eliminate things from your life that you've outgrown or you no longer need, and you are likely to feel more self-confident because you have a realistic grasp of your priorities and abilities to fulfill them. You're less likely to take on burdens which are not yours to carry, and may find that you're actually capable of saying "no" when you really mean it! If you've been postponing your commitment to your physical needs, this is the perfect year to get into a routine that yields better health and to eliminate habits which have been undermining your vitality. It's also a great time to make meaningful relationship commitments or to renew your vows of love.

If you were born from September 28 to October 3, the influence of Neptune transiting in trine aspect to your Sun brings a sense of peace and heightened compassion into your life. This influence can be especially noteworthy if you're involved in work where reaching out to others plays a significant role, and you may also find that you're feeling more charitable and need a method to show your care and concern that will make a difference in the world. Creative endeavors can be especially gratifying now, although you may not feel much like working really hard to make things happen. While one element of this cycle is a tendency to "drift" a bit more than usual, if you are focused on showcasing your talents and abilities you'll see tremendous rewards by putting extra energy into making things happen. The beauty of this time is that you seem to attract the right situations. All you have to do is allow your light to shine! You are also feeling an irritation signified by Uranus transiting in sesquiquadrate to your Sun which can show up as unanticipated interruptions or inconsiderate behaviors from others, although this is usually a minor influence. Just watch out for your reactions, since you may be responding in an uncharacteristically uncaring manner if you feel pushed too far. Fortunately, the Neptunian influence increases your sensitivity, and you're likely to have a better feel for the best way to respond to people or circumstances that seem to trigger feelings of irritation.

If you were born from October 6 to 10, you're experiencing the empowering cycle of Pluto traveling in sextile aspect to your Sun.

The transformational changes you're making in your life now can have a lasting effect, since you're getting into the deeper layers of your psyche and you're learning how to call upon your will power at the right time to bring about necessary change. You're ready for more than a "make-over": you're being reborn! From modifying your image to altering your priorities, this is the year to make changes that will give you more room to express yourself and fulfill your needs. It's the perfect time to add the refinements to your life which allow you to feel more like yourself. Setting goals that reflect your evolving self-concept can provide the perfect mechanism to affirm that you deserve to experience a life which you create on your own terms. Your relationships are ripe for alterations, too, and although you may embrace new friends, the old friends who also welcome growth can become an even more important element in your life than you previously realized.

If you were born from October 11 to 19, you may feel that you're on top of the world while Uranus transits in trine aspect to your Sun. The most significant aspect of this cycle may be felt in your desire to finally experience life as you want it on your own terms. Since you usually like to be accommodating, you're not likely to drop your sense of consideration for others, but may put your own tastes, desires, and priorities ahead of their opinions for a change! Exercising your independence can also mean that you'll be more comfortable in relationships that allow for true autonomy, instead of just giving lip-service to the idea. Stepping into career opportunities that will call upon your special talents is easier during 2001, since you'll relish the idea of working more independently and allowing your light to shine on your own merits. However, you can also work in harmony with others and may experience your greatest successes while participating in endeavors which benefit the common good.

If you were born from October 20 to 23, you're completing a cycle which began last year—Saturn transiting in quincunx to your Sun. The influence of this cycle is complete by the end of May, and after that time you may feel that you're finally on a life path which is no longer "under construction." During the first quarter of the year you'll benefit from addressing any health concerns when they emerge, since this is the perfect time to make necessary adjustments to improve your quality of life. You'll also benefit from targeting the first four months of the year as the time to clear out projects that are overdue or which have been delayed, since from May onward you'll be eager to move forward. Clear the pathways early for smooth sailing during the second half of 2001.

Tools to Make a Difference

You're probably feeling more open to "experimentation" with all sorts of alternative options, since you're eager to maximize your potentials. Nourishing your spirituality may be top priority this year, and your awareness of the necessity of balancing the elements of your life is exceptionally strong. For this reason, you are likely to benefit from utilizing tools that bring harmony and balance between the spiritual, emotional, mental, and physical realms of your life. Healing therapies such as chakra balancing (as in the work of Deepak Chopra) or therapeutic touch or energy balancing with reiki can be especially beneficial. You'll also gain tremendously by working toward a free-flow of chi that can be opened through acupuncture or chi gung. Working with polarity therapy or using copper polarity screens can be helpful as well.

Your physical target zone is the kidneys and lower back, and if you're under extra stress, these will be the areas that are likely to show strain first. Keep your kidneys in good shape by drinking plenty of fluids, especially when you're traveling or sitting for long periods. For lower back, maintaining flexibility is top priority, but you also need to keep your abdominal and pelvic girdle muscles in good shape. Incorporate more stretching, and consider looking into Pilates to keep yourself going.

Working with symbols can be especially interesting and rewarding now, and one of the primary symbols that will resonate very clearly for you is the sacred ankh, the Egyptian symbol of eternal life and the balance of the masculine and feminine. Whether wearing this symbol as jewelry or keeping it around your environment as art, you'll enjoy the reminder of the power of love and harmony as the most eternally enriching experiences of life. You might also feel strongly drawn to the Chinese Tao, another symbol of wholeness through balance, and studying or utilizing the principles of traditional oriental medicine as a complement to your total well being can be especially useful.

Affirmation for the Year

I love unconditionally. Accepting myself and others allows me to open to endless possibilities.

Libra/January

In the Spotlight
With your focus on exercising your considerable talents, you may forget about the necessary time, money, and energy required to accomplish everything on your agenda. Attention to how quickly you're expending your resources will save you a lot of grief!

Wellness and Keeping Fit
Concentrate on extending your endurance, but remember to balance strength-building with enhanced flexibility. If exercise is insufficient to diminish feelings of tension, schedule a massage near the time of the Moon's eclipse on January 9.

Love and Life Connections
Family tensions can wreck your need for bliss, although there may be no way to avoid dealing with the issues from January 1-10. Fortunately, your diplomatic manner allows you to address what could be unpleasant. In the romance department, you're feeling positively electric and may have little patience if your intended is reluctant to enjoy the games of love. The New Moon on January 24 is a positive time to let love's light shine brightly in your life.

Finance and Success
Improvements in the work place can range from remodeling to new personnel, and you're the perfect person to direct the proceedings. Watch for potential budget overruns or misunderstandings about contracts. After January 11 you'll have excellent results from marketing or promotional activities, and will benefit from business conferences or meetings with others in your field.

Cosmic Insider Tip
A window of opportunity emerges from January 23-31, when showcasing your talents or promoting your ideas can advance your reputation almost overnight!

Rewarding Days: 6, 7, 10, 11, 14, 15, 19, 24, 25

Challenging Days: 2, 3, 8, 9, 17, 21, 22, 29, 30

Affirmation for the Month
My creative impulses emerge from a heart filled with joy and love!

Libra/February

In the Spotlight
Further development of a current project or idea can lead to breakthroughs—personally and professionally. The support you need is right in front of you, and by showing your gratitude you're forging strong connections.

Wellness and Keeping Fit
Your time seems to be in a crunch, and it's easy to rationalize that there's just not enough time for workouts . . . or sleep for that matter! Before you give up, try letting go of a few lower priority items. Your commitment to your health is better focused after February 15.

Love and Life Connections
Partnership gets easier, although there may be extreme differences about the best ways to handle finances. Before you decide it's all about money, explore the deeper issues. Take time during the Full Moon on February 8 to let love fill your heart. Concentrate on your shared ideals and dreams as a means of uplifting your relationship.

Finance and Success
With Mercury in retrograde from February 3-25 you may feel that you're just not getting anything accomplished. Rather than trying to start new projects, focus on clearing your list of commitments so you can be free to develop fresh ideas later. Conflicts at work can stall progress from February 22-26. However, maintaining clear lines of communication helps to diffuse the larger problems so that productivity ultimately improves.

Cosmic Insider Tip
Delays, missed appointments, and equipment breakdowns can be irritating. While you're waiting for repairs you may actually uncover something that's been missing. Ah . . . serendipity!

Rewarding Days: 3, 4, 7, 8, 11, 12, 16, 20, 21, 22

Challenging Days: 5, 6, 18, 19, 25, 26, 27

Affirmation for the Month
I am open to different perspectives.

Libra/March

In the Spotlight
Fast-paced developments lead to an important exchange of information and ideas. Social interaction provides a perfect backdrop for connections that should prove to be quite valuable over the coming months.

Wellness and Keeping Fit
Getting involved in a fitness class or team sport can be a lot of fun, and may be your best motivation for staying active. You'll enjoy it even more if you can talk a friend into sharing the experience.

Love and Life Connections
Venus, your ruling planet, is retrograding from March 8 to April 19, marking a period of questioning in your relationships. Whether you're seeking change or just want to make things better with your partner, it's unlikely that you'll be satisfied with the same tiring routine. Resistance may come from your own fears that if you make alterations or go after what you really want that you'll be rejected. Your smile will be more genuine if you're being yourself!

Finance and Success
You may be fired up and ready to get moving from March 1-12, when initiating an important project gains the greatest momentum (culminating with the Full Moon on March 9). However, conservative factions raise questions or block your progress from March 11-17 out of fear that innovative changes will be either too costly or "not the way we're used to doing things." Back at the drawing board, you'll have solutions by the New Moon on March 25.

Cosmic Insider Tip
A careful look at the way you're spending money may expose a pattern you're ready to change. You'll be ready to get rid of clutter from March 25-31, so you'll have room to breathe.

Rewarding Days: 2, 3, 6, 7, 10, 11, 15, 20, 21, 29, 30

Challenging Days: 4, 5, 9, 17, 18, 19, 25, 26, 31

Affirmation for the Month
My values arise from a pure quality of love and acceptance.

Libra/April

In the Spotlight
Relationships take front and center stage. Allowing ample time to explore your feelings and your current needs will give you a chance to create the most appropriate options—whether you're starting anew or reviving an existing commitment.

Wellness and Keeping Fit
An adventure lifts your spirits. Of course, you prefer lights and running water, but getting outdoors can be positively invigorating. Gardening might be a reasonable option, plus you gain the benefit of gorgeous flowers!

Love and Life Connections
While you may be having second thoughts about your current relationship, if there's strong love and reasons to make it work this can be the perfect time to air issues and work toward resolutions so you'll both be happier. You're especially sensitive near the Libra Full Moon on April 8, although you'll find that others can be more receptive to you at this time. After April 20 you may feel that you're ready to take an intimate relationship to the next level.

Finance and Success
Contract negotiations can be hung up on details about roles and responsibilities, although you'll be reluctant to agree until these are defined. Agreements involving joint property are most auspicious after the New Moon on April 23. Review your investment portfolio and work toward eliminating low-performance items unless they appear promising in the long run.

Cosmic Insider Tip
You may be breathing a sigh of relief after Saturn moves into Gemini on April 20, when you'll find that your focus turns toward future developments and spiritual growth.

Rewarding Days: 3, 7, 8, 11, 16, 17, 25, 26, 30

Challenging Days: 1, 13, 14, 15, 21, 22, 27, 28

Affirmation for the Month
I am grateful for my good fortune and share my luck with others.

Libra/May

In the Spotlight
Strengthening your network of supporters builds the platform you need to move forward on an important project. This is the perfect time for conferences or presentations that give you or your products a more diverse audience.

Wellness and Keeping Fit
Your physical vitality is likely to improve, and if you have time for a recreational vacation you can boost your energy even more. Nourish your spirit by taking time to drink in the beauty of life.

Love and Life Connections
Shared ideals enhance the quality of your intimate relationship, and if you're looking for love you may discover a meeting of heart and soul in the process of delving into your spiritual quest. During the Full Moon on May 7 you're confronting the question of trust, although your desire to forgive can help you move further toward your goals of getting closer. Keeping an open mind can lead to all sorts of possibilities after May 23, when new love is on the horizon.

Finance and Success
Your principles may be different from those who are in positions of leadership, although your attitudes can be highly influential in shaping the direction or policies currently emerging. Finances require special consideration through May 5. Your greatest successes are likely to come from May 12-26, when novel ideas and innovative actions place you center stage.

Cosmic Insider Tip
Tensions run highest through May 9, and situations can get out of control due to differences in philosophy or problems with interpreting the meaning of agreements.

Rewarding Days: 1, 4, 5, 8, 13, 14, 23, 24, 28, 31

Challenging Days: 6, 11, 12, 18, 19, 25, 26

Affirmation for the Month
I am whole, perfect, strong, and powerful, and I walk in the Light of Divine Truth.

Libra/June

In the Spotlight
Your diplomatic skills may be in high demand, especially in circumstances where injury has resulted from others jumping to the wrong conclusion or taking ill-advised action. The trick will be coming out of the situation unscathed!

Wellness and Keeping Fit
Since you're likely to be burning that candle at both ends, it's a good idea to take a few moments for rejuvenation whenever you can. Pushing beyond your limits now can lead to exhaustion before you know it. Be especially careful when driving.

Love and Life Connections
If you have unfinished business in matters of the heart, you're revisiting the situation to determine where you want to go from here. Sometimes it takes a while before you're ready to move on, and sometimes you actually do need to open another door to learn what's in your heart. A meeting before and during the Full Moon on June 6 can be illuminating. Your perspective concerning your priorities shifts, and you'll feel that it's a new dawn by the solar eclipse on June 21.

Finance and Success
Volatile communications keep you on your toes, and during Mercury's retrograde from June 4-28 you may find that you're doing little more than troubleshooting. The good thing is that you can thoroughly examine legal and contractual matters; waiting until next month for a final agreement may be your best option.

Cosmic Insider Tip
You're in the perfect position to bring up possibilities others have missed. Integrating new technologies or unusual choices into situations puts you in a league of your own.

Rewarding Days: 1, 5, 9, 10, 11, 19, 20, 24, 27, 28, 29

Challenging Days: 7, 8, 14, 15, 16, 21, 22

Affirmation for the Month
My thoughts, ideas, and words are inspired by Truth and Wisdom.

Libra/July

In the Spotlight
Career developments enhance your reputation, or you may be in a more influential position in family matters, taking the lead while others seem aimless or uncertain. Establishing a comfortable position philosophically adds stability.

Wellness and Keeping Fit
The pace calms down a bit, although you may still feel restless. Strengthen your nervous system, and include ample time to renew your vitality. A massage can work wonders. Pay extra attention to those muscles in hips and lower back.

Love and Life Connections
Sharing a special time away from home with the one you love can be just what you need to revitalize your romance. It's time to break up your routine with something that says, "Let's play," or to change the ambience to a more dramatically enticing setting. Family matters may take precedence during the Moon's eclipse on July 5, but after that, you're eager to devote more attention to your love life.

Finance and Success
Launching your pet project meets with good success from the July 1-12, although the momentum generated can get out of hand. Special excitement emerges from July 14-28, when your special talents are shining and your reputation is growing. Changes in leadership may emerge after the New Moon on July 20, although this can make a positive difference. Just remain on the alert for potentially misleading directions after July 29.

Cosmic Insider Tip
Mars turns direct on July 19, and situations which may have been stalled or moving too sluggishly finally show progress.

Rewarding Days: 2, 3, 7, 8, 16, 17, 23, 25, 26, 29, 30

Challenging Days: 4, 5, 12, 13, 14, 19, 20, 31

Affirmation for the Month
I am eager to learn and invite positive change into my life.

Libra/August

In the Spotlight
By taking an active role in community affairs you can advance your reputation while making a difference in the quality of life around you, too. Your creative ideas inspire plenty of action on your part, and you're also eliciting a great response from others.

Wellness and Keeping Fit
Enrolling in a fitness class, participating in team sports, or working out with a buddy are great options to keep your commitment to fitness. A little competition from others helps you push your limits.

Love and Life Connections
Making connections with your friends is just what you need, although it's also a good time to touch base with siblings and catch up on the news. Your first priority near the Full Moon on August 4 is likely to be love-related, since you're feeling especially amorous and will adore the attentions of your sweetheart. Looking for love? Consider attending a party or gathering on August 19 (New Moon) wearing your favorite colors and featuring your most alluring smile.

Finance and Success
Although there are significant potentials for advancing your career from August 1-8, it's crucial to identify expectations from all sides, since you could run into empty promises or seemingly impossible options. Structures are transforming, and whether you're working under new circumstances or different objectives, you may feel ready to step into a more challenging position where you can make alterations of your own.

Cosmic Insider Tip
Insecurities can be stimulated early in the month, especially in areas where you expect things to be "permanent." Just remember that the only consistent feature these days is change!

Rewarding Days: 3, 4, 13, 14, 17, 18, 21, 22, 26, 30, 31

Challenging Days: 1, 2, 8, 9, 15, 16, 28, 29

Affirmation for the Month
I am open to renewal and welcome change leading to growth.

Libra/September

In the Spotlight
With plenty of room to exercise your creativity and self-expression, you may feel that you're on fire with ideas and opportunities to turn them into reality! Your smooth manner and special talents can be in high demand.

Wellness and Keeping Fit
You can be more accident-prone this month, especially if you're moving too quickly or participating in activities that are out of your normal realm. Taking the time to center and ground your energy can make a big difference.

Love and Life Connections
Changes in a friendship can open the way for unanticipated experiences, and a friend may be the link to the romance of your dreams. Clarifying expectations helps assure that you'll avoid misunderstandings from September 6-18. Tensions at home can escalate after September 8, but may be due to increased activity, moving, or disruptions in schedules.

Finance and Success
Advancement in career and rewards for your efforts leads to greater satisfaction, and you may be able to take advantage of an opening arising suddenly or as the result of reorganization. Negotiate contracts or payments from September 4-20, when you're feeling more confident about what you want. Pull together details after the New Moon on September 17 in preparation for presentations, and be ready to initiate projects after September 23.

Cosmic Insider Tip
Mercury transits in your sign for the next ten weeks, marking a time when your ideas and communicative abilities can be particularly valuable.

Rewarding Days: 1, 9, 10, 14, 17, 18, 22, 23, 26, 27, 28

Challenging Days: 4, 5, 6, 11, 12, 24, 25, 30

Affirmation for the Month
My goals are motivated by my highest needs.

Libra/October

In the Spotlight
You may feel that you're caught in the vise of trying to please too many people at once. Prioritizing your responsibilities and identifying your goals helps you determine when and where to say "no." Sometimes you simply cannot keep everyone happy!

Wellness and Keeping Fit
Tension is not your friend, although it may be your constant companion. Increasing your flexibility while maintaining your fitness schedule is important, even though you may not think you have enough time. Oh, yes . . . remember that sleep is necessary, too!

Love and Life Connections
Changes at home continue to add to your stress levels, although some of them may be welcome—especially the improvements. Relationships are emphasized during the Full Moon on October 2, and while you may be keeping your secret hopes under wraps, fortune smiles after October 14, when Venus enters your sign and love blossoms. You're eager to keep things moving, especially after the Libra New Moon on October 16. Finally—it's your turn!

Finance and Success
With Mercury retrograding in your sign from the October 1-22 you may feel that you're personally singled out as the one who seems to be in the middle of all the breakdowns. When you look around, you'll realize you're not alone after all! Mostly, watch out for competitors who can steal your thunder. Negotiations fare best after October 15, but wait until October 24 to finalize anything.

Cosmic Insider Tip
Although you may be tempted to jump into a new project early in the month, concentrating on completing the tasks at hand will serve you better, leaving time for new ventures after October 24.

Rewarding Days: 6, 7, 12, 15, 16, 19, 20, 24, 25

Challenging Days: 1, 2, 9, 10, 18, 21, 22, 29, 30

Affirmation for the Month
I am confident in my choices and decisions.

Libra/November

In the Spotlight
Exercising your special talents not only makes your heart sing but can be quite profitable. Children and lovers play an important role this month, and much of your delight may result from sharing special times with your loved ones.

Wellness and Keeping Fit
If your exercise routine has become drudgery, then change it. You need to have fun now, and anything that seems dreadfully boring will simply not stand up to the challenge.

Love and Life Connections
Retreating with your lover to a place which allows you to luxuriate in your most delightful fantasies can certainly be a top agenda item during the Full Moon on November 1. You might even want to take a long weekend away! Love's definitely in the air until November 9, but after November 23 you may have to fit romance in between all your other obligations. Then you get another reprieve that's perfect for savoring special indulgences.

Finance and Success
Speculative endeavors fare best from November 1-9, although you might be tempted to make a buy which is more air than substance. Agreements can break down or may be ignored altogether this month, since Saturn and Pluto are embattled, exposing the weak links in contracts you've previously signed. Special care with finances is necessary after November 8, and impulse shopping is definitely your enemy. Consider keeping those credit cards on ice!

Cosmic Insider Tip
Alterations in the power structure makes business as usual, unusual. After the dust settles, you can see your way clear to make a positive move, but caution is still a good idea.

Rewarding Days: 3, 4, 8, 11, 12, 17, 20, 21, 30

Challenging Days: 1, 2, 5, 6, 18, 19, 25, 26, 27

Affirmation for the Month
I am making the most of all my resources.

Libra/December

In the Spotlight
Connections with others keep you on your toes, but you're having a good time with all the social interaction. Extra care with communication is necessary to avoid stepping on the wrong toes.

Wellness and Keeping Fit
Your physical vitality is strong initially, although you may feel that you're running out of steam midmonth. Pacing yourself is harder after December 9, since you may not know where to draw the line.

Love and Life Connections
Fortunately for you there's marvelous support for social activity from December 1-25—just in time for parties and other holiday exchanges. However, the solar eclipse on December 14 can mark a time of sudden changes and disruptions, and keeping things simple near that time will help you cope with anything unexpected. The lunar eclipse on December 30 brings family matters to the forefront, when you may decide to alter a long-standing tradition.

Finance and Success
Meetings and presentations fare best from December 1-15, when you're building a positive network of support for your pet projects or new ideas. Pulling together details and plans works rather nicely through December 20, but after that time you'll uncover the trouble spots and may need time to make repairs or eliminate unnecessary items or change personnel. Your patience for lacking productivity is exhausted by month's end.

Cosmic Insider Tip
It's highly conceivable that the solar eclipse on December 14 will mark a turnaround in a situation that's been at a stalemate, but you may have to take the initiative to get the ball rolling.

Rewarding Days: 1, 5, 8, 9, 13, 14, 17, 18, 19, 27, 28

Challenging Days: 2, 3, 15, 16, 22, 23, 29, 30

Affirmation for the Month
I clearly communicate my thoughts and feelings.

Libra Action Table

These dates reflect the best—but not the only—times for success and ease in these activities, according to your Sun sign.

	JAN	FEB	MAR	APR	MAY	JUN	JUL	AUG	SEPT	OCT	NOV	DEC
Move	1-9											15-31
Start a class					22, 23						26-30	1-15
Join a club								18, 19				
Ask for a raise										16, 17		
Look for work		1-3	17-31	1-5			13-29					
Get pro advice	2-3, 29-30	25, 26	24-26	21, 22	18, 19	14-16	12, 13	8, 9	4-6	1-3, 29-30	25, 26	22-24
Get a loan	4, 5, 31	1, 2, 28	1, 27, 28	23, 24	20-22	17, 18	14, 15	10-12	7, 8	4, 5, 31	28, 29	25, 26
See a doctor		1-6	17-31	1-5				14-31				
Start a diet	26-28	23, 24	22, 23	18-20	16, 17	12, 13	9-11	5-7	2-3, 29-30	26-28	23, 24	20, 21
End relationship										1-3		
Buy clothes	10-31	26-28	1-16									
Get a makeover										15-31	1-7	
New romance	1-2, 24-25											
Vacation	6, 7	3, 4	2-3, 29-30	25, 26	23, 24	19, 20	16-18	13, 14	9, 10	6-8	3, 4, 30	1, 27, 28

Scorpio

The Scorpion
October 23 to November 22

♏

Element:	Water
Quality:	Fixed
Polarity:	Yin/Feminine
Planetary Ruler:	Pluto (Mars)
Meditation:	I achieve mastery through transformation.
Gemstone:	Topaz
Power Stones:	Obsidian, amber, citrine, garnet
Key Phrase:	I create
Glyph:	Scorpion's tail
Anatomy:	Reproductive system
Color:	Burgundy, black
Animal:	Reptiles, scorpions, birds of prey
Myths/Legends:	The Phoenix, Hades and Persephone, Shiva
House:	Eighth
Opposite Sign:	Taurus
Flower:	Chrysanthemum
Key Word:	Intensity

Positive Expression:
Regenerating
Incisive
Creative
Transforming
Impassioned
Sensual
Perceptive

Misuse of Energy:
Destructive
Extremist
Obsessive
Jealous
Lascivious
Vengeful
Vituperative

Scorpio

Your Ego's Strengths and Shortcomings
Not only do you enjoy the intrigues of life, but you are rather intriguing yourself! Your creative drive is fueled by your ability to tap into energy beneath the surface, as you explore and expose the essential nature of life itself. You have the capacity to bring things back to life, and it is this healing quality which is an extension of your role as "The Catalyst" of the zodiac.

You can develop piercing insights into human nature, although you have a tendency to keep your deeper feelings controlled under a cool veneer, especially when you feel vulnerable. Exposing the details of your own life to anybody requires an exceptional measure of trust, and you'll thoroughly test anyone before you grant admittance to your inner circle. As a result, others may feel that you're operating with a hidden agenda, which can create a gap that's virtually impossible to bridge when you finally decide that you want to allow someone to be close. Fortunately, with your ability to tap into the qualities of Pluto's energy, you're capable of transformational change, and can rise above circumstances that may have previously limited your ability to express your deepest feelings, most intense emotions, and strongest needs.

Your inner strength allows you to rise to heroic action in support of others who may be incapable of protecting themselves or making the strides necessary to heal their lives. You're walking the shamanic path: the way of regeneration and ability to tread between the worlds of joy and sorrow in search of truth. The ultimate emotional and spiritual rebirth you hope to accomplish is most likely to emerge once you embrace forgiveness of yourself and others.

Shining Your Love Light
You have the kind of charisma that readily lures others, but your yearning for a true soulmate may prompt you to protect your heart until you're sure that the right person has come along. Once you make a commitment, you intend to keep it and nourish it through time. As a lover, your sensuality and intensity leave an indelible impression, since your sensibilities can allow you to open the gates

of rapture. But unlocking the doors to your heart can be difficult if you've been hurt. Learning to trust that love will heal ultimately makes all the difference!

The water signs—Cancer, Scorpio, and Pisces—are the most at home with your intensity and emotionality. However, you're capable of enticing almost anyone! The teasing of an Aries can be fun, but you may yearn for more consistency. Your zodiac opposite, Taurus, attracts you with a steadfast persistence and strong sensuality, although if you disagree you can both be monumentally stubborn. Gemini's wit is entertaining, but you may distrust his or her variability. Cancer's care inspires feelings of security and closeness and may become a lifelong companion. Although Leo's magnetism can make you tremble, the relationship won't go far if you feel he or she is too self-absorbed.

With Virgo, you can develop a relationship that's a powerful blend of passion and friendship. Libra can put you at ease, but you may grow to resent the feeling that you have to make all the decisions. With another Scorpio you may feel that you've found a soulmate, but the relationship can run the gamut from volatile power struggles to extreme passion. The fun-loving and self-reliant attitudes of a Sagittarius can be appealing unless you feel left out. Capricorn confirms your security needs and can support your desire to fulfill your ambitions. You feel strangely at home with Aquarius, but may not achieve the passion you require if there's too much emotional distance. Your ultimate lover may be Pisces, who stimulates your romance and creativity while providing endless imaginative sensitivity.

Making Your Place in the World

Since you're an excellent strategist, you'll appreciate a career path that requires creativity, probing, or restoration. Your artistic work can have a healing effect—whether you're a writer, sculptor, painter, or musician. You could become an exceptional producer, director, or performer and may have a special ability to create mystery or science fiction.

You're well suited to positions of influence, and have the knack of making the most of others' resources. Whether you're drawn to the healing arts, including counseling, or fields like financial counseling, investment banking, career management, insurance, corporate law, or politics, others may sense that you can help them renew their lives. Or, you may decide to fulfill your need to peek beneath the surface through research, the sciences, archaeology, or history.

Power Plays

Power is a Scorpio thing. True power is easy for you to spot, but you also know an abuse of power when you see it, and may shun those who would steal power from others. Since childhood, when superheroes and powerful people held your fascination, you've secretly identified with the heroine or hero capable of transforming from ordinary to extraordinary in a flash. You know whether or not someone holds his or her own power, and hope that others will understand that you, too, have the ability to create and shape your own life. However, you're more at ease when your life and the total extent of your being is not open to the scrutiny of prying eyes. You have every intention of keeping your secrets!

While some may shun looking into the mysteries of life and death, you're fascinated, and understand that it's only when you embrace the transcendent that you are fully empowered. Yet your desire to hold onto life's richest treasures can actually get in the way of experiencing a natural flow with these processes, and that can weaken you. It is the essence of healing—releasing what is no longer needed—that allows you to restore your own life when you've experienced loss or pain. Your warrior spirit continually guards you, but it is compassion that sustains your ability to impart hope in a world filled with doubt, filling your cup to overflowing.

Famous Scorpios

Charles Atlas, Tina Brown, Chiang Kai-Shek, Jamie Lee Curtis, Dorothy Dandrige, Larry Flynt, Martin Luther, Demi Moore, Chris Noth, Tim Rice, Srisathya Sai Baba, Kurt Vonnegut, Sam Waterston, Alfre Woodard

The Year Ahead for Scorpio

The persistent effort you've been applying toward bringing balance into your life is repaid through enhanced opportunities to broaden and explore new horizons during 2001. You may still feel that you're coping with a series of shifting paradigms, which can serve to feed your creativity—despite the fact that you may complain that life is simply not predictable any longer!

Your ability to draw upon the support and resources of others is strengthened from January to July, as Jupiter's travel highlights the Eighth House of your solar chart. The downside to this cycle is what's expected of you in return, so before you commit to formal contracts or friendly promises, make sure you understand the implications and expectations involved. In monetary matters, you may be tempted to spend beyond your limits, and if you do, then you'll feel the pinch before you know it! Fortunately, Jupiter's cycle moves along on July 12, 2001, forming a supportive connection to your Sun, enhancing your confidence and inspiring a hopeful future. This is an exceptional period for travel or reaping the benefits of publishing or education.

Saturn's long transit in opposition to your sign is complete in April, after which time you may feel you're exchanging one set of obligations for another. If you've been involved in cooperative or partnership endeavors which have been healthy, you're making this transitional change under better circumstances. If not, you may feel that you're forced to come to grips with trust issues and questions about intimacy. The work of untangling yourself from ties that inhibit your growth can have rewards of its own, but if you're trying to avoid the fear-inducing ghosts of your past, they will persist in haunting you until you finally acknowledge and embrace the shadow of your own psyche. It can be a healing and rewarding time, but the next two years will definitely be a time when you'll understand the rewards of joining your energy with others in your life.

Although the most influential periods for the long cycles of Uranus, Neptune, and Pluto will be when those planets make exact aspects to your Sun by transit, you're feeling the effects of these cycles in part of your life for long periods of time. (To find out when those cycles are exact, check for your birthday in the notes which follow.) The awakening energy of Uranus continues along its path, bringing a shakeup in your personal environment and family structure. Neptune's energy of enchantment (and sometimes confusion!) can leave you feeling lost in new territory, particularly if you're letting go of traditions or structures that have been your foundation for a long time. Pluto's cycle emphasizes a revamping of your personal value systems.

The solar eclipses add emphasis to your need to determine the manner in which you're strengthening or undermining your sense of self-worth, but look to the months of June and December to find out how to handle these influences this year. At a deeper emotional level, it is the transit of the Moon's Nodes through your solar Ninth House that leaves the strongest impression, helping you overcome old prejudices that stood in the way of spiritual enlightenment.

If you were born on October 23 to 24, you're experiencing a period of breakthrough while Pluto transits in semisquare aspect to your Sun. This influence can be unsettling, especially if you feel that situations outside your control are forcing you into circumstances you would not otherwise choose. If this affects your finances, you may discover that what you thought you once could not live without is not quite as necessary as you believed. In fact, the essence of this cycle is about learning to accept the origins and impact of your values. Where you've been too strongly influenced by others, you may finally take control. Also, your connection to the environment, and your desire to blend your energies and priorities more harmoniously with your surroundings, can put you in touch with the Laws of Abundance in a profound way. Saturn's cycle in quincunx to your Sun during April and May adds a period of trial and testing, so you'll discover exactly how far you've come in your quest to strengthen your self-worth. This can also mark a time when physical problems are most troubling. However, since this cycle is a completion of one which began last summer, you'll feel that you're moving to the other side of the most difficult tests.

If you were born from October 25 to November 8, you're experiencing the limitations of Saturn transiting in quincunx aspect to your Sun. In advance of this cycle, Jupiter's transit will open the way with opportunities and invitations from January through the end of April, and the choices you make during the first quarter of the year will set the stage for what is to follow. To take advantage of the best possible options, it's necessary to identify your motivations and goals. Otherwise, you may get into situations that overextend your time or overtax your resources for the remainder of the year. The same is true of your expenses: if you're overspending in the early part of 2001, you'll feel the burdens much more quickly than you intended, or other expenses or obligations may materialize which stretch your resources to their limit. Once Saturn's cycle is in full swing starting in May 2001, it's crucial to pace yourself, making adjustments which allow you to honor your priorities in the best possible manner. You may have to let go of some of the things that have been part of your life for a long time in favor of simplifying or organizing your time and energy in a more efficient way. It's also conceivable that you'll find it necessary to eliminate some of the responsibilities you've been carrying for others, identifying exactly where your obligations should end and another person's should begin.

If you were born from October 28 to November 2, you're feeling the sensitizing influence of Neptune transiting in square aspect to your Sun. Your awareness of the subtle planes of existence grows stronger during this cycle, and your dreams should be particularly powerful. Your creative impulses can be amazing, and you'll have ideas that are truly out of this world! However, it's easy to get lost when you're trying to determine the difference between reality and fantasy, especially where other people are concerned. In some respects, you're ready to escape from the heaviness of daily life, and you'll benefit from adding meditation to your daily schedule or by dedicating more time to your artistic pursuits. Choosing healthy escapes is important, though, since you may also find that this cycle triggers addictive behaviors or weaknesses. While it's tempting to just let go of everything, your responsibilities may dictate otherwise. The problem can be keeping your feet on the ground, since your inner life may seem more interesting than the physical plane. The same is true of maintaining a positive connection to your physical health, since it's easy to ignore some of your physical needs, which can ultimately lead to a loss of vitality. If you're concerned about your health, this is the time to find out what's really happening, since denial can be costly in the long run. In your relationships, maintaining your personal boundaries can become an issue. Knowing where and when you can make a difference and when to step away will lead to healthier connections in the long run, but sacrificing yourself for someone else right now could be a disabling choice for all concerned. The same is true of financial relationships, since you may be swayed by the influence of someone whose objectives can be counterproductive to your best interests. Seeking objective counsel can save your hide!

If you were born from November 5 to 9, Pluto's transit in semisextile to your Sun brings a period of healing and a change in perspective on yourself and your priorities. You're creating a new platform, and taking the steps to bring everything in your life to a new level can be positively invigorating. Getting used to situations that contrast with what may seem like your "previous life" may take some time, although you may be intrigued by the prospects and creatively inspired to make alterations which allow you to convey qualities you've never fully expressed. This can be a time of experimentation, although you're realizing that the effects of the changes you're making are likely to be very long-lasting.

If you were born from November 10 to 18, Uranus' energy is opening a series of disruptions during its transit in square aspect to your Sun. This cycle can be a bit mind-boggling, since each day can seem like a new day or you may feel that you're literally unmasking yourself and discovering things you've never fully acknowledged. Actually, you're finally allowing your individuality to emerge, and it could be that the world around you is simply responding with surprise! In your heart, you've always known who you are, but now the restrictions, old feelings of guilt, or other inhibitions which have prevented you from expressing yourself are barriers you're tearing down. You're ready to break away from the past and experience life on your own terms. Whether you decide to move, renovate, change your family structure, alter your relationships, or just toss your wardrobe and reinvent yourself, it's time to release the things that no longer support the truth of your self. The trick is to make these changes without destroying too much in your path. In other words, before you torch that bridge, be sure you won't need to cross it again—and that you're not standing in the middle!

If you were born from November 17 to 22, you're completing the cycle of Saturn transiting in opposition to your Sun. This cycle, which began last spring, will finally be complete at the end of April 2001. The restraints of Saturn's opposition have been like a test. By now, you know your priorities and may be completing some long-standing obligations. For the second half of the year, you may feel you're breathing freely for the first time in quite a while!

Tools to Make a Difference

In some respects, you're tearing down your old foundations and building new ones. This can affect everything from your personal environment to your daily routine. For this reason, you'll reap tremendous benefits by making choices that encourage your energy to flow more freely. Simplifying your life can give you greater freedom on every level, and you may feel most at ease if you're altering your lifestyle to reflect a lack of dependency on situations you cannot control. Whether you're deciding to "live off the grid," or just becoming more conscious of making better use of your resources and helping the environment by doing things like recycling, you'll feel best when you know you're not wasting anything—including time.

Since your sensitivity to vibrational influences is enhanced, you might benefit from working with tuning forks, chimes, or similar tools to help you equalize your physical and subtle bodies. Tools like acupuncture can be especially useful now to bring your chi into balance. You may also respond strongly to magnetic therapy. Since Uranus and Neptune are activating your solar Fourth House, you're much more sensitive to the way your personal and work environments support your health and energy. Working with feng shui can be especially beneficial this year, even if you're only creating minor alterations using colors, fountains, mirrors, or simple decorating devices. In relationships, this is the perfect time to explore the benefits of tantra with your intimate partner, since you're ready to go beyond surface connections and experience a genuine bonding of heart and soul.

♏

Affirmation for the Year

I am creating a safe space for healthy change in my life.

Scorpio/January

In the Spotlight
You're beginning 2001 with love in your heart, inspired to express your most powerful creative impulses and driven in positive ways toward fulfilling your desires. The momentum created by your actions and thoughts now will have a powerful impact throughout the year.

Wellness and Keeping Fit
Since Mars is transiting in your sign for the next six weeks you can be more energetic and driven, but there's a potential problem: you can also burn out more quickly. Stay aware of your limits.

Love and Life Connections
Your passion can be all-consuming, and if you're in a healthy relationship you may finally cross over barriers which have prevented your expression of your deepest feelings. It's easy to be misunderstood from January 1-5, but clarifying your intentions during the lunar eclipse on January 9 puts you back on track. You may feel that you're walking between two worlds for a while. Listen: your heart sings the purest song.

Finance and Success
Before finalizing agreements, define your aims, since vague or misleading communication can place you in a financially vulnerable situation from January 3-14. Investments promise strong returns from January 6-22, but after the New Moon on January 24 there may be a change of direction that prompts you to reconsider some of your options.

Cosmic Insider Tip
Showcasing your talents works to your advantage, and you'll be most visible from January 8-22, when others are most likely to understand and appreciate your offerings.

Rewarding Days: 1, 8, 9, 13, 16, 17, 18, 22, 27, 28

Challenging Days: 4, 5, 10, 11, 24, 25, 31

Affirmation for the Month
My words and actions are motivated by love.

Scorpio/February

In the Spotlight
Resistance from others can present the type of challenge that brings forth the best you have to offer. You're being tested, and if you're prepared you'll find that the test actually strengthens your position.

Wellness and Keeping Fit
If you feel that you've become a magnet for stress, then it's a good idea to bring balance into your life by releasing tension. A massage or day at the spa can be just what you need to rejuvenate your energy, and staying active keeps your energy strong.

Love and Life Connections
At home you may feel that you're dealing with a series of mishaps or disruptions which leave your nerves jangled and spirits unsettled. Situations escalate near the Full Moon on February 8, when you may feel that you're being pulled in several directions at once. Your perspective shifts during the New Moon on February 23 when love shines its light on your true feelings.

Finance and Success
Competitive situations challenge your best-laid plans, but if you know the limits of your rival you'll endure. Mercury's retrograde from February 4-25 marks a time to reconsider your career path. If you're not getting what you want or need, you may decide that it's time to finish up and move on. Rash actions from February 21-25 can thwart your progress. You've heard about counting to ten? Well, try twenty-five this time!

Cosmic Insider Tip
Mixed messages can be a problem for everyone, but it's your past experiences that provide valuable insights into what's happening beneath the surface. Trust what intuition whispers.

Rewarding Days 5, 6, 9, 13, 14, 18, 23, 24

Challenging Days: 1, 2, 7, 8, 20, 21, 28

Affirmation for the Month
Exploring my deepest motivations helps me make positive alterations in my course of action.

Scorpio/March

In the Spotlight
While reconsidering your deepest needs and exploring your value systems, you may discover that you want something more from your life. Reckless attitudes expose your vulnerabilities, while persistent efforts help you persevere in the midst of crisis.

Wellness and Keeping Fit
Defining your limitations is necessary to avoid accident or injury, since you may feel driven to increase your endurance but fail to heed your personal limits. Moderation works to your advantage, but inactivity creates bigger problems.

Love and Life Connections
It could just be a difference in style—the way you express yourself versus the way your sweetheart shares affections. Regardless, the barrier between you can lead to bewilderment near the Full Moon on March 9, when a friend might offer the best counsel if you're needing objectivity. If the problem seems to be money, look further—since it's probably a deeper sense that you're not truly satisfied on more intimate levels.

Finance and Success
Alterations at work can leave you feeling displaced, or your heart may simply not be in what you're doing. Considerations of what you hope to accomplish beyond just making a living come into play. Ideas emerging after March 17 have greater validity and may get your enthusiasm going again. Eliminate nonproductive attitudes or situations, and regroup after the New Moon on March 25.

Cosmic Insider Tip
The manner in which you're handling your resources says a lot about your basic security needs. This is the time to change behaviors which undermine your self worth.

Rewarding Days: 4, 5, 8, 9, 12, 13, 17, 18, 22, 23, 31

Challenging Days: 1, 6, 7, 19, 20, 21, 27, 28

Affirmation for the Month
My desires are stimulated by my highest needs.

Scorpio/April

In the Spotlight
Your "want" list may be larger than your budget, but you're perfectly willing to put the extra effort into getting all that you desire! The problem lies in whether or not others are willing to do their part.

Wellness and Keeping Fit
You're feeling driven by a longing to make everything happen the way you want, and can run into problems if you're tapping into your energy reserves. Rejuvenation is the key to your endurance, so take time to rebuild your vitality every chance you get!

Love and Life Connections
Your work may get in the way of the time you'd like to spend enjoying your loved ones, although near the Full Moon on April 8 you may need quiet time to yourself to regroup. A secret rendezvous might be in order if you're willing to drop your defenses. You'll feel more like reaching out after April 22, and your perspective on your partnership is likely to shift during the New Moon on April 23.

Finance and Success
Pushing your ideas or initiatives through the proper channels works best from April 1-6, and after that you're organizing the efforts of everyone else involved in your special project or working to establish better communication with them. It's time to put on finishing touches, since after April 20 you're ready to look toward a different horizon for satisfaction. Help from partners is likely to arrive after April 22, but first find out what they want in return!

Cosmic Insider Tip
You may feel that you're undercutting or compromising in order to get what you want. Planetary cycles shift on April 20 when your values may seem more in line with possibility.

Rewarding Days: 1, 5, 9, 10, 13, 18, 19, 20, 27, 28

Challenging Days: 2, 3, 8, 16, 17, 23, 24, 30

Affirmation for the Month
I openly seek out cooperative relationships.

Scorpio/May

In the Spotlight
Sensitive issues regarding contracts and finances can emerge, triggering disputes. While you definitely have your feelings about these matters and the people involved, you may find the solution you seek by first researching the details of agreements.

Wellness and Keeping Fit
Probing into root causes of physical distress can lead to the most direct method of treatment. It's a good time to have a complete physical in order to establish base line values, but delving into psychological issues can also speed your healing.

Love and Life Connections
You're not taking anything lightly right now, and with the Scorpio Full Moon on May 7 you can be particularly sensitive. Protecting your sense of vulnerability may seem more important than sharing secrets, and if you're concerned about trust issues, then you'll be even less open. Circumstances which trigger past traumas can lead you to overreact, so before you shut out someone you care for, determine if your reactions are appropriate now.

Finance and Success
The commitments you're making are likely to last, although you are unlikely to agree until you're satisfied with all the details. This is an excellent time for investigation or exploration, and if anybody can get to the core of perplexing problems, it's likely to be you. Tax matters or issues related to debts or inheritance may arise, even if you're only updating your will or changing beneficiaries.

Cosmic Insider Tip
You may be surprised to discover exactly who's been digging up the dirt, and with Jupiter opposing Pluto, you're probably holding at least one ace up your own sleeve!

Rewarding Days: 2, 3, 6, 7, 11, 16, 17, 25, 26, 29

Challenging Days: 1, 13, 14, 20, 21, 22, 27, 28

Affirmation for the Month
I am honest with myself about my true feelings.

Scorpio/June

In the Spotlight
Money matters take center stage. You can experience a rush of energy in the financial department and may be producing strong income. Disputes over finances can be a problem if you and your partner have divergent ideas about your priorities.

Wellness and Keeping Fit
Sports or fitness activities are invigorating, and you'll appreciate a positive challenge. Knowing your limits is necessary, though, since you can quickly get in over your head!

Love and Life Connections
Although you may be drawn into arguments, you discover that there are issues hiding beneath the surface that come into view once you're in the midst of a dispute. Your passionate desires grow stronger during the Full Moon on June 6, but you may feel inhibited about expressing yourself. It could be that you're hoping to forge a spiritual and emotional attachment, and the solar eclipse on June 21 opens the way for that possibility.

Finance and Success
With Mercury and Mars both retrograding in financial departments of your life, you need to be especially conscious about the way you're handling your resources. Impulse is your enemy when it comes to spending, although you may be generating a strong income or having good luck in the markets. However, you may be more easily drawn into a web of deception from June 6-16, and can spend more than necessary after June 18.

Cosmic Insider Tip
Overreaction is everywhere with Mercury, Mars, and Jupiter creating what can be a stormy circumstance or fast-paced change. Operating from your "center" keeps you on a steady course.

Rewarding Days: 2, 3, 7, 12, 13, 21, 22, 25, 26, 30

Challenging Days: 5, 6, 9, 10, 11, 17, 18, 23, 24

Affirmation for the Month
I am clearly aware of my reasonable limitations.

Scorpio/July

In the Spotlight
It's a month of discovery, and thorough investigation can open the way to inspiring possibilities. Getting beyond inhibiting circumstances allows you to move toward horizons you've always dreamed of exploring.

Wellness and Keeping Fit
If your vitality is waning you'll need more rest, and rebuilding your energy will be easier after July 20 when Mars turns direct. Consider time away from your routine as a means of refreshing your energy and altering your perspective.

Love and Life Connections
Feelings of mistrust may be triggered by situations that remind you of the past, but you're ready to move beyond old fears during the lunar eclipse on July 5 if you feel a new understanding emerging with your lover. If you're single, you're uncovering more reasons to feel good about yourself, and after July 13 may be more interested in exploring what the world has to offer. Your quests can lead to an exciting meeting near the New Moon on July 20.

Finance and Success
Negotiate final details, but try to postpone important contracts until after July 20, when legal or less formal agreements have more auspicious qualities. You may still be wrangling with budget details and feel that others are not as forthcoming as you'd like from July 10-20. Leave enough room for a change in leadership or a reorganization of priorities.

Cosmic Insider Tip
Conversations early in the month have all sorts of promise, although you won't see a manifestation of anything substantial until after the New Moon on July 20.

Rewarding Days: 1, 4, 5, 9, 10, 19, 20, 23, 27, 28, 31

Challenging Days: 7, 8, 14, 15, 16, 21, 22

Affirmation for the Month
I gratefully acknowledge the value of what my past has taught me.

Scorpio/August

In the Spotlight
Reaching toward your most cherished aspirations leads to an excitement all its own, and you're receiving recognition for your efforts and accomplishments. Anchor your hopes to your faith in what you know to be honest and true; changes test your values.

Wellness and Keeping Fit
Spiritual renewal enhances your well-being. Whether you're accomplishing this through time away (a vacation? what's that?!), or you're dedicating more time to meditation or inner focus, your connection to your higher needs infuses you with vitality.

Love and Life Connections
Your love life is magnified by a multifaceted joining of body, mind, and spirit. To strengthen your current relationship, consider a retreat from your daily routine, which will allow ample time to talk about your dreams and feed your shared vision. Love connections you make while traveling can be especially significant. At home you're feeling the need to make alterations, and you're restless if you are not happy with your current situation.

Finance and Success
If you thought something was in the bag, you'll feel unsettled if you discover that someone's changing the rules or the workings of an agreement. It's easy to overreact near the Full Moon on August 4, but before you jump to any conclusions, look further into the matter. There may be a silver lining, and after the New Moon on August 19 there's an entirely different horizon to explore.

Cosmic Insider Tip
Reorganization or changes in leadership can interfere with your plans, especially if your budget depends on the old structure. New agreements made after August 20 have fewer loopholes.

Rewarding Days: 1, 6, 7, 15, 16, 19, 23, 24, 28, 29

Challenging Days: 3, 4, 10, 11, 12, 17, 18, 19, 30, 31

Affirmation for the Month
My view of the larger picture allows me to clearly see the truth.

Scorpio/September

In the Spotlight
The hard work you've been doing for the last few months pays off when you realize that the support for your efforts ranges further than you knew. Keep the momentum going by linking your ideas and efforts with those others who share your enthusiasm.

Wellness and Keeping Fit
Spending time getting back to nature is especially enjoyable, and you'll feel more grounded as a result. Your health is improving, and during the next few weeks you may want to target new fitness challenges that add endurance and strength.

Love and Life Connections
Romantic ventures leave a powerful impression, and during the Full Moon on September 2 you may be feeling wickedly amorous. Spiraling into ecstasy can be delicious, but changing your life may be out of the question. Honesty allows you to experience the best of both worlds. A weekend away around the New Moon on September 17 gives you a chance to lay the groundwork for the future.

Finance and Success
If you feel you're wanting more from your career, take a careful look at the big picture on September 1-3, when you're also more in touch with your long-term goals. Your accomplishments will be more impressive after September 9, and rewards for your efforts should be forthcoming after September 21. Be alert to unexpected challenges from September 12-18, when finding a way to incorporate innovations into an existing situation works to your advantage.

Cosmic Insider Tip
A rush of energy after September 20 can lead you to believe that you're running out of time, but you'll do yourself a favor by maintaining a reasonable pace while others take the risky path.

Rewarding Days: 2, 3, 11, 12, 16, 19, 20, 21, 24, 29, 30

Challenging Days: 1, 7, 8, 13, 14, 26, 27, 28

Affirmation for the Month
My intuitive insights are a valuable guiding light.

Scorpio/October

In the Spotlight
Community projects and work with peers provide excellent options for advancing your reputation and accomplishing your aims. Even from behind the scenes you can be politically influential, and you may enjoy the power of some anonymity.

Wellness and Keeping Fit
Persistently working toward the goals of building your endurance, you're also feeling more open to the idea of indulging your sensual needs. A day at the spa, a massage, or other body work can be especially beneficial, immediately boosting your vitality.

Love and Life Connections
An adventure with your lover from October 1-15 ignites your passion, although you don't really have to do anything outrageous. After all, when you're in the groove, love's an adventure all by itself! Conflicts or misunderstandings midmonth may be the result of circumstances that inhibit your ability to spend as much time as you like together, or you may simply be in uncomfortable surroundings. Improvements come after October 24.

Finance and Success
Since Mercury is retrograding from October 1-22, you'll be more inclined to deal with ongoing situations or troubleshooting when problems arise, instead of trying to get new projects off the ground. You may still be pretty busy promoting your current ideas anyway, and adding more to your plate now will just dilute your effectiveness. Intriguing information uncovered in the course of investigations can lead you toward different circumstances later.

Cosmic Insider Tip
Careful preparation and research now gives you an advantage next month. Think of this as a gestation period.

Rewarding Days: 9, 10, 13, 17, 18, 21, 22, 23, 26, 27, 28

Challenging Days: 4, 5, 11, 12, 24, 25, 31

Affirmation for the Month
I am aware of my motivations and allow love to guide me.

Scorpio/November

In the Spotlight
You're feeling driven toward the accomplishment of your goals, and you may be attracting more attention than you realize. Purity of intention is important, since you'll feel more in control if others clearly understand who you are and what you represent.

Wellness and Keeping Fit
Stress levels are on the rise, and although you may feel that you've become a magnet for tension, you can release it by staying active and concentrating more attention to increasing your flexibility. Yoga class or more stretches during workouts do the trick nicely.

Love and Life Connections
Venus and Mercury shed their rays in the most complimentary manner, emphasizing your allure from November 6-30. If the Full Moon on November 1 left you feeling a little exposed, you'll want to wait until November 9 before you try to alter another person's perceptions or to ask those questions that are driving you crazy. It's tempting to overreact during the Scorpio New Moon phase from November 15-26, so take a deep breath before you form an opinion.

Finance and Success
Your finances should certainly improve after November 7, although you could make ill-advised decisions from November 10-13, when the facts may be altered to suit another's interests. Investment options are most advantageous from November 14-24. At work, showing special sensitivity to those in positions of influence allows you to step in or step back at the most auspicious moments.

Cosmic Insider Tip
Saturn and Pluto continue their intense opposition, marking a time when the hierarchy is changing due to power struggles. When possible, watch from the sidelines.

Rewarding Days: 5, 6, 9, 13, 14, 18, 19, 23, 24

Challenging Days: 1, 7, 8, 20, 21, 28, 29

Affirmation for the Month
My life is filled with beauty and joy!

Scorpio/December

In the Spotlight
Your vision for the future may be stalled during a momentary change of direction brought on by circumstances you cannot control. Fortunately, your confidence is supported by favorable ideals, and your creative impulses help turn the tide.

Wellness and Keeping Fit
Find fitness activities that are enjoyable, since the drudgery of repeating stale routines discourages your enthusiasm. Laughter is your best medicine, and your sharp wit also encourages healing in the lives of others.

Love and Life Connections
Mundane activities monopolize your attention early in the month, although your first priority is toward those you love, after December 8. Connect with siblings: this is a good time to forge an understanding. After December 22 a romantic rendezvous can be just what you need to jump-start your affections. Overtures made during the lunar eclipse on December 30 are especially meaningful.

Finance and Success
Dealing with others who see you as a threat may be a necessary task from December 1-8, and if you can establish a strong position you'll be able to garner further support. Review your finances and budgets, since the solar eclipse on December 14 marks a time when you're ready to ditch plans that are not working in favor of a more optimistic long-range plan. Watch for a turn in investments after December 27, but avoid making radical changes.

Cosmic Insider Tip
There's a sense of hope for the future during the lunar eclipse on December 30, although you may see signs that everything is not exactly rosy. Cautious moderation works to your benefit.

Rewarding Days: 2, 3, 6, 11, 12, 15, 16, 20, 21, 30, 31

Challenging Days: 4, 5, 14, 17, 18, 19, 25, 26

Affirmation for the Month
I release negative thoughts and replace them with hope.

Scorpio Action Table

These dates reflect the best—but not the only—times for success and ease in these activities, according to your Sun sign.

	JAN	FEB	MAR	APR	MAY	JUN	JUL	AUG	SEPT	OCT	NOV	DEC
Move	10-31	26-28	1-16									
Start a class	1-9					21, 22						15-31
Join a club									17			
Ask for a raise											15	
Look for work				6-20			30, 31	1-13				
Get pro advice	4, 5, 31	1, 20, 28	1, 27, 28	23, 24	20-22	17, 18	14, 15	7, 8	7, 8	4, 5, 31	1-2, 28-29	25, 26
Get a loan	6, 7	3, 4	2-3, 29-30	25, 26	23, 24	19, 20	16-18	13, 14	9, 10	6-8	3, 4, 30	1, 27, 28
See a doctor				6-20					1-30	23-31	1-6	
Start a diet	2-3, 29-30	25, 26	24-26	21, 22	18, 19	14-16	12, 13	8, 9	4-6	1-3, 29-30	25, 26	22-24
End relationship											1, 2	
Buy clothes		1, 2	17-31	1-5								
Get a makeover											8-30	1
New romance	3-31	1, 23, 24										
Vacation	8, 9	5, 6	4, 5, 31	1, 27, 28	25, 26	21, 22	19, 20	14, 15	11, 12	9, 10	5, 6	2-3, 29-31

Sagittarius

The Archer
November 22 to December 21

♐

Element:	Fire
Quality:	Mutable
Polarity:	Yang/Masculine
Planetary Ruler:	Jupiter
Meditation:	All things are possible.
Gemstone:	Turquoise
Power Stones:	Lapis lazuli, azurite, sodalite
Key Phrase:	I understand
Glyph:	Archer's arrow
Anatomy:	Hips, thighs, sciatic nerve
Color:	Royal blue, purple
Animal:	Fleet-footed animals
Myths/Legends:	Athena, Chiron, the Centaurs
House:	Ninth
Opposite Sign:	Gemini
Flower:	Narcissus
Key Word:	Optimism

Positive Expression:
Adventurous
Philosophical
Scholarly
Charitable
Jovial
Broad-minded
Wise

Misuse of Energy:
Foolish
Bigoted
Self-righteous
Extravagant
Condescending
Inconsiderate
Blunt

career in politics, diplomatic service, or the ministry can be fulfilling. Or you might enjoy acting, sports, or promoting the talents of others. Whatever your choice, you think big!

Power Plays

Defining power is an active philosophical exercise, but in your heart of hearts, liberty and power are inextricably linked. Ideally, you feel that power works only when accompanied by a sense of higher truth, and you can feel almost personally insulted when others use their power to limit human potential or to serve their own greed. While the highest level of your personal power may be an accomplishment of spiritual enlightenment, you are very likely to run into a series of blind alleys fueled by useless double talk along the way. Truth always lights the higher path, freeing you of prejudicial ideas and beliefs.

Keeping an open mind is an important part of finding personal strength, and narrow-minded or condescending attitudes can be terrible traps for you. Real abundance can be just as puzzling until you feel a harmony between your highest needs and your desires and actions. It is through sharing your bounty with others that you experience the power of joy, which leads to even greater prosperity! In the interim, your study, writing, travels, and teaching light the fires of inspiration, allowing you to reach toward others as an architect of a healthy future of understanding for all humankind.

Famous Sagittarians

Woody Allen, Tracy Austin, Ludwig von Beethoven, Surya Bonaly, Jeff Bridges, Maria Callas, Benjamin Disraeli, Walt Disney, Berry Gordy, Jr., Jimi Hendrix, Lucky Luciano, Stephen Spielberg, Eli Whitney

The Year Ahead for Sagittarius

The year 2001 is a period of personal breakthroughs for you, with new horizons to explore and innovative ideas to assimilate. Establishing the right pace can be challenging, since it will be easy to move too quickly or to feel that you're somewhat out of step with everyone else around you. Certainly your sights are set on the future, and your inspirational ideas and leadership can be the perfect stimulus to gather the support you need to make your dreams come true.

You're still feeling the force of Pluto's very long transit in your sign, marking a decade of personal transformation. The most significant two years of this cycle will be the time Pluto makes an exact conjunction to your Sun (look for the birthdays undergoing this exact influence below), but the essence of this cycle has a long-lasting impact. As a result, you'll feel a bit vulnerable until Pluto moves out of Sagittarius in 2009! This does not mean that your life will be a mess until then. In fact, this influence can be exceptionally positive, since you may finally be less inclined to take on things you cannot accomplish effectively.

Jupiter, your planetary ruler, is traveling in opposition to your Sun sign from January through July 12, adding a boost of confidence with the potential for growth in your relationships. The major pitfall of this cycle is a strong tendency to overdo it, and you can experience what seems like "instant karma" if you overextend yourself. Moderation is the key to making this cycle work for you. From July through December, you're experiencing a different influence from Jupiter, learning how to extend true appreciation for the efforts and resources others share with you.

Saturn's cycle brings well-defined tests. There's little mystery about Saturn's influence, since by the spring it moves into an opposition to your Sun sign. For the next two years you're learning about your limitations and can take steps to assure that you're standing on solid ground before launching your heartfelt hopes. Either this year or next year (look for your birthday below to see if it's this year), you'll be feeling the burden of responsibility testing your resolve to know what's really good for you.

The slow-moving cycles of Uranus and Neptune highlight your desire to expand your consciousness. Whether you're applying innovative technologies to further your outreach, learning a different language, or exploring relationships with unique individuals, you're ready to experiment with the world of possibilities. You may even become an innovator yourself: with your ideas and insights setting the parameters, others will follow!

The eclipses of the Sun and Moon are especially significant for you this year. In fact, the December 14th solar eclipse is in Sagittarius, indicating a time when you're realizing the things that are standing in the way of your spiritual and personal growth. It is the cycle of the Moon's Nodes that tells the story of your deeper feelings regarding your spiritual evolution, and this year you're exploring your emotional attachments, fears, and inhibitions. It's a good time to work with a psychotherapist, to probe into metaphysical teachings, or to develop your psychic and intuitive insights to help you release the old traumas that have inhibited your ability to know true freedom and connection to the Source.

If you were born from November 22 to 27, you're experiencing Saturn's restrictive transit in opposition to your Sun from January through the end of May. After that time you're likely to experience a sense of relief, especially if you take advantage of Saturn's cycle to complete obligations, finish school, or eliminate things that are no longer advantageous to your personal growth. This cycle began last summer, and its strongest impact will be during the spring of 2001. Relationships can be a key issue during this time, and your real feelings about a marriage, including your role and needs in the relationship, will be difficult to ignore. If you're single, you may be seriously exploring what you want or need from commitments, and if you're involved in a relationship, you may feel that it's testing you—or you're testing it! Sometimes it's virtually impossible to get out of situations until Saturn's cycle is complete, and obligations for which you hold true responsibility are chief among the tenacious issues you'll be addressing. Saturn's opposition cycle marks an important period, since now you're completing things in preparation for your climb up the ladder of personal success. This is the time to pay attention to all the details.

If you were born from November 27 to December 9, you'll feel Saturn's transit in opposition to your Sun from May 2001 through May 2002. During this time you're likely to experience a series of restraints that appear to slow your progress. In actuality, you're invited to take a serious look at yourself and your priorities, since this is the period in which you can see yourself most clearly. While there may be different cycles affecting other points in your natal chart, this influence can be the overriding one, challenging you to make choices that are in harmony with your needs and to understand the nature of the obligations to which you're making a commitment. Of course, relationships can be a key factor, and whether you're connected or single you're testing the qualities in a relationship that fit who you are. In many respects you're also seeing the fruits of your labors and the areas in which you've failed to meet your obligations. Fortunately, you can now take steps to solidify your security base or work toward your goals. Physically, it's also time to take a serious look at your health and the manner in which you're caring for your body's needs. Destructive habits or attitudes can create a more significant block than they have in the past, prompting you to make an honest assessment of your needs from a holistic viewpoint. Circumstances which add stress may be difficult to avoid, but the manner in which you deal with the stresses is up to you!

If you were born from November 27 to December 2, you're experiencing the influence of Neptune transiting in sextile aspect to your Sun for the entire year. This influence adds a level of serenity and heightens your connection to your spirituality and creativity. It's fortunate that you're working with Neptunian energy during this time of Saturn's testing, since your inner voice can be a powerful asset. In fact, by applying a reasonable level of self-discipline to your personal development, you may feel that your consciousness is expanding in ways that seem almost miraculous. Your devotion to your spiritual path can, literally, be your saving grace! Since Uranus is also transiting in quintile aspect to your Sun, special talents and abilities can be more easily developed now, as well. If you've wondered about the best time to study with a master teacher or to fine-tune your own talents, this can be an exceptional period of progress and insight. It's much like the difference between learning the notes in a piece of music and merging with the essence of the music. Certainly getting the technical aspects right can be helpful, but your muse invites you to dance in your own special way and to fully surrender to the song of your heart.

If you were born from December 4 to 9, Pluto is transiting in exact conjunction to your Sun during 2001. This cycle can only happen once in a lifetime, and marks a powerful period of personal transformation. You may feel that your life is changing in ways that are difficult to describe, and some changes may be happening outside your own control. Since Saturn is also transiting in opposition to your Sun, it's absolutely crucial that you take a careful look at your priorities and needs, and that you find the best possible responses to the changes happening in your life. It's also likely that you'll develop a clearer understanding of the nature of life itself—from birth to death. This does not mean that you are dying or that anyone you love is necessarily dying, but at some level, a part of your life is dying away. It's the deeper spiritual and psychological changes which are the significant ones: you're eliminating the factors from your life that will not be part of the new you emerging. In many ways, you're experiencing a kind of gestational stage in preparation for rebirth. For that reason, the people and situations which no longer fit are simply dropping away. Think of this as a cocooning stage, when you're changing from caterpillar to butterfly. During this time, you'll feel more vulnerable, while also experiencing a connection to the power which originates from the Source of Life itself. Envision who you want to be on the other side, since, after all, you're also learning that you're the creator of your life.

If you were born from December 10 to 17, you're feeling a surge of excitement while Uranus transits in sextile to your Sun. The freedom you're feeling arises from a sense that it's finally your turn to experience acknowledgment of your individuality. The things that make you special grow stronger. It's an excellent year to unleash your unique ideas or to experiment with positive applications of technology that strengthen your accomplishments. Since Neptune is also transiting in semisquare to your Sun, you'll feel an increased artistic and spiritual sensibility. The primary downfall of Neptune's influence can be that saying "no" is more difficult—especially if you need to deny anything to someone you care about. Breaking old habits, especially codependent behaviors, is necessary if you are to avoid falling victim to another's tendency to usurp your personal power. In addition, you're experiencing a direct connection to the solar eclipse on December 14th, since it is in conjunction to your Sun, and marks a relatively rare cycle. The eclipse may signify a point of realization or change, and some of the things you want to clarify will become more apparent during December.

If you were born from December 18 to 21, you're experiencing a need to make a few adjustments while Saturn transits in quincunx to your Sun from January through April. After that time, you may feel that you have the world on a string—relatively speaking. The manner in which you've handled Saturn's tests since June of last year will determine where you're standing when this cycle is completed in April. One thing is certain: you'll feel relieved!

Tools to Make a Difference

Remaining flexible—physically and emotionally—is your big assignment for this year. Your life is undergoing changes and outside forces are providing their own stressful elements, giving you every opportunity to become more tense. To offset the tension, you'll benefit from a routine which includes stretching, breathing, and relaxation, in addition to staying physically active. You may even rationalize that you just don't have time to take care of yourself—and it's during such periods that you need to be even more loving toward yourself! First things first: make every attempt to create a consistent schedule of exercise, enroll in a fitness or yoga class, or make an agreement with a buddy to keep each other on track. So, yes, your friends or partners may act as "tools" to help you maintain balance in your life.

Your target zone physically is hips and thighs. While you may not think you hold much tension in these areas, they're the first place you're likely to store tense energy. You're also a candidate for sciatica, especially if you've been carrying burdens inappropriately—emotionally or physically. Schedule regular visits with your massage therapist, and promise to see an acupuncturist at least once each season to keep your chi flowing properly. You'll also benefit from enhancing graceful movement, and anything from dance to tai chi classes can help you get more in touch with your body.

Removing energy blocks from your work space and enhancing the flow of energy around you in your work environment can make a huge difference, too. Apply principles of feng shui both at work and at home. You might be surprised at the change in your productivity, attitude, and prosperity!

Affirmation for the Year

In all things, my consciousness is open to guidance from my Higher Self.

Sagittarius/January

In the Spotlight
Careful attention to financial details assures that you'll avoid costly mistakes, especially if your partner or others have taken actions which affect your resources. Initiate the year with new budget plans.

Wellness and Keeping Fit
Inner fitness draws your concentration toward your need to let go and surrender to a process of renewal. By allowing private time to explore your inner self now, you'll feel more balanced and become better integrated. Consider a massage to offset tension.

Love and Life Connections
Setting priorities between family concerns and time with your partner can leave you feeling that you're caught in the middle, ultimately pleasing nobody. At the innermost core may be intimacy issues—getting into the roots of your feelings and needs—stimulated by the Moon's eclipse on January 9. After January 21, communication improves, although you may still feel frustrated if others insist on argumentative or hostile interaction.

Finance and Success
Improvements or repairs to your personal environment are more expensive than you anticipated, especially if your aims clash with your partner's. If you're dissatisfied, get an expert opinion. Contracts and negotiations fare best after the New Moon on January 24, although others are likely to show support for your ideas early in the month. If your position depends upon making a solid presentation, set the meeting for January 24 or 25.

Cosmic Insider Tip
It's a mixed picture this month, since you're reasonably confident, but may not be receiving the assurance you need from someone who matters. Evaluate your worth on your own terms!

Rewarding Days: 2, 3, 10, 11, 19, 20, 24, 25, 29, 30

Challenging Days: 6, 7, 8, 9, 12, 13, 17, 26, 27, 28

Affirmation for the Month
I am whole, energetic, and getting stronger with each moment.

Sagittarius/February

In the Spotlight
Your heart opens to love, and through sharing your feelings of affection you're not only improving your relationships but opening the way to enhanced creativity. Your enthusiasm can run away with you, though—so be sure that your overtures are welcome!

Wellness and Keeping Fit
The key to feeling sufficiently energetic is the pace you choose, since you may not be aware of exhausting your energy until it's too late. Take extra care evaluating risk situations to avoid running into problems which can be difficult to control.

Love and Life Connections
Venus and Jupiter add enhancement to your relationships, bringing you into the good graces of others. You feel more open to making a connection, but can have trouble reading the signals from the shy types. The intrigues of romance are rather enjoyable from the Full Moon on February 8 until February 17. Slow the pace after February 18 to avoid getting in over your head.

Finance and Success
Despite Mercury's retrograde during February 4-25, it's a great time to let your talents shine or to continue developing a pet project. You're likely to feel most confident after February 14, although you'll be tempted to rush, and could miss important details as a result. Business presentations and written communications are well received after February 5, although those resistant to futuristic ideas may need further explanation. Patience works to your advantage.

Cosmic Insider Tip
Mars enters Sagittarius on February 14, beginning an unusually long cycle lasting into September and creating the Energizer Bunny effect. Moderation keeps your energy consistent.

Rewarding Days: 7, 8, 11, 15, 16, 17, 20, 25, 26

Challenging Days: 3, 4, 9, 10, 14, 23, 24

Affirmation for the Month
I have faith in true love.

Sagittarius/March

In the Spotlight
Creative ideas permeate your consciousness, and you're beginning a long period of heightened enthusiasm, coupled with increased artistry. Whatever your talents or expressive abilities, this is definitely the time to start making the most of them!

Wellness and Keeping Fit
Enhance your physical strength through your dedication to fitness. A personal trainer can be especially helpful. This is also a good time to detox, since you may feel that your body is ready to regenerate.

Love and Life Connections
Venus and Mars work their magic, opening your heart and sparking your confidence in your feelings. However, the pace may be uncomfortable: changes can be happening too quickly, or if you're ready and he/she is hesitating you can be exceptionally impatient—especially if the question involves pesky practicalities. Make an effort to establish a clear understanding after the New Moon on March 25. Speak from your heart.

Finance and Success
Investments are on the right track, although you may need to evaluate your portfolio to determine whether it's suited to your current aims. If your work requires innovation or strong personal expression, you're capable of impressing the right people, but you'll have to scale back if you're still in the middle of something yet unfinished. Test any situation before jumping into it, concentrating on establishing strong connections which can serve you in the future.

Cosmic Insider Tip
With Mars transiting in Sagittarius until September, you're poised to assert yourself; the trouble is knowing how far to go. Power plays made midmonth will be tested in August.

Rewarding Days: 6, 7, 10, 11, 14, 15, 16, 20, 25, 26

Challenging Days: 2, 3, 8, 9, 22, 23, 29, 30, 31

Affirmation for the Month
I am conscious of the effects of my words and actions.

Sagittarius/April

In the Spotlight
Part of you is running full steam ahead while around you circumstances require a series of adjustments. Your intuition is working like a charm despite the fact that the messages from your inner self may defy logic—at least in the early stages!

Wellness and Keeping Fit
You can be a little more accident prone, especially if your head is one place while your body's in another! Grounding your energy can be your saving grace; try getting back to nature, or at least have lunch in the park or spend some weekend time in the garden.

Love and Life Connections
Having second thoughts about a love relationship? Join the crowd! It's part of Venus retrograde—but you're also dealing with discoveries that cause you to question whether this love is good for you. Romance fares best from April 6-20. After that, you can almost hear the squeal of the brakes while you look around and wonder just how long you can tolerate the same old problems. Emotional house cleaning is rarely easy, but it can shed light on your needs!

Finance and Success
Review the financial details of your proposal or current project, getting rid of excess and opening the way for the innovations which tell you that you're right where you want to be: on the leading edge. Involving others is inevitable, but you can define the roles you want to take in the changing hierarchy. For a while at least you may have to scale back just a bit, but as long as your eyes are on the future, you'll keep advancing!

Cosmic Insider Tip
Establish firm agreements concerning work after April 19, since you'll function best when you know what's expected.

Rewarding Days: 2, 3, 7, 8, 11, 12, 16, 17, 21, 22, 30

Challenging Days: 4, 5, 6, 18, 19, 20, 26, 27

Affirmation for the Month
I am honest about my intentions.

Sagittarius/May

In the Spotlight
With momentum slowing, you have a chance to add a layer to an existing project or to take a relationship to a more substantial level. Don't be surprised if you're feeling that you're being tested. You are! Fortunately, you have a while to complete your assignment.

Wellness and Keeping Fit
If you've been pushing past your limits you'll feel it after Mars turns retrograde on May 11. There's no reason to give up—but you may have to alter your goals to fit your current situation.

Love and Life Connections
Commitment to your relationship becomes an issue, particularly if you need or want your role to change, or feel that it's finally time to identify where you're going. Outside pressures can play a part in your priorities, and although you may feel a profound love, you may not like certain things about your partner's life. Talking over your concerns allows you to clear the way for an honest promise made during or after the New Moon on May 23.

Finance and Success
Contracts finalized now are likely to have a lasting impact, although the hierarchy or priorities of your work situation are under construction. Airing your ideas draws criticism and support, since the lines are definitely established, and your moral dictates are not likely to allow you to follow leadership which seems counterproductive or abusive. Your creative impulse works to your advantage, and those who thrive on similar values come to your aid.

Cosmic Insider Tip
Some of the rhetoric spouted last fall is tested when Jupiter opposes Pluto on May 6, when you're ready to walk to the beat of your own drum. Just keep your eyes open!

Rewarding Days: 1, 4, 5, 8, 9, 13, 14, 18, 19, 27, 28, 31

Challenging Days: 2, 3, 16, 17, 21, 23, 24, 25, 29, 30

Affirmation for the Month
I am clearly aware of the needs and concerns of others.

Sagittarius/June

In the Spotlight
If you're scattering your energy and resources due to a lack of focus, it's time to evaluate your priorities. Although your versatility will come in handy this month, your responsibilities will not take a back seat—so make room for them!

Wellness and Keeping Fit
A feeling that you're running on empty can perpetuate a vicious cycle. Sometimes you simply have to stop, give yourself time to heal (or at least take a breath!), and then get back in the groove. Otherwise you won't enjoy the ride.

Love and Life Connections
Your inner voice may be hoarse from screaming, "Slow down!" Certainly you're allowed to have fun—in fact, it may be the overriding force during the Sagittarius Full Moon on June 6—but you have to know the cost of your pleasure. Mars, Mercury, and Jupiter work like high test rocket fuel, and your eagerness can be irritating to those who are not as comfortable with adventure as you may be. If they're important to you, listen to their pleas.

Finance and Success
Your timing can be off, since Mercury and Mars are both retrograding, and their cycles are directly impacting your life. Other people seem to drop out just when you need their resources, or want more from you than you feel you can deliver. Review contracts, and explore problems which are arising around the time of the Sun's eclipse on June 21. Research before taking action.

Cosmic Insider Tip
If somebody's pushing for your signature, ask them why they're in such a hurry! Anything substantial will be better served if you wait on final decisions until next month.

Rewarding Days: 1, 5, 6, 10, 11, 15, 16, 24, 28

Challenging Days: 12, 13, 17, 19, 20, 25, 26, 30

Affirmation for the Month
I value my integrity and that of meaningful relationships in my life.

Sagittarius/July

In the Spotlight
You're unwilling to commit your time and resources if you anticipate that you'll be getting the short end of the bargain, although ascertaining the best alternatives may require a team of experts. Making the best use of wise counsel requires a measure of patience.

Wellness and Keeping Fit
Getting to the source of a bothersome complaint is easier after July 5—you'll be more assured after obtaining several opinions. Complementary healing techniques are likely to offer the best results, since you want long-term satisfaction!

Love and Life Connections
Overtures from others may cause you to wonder if you're on the same page! It's by listening to your partner's needs and desires that you determine where the relationship is heading. Trust issues emerging during the Moon's eclipse on July 5 can shed light on whether you're still upset about the past. Only when you're satisfied that your spiritual aims are harmonious will you let go and trust. Take another look after July 21.

Finance and Success
Your confidence in agreements is strong from July 1-12, although your best time for legal dealings is after July 23. Double-check all details and research the current economic trends. Your career advancement may depend upon how well you're dealing with outside competitors, and you're likely to discover their weak links if you look closely.

Cosmic Insider Tip
You're understanding the value of knowing the enemy. Of course, that starts by identifying the precise nature of all your relationships, including your knowledge of yourself!

Rewarding Days: 3, 4, 8, 9, 17, 18, 21, 22, 25, 26, 30, 31

Challenging Days: 5, 6, 7, 13, 14, 19, 20, 24

Affirmation for the Month
I am clear about my own motivations.

Sagittarius/August

In the Spotlight
Your energy is getting stronger, and you're in a great position to finish up an important project or to complete the final leg of a significant journey. Profound questions are the first priority of your consciousness, awakening yet another important quest.

Wellness and Keeping Fit
Delving into your psyche can be the key to healing. Deep tissue body work like Rolfing is helpful, or you might respond to unlocking your energy through martial arts, Chi Gung, yoga, or working with an acupuncturist.

Love and Life Connections
Travel can awaken or renew a love connection from August 1-14, with romantic intensity opening the way to an uplifting understanding during the Full Moon on August 4. Redefining your role in close relationships makes room for your vision of the future, and your hopefulness opens the way for positive change. You're ready to move forward, transforming your life through true and joyful love. (But, first—look in the mirror and reflect love back to yourself!)

Finance and Success
Pooling your resources with others can give you a substantial platform, especially if your ideals are forged from the same mettle. Yielding to the need to make major alterations in corporate or hierarchical structures makes way for a more smoothly running organization, although some may resist what feels like displacement. Your ideas can inspire change from August 17-19.

Cosmic Insider Tip
Extending your gratitude to others who offer support can quell a potentially disruptive situation, setting a positive platform for excellent long-term growth.

Rewarding Days: 3, 4, 8, 9, 17, 18, 21, 22, 25, 26, 27, 30, 31

Challenging Days: 5, 6, 7, 13, 14, 19, 20

Affirmation for the Month
Through love, I release the things I no longer need.

Sagittarius/September

In the Spotlight
Community outreach and involvement with special interest groups adds a measure of excitement. Expanding your options through academic pursuits, publishing, travel, or international relations can renew your goals or stimulate new directions.

Wellness and Keeping Fit
Consolidate your energy by creating a more balanced regimen—one that includes rest! You may need to supplement your diet with nutrients like ginkgo biloba or DHA, which boost mental function.

Love and Life Connections
Sharing a journey with someone you adore can be wondrous if there's room for spontaneity; your adventurous spirit will relish the idea of heading out toward unexplored horizons. A provocative attraction arouses your interest from September 1-5 and then from September 13-20. This can bring renewal to a healthy relationship or mark a time when you're ready for new love. You're dropping some of your strongest inhibitions in favor of enjoying the pure pleasures of love.

Finance and Success
Conferences or business presentations provide an excellent forum to share your research or theories, and you're in line for more substantial financial support to further your ideas, particularly if your boss considers you part of the family! Incorporating futuristic concepts works to your advantage, although you'll need to watch the numbers, since budgets can quickly loom out of control.

Cosmic Insider Tip
Your display of expertise and convincing rhetoric inspires others to follow your lead, but you'll go further if you have solid research and understanding to back up your claims.

Rewarding Days: 1, 4, 5, 13, 14, 18, 22, 23, 27, 28

Challenging Days: 2, 3, 9, 10, 11, 15, 16, 29, 30

Affirmation for the Month
My words are inspired and guided by Truth and Wisdom.

Sagittarius/October

In the Spotlight
The manner in which you're handling your resources says a lot about your personal security; if you're feeling good about yourself you'll be more likely to avoid wasting time and money. Otherwise, keep those credit cards on ice.

Wellness and Keeping Fit
If you've been overdoing it or giving in to your indulgences too frequently, you may feel that your energy is waning. Regenerate by initiating a holistic program of self care which will elevate your vitality to reliable levels.

Love and Life Connections
Fitting in time for your friends around the Full Moon on October 2 can spark jealousy from your partner if he or she is too dependent (or if you're codependent!). You're discovering where you need to create more realistic boundaries, and may finally be breaking away from negative patterns adopted from your family of origin. You'll feel more confident expressing your heartfelt desires after October 15, and may even have a second chance with your true love.

Finance and Success
During Mercury's retrograde cycle from October 1-22, take time to address pending issues or review ongoing projects in hopes of reaching a conclusion. Taking on too much early in the month will leave you feeling overburdened after the New Moon on October 16, since it's easy to underestimate the types of resources necessary to adequately complete the job at hand.

Cosmic Insider Tip
It's interesting to observe that things seem to be moving too quickly, but are somehow at a standstill at the same time. Moderation saves your hide more than once this month.

Rewarding Days: 2, 3, 11, 12, 15, 16, 19, 20, 24, 29

Challenging Days: 1, 13, 14, 18, 21, 26, 27

Affirmation for the Month
I replenish and renew spent resources.

Sagittarius/November

In the Spotlight
Extra hours working behind the scenes proves worthwhile, since it's time to repair weak links or to complete anything requiring extra attention to creative detail. This also applies to your connection to your spirituality: your inner voice is speaking volumes.

Wellness and Keeping Fit
Time away from the daily grind is in order. At the least, pull back a little and give yourself extra time to take a few detours. Refresh your workouts with different exercises, and try to get outdoors, since nature is an excellent source of renewal for you now.

Love and Life Connections
Connect with friends from November 1-7 to catch up on the news and enjoy your shared interests. Your love life seems to be more fantasy than reality from November 8-25, especially if an unattainable someone has caught your eye. Enjoy the reveries, but put your desires to the test of reality after November 22. Give yourself time for a retreat during the Full Moon on November 15.

Finance and Success
Make presentations or attend conferences from November 1-8 and then after November 27. Your support network grows stronger throughout the month, and interactive communications give you the links you need to continue developing your ideas—even if you're not in immediate contact (take advantage of cyberspace!). Contractual agreements define how far you can advance at the moment, but there's room for change next month.

Cosmic Insider Tip
Be especially wary of overtures from those who seem to offer the impossible from November 7-15, trusting your intuitive sense of situations to show you where to investigate.

Rewarding Days: 8, 11, 12, 15, 16, 17, 20, 21, 25, 26, 27

Challenging Days: 1, 3, 4, 9, 10, 23, 24, 30

Affirmation for the Month
I give reassurance to those I care about.

Sagittarius/December

In the Spotlight
You're feeling especially generous, but you're also experiencing a wake-up call! It's time to address situations you've been ignoring: dealing with them now is empowering, but waiting can be costly.

Wellness and Keeping Fit
Emotional components play a huge role in your well-being, and the manner in which you're handling frustration or anger can make a difference in your vitality. Staying active is more important than ever, but you have to honor your limits to avoid accident or injury.

Love and Life Connections
The Sun's eclipse in Sagittarius on December 14 marks a time when the circumstances that have been brewing finally reach their peak. Crisis periods can be extremely invigorating, and this is an excellent time to address the issues that you've been trying to keep hidden. It's time to take the reins, directing your life along a course which fulfills your most powerful and urgent needs.

Finance and Success
Making alterations in your career path is a natural conclusion to the hard work you've been doing. However, you may also be ready to walk away from circumstances which have failed to provide the kind of advancement you deserve. Setting out with a plan of action gives you direction, and if you're to avoid feeling that the bottom has dropped out, you'll do yourself a favor and at least have an idea of your course. Goals are indispensable now.

Cosmic Insider Tip
While the Sun's eclipse is a time of new direction, the lunar eclipse on December 30 stimulates an urge to review how you're using your resources. Making the most of what you have has never made as much sense as it does now!

Rewarding Days: 4, 5, 9, 10, 13, 14, 18, 19, 23, 24

Challenging Days: 1, 6, 7, 8, 20, 21, 27, 28, 30

Affirmation for the Month
I know what I want and where I'm going.

Sagittarius Action Table

These dates reflect the best—but not the only—times for success and ease in these activities, according to your Sun sign.

	JAN	FEB	MAR	APR	MAY	JUN	JUL	AUG	SEPT	OCT	NOV	DEC
Move		1-3	17-31	1-6								
Start a class	10-31	26-28	1-16					18, 19				
Join a club										16		
Ask for a raise												14
Look for work				21-30	1-5			14-31				
Get pro advice	6, 7	3, 4	2, 3, 31	1, 25, 26	23, 24	19, 20	16, 17	13, 14	9, 10	6-8	3, 4, 30	1, 27, 28
Get a loan	8, 9	5, 6	4, 5, 31	1, 27-29	25, 26	21, 22	19, 20	15, 16	11, 12	9, 10	5, 6	2-3, 29-31
See a doctor				22-30	1-5						8-25	
Start a diet	4, 5, 31	1, 20, 28	1, 27, 28	23, 24	21, 22	17, 18	14, 15	10-12	7, 8	4, 5, 31	1-2, 28-29	25, 26
End relationship											30	1
Buy clothes				6-20								
Get a makeover												2-25
New romance		3-28			24-31	1-5						
Vacation	10, 11	7, 8	6, 7	2, 3, 30	1, 27, 28	23, 24	21, 22	17, 18	13, 14	11, 12	7, 8	4, 5

Capricorn

The Goat
December 21 to January 20

♑

Element:	Earth
Quality:	Cardinal
Polarity:	Yin/Feminine
Planetary Ruler:	Saturn
Meditation:	I master the challenges of the physical plane.
Gemstone:	Garnet
Power Stones:	Diamond, quartz, black obsidian, onyx
Key Phrase:	I use
Glyph:	Head of goat, knees
Anatomy:	Skeleton, knees, skin
Colors:	Black, forest green
Animal:	Goats, thick-shelled animals
Myths/Legends:	Chronos, Vesta, Pan
House:	Tenth
Opposite Sign:	Cancer
Flower:	Carnation
Key Word:	Structure

Positive Expression:	Misuse of Energy:
Disciplined	Controlling
Ambitious	Rigid
Patient	Miserly
Conscientious	Repressed
Responsible	Fearful
Sensible	Machiavellian
Thrifty	Severe

Capricorn

Your Ego's Strengths and Shortcomings

In your steady rise up the ladder of your ambitions, your ability to succeed is strengthened by your desire to achieve a sense of mastery. Settling for second best will never do, and by coupling your determination with your sense of structure, you can accomplish things others may never begin! Putting your talents to work, you're "The Pragmatist" of the zodiac, effectively getting the job done and making the most of the materials at hand.

Because you value things that withstand the tests of time, you're willing to wait if something is truly worthwhile. This does not mean that you are always patient, but you are learning how to set priorities which will help you get what you want from life. Your connection to the disciplined energy represented by Saturn works to your advantage when you embrace responsibilities in the best way possible. However, this same energy can lead you to be resistant or controlling—especially if you're struggling within yourself over issues about personal worth. While you understand the reasons for rules, you may be the first to go against arbitrary limitations if they're standing in your way. In fact, others may even complain that you're taking unfair advantage of them, if your desire to have what you want blinds your ability to be fair-minded. It is when you're sharing and working in concert with the talents of others that your ability to direct can lead to exceptional accomplishments for all.

You take great pleasure in watching your friends, students, or children reach their own pinnacles, finding that true immortality rests in the seeds you've planted and nourished during your time on Earth. For yourself, the pleasures of the simple joys of life, and the knowledge that you've carved your own niche, can keep the eternal flame that shows in the glint of your smile.

Shining Your Love Light

The pleasures of love are definitely not wasted on you! Your sensual, steadfast embrace is reassuring to the person you choose as a partner, although you may take your time finding that individual. You're seeking love that will endure and become the foundation of the values you hold dear. Your reserved, matter-of-fact manner can leave the impression that you are not particularly romantic, but this is simply your guarded nature protecting a truly sensitive heart. Once you're open to love, a childlike playfulness and joy in building a lasting commitment can lead to a lifelong promise of love.

With the earth signs—Taurus, Virgo, and, Capricorn—you share a mutual appreciation for down-to-earth virtues and practical ideas. Yet it is with Cancer, your zodiac opposite, that you feel the most intense attraction, and with whom you can create a partnership based upon a mutual desire for security and lasting family values.

Playing delightful, teasing games with Aries can be fun, but your mutually headstrong attitudes lead to locked horns if you disagree. Taurus can be your eternal lover, engaging your earthiness and strengthening your personal worth. Mutual frustration may be your lot with Gemini, but you might be able to work together if you have a common goal. A strong attraction to Leo can lead to passion, but control issues are likely to emerge. Virgo is the perfect companion for your life's journey, and you'll treasure the same things.

Your attraction to Libra is legendary, but getting close emotionally can take on the vestiges of an epic quest. Scorpio offers the potential for magical alchemy and passionate devotion. With Sagittarius you're inspired to seek your dreams, but you may not understand her or his needs for independence. Reaching an understanding with another Capricorn can be easy, but your love will tarnish if your life falls into stale routine. Aquarius is your lifelong and cherished friend. Love's magic flows with Pisces, the mystical journey leading you toward your heart's desire.

Making Your Place in the World

Since you don't often feel that you can relax and enjoy life until you're satisfied with your career, finding a field which promotes your self-respect while offering you a chance to exercise some authority is among your ultimate priorities. The world of business has its appeals, particularly if you can exercise your executive and administrative abilities. Managing a ranch, farm, zoo, or forest can answer your need to stay in touch with nature. Yet you can also enjoy teaching, with particular emphasis on life sciences, geology, physics, and the healing arts.

If you opt for politics or the ministry, your ambition supports your desire to reach the heights. In healing arts, you'll enjoy holistic medicine or working as an herbalist, naturopath, chiropractor, or counselor. Fields like the construction industry can also be rewarding, ranging from contracting and carpentry to design and development. Your choice made, you're determined to succeed!

Power Plays

You feel most happy when you're in control of something, but determining the nature of power is an arduous task if you're going to do it right. If you're too rigid, then you can fall behind the times or lose the valuable support of others, but you also know that if you're not using your power, somebody else will want it! By maintaining an open mind and attitudes that allow room for growth and experimentation, you understand that power is actually a means to an end. Once you achieve the position you desire, it becomes readily apparent why you're there, and others move toward your leadership.

Ultimately, you can become a kind of icon if you temper your personal power through a loving heart. Since you have no interest in undermining what you've worked so hard to achieve, you appreciate situations in which others are making the most of their power. By honoring the traditions of the past but moving beyond outworn or archaic practices or attitudes, you will keep a strong power base. Lording power over others ultimately weakens your ability to lead effectively, and as you take full responsibility for yourself, you can reflect attitudes which attract steadfast respect.

Famous Capricorns

Carlo Benetton, Robert Bly, Humphrey Bogart, David Bowie, Al Capone, Tia Carrere, A. J. Foyt, Cuba Gooding, Jr., Conrad Hilton, Diane Keaton, Mao Zedong, Henri Matisse, Sir Isaac Newton, Edgar Allan Poe, Sulamith Wulfing

The Year Ahead for Capricorn

Shaping a new platform for your personal progress can be exciting during 2001, since you'll have ample opportunities to exercise your creative abilities and hone your special talents in the process. It is your uniqueness, coupled with common sense, that opens doors, but you're also confirming the value of your preparation and hard work, and you may finally experience the mutual benefits of a supportive partnership.

From January through July, the planet Jupiter moves through the work-related area of your solar chart, bringing better working conditions while challenging you to strengthen your productivity. This can also be a period of improvement in your overall health, especially if you're building positive attitudes and adopting a fitness regimen which increases your endurance. It's tempting to be self-indulgent, or to ignore your body's needs, since this cycle can indicate general good health—but if you do fall into such behaviors, the price you pay can be the creation of cumbersome burdens. From July 12 through the remainder of the year, Jupiter transits in the sign of Cancer, marking a time when your life can be enhanced through cooperative partnership endeavors and expanded social opportunities. Attracting good fortune is one element of this transit, and the more you show gratitude and generosity, the more likely you are to strengthen the positive influence of this cycle.

Saturn, your planetary ruler, completes its transit in complementary connection to your Sun in April, and then moves into the sector of your life dealing with self-improvement and daily routine. For the next two years you'll experience a series of situations which help you fine-tune your priorities until they are in harmony with your higher needs. It can be much like the effect of taking lessons to improve your abilities in any field, learning techniques and tricks of the trade to become more proficient—except the abilities are life skills, and your talent is to express yourself with greater effectiveness and clarity.

The outer planets—Uranus, Neptune, and Pluto—are moving through their slow paces, stimulating changes in the way you're connecting to your spirituality and the manner in which you're using your resources. Think of the next few years as the time when you're "getting up to speed" on multiple levels.

The eclipse cycles and transits of the Nodes of the Moon have strong significance for you during 2001. The Moon's eclipses in January, July, and December help you uncover some of your hidden motivations in connection with your personal relationships, and actually have a greater significance for you this year than the Sun's eclipses. These influences will be further defined in the monthly sections which follow. The influence of the Moon's Nodes involves a stronger awareness of your deeper feelings. You may be more willing to let others get close to you, since you're discovering what you truly need from them. However, you're also ready to become the kind of partner you need and want to be, and that can bring significant changes in the way you're responding to relationships.

If you were born from December 21 to 29, you're experiencing positive reinforcement of your self-discipline and receiving rewards for maintaining your priorities. Saturn's cycle is transiting in biquintile aspect to your Sun from January through April, when extra attention to developing your talents can take you to a new level. This cycle began last summer, and if you feel you still need more time to work with a mentor or guide, take advantage of the influences during the first quarter of 2001. Then, from April through July, Saturn moves into a quincunx aspect to your Sun, marking a time when you're making adjustments in order to make the most of your resources and abilities. Health issues can emerge, prompting you to take a careful look at your physical needs and to make alterations that will ultimately strengthen the flow of your energy. You'll see excellent results if you eliminate factors blocking your energy—whether they're psychological or physical. After August, you're feeling freer, and may see faster progress and less complex circumstances. Finally, you're getting a few breaks!

If you were born from December 26 to January 2, Uranus transits in semisquare to your Sun, interrupting the status quo with a series of unanticipated changes. Although some effects of this cycle can be enjoyable, the feeling that you're not in complete control of your life can be disconcerting. Learning to flow with the changes can be difficult, particularly if you do not understand them. Since this influence lasts all year, you may be more comfortable with it as the months move along, but the quality of Uranus that's most troubling is the unexpected. You prefer to follow a reasonably predictable course, and you're discovering that either the path toward your goals is changing or your sense of what you want is undergoing a kind of revolution. Allowing room for spontaneity can make a huge difference, since your attempts to keep everything and everyone in order are likely to be disrupted on a regular basis. In sports, coaches suggest rolling with the punches—a concept that can save you lots of energy this year. Excessive resistance is likely to work against you!

If you were born from December 28 to 31, Neptune is transiting in semisextile aspect to your Sun. Your spirituality and creative sensibilities are deepened under this influence, although you may feel a little disoriented while you're getting used to the energy shift. Any artistic endeavor can be enhanced if you're applying yourself, but you cannot expect to make improvements by osmosis alone! Your search for inner peace may also be met with wondrous experiences, but if you enter with an unrepentant soul you won't fully enjoy the potential benefits. It's time to forgive and to welcome pure compassion into your life. You can also feel like you're entering a rather foggy period, but fortunately there should be sufficient visibility to navigate safely, as long as you're moving with deliberate caution. When stepping into new relationships or dealing with unfamiliar circumstances, you may see only what you want to see now, and can be misled by your own fantasies or the deceptions of others. In many ways, your strengths and weaknesses are all mirrored in the circumstances of your life at this time, and if you look upon those reflections with a pure heart, you'll see the truth.

If you were born from January 1 to 6, you're feeling the challenge of Saturn transiting in quincunx to your Sun. However, this cycle does not come into full focus until June, and then will last through May 2002. During the first part of the year, make every effort to examine your priorities, clear your path, and strengthen your support network. Because this influence lasts about a year, it may take a while to see the full effects, and after June you'll feel a need to tailor your priorities to your current situation. Completing your obligations will set you on a strong path, and this is the perfect time to eliminate things you no longer need. You'll also benefit from an assessment of your overall health, and altering your routine, diet, and attitudes can bring amazing improvements. Resisting the need to make changes can, instead, undermine your vitality, and you could discover that you're standing in the way of your own growth and progress.

If you were born from January 2 to 7, Pluto's influence helps you express a new level of personal strength. Transiting in semisextile to your Sun this year, Pluto's transformational energy helps you take steps that will allow you to move to a different platform. In many respects you're working from the inside, out—and you can become much more aware of the power of your inner guidance. You're removing many layers of resistance that have built up over the years, and uncovering your wholeness. Have you ever refinished a piece of vintage furniture? This influence is much like that process—you're working away, getting rid of layers of worn or damaged lacquer and exposing the beauty of the wood beneath. What you do during the restoration process is up to you! Envision what you want your life to become and who you want to be. This is your chance to recover your power on your own terms, leaving behind the vestiges of the past.

If you were born from January 8 to 16, you're altering the way you express yourself while Uranus transits in semisextile to your Sun. There's a quality of excitement in your life, and you may feel that you're ready for innovative directions. The changes you made in the early 1990s need to be brought up to date, or, if you were resistant to new technologies or did not have an opportunity to fully break free, you can now take the next steps. The manner in which you're using your resources is of crucial importance, since you need to feel free, and making wasteful decisions can have a dear price—accumulating excessive debts will be entirely too burdensome. You're the master at discovering the many uses of anything, and now you can put that talent to work through measures that emphasize the value and worth of anything or anyone—including yourself.

If you were born from January 15 to 20, you're beginning to feel that your life is more under your control. Saturn continues its cycle in trine aspect to your Sun which began last summer, and from January through May you're building on the progress that started in 2000. The foundations you establish now can serve you for some time to come; it's important that you target the development of situations which will support your hopes and dreams. Additionally, the discipline and focus you show now can act to accelerate your progress in career and in matters of personal development. You're in your element—enjoy it!

Tools to Make a Difference

You have a keen appreciation for anything that will improve the results of the task at hand, and have an uncanny knack of finding multiple uses for just about everything. This is the perfect time to put those talents to work as you seek ways to increase your effectiveness and productivity. Shifting your habits can become an amazing tool for proficiency, and observing when and how you're wasting your resources is a good beginning. That accomplished, you can make highly effective alterations!

Your target this year is your overall endurance and vitality. You may be rather accident-prone, too, and developing a more graceful connection to your physical form can be helpful. Study martial arts, dance, yoga, or tai chi. If you've been ignoring any "repairs"—like knee or hip repairs—this is the time to put them on the agenda so you can regain your full momentum. Or, you may simply need to exercise and fortify the muscles of the legs, hips, abdomen, and lower back to provide better support for your skeleton. Strengthen your bones by supplementing your diet with additional calcium and vitamin D, and help eliminate the effects of inflammation by including foods high in Omega-3 fatty acids (fish, flax seeds, and walnuts are great sources).

Chakra balancing and polarity therapy may be especially helpful for you now, and unlocking your body through flexibility and relaxation can have an amazing effect on your overall sense of well-being. To diminish the effects of gravity and aging, considering using devices such as a slant board, an antigravity swing, or gravity boots which can aid you in reversing blood circulation. The final tool that will be exceptionally helpful for you this year is one of outreach. It's time to experience the benefits of reaching out to help teach or mentor others. What you'll gain in the process will be unequaled by anything you've experienced before.

♑

Affirmation for the Year

I embrace my responsibilities with love!

Capricorn/January

In the Spotlight
Your enthusiasm about manifesting your goals gets your year off to a fantastic start! Concentrating on your top priorities, you're making a bold statement and can advance your reputation.

Wellness and Keeping Fit
Whether you're involved in team sports, fitness class, or working on an individual program, you'll benefit from the guidance of a coach or trainer, and will appreciate the challenge of meeting new fitness goals. It's time to bring yourself to the next level.

Love and Life Connections
You may fall head over heels from January 1 through the lunar eclipse on January 9, and things can get serious before you know it. While the thrill can be delicious, watch for signals that shed light on whether or not it's the real thing. An existing relationship is tested, especially if you've been feeling dissatisfied or have been reluctant to expose your vulnerability. If you find you have a roving eye after January 23, ask yourself what you're really looking for.

Finance and Success
Before you pay too much, explore options on expenditures made from January 1-6, since you might be missing a great bargain if you're in a hurry. There's another temptation, but this one's an impulse buy near the New Moon on January 24, and you might be drawn to something you don't really need. Presentations and meetings give you a chance to strut your stuff, and you're most persuasive from January 8-26.

Cosmic Insider Tip
The lunar eclipse on January 9 can indicate a turnaround in a relationship or an ending regarding a contract. Reaching conscious closure makes all the difference.

Rewarding Days: 4, 5, 12, 13, 17, 21, 22, 23, 27, 31

Challenging Days: 1, 2, 8, 9, 14, 15, 25, 29, 30

Affirmation for the Month
I am clearly aware of the impact of my words and actions.

Capricorn/February

In the Spotlight
Money matters require extra time and attention, and contractual arrangements can prove frustrating. Your patience with the process allows you to take a steady course, even if the situations (and people) around you are stormy.

Wellness and Keeping Fit
Slowing your pace makes a huge difference, especially if circumstances at work are more stressful and demanding. You need ample time to rejuvenate, and a bit of pampering is in order. Schedule a massage at least once this month.

Love and Life Connections
Beautify your home, adding the comforts that make you feel positively secured in your personal space. A gathering of steadfast friends can be enjoyable from February 1-14, although you'll be happier if plans are simple and down-to-earth. After February 15 you might feel better withdrawing from the public eye to enjoy your most intimate relationships without interference from the outside. A getaway on February 24 can be romantically inspiring.

Finance and Success
With Mercury retrograding from February 4-25 and frustrating aspects involving Mars and Saturn, there are likely to be financial blocks and disagreements over costs. You're not likely to waste your own resources, but may still end up spending more than you want. Avoid signing contracts this month.

Cosmic Insider Tip
The past can rear its head from February 6-17, and if unfinished business arises, you'll do yourself a favor by addressing it and getting it out of the way once and for all!

Rewarding Days: 1, 9, 10, 13, 18, 19, 23, 24, 28

Challenging Days: 5, 6, 7, 11, 12, 25, 26, 27

Affirmation for the Month
I am protective of all that is most precious and valuable to me.

Capricorn/March

In the Spotlight
Problems behind the scenes can make you nervous, although open discussion allows everyone to know where things stand. Your unrest may stem from knowing that others are envious of you, but you're not likely to give them reasons to undermine your position.

Wellness and Keeping Fit
You'll rest easiest in familiar surroundings. Create the feeling of vacation by making room for retreat or meditation. Your inner fitness directs your overall health, with your spirituality playing a significant role in healing.

Love and Life Connections
Sharing your ideals and philosophies can forge a powerful bond with those of like values near the Full Moon on March 9. However, you're likely to experience a separation if your spiritual path is divergent from another's, and this can include breaking from a family tradition. It's necessary to be true to yourself first, since those who appreciate you for who you are will make room for your differences. The question remains if you can do the same.

Finance and Success
On first impression you may wonder if they're really serious about a contract offer, so before you agree you'll need to research all the particulars. Job descriptions can be an uncomfortable issue, especially if your expectations do not mesh. Practical considerations work to your advantage, so show others the value of what you're bringing to the table.

Cosmic Insider Tip
This is the perfect time to repair anything that's not working properly. Temporary fixes fall apart during the Full Moon on March 9, but at least you'll know precisely what's wrong!

Rewarding Days: 1, 8, 9, 12, 17, 18, 22, 27, 28

Challenging Days: 4, 5, 6, 10, 11, 24, 25, 26, 31

Affirmation for the Month
I am releasing the past with love.

Capricorn/April

In the Spotlight
Family matters take center stage, and although you may be focusing on activities at home, you'll have to make an effort to squeeze in time for yourself. Rewards are forthcoming, and all your hard work pays off with entertaining results before month's end.

Wellness and Keeping Fit
To balance your energy, consider integrating techniques like chi gung, hatha yoga, or tai chi into your daily routine. In your work and home environments, energy flow can also be in need of redirection. Feng shui principles can make a significant difference.

Love and Life Connections
Whether you're moving, redecorating, rearranging furniture, or altering the particular purpose of rooms to suit the changing needs of your family, it's time to eliminate clutter, clean closets, and bring a fresh energy to your home. By the New Moon on April 23, you're more settled and ready to enjoy the love surrounding you. You may even find yourself rather enamored with a charming relationship stemming from shared ideas from April 22-30.

Finance and Success
Like storm clouds gathering, you sense a change in the atmosphere at work or in the world around you. New procedures, alterations in leadership, or integration of different goals can give you reason to question your level of dedication. If you're excited about the possibilities arising after April 20, you may redouble your efforts. If not, it's likely that you'll be seeking alternatives of your own fairly soon.

Cosmic Insider Tip
Venus turns direct, Saturn moves into Gemini, and the Sun enters earthy Taurus—all on April 20. New trends emerge, with a collective focus on knowledge, travel, and information exchange.

Rewarding Days: 5, 6, 9, 13, 14, 15, 20, 23, 24

Challenging Days: 1, 7, 8, 21, 22, 27, 28, 29

Affirmation for the Month
My mind is open to innovative ideas and fresh faces!

Capricorn/May

In the Spotlight
Putting your security needs at top priority helps you identify immediate goals which will form the stepping stones to your advancement. Your creative, no-nonsense approach to the tasks at hand is in high demand from everyone.

Wellness and Keeping Fit
An old injury or physical weakness can flare up, especially if you've been ignoring your body's needs. There's information available that can help. Couple this with knowledge and a responsible attitude, and you're heading toward healing.

Love and Life Connections
Venusian influences soften stress at home, helping to ease tension and invite greater comfort and sharing. Passions are strong during the Full Moon on May 7, but there can be disagreements involving personal tastes which lead to disputes. It's probably not the color of the upholstery that bothers you as much as your sense that you're not being appreciated! Before you withdraw into your shell, make an attempt to determine what's really troubling you.

Finance and Success
Instituting different procedures or integrating technological changes may ultimately upgrade productivity, but you're likely to be wondering what "they" are thinking if the new organization leaves everyone confused. It's a good time to slow down and concentrate on mastering skills, training those who need direction, or setting up routines which lead to improvements.

Cosmic Insider Tip
Surface answers will not satisfy you, and instead of dressing up the facade, you're looking for ways to improve things at the most fundamental level. Your insights are not going unnoticed!

Rewarding Days: 2, 3, 6, 7, 11, 12, 17, 21, 22, 29, 30

Challenging Days: 4, 5, 18, 19, 20, 25, 26, 31

Affirmation for the Month
I am tolerant of others.

Capricorn/June

In the Spotlight
Tackling a creative project can lead to success, and you'll enjoy taking advantage of entertaining options as a reward for your efforts at work. Distractions can frustrate your ability to maintain your concentration, especially if equipment fails to operate correctly.

Wellness and Keeping Fit
Watching for detours or breakdowns saves you the potential for accidents or agitation. An undercurrent of anxiety leaves you feeling out of sorts, but balancing rest and work keeps tension at bay.

Love and Life Connections
Misunderstandings over the most ridiculous things can run rampant, and you may feel that you're making matters worse. Although thinking before you speak is a great idea, you do still need to keep lines of communication open, since your partner might interpret your silence as a lack of caring. Brewing problems can reach a critical point during the solar eclipse on June 21, although this is a time to clarify exactly what you want.

Finance and Success
While Murphy's Law usually seems laughable, you're seeing ample evidence that it's working quite well. Mercury's retrograde from June 4-28 seems to mark a period when things are not only going wrong, but when you're also uncovering information that causes you to question how effectively anybody is doing his or her job. You're not usually one to jump to conclusions, so take your time before determining the best course of action.

Cosmic Insider Tip
Governing your pace can be quite a task, since you may discover that moderation places you in the slow lane. That's fine. The fast lane is where all the accidents are happening this month!

Rewarding Days: 3, 7, 8, 13, 17, 18, 25, 26, 30

Challenging Days: 1, 6, 14, 15, 16, 21, 22, 27, 28, 29

Affirmation for the Month
I am a caring and loving person.

Capricorn/July

In the Spotlight
Partnerships and social situations can demand more than you're willing to give. You're discovering the limits of your flexibility, which means you're also running into your boundaries and where others may be showing a lack of consideration.

Wellness and Keeping Fit
Competitive situations providing a healthy challenge may be just the impulse you need to attain better performance levels. However, you may opt out if anyone fails to comply with rules of fair play. Consider working with a personal trainer after July 20.

Love and Life Connections
You may be feeling extrasensitive during the Moon's eclipse in Capricorn on July 5, although it can be a good time to define the best direction for a relationship. A time-out can help if you simply need to sort through priorities, and after July 13 better circumstances can lead to greater acceptance of your needs and openness in communication. If you're single, playing the field may be more comfortable than commitment, but that's likely to change!

Finance and Success
Backtracking and trouble-shooting is paying off, and you're seeing the advantages of combining your efforts with others whose dedication matches your own. Contracts and partnerships fare best after July 14, and the New Moon on July 20 is highly auspicious. Consult with experts if you cannot satisfy your concerns through your own research. Temporary arrangements may be the least risky.

Cosmic Insider Tip
Cooperative ventures work like a well-oiled machine if roles are clarified and your values are unified.

Rewarding Days: 1, 4, 5, 6, 10, 14, 15, 23, 24, 28, 31

Challenging Days: 2, 3, 12, 13, 19, 20, 25, 26

Affirmation for the Month
I am attracting good fortune and abundance to share with others.

Capricorn/August

In the Spotlight
Through joining your resources with others your accomplishments increase and your opportunities expand. Partnership options not only improve, they light up your life. Your commitments open new doors, love grows, and abundance flows!

Wellness and Keeping Fit
Joining a class or pairing up with others whose skills complement your own can spark your enthusiasm. Your vitality improves by leaps and bounds—but only if you're taking an active role in the process. Watching sports on TV doesn't count!

Love and Life Connections
Old emotional wounds resulting from a breach of trust require you to look deep within your heart: are you holding unrealistic expectations of yourself or others? Open agreements and a clear understanding help you to decide if you can move into real intimacy. Clarify expectations in the social realm and with your sweetheart from August 1-5, then, after August 14, love can readily soothe your heart and allow you to forge an uplifting bond.

Finance and Success
Presentations and proposals advance your position, although you may be working on details of the budget through August 14. Leave ample room for reasonable overruns and you'll be ready to move forward from August 15-31 with a plan that can grow quickly toward success. Business travel, advertising, and promotional activities give you a chance to advance your career after August 24.

Cosmic Insider Tip
Putting outstanding resources to work can bring prosperity to your partner, but you may also experience exceptional benefit from a partner's good fortune.

Rewarding Days: 1, 2, 6, 10, 11, 12, 19, 20, 23, 24, 28, 29

Challenging Days: 8, 9, 13, 15, 16, 21, 22

Affirmation for the Month
I am grateful for the abundance flowing through my life.

Capricorn/September

In the Spotlight
Your outreach and opportunities to grow professionally improve, and through sharing your knowledge and expertise with others you're establishing a more secure position. Taking an assertive but considerate posture advances your reputation.

Wellness and Keeping Fit
After a long period of compensating for physical limitations, you're on the other side and ready to set more challenging goals. Mars activates your Sun, and your vitality gets a big boost. Pace yourself to avoid burning out too quickly!

Love and Life Connections
Delving into the insecurities which trigger your inhibitions can lead to a more intense connection with your true love during the Full Moon on September 2. Consider getting away for the weekend to explore your connection from a fresh perspective. Looking for love? Travel, cultural pursuits, or activities which develop your mind and spirit can lead to an amazing meeting of heart and soul.

Finance and Success
A message or review of an agreement opens the way for discussions, which lead to fresh professional terrain. Your capacity for positive leadership emerges with a flourish after September 9, although you might surprise some in authority who thought they had you pegged as something else! Take care with the manner in which you assert yourself, since you can accidentally step on sensitive toes on your way up the ladder.

Cosmic Insider Tip
As one situation runs its course, new directions emerge. The lag time during September 2-17 is filled with networking activities that set the stage for your next endeavor.

Rewarding Days: 2, 3, 7, 8, 15, 16, 20, 24, 25, 29, 30

Challenging Days: 4, 5, 6, 11, 12, 13, 17, 18, 19

Affirmation for the Month
I am clearly aware of the manner in which I use my power.

Capricorn/October

In the Spotlight
Your desire to get things moving quickly may be thwarted by those who are not yet up to speed. Keep progress going by delegating responsibilities in accordance with ability, giving yourself time to focus on developing your own talents and ideas more fully.

Wellness and Keeping Fit
While you know your limits, you may decide to ignore them. High-risk activities can be a problem and result in setbacks, like accidents. Read the instruction manual before proceeding!

Love and Life Connections
The spiritual flow of energy with another who shares your ideals or beliefs can bring you into a more profound experience of love. Breaking away from old restraints during the Full Moon on October 2, you can also see the value of everything that has gone before, and may decide that it's time to embrace your roots and those who have nourished your real needs. You're ready to be the protector for those who rely on your support and care.

Finance and Success
The frustrations of Mercury's retrograde from October 1-22 are most annoying after October 13, when the momentum of a project can come to a screeching halt due to a breakdown in communication. Reconfirming appointments, travel plans, and other details helps you avoid some of the hassles. In the meantime, be sure the battery on your cell phone is fully charged and take important documents with you instead of just sending them ahead.

Cosmic Insider Tip
If an impasse is meant to be broken, you can probably accomplish that task after October 14. Before you take it on, however, study the situation carefully. Stopping might actually serve a purpose!

Rewarding Days: 4, 5, 13, 14, 17, 18, 21, 22, 23, 27, 31

Challenging Days: 1, 2, 9, 10, 11, 15, 16, 29, 30

Affirmation for the Month
I am reasonably cautious in questionable situations.

Capricorn/November

In the Spotlight
Involvement with community activities or friends whose interests complement your own has mutual advantages. You may even be drawn into political circumstances, although it could be your preference to be the power behind the throne.

Wellness and Keeping Fit
Fitness classes or team sports continue to be appealing and worthwhile. Concentrate on building your endurance. You may still be accident-prone from November 11-17, when carefully assessing conditions helps you avoid trouble.

Love and Life Connections
Although close friends bring significant joy into your life, a disagreement over fundamental values could lead to a falling out. A strong relationship survives, but a connection based upon surface attachments is likely to end. Romance can flourish if you fully trust the love you share, but in matters of the heart you may feel a bit guarded from November 1-15 and feel like just testing the situation. Could it be that you don't trust yourself?

Finance and Success
While others may respect your ideas and give indications that they're supporting you, you're looking for true allies who will use their talents and influences in the good times and the tough times. Hammering out budget details gives you a look into the true motivations of others, and may tell the real story of who's in the same ball park. Forge alliances after the New Moon on November 15.

Cosmic Insider Tip
The rules seem to be changing along with a shift in the hierarchy. During this fruit basket turnover you discover that a new plan is necessary. The question is, "Who's making the rules?"

Rewarding Days: 1, 2, 9, 10, 14, 18, 19, 23, 28, 29

Challenging Days: 5, 6, 11, 12, 13, 25, 26, 27

Affirmation for the Month
I am willing to work for the things that have true value in my life.

Capricorn/December

In the Spotlight
As the tension subsides, you're eager to let go of the past and move toward a new dawn. Your dreams show the way, and although they may paint a picture of unfamiliar territory, you'll feel excited by the prospect of uncovering and developing your talents to their fullest.

Wellness and Keeping Fit
Getting back to nature is at the top of your agenda, and enjoying the brisk days of winter can be completely invigorating. Your energy and vitality are improving, and overall health should be in the pink after December 8.

Love and Life Connections
Your fantasies can outdistance reality by a mile, but some dreams sow the seeds of fresh possibilities. Others are about letting go, and during the solar eclipse on December 14 you're releasing your attachment to an old bond and opening your heart to the embrace of pure love. Whether it's a call, an e-mail, or a chance meeting, a significant connection paves the way for understanding and lasting ties. Listen to your heart during the lunar eclipse on December 30.

Finance and Success
You may have regrets over impulsive expenditures, but after December 7 you'll feel more in control of your finances. Take the lead after December 9 by making overtures to those who can be positively influential in a project or venture. Brainstorming after December 16 leads to all kinds of exciting possibilities, and improvements in finances are only a portion of your reward. The rest is pure joy!

Cosmic Insider Tip
Actions and circumstances which flow in harmony with your true needs seem to work like a charm, but those things that are not part of your growth just don't come together. Call it destiny!

Rewarding Days: 6, 7, 11, 15, 16, 20, 21, 25, 26

Challenging Days: 2, 3, 8, 9, 10, 14, 22, 23, 29, 30

Affirmation for the Month
I am always directed by the wisdom of my Higher Self.

Capricorn Action Table

These dates reflect the best—but not the only—times for success and ease in these activities, according to your Sun sign.

	JAN	FEB	MAR	APR	MAY	JUN	JUL	AUG	SEPT	OCT	NOV	DEC
Move				6-21								
Start a class		23, 24	17-31	1-5								
Join a club									17	17, 18		
Ask for a raise											14	
Look for work					6-31	1-3, 29-30	1-12		1-30	24-31	1-6	
Get pro advice	8, 9	5, 6	4, 5, 31	1, 27, 28	25, 26	21, 22	18-20	15, 16	11, 12	9, 10	5, 6	2-3, 29-31
Get a loan	10, 11	7, 8	6, 7	2, 3, 30	1, 27, 28	23, 24	21, 22	17, 18	13, 14	11, 12	7, 8	4, 5
See a doctor					6-31	1, 2	1-12				27-30	1-14
Start a diet	6, 7	3, 4	2-3, 29-30	25, 26	23, 24	19, 20	16-18	13, 14	9, 10	6-8	3, 4, 30	1, 27, 28
End relationship	20											30, 31
Buy clothes				22-30	1-5							
Get a makeover												26-31
New romance				23, 24		6-30	1-4					
Vacation	12, 13	9, 10	8, 9	4-6	2-3, 29-30	2-4, 25-26	12, 13	19, 20	15, 16	13, 14	9, 10	6, 7

Aquarius

The Water Bearer
January 21 to February 19

≈

Element:	Air
Quality:	Fixed
Polarity:	Yang/Masculine
Planetary Ruler:	Uranus
Meditation:	I create unique paths by focusing my mind.
Gemstone:	Amethyst
Power Stones:	Aquamarine, black pearl, chrysocolla
Key Phrase:	I know
Glyph:	Energy currents
Anatomy:	Ankles, circulatory system
Color:	Iridescent blues, violet
Animal:	Exotic birds
Myths/Legends:	John the Baptist, Ninhursag, Deucalion
House:	Eleventh
Opposite Sign:	Leo
Flower:	Orchid
Key Word:	Unconventional

Positive Expression:	Misuse of Energy:
Humanitarian	Subversive
Self-reliant	Extremist
Ingenious	Aloof
Congenial	Undirected
Liberal	Thoughtless
Futuristic	Anarchistic
Altruistic	Deviant

Aquarius

Your Ego's Strengths and Shortcomings
Your distinctive personality is no accident. You are the consummate individualist, fascinated by the extraordinary, shining light on the untrodden paths. You're "The Reformer" of the zodiac, fanning the fires of evolutionary change, assuring that the momentum of progress continues. It is the clear and quiet whisper of your intuitive voice which guides your journey, and the pure quality of unconditional love that animates the song of your heart.

As a trendsetter, you can be comfortable wearing the expressions of your unique self. Some may see you as revolutionary, while others emulate your unmatched style. Following the herd is not your way, and situations or traditions that restrain your ability to express your creative individuality can lead you to take steps which fly in the face of the established order. It is the value you place on freedom that tests your ability to channel rebellion through responsible action. Otherwise, your tendency to rebel can leave you feeling isolated and unsupported by the world. Walking the fine line between future possibility and the acceptable bounds of reality is something you can definitely accomplish, while others use tradition as an excuse for a lack of progress. It's your unique perspective on life, forged through a universal frame of reference, which challenges you to be part of establishing a new order.

When you're light years away in your mind—reaching out to connect with your higher consciousness—you can seem aloof to those who want to hold you close. Those who understand that your quest takes you into a space of universality will become your lifelong friends and have your undying support. Through these connections your originality emerges, and your ideas and creative efforts illuminate the wisdom of unconditional love.

Shining Your Love Light
Forging a connection to a life partner requires that you feel an extraordinary bond of friendship and passion. You need to know that your relationship supports the individuality of both partners and honors your autonomy, otherwise you'll keep the doors to your

heart guarded. It is through a meeting of the minds that you first learn to trust love, and in the space of shared ideals that you can truly experience love's transcendent joy. Until then, your logical mind can actually talk you out of loving, since the idea of "bonding" to another can seem more like prison than freedom! You know when you're looking into the eyes of love. The question is whether you're ready for the commitment necessary to allow it to blossom.

You're an air sign person, and need relationships centered around communion of ideas. With Gemini, Libra, and Aquarius you're in common territory, since you share the nature of air: mentality, sociability, and communication. Aries invites your passionate need to express yourself and keeps you on the move. Taurus holds onto everything, including you, and that can feel too restrictive. Gemini's love of ideas is delightful and engages your heart and mind. You may have to work too hard to keep Cancer's need for constant contact satisfied. With Leo, your opposite, you feel magnetic attraction but can be frustrated if he or she requires too much attention without returning the same to you. Virgo invites you to probe the depths of your soul, although intimacy is sometimes uneasy.

Your spiritual connection with Libra inspires you to explore the richness of human endeavor and your relationship is based on sharing life's beauty. Scorpio's intensity can leave you feeling inundated by a sea of implied complexities. Sagittarius can be pure fun and an unequaled friend. Although Capricorn can become a steadfast friend, control issues can prompt you to keep your distance. Connecting with another Aquarian is sometimes difficult, since there can be so much electricity that you short-circuit before you become partners. With Pisces, you share universal ideals and concerns, but you may feel that you're light years away from intimacy.

Making Your Place in the World

You're seeking a life path that will allow you to make a difference in the world. If your work gives you room to fully express your originality, then that's even better! Communications fields such as broadcasting, advertising, public relationships, sales, writing, or internet applications can provide an excellent forum for expressing your ideas. Or, you might be drawn into public service through politics, social work, or civil service. Owning your own business can be rewarding, especially if you're marketing your uncommon creations or working in human outreach fields like psychology or astrology.

Developing your talents in the arts—from visionary art to theater to original music—can be right up your alley. Also, scientific fields can be suitable to your abilities: electronics, theoretical mathematics, meteorology, aviation, computer science, astronomy, or the space industry all have their appeal. Wherever you let your light shine, your uniqueness will not be overlooked.

Power Plays

When there is a cause tugging at your soul, there's little that will stop you from using all the power you can muster to make a difference. It is your soul's challenge to learn how to harness evolutionary energy and create a climate ripe for change. You're not here to maintain the status quo, but were born instead to a life dedicated to opening the pathways few have seen. Your piercing visionary sensibilities allow you to see the places and circumstances where power is abused or wasted, and to feel a union with your life purpose you make it your quest to eliminate as many of those abuses as possible.

While you may not seek power for the sake of personal recognition, you may want to use your influence to make a difference in the path of human evolution. It is important, though, that you watch out for your ego, since your inner shadow, driven by selfish motives, can steal the light you long to show the world.

Famous Aquarians

Richard Dean Anderson, Jack Benny, Lewis Carroll, Geena Davis, James Dean, Clark Gable, Minnie Driver, Andrew Greeley, Gene Hackman, Jerome Kern, Jack Lemmon, Abraham Lincoln, Bill Maher, Oral Roberts, Rip Torn

The Year Ahead for Aquarius

After keeping a firm rein on your self-expression, you're finally breathing easier and finding that you can soar to greater heights. The breakthrough can catapult you into experiences which challenge your abilities, providing exceptional opportunities to let your unique talents shine like never before. Think of this as your time to experiment with all you've ever dreamt of becoming!

Jupiter's cycle of expansion focuses its energy through urging you to open the doors to your heart from January through July. Whether you choose to apply your heart's desire to developing love relationships or enhancing your artistic expression, it's time to move into a broader arena and allow yourself to give all you can, remembering that the flow also begs you to open and receive. It can be a process of pure beauty! Then, in July, Jupiter moves into Cancer for the remainder of the year, and during this cycle you'll be making a series of adjustments, determining exactly how far you can go and when you need to pull back to regroup. Watch your indulgences, since these cycles each tempt your desires, and you may find that you're overdoing it, thereby limiting yourself in the long run!

Until April, Saturn is completing its cycle in Taurus, but then, on April 20th, Saturn finally moves into a friendly element, making its ingress into Gemini, where it will continue for another two years. This is a significant change, since many of the restraints and blocks which have been standing in the way of your progress are finally ending. Completing the steps that will allow you to move onto a more stable platform of self-expression will be easier, and your experience and expertise grow as a result. It's a good time to make long-term commitments or to become involved in guiding others toward their own self-development.

Uranus, your planetary ruler, continues its cycle in Aquarius, stimulating your urge to express your most individualistic traits and abilities. Neptune's slow cycle in Aquarius adds an element of sensitivity and an urge to surrender to your spirituality. Pluto, the energy of transformational change, targets your sense of direction and is indicative of a time when you're altering your life path so that you can fulfill your hopes of making a difference in the world. The years when these three planetary transits have their strongest impact are during the times they make exact aspects to your Sun. Check the lists below to determine when it's your turn!

The influence of the solar and lunar eclipses is explained in the monthly forecasts which follow. However, the area of your life stimulated by the eclipses is symbolized by the cycle of the Moon's Nodes. During 2001, the transit of the nodes of the Moon puts you in touch with how you feel about taking care of yourself. Your physical weak links are more exposed now—and it's the psychological and physical connection to your sense of well-being that becomes more apparent. This is the perfect time to delve into your repressed memories, or the unresolved emotional issues you've failed to address. Think of this as your year of "self-improvement," and a time when you're ready to alter your lifestyle to support and reflect your health needs.

If you were born from January 21 to 24, it is during the first six months of 2001 that you'll feel most strongly empowered. From January through March, Jupiter transits in trine aspect to your Sun, continuing a cycle which began in July of last year, and you're experiencing exceptional opportunities to expand your horizons. This influence encourages you to feel more self-confident, and you're more capable of attracting situations which lead to advancement and personal growth. Target the first quarter of 2001 as the time to make presentations or initiate important new directions. Then, during April and May, while Saturn transits in trine aspect to your Sun, you'll be ready to focus your energy and attention on the most advantageous situations. Your ability to determine your priorities is stronger, and it is during April and May that contracts and commitments can clearly reflect your aims while supporting your personal needs.

If you were born from January 25 to 30, Neptune's transit in conjunction to your Sun heightens your creative sensibilities. This cycle can only happen once in your lifetime, and marks a period when you're experiencing true grace. If you've been uncertain of the role Spirit plays in your life, you're seeing evidence of the intangible, and can surrender your ego to the needs of your inner and higher self. If you've been struggling with old hurts, now you can forgive and move on. As a time of developing your artistry, this cycle is unmatched. Moving into the flow, dancing with your muse, now seems natural. You're also feeling the stabilizing influence of Saturn in trine aspect to your Sun from May through July. This can be helpful, since one effect of living under Neptune's rays is a lack of clarity in mundane matters. Saturn's influence provides a kind of "reality check," so if you're wondering whether or not your urge to sell everything and move to the mountains is a good idea, look at it very seriously from May through July, when you can weigh your dreams against a backdrop of realistic needs. Because Neptune's cycle lasts all year, its effect on your health can be more marked. There's a tendency to ignore the the physical, since your focus is on the otherworldly. You can become sensitive to environmental influences, and substances that you cannot see or taste can more easily penetrate your body. You might even discover that you cannot tolerate certain medications or foods. Even though you may usually be fairly realistic about your health, this year you can fall into denial if your energy is faltering, and can be tempted to avoid seeking a professional opinion. Chances are, you're fine. But it's still a good idea to have that annual physical.

If you were born from January 31 to February 5, you're feeling more focused and self-disciplined while Saturn transits in trine aspect to your Sun. This influence does not begin until June, but it will last until May of 2002. One of the key factors of Saturn's trine is that you will feel more in control of your destiny, or, at the least, that you'll be able to apply sufficient self-discipline and clarity to your choices. You'll be able to see the effects of taking charge of your life. It's the perfect year to make serious alterations in your career—the kinds of changes that fortify your reputation or enhance your abilities. Educational options can be especially important, or you may take actions which serve as the types of landmarks usually attributed to completing academic accomplishments. Taking on the responsibilities which allow you to exercise greater influence and utilize your talents to the fullest can be exceptionally gratifying, or you may finally be ready to make commitments because they fit your life now. You're also poised to eliminate attitudes, habits, and circumstances which you've outgrown or which create stumbling blocks. Now, it's time to build reliable stepping stones which lead to the fulfillment of your potential.

If you were born from February 1 to 6, Pluto is transiting in sextile aspect to your Sun. This period represents a cycle of transformation in which you can make marvelous alterations to your life. There may also be shifts in the world that make it easier for you to change, or others may be more cooperative and supportive. In fact, your connection to influential people can seem almost miraculous if you're putting forth sufficient effort and energy. It's not a time when things just drop in your lap. Rather, this is one of those cycles which stimulates your need to become whole, but you have to do the work if you're going to feel the full effect of personal transformation. The manner in which you use your own influence is also critical, since you can be in a position to make a difference for others, and by doing so, you can experience amazing rewards. Think of this as the time when you are able to access all the tools necessary to heal and revitalize your life. All you have to do is use them!

If you were born from February 7 to 15, you're experiencing a year of exciting change while Uranus transits in conjunction to your Sun. You've felt this energy building for a while, but now your personal voltage level is reaching maximum intensity. It's not likely you'll have a repeat of this cycle, since it can only happen once every eighty-seven years, but the effects of the actions and decisions made this year are likely to have a lifelong influence. You may feel more rebellious, and are certainly not as likely to allow anyone to tell you what to do or how to do it. It's your turn to show the world what you have to offer, and using all resources available (and developing a few of your own)—you're singing your own song with gusto! Relationships undergo change, although you may simply end situations which have felt too inhibiting. Surprisingly enough, sometimes it's the other people around you who change—since the universe tends to help you break ties you no longer need. The most amazing quality of this cycle can be the manner in which you take advantage of unexpected happenings, and whether or not you're making freedom-oriented responses to the things you cannot control. Your ingenuity functions at its ultimate level, and you're also primed to develop your intuitive abilities. This is a cycle of awakening. The lights are on, and you can see your options. All you have to do is take a deep breath and take the actions that transport you into a pure expression of your true essence.

If you were born from February 16 to 19, the period of testing represented by Saturn transiting in square aspect to your Sun is almost at an end. This cycle began in June of last year, and will finally be complete in April of 2001. While the restraints and limitations of Saturn subside during the spring, it may take a few months to feel that your momentum is re-established. Take a good look, regroup, and use the rest of the year to make stabilizing choices. Next year you'll be making radical change, and you need a steady platform for launching your dreams!

Tools to Make a Difference

You may actually invent a few devices of your own to alter and heal your life during 2001. Or, it's quite possible you'll rediscover some old techniques and tools, bringing them into twenty-first century applications. Since you're getting past many of your own barriers, you can also begin to take advantage of things which may have been interesting to you in the past, but now you're ready to actually take advantage of or fully develop them. You're hungry for ideas, and studying ancient wisdom can be enlightening. Philosophical and metaphysical concepts can take your consciousness to the space that allows you to unify your mind with the Source.

Your target zone physically is the nervous system and circulatory system, and it's time to heal these areas of your body. Whether you're changing your diet to support these needs or improving the balance of work, rest, and fitness activity, now is the time to take charge of your health. Adding foods rich in Omega-3 fatty acids is especially important. Additionally, keeping your synaptic and brain functions up to par with ample B-vitamins, or supplements like ginkgo biloba can be helpful. Your body is also likely to respond more favorably to healing techniques like acupuncture, magnetic therapy, and polarity therapy. Using tools such as tuning forks to help alter your vibrational level can be especially invigorating and relaxing, depending on which your body needs most.

To gain deeper insights into the functioning of your mind and consciousness, spend more time with your inner self. Learn mindfulness. Whether you're meditating or taking a daily time-out, your reflections can help you let go of tension and open to your creative flow. Using images from divinatory cards or runes can help you probe your connection to higher mind. You might also feel more inclined to release your creative ideas when listening to music appropriate for your expression—or through creating music of your own. The alterations you make on subtle vibrational levels can allow you to move into a profoundly sacred expression of life.

≈

Affirmation for the Year

I am an instrument of Divine Love.

Aquarius/January

In the Spotlight
Pressure on the career front can arise from circumstances which seem unreasonably competitive, or you may be working against deadlines and under scrutiny from those fighting progress. Your introduction of objectivity into the situation can diffuse conflicts.

Wellness and Keeping Fit
The harbingers of stress are everywhere, and your salvation arises from the time you take to pull away from daily turmoil. Release frustrations through exercise, but avoid mishaps by staying away from high-risk situations after January 18.

Love and Life Connections
Family concerns and dealing with unfinished business can take up your free time, and you may be feeling rather spent if you're around emotional outbursts from others. Knowing when you can have an effective influence and when to step away saves you from getting involved in disputes which are not your own. You're feeling more in charge of your life after January 21, and in a great position to set new ground rules during the Aquarius New Moon on January 24.

Finance and Success
You may be concerned that a project is lagging behind due to unreliable or inefficient actions from others, although problems come to the surface with the Moon's eclipse on January 9. To some extent, after January 22, you can extricate yourself from the situation and focus on the areas where you can make a difference—even though outside resistance still looms.

Cosmic Insider Tip
Despite your growing impatience with the old school, it's still necessary to give them their due. Excessive push only results in friction. Let innovations speak for themselves.

Rewarding Days: 2, 6, 7, 14, 15, 19, 24, 25, 29, 30

Challenging Days: 4, 5, 9, 10, 11, 16, 17, 18, 31

Affirmation for the Month
I am making the best use of my strengths.

Aquarius/February

In the Spotlight
Affiliations with others who appreciate and support your talents can lead to significant rewards. Advancement may be promised, but not yet fully realized, since there are a few things to finish before you're at your pinnacle.

Wellness and Keeping Fit
You may be worrying more than you realize. Free your mind by actively letting go of physical tension. A massage, extra time in the hot tub, or daily stretching can help. And remember to breathe!

Love and Life Connections
Dragging the vestiges from the past into the present can seem like swimming with concrete fins. Releasing self-defeating attitudes is getting easier, but old hurts can creep into your heart during the Full Moon on February 8. To trust love you must first trust yourself. Objectivity comes from a dear friend whose presence activates true joy, making it easier to find contentment. Consider returning to a meaningful place as a stepping stone toward reshaping your future.

Finance and Success
While Mercury retrogrades from February 4-25 you're given a second chance to explore the reasons for your own or another's hesitation. Fortunately, calling in others whose resources can fill in the gaps works to your advantage, and by February 17 you're moving forward with great composure. Returning a favor builds the kind of loyalty you crave, although you may have to forgive a few shortcomings in the process.

Cosmic Insider Tip
The tendency for getting carried away can be epidemic from February 18-25, although unifying your efforts with others to assure logical actions helps—a little.

Rewarding Days: 3, 4, 11, 12, 15, 16, 20, 21, 25, 26

Challenging Days: 1, 2, 7, 8, 13, 14, 28

Affirmation for the Month
My words and actions arise from a heart filled with joy!

Aquarius/March

In the Spotlight
Forging a close connection with others strengthens your network of support. You're making breakthroughs despite slow progress from those insistent on clinging to the past.

Wellness and Keeping Fit
If you've been waiting for the perfect time to enroll in a fitness class or instruction in martial arts or sports, this is the time to get the ball rolling. You're eager to embrace a challenge and will appreciate the encouragement of an instructor.

Love and Life Connections
Spend time in the company of friends or connecting with siblings as a means of creating a matrix of collaboration and communication. Through providing complementary supports you can all prosper, and find that you're redefining a meaningful sense of family in the process. Your love life moves into more rewarding territory, too, and it's time to break old patterns of interaction in order to forge a better understanding of your mutual needs.

Finance and Success
Equipment purchases or repairs can be costly, and expenditures near the Full Moon on March 9 may be a source of worry or concern, especially if you're rushed through the process. Revise budgets early in the month, and then after the New Moon on March 25 you'll be ready to put your plans into action with greater confidence. Business meetings fare best after March 19, but be alert to the hidden agenda held by those who seem to be power hungry.

Cosmic Insider Tip
For the next three months your energy and vision can be the beacon guiding a high-impact program or project, and you're attracting others whose talents complement your own.

Rewarding Days: 2, 3, 10, 11, 14, 15, 16, 19, 20, 21, 29, 30

Challenging Days: 1, 6, 7, 8, 12, 13, 27, 28

Affirmation for the Month
I am making the best use of all my resources.

Aquarius/April

In the Spotlight
Fueled by a series of inspirational ideas sparked by your interaction with others, you're eager to bring factions together and can be instrumental in creating significant improvements. It's good to know you're not alone, after all!

Wellness and Keeping Fit
A gradual improvement in your abilities instills confidence to pursue more challenging feats, although honoring your limitations will help you avoid injury or accidents. You're probably willing to risk a few scrapes or sore muscles in the name of progress, though.

Love and Life Connections
Return to your deeper feelings, reminding yourself why you're with your partner. It's time to release the weight of your defenses and open up. Taking time away, or returning to your favorite place for a romantic weekend or dinner, sparks an urge to renew your commitment during the Full Moon on April 8. If you're free and looking for romance, you're ready to determine why you've been keeping your heart locked away. Love sometimes needs an invitation!

Finance and Success
To strengthen your career foundation, dust off little-used skills and put them to work. In fact, bringing your skills and knowledge up to date by attending a workshop or convening with others in your field can be especially helpful from April 1-20. The economic climate changes after April 20, and then you can bring everything closer to your vision of the future!

Cosmic Insider Tip
Take a look at your database or stack of projects, and get rid of the things just taking up space. Or, delegate ventures which do not hold your interest to someone who might enjoy them.

Rewarding Days: 7, 8, 11, 12, 16, 17, 25, 26

Challenging Days: 2, 3, 9, 10, 23, 24, 30

Affirmation for the Month
My thoughts originate from a space of loving wisdom.

Aquarius/May

In the Spotlight
Flying high on the wings of your creativity, it's time to let the world in on your unique abilities. Through integrating your sense of the artistic with what you're feeling from the collective, you're right on target. You *know* if something will work. Trust that feeling!

Wellness and Keeping Fit
Recreational activities, or exercise which feels more like fun than work, enhance your fitness level and serve to raise your spirits. Laughter proves to be phenomenally healing, too, and spending time uncovering and creating joy makes you feel whole.

Love and Life Connections
Your declarations of love can arise through several sources, and your feelings can inspire your artistry. The connection to your soul is especially powerful, and through this quality you're translating the part of you that is immortal: you're building your lineage. Return to the Source during the Full Moon on May 7, and then as you emerge unified with your true self you can initiate amazing changes through love during the New Moon on May 23.

Finance and Success
An alignment with others whose ideals reflect your own truth places you on a different platform from the 1st to 8th. Whether you're working in a different unit or stepping out on your own, it's time to keep the lines of communication open and pull together resources so that everyone benefits. Eliminate dead weight from May 8-20, and set up a new long-term strategy after May 23.

Cosmic Insider Tip
If you're bidding goodbye to an old group of friends or associates you may actually feel a great sense of relief. Target the period from May 5-12 to close a chapter.

Rewarding Days: 4, 5, 8, 9, 13, 14, 15, 18, 19, 23, 24, 31

Challenging Days: 1, 6, 7, 20, 21, 22, 27, 28

Affirmation for the Month
I invite others to share the abundance of my good fortune!

Aquarius/June

In the Spotlight
Building on the momentum launched last month, this is the time to fine-tune and strengthen your efforts. Pooling your resources continues to bring positive results. Your dreams are coming to life, and your gratitude invites even greater abundance and fulfillment.

Wellness and Keeping Fit
Although you may be feeling fairly invincible, on some level your mortality whispers, reminding you that some caution will keep you safe. An adventure is in the works, and you'll enjoy it more if you have an idea of the best way to fully experience it.

Love and Life Connections
Vacationing or traveling can be just what you need to take your relationship to the level of pure ecstasy from June 1 through the Full Moon on June 6. Lighthearted entertainment brings you closer, as you experience pleasures unique to your special relationship. Although you might get a bit carried away envisioning your hopes, a need for stability helps you keep your feet on the ground when projecting your dreams with your partner.

Finance and Success
While excitement builds it's easy to forget about the lessons of the past. Fortunately, you can integrate your experience into the framework of current projects when trouble-shooting or testing your plans during Mercury's retrograde from June 4 to 27. It's time to finish what you've started if you want to maintain ultimate quality. Institute changes in routine after the Sun's eclipse on June 21.

Cosmic Insider Tip
The world of possibilities has captured everybody's imagination, and you're making a list of potential spin-offs. Meanwhile, you're drawing the support of the right people at the right time!

Rewarding Days: 1, 5, 6, 9, 10, 11, 15, 16, 19, 20, 27, 28

Challenging Days: 2, 3, 17, 18, 21, 23, 24, 25, 30

Affirmation for the Month
My intuitive insights are a powerful asset.

Aquarius/July

In the Spotlight
Love continues to grow and your commitments reshape your life. To keep your workload under control, re-evaluate your priorities and delegate tasks appropriately while your support is strong. You're making room to exercise your creativity in different directions.

Wellness and Keeping Fit
Pulling away from the action provides a chance to rejuvenate during the lunar eclipse on July 5. By concentrating on your inner self for a while you can create a new balance in your priorities and will be able to sustain the pace necessary to nourish your creativity.

Love and Life Connections
Communicating your needs and concerns with those you love keeps your connection strong from July 1-12. However, your romantic intentions are powerful all month long, and from July 10-27 you need to affirm the strength of your love. Your work can draw you away and you might seem too aloof: unless you're maintaining contact your relationship can suffer. Sometimes it's the little things that can make all the difference.

Finance and Success
Your enthusiasm can wane, particularly if you feel you're carrying excessive responsibility. After Mars turns direct on July 19 the pace begins to pick up again, with your attention focused on increasing productivity. Finances and investments grow steadily, although you're not very interested in giving them too much time since you're concentrating on improving day-to-day operations.

Cosmic Insider Tip
Take a careful look at efficiency, since it's time to reorganize and regroup. You may even be shuffling people into more appropriate jobs, although not everyone may be pleased.

Rewarding Days: 2, 3, 7, 8, 12, 13, 17, 18, 25, 26, 30

Challenging Days: 1, 14, 15, 21, 22, 27, 28

Affirmation for the Month
My values originate from pure love shining from my heart.

Aquarius/August

In the Spotlight
Cooperative interaction with others requires finesse, since you often grow impatient with anyone dragging their heels on important matters. Arrangements take on significant importance, and abuses of power sting more bitterly if you're feeling unappreciated.

Wellness and Keeping Fit
Staying active takes the edge off tension, but you're also feeling a bit competitive and will appreciate a physical outlet. Indulge your need for pampering, since a day at the spa, a massage, or other services can be remarkably rejuvenating to body, mind, and spirit.

Love and Life Connections
The Aquarius Full Moon on August 4 is a time to test the balance within your relationships and life experiences. Disproportionate situations are felt more intensely and you're ready to take action to change them, even if that means leaving behind a friend who simply cannot keep up with your transformation. Although you may not be torching the bridges, some seem to be burning on their own, altering your responsibilities and priorities.

Finance and Success
Review contracts, since you may need to negotiate different terms before agreements come up for renewal, and could decide that you are not interested in continuing in the same roles as before. Bureaucratic structures are shifting, too, and with the change in leadership you may decide that it's time to work more independently. Joint resources and tax matters need extra attention after August 14.

Cosmic Insider Tip
Saturn has begun its long opposition to Pluto, signifying a time of repair of the power structures of life. "Old reliable" methods are not so reliable now!

Rewarding Days: 3, 4, 8, 9, 13, 14, 21, 22, 26, 30, 31

Challenging Days: 10, 11, 12, 17, 18, 19, 23, 24

Affirmation for the Month
I understand and honor my promises.

Aquarius/September

In the Spotlight
Contractual agreements help clarify your direction, and dealing with legal matters now places you on solid footing for the future. In addition, business travel and educational pursuits offer opportunities to advance your reputation and career.

Wellness and Keeping Fit
Knowing when to pull back and develop your connection to your inner self helps you maintain the focus and lucidity necessary to remain creatively sharp. Extra sleep (or at least adequate sleep!) may be necessary, since your body is craving a recharge.

Love and Life Connections
By directing your focus to the spiritual quality of your love relationship you're opening the way to the visions and hopes you share as a couple. Traveling to a romantic hideaway can provide the right place to indulge your fantasies, especially if you've been feeling that things are getting entirely too routine. After September 22, reaching into a deeper level of intimacy helps to build your trust and reinforce the oneness of your relationship.

Finance and Success
Financial disputes can arise during the Full Moon on September 2 if too many loose ends remain. You're looking for definition and will be uncomfortable if you sense that you're the one holding all the responsibility while a partner or others ignore their obligations. Firm up your roles during the New Moon on September 17, so you're free to concentrate on outreach.

Cosmic Insider Tip
Share your ideas or talents only when you feel protected and sufficiently prepared. That's why contracts can be helpful!

Rewarding Days: 1, 4, 5, 9, 10, 17, 18, 22, 23, 26, 27, 28

Challenging Days: 2, 7, 8, 13, 14, 19, 20, 21

Affirmation for the Month
My thoughts, words, and actions are guided by Truth.

Aquarius/October

In the Spotlight
Knowing when to reach toward new horizons and when to wait can be difficult since you're getting mixed signals from others. Fortunately, this is a month of second chances, although you don't really like repeating yourself!

Wellness and Keeping Fit
You can exhaust your energy before you know it, or may be in circumstances where you feel more exposed. If you're out of sorts, consider scheduling time for bodywork to help balance your energy.

Love and Life Connections
Safeguarding your privacy is a high priority, since you're not interested in having prying eyes invade your personal life. You may not even feel all that comfortable talking about your deeper concerns with your partner, particularly if you know you're dealing with sensitive issues. While you can reach a breakthrough during the Full Moon on October 2, you'll feel less exposed during the New Moon on October 16.

Finance and Success
Not only is Mercury retrograde from October 1-22, but you may feel an undercurrent of mistrust—particularly with someone who seems to be operating from a hidden agenda. If you're uncertain, waiting to give the go-ahead will be to your advantage. Simple measures and small steps make more sense than making sweeping moves. After October 27 you'll be in a better position to launch new and exciting ventures.

Cosmic Insider Tip
Angry outbursts can arise after October 13 and may seem out of place with the circumstances. This is likely to be a battle that's not yours to fight, but observation can be illuminating!

Rewarding Days: 1, 2, 6, 7, 15, 16, 19, 24, 25, 29, 30

Challenging Days: 4, 5, 11, 12, 13, 17, 18, 31

Affirmation for the Month
I am grateful for the energy, care, and love shown to me by others.

Aquarius/November

In the Spotlight
You're maintaining a higher profile and can make excellent strides developing your career. However, some of your actions or ideas fly in the face of convention and can create quite a stir—but wasn't that your idea in the first place?

Wellness and Keeping Fit
With Mars in your sign this month you're feeling fired up and ready to go. It's easy to reach burnout if you're pushing past your limits, especially if you're underestimating the energy expenditure required by emotionally intense situations. Pace yourself; energy is energy!

Love and Life Connections
Getting your point across and accomplishing a meeting of hearts and minds is much easier from November 1-7. Show your lover how you feel—clearly, and with at least a little drama! Insecurities are flying around all over the place, and you may feel like you're walking through a minefield after November 9, especially if family issues have exploded. You're discovering a few sensitive spots of your own from November 10-15, but will be ready to distance yourself from situations you've outgrown afterward.

Finance and Success
Schedule conferences and sign agreements from November 2-6 or after November 23. In the interim, you're gaining recognition and credibility, but your superiors have a long list of requirements. By the New Moon on November 15 you have a handle on who wants what, and will feel more confident following your own agenda.

Cosmic Insider Tip
Taking actions without considering their impact gets you into trouble from November 5-16, and even though you feel ready to get out on your own, others may need your time and attention.

Rewarding Days: 3, 4, 11, 12, 16, 17, 20, 21, 25, 26, 27, 30

Challenging Days: 1, 2, 7, 8, 13, 14, 15, 28, 29

Affirmation for the Month
I know how to safely assert myself.

Aquarius/December

In the Spotlight
Your supporters come to your aid, and the plans and projects at the top of your priority list have a dramatic impact on your reputation. It's time to take the lead in political or special interest situations.

Wellness and Keeping Fit
Work toward building your endurance and strengthening your muscles. It's a great time to concentrate on weaker areas that need extra toning. Also, evaluate whether or not you're getting sufficient B-vitamins and add a supplement if your diet is inadequate.

Love and Life Connections
Enjoying your friends is purely magical, and you may have a chance to be with a good friend who's been distant or away for a while. Celebrate your own and other's successes during the solar eclipse on December 14, when the powerful love and support you're feeling comes full circle. After December 16 you'll be likely to crave some quiet time with your sweetheart, and will appreciate getting away from your routine during the Moon's eclipse on December 30.

Finance and Success
Bold moves from December 1-8 can leave a lasting impression on others whose influence helps to advance your reputation. You're feeling greater satisfaction with your rewards from career, and although your finances appear to improve, you may tend to overspend on impulse after December 9. Careful consideration of your long-term goals goes a long way toward determining the best ways to use your increasing resources.

Cosmic Insider Tip
Positive situations and fears alike can be blown out of proportion near the time of the solar eclipse on December 14. Stay alert to your personal boundaries to avoid feeling unduly influenced.

Rewarding Days: 1, 9, 10, 13, 14, 18, 19, 23, 27, 28

Challenging Days: 4, 5, 11, 12, 25, 26, 30

Affirmation for the Month
My goals reflect the love in my heart.

Aquarius Action Table

These dates reflect the best—but not the only—times for success and ease in these activities, according to your Sun sign.

	JAN	FEB	MAR	APR	MAY	JUN	JUL	AUG	SEPT	OCT	NOV	DEC
Move				22-30	1-5							
Start a class			25, 26	6-20						16		14
Join a club												
Ask for a raise	24, 25											
Look for work							13-29				7-25	
Get pro advice	10, 11	7, 8	6, 7	2, 3, 30	1, 27, 28	23, 24	21, 22	17, 18	13, 14	11, 12	7, 8	4, 5
Get a loan	12, 13	9, 10	8, 9	4, 5	2-3, 29-30	25, 26	23, 24	19, 20	15, 16	13, 14	9, 10	6, 7
See a doctor	1-9						13-29					16-31
Start a diet	8, 9	5, 6	4, 5, 31	1, 27-29	25, 26	21, 22	19, 20	15, 16	11, 12	9, 10	5, 6	2, 3
End relationship		8										
Buy clothes					6-31	1-2, 29-30	1-11					
Get a makeover	1-3, 24-25											
New romance					23, 24		5-31					
Vacation	14, 15	11, 12	10, 11	7, 8	4, 5, 31	1, 27, 28	25, 26	21, 22	17, 18	15, 16	11, 12	8, 9

Pisces
The Fish
February 19 to March 20

Element:	Water
Quality:	Mutable
Polarity:	Yin/Feminine
Planetary Ruler:	Neptune
Meditation:	I surrender to the heart of divine compassion.
Gemstone:	Aquamarine
Power Stones:	Amethyst, bloodstone, tourmaline
Key Phrase:	I believe
Glyph:	Two fish joined, swimming in opposite directions
Anatomy:	Feet, lymphatic system
Color:	Violet, sea green
Animal:	Fish, sea mammals
Myths/Legends:	Aphrodite, Buddha, Jesus of Nazareth
House:	Twelfth
Opposite Sign:	Virgo
Flower:	Water lily
Key Word:	Transcendence

Positive Expression:
Imaginative
Idealistic
Empathetic
Mystical
Visionary
Forgiving
Flexible

Misuse of Energy:
Escapist
Codependent
Gullible
Unconscious
Confused
Addictive
Victimized

Pisces

Your Ego's Strengths and Shortcomings
Your acute sensibilities allow you to experience life in a multidimensional manner. There's little doubt in your mind that there's more to life than tangible existence: you're connected to the realm of the spiritual through your perception and imagination. Your self-expression can range from whimsical artist to compassionate world server, and you often prefer to think of yourself as an instrument through which your higher self is expressed. These magical and mystical expressions are your connection to Neptune, the planet representing the energy of the spiritual plane.

Your inner senses have always been strong. In childhood, everyone probably said you had a vivid imagination. Has anything changed? What you're learning to express as an adult is the best way to trust and develop these sensibilities so that you're making a difference. As a result, others may seek your insightful support. In fact, in your role as "The Illusionist" of the zodiac, you're the one who can paint a picture of hope when the world is crying in despair. Sometimes the dream is necessary as a beacon to light the way beyond pain and suffering. However, you can fall victim to unscrupulous individuals who would take advantage of your sensitivity, and it's easy to lose the way if your personal boundaries are lost to situations which rob you of your power. You need a space which serves as a haven to soothe you when the world is too much to take. Whether you take time for solitude or retreat into your artistry, letting go of the heaviness of life is necessary in order to keep your spirit alive. Choosing healthy escapes can be difficult, but by following the transcendent beauty of your inner light you can connect your spiritual power to your physical existence, and from this source you can express the real magic of changing the world.

Shining Your Love Light
While the ideals of true love are enchanting, your search for a soulmate can lead to disappointments when another fails to understand or appreciate your depth. Yet this is unlikely to diminish your yearning to experience pure and true love. Your ability to see beauty in

the eyes of others can be spellbinding, and once you find one worthy of your trust you can create a world together that allows you to retreat into the ecstasy of loving one another.

You feel an instant kinship with the water signs—Cancer, Scorpio, and Pisces, since your experience of emotion can bind you into a powerful understanding. Aries quickens your joy in spontaneous passion, but when the flames cool you may be disappointed. With Taurus, you feel a foundation and safety which allows you to express and fulfill your needs. Gemini keeps you on your toes and leaves you dizzy with laughter, although you may never really trust your connection. Cancer nourishes your self-expression, and creating a family together can fulfill your heart. With Leo, you sometimes sense that you have few chances to express your own needs and that she or he demands all your energy.

Virgo, your zodiac opposite, can become the consummate partner with whom you build your dreams, although you sometimes frustrate one another if you're not on the same wavelength. You're intrigued by Libra's elegance and artistry, but feel ill at ease if demands for perfection get in the way of just being yourself. Scorpio can fill your thirst for passion and inspire you to express your own sensuality as a means of becoming spiritually united. Keeping up with Sagittarius is challenging, since what seemed real yesterday can be miles away today. Capricorn helps you feel safe, and a trusting and stable love can grow as long as you feel you each are in control of your own lives. Aquarius can be a lifelong friend, but as lovers you may feel awkward. Another Pisces can invite you to find the place where your dreams are accepted and encouraged, but if your spirits are not in harmony you can drown in confusion.

Making Your Place in the World

Your dreams and hopes run more along the lines of creating a life work than accomplishing worldly ambitions. However, finding work which allows you to develop and express your imagination and care will provide a fulfillment that inspires your faith in life itself. You may even change career paths more than once. Exercising your imagination and bringing beauty into the world can lead you into fields like acting, art, music, dance, photography, film-making, the fashion industry, interior design, or set or costume designing.

You might be drawn into service fields such as the ministry, medicine, social work, psychology, or charitable or missionary work. A desire to sustain the quality of life and an interest in other life forms draws you toward fields like veterinary medicine, zoo-keeping, or environmental concerns. You might enjoy the restaurant or club business, or find that an eclectic metaphysical store suits your interests and energy.

Power Plays

You're more aware of power than people may realize, and, in truth, you possess the power of faith, which can sustain you when everyone else is faltering in apathy. It is the strength of divine compassion that gives you energy and hope, and when you surrender to the radiant vision of transcendent love, your destiny emerges and guides you along your path. Power-hungry people can make you feel uncomfortable, since you're very sensitive to those who seem to be abusive or who take unfair advantage of others. In your utopia, the world is a place of harmony and peace where everyone joins together to help one another.

It's seeing yourself that can be the problem, particularly if you feel disconnected from the Source. Finding yourself begins through self-acceptance—a process which allows you to merge your inner and higher self. When others influence you in negative ways your power wanes; learning that surrender does not mean becoming a victim is the key to keeping your light shining. The light you seek is always glowing in the depths of your own soul, evoking peace and emanating the harmony you know as the essence of power.

Famous Pisces

Ansel Adams, Jon Bon Jovi, Mary-Chapin Carpenter, Buffalo Bill Cody, Sam Donaldson, George Harrison, Victor Hugo, Dame Kiri Te Kanawa, Bernadette Peters, Maurice Ravel, John Updike

The Year Ahead for Pisces

The year 2001 is a time to lay the foundations which will sustain your ability to develop your dreams. In the process, you're dismantling some of the structures in your life and finding better ways to approach and express your artistry. Some cycles challenge you to face your illusions, while others inspire visions that give your heart wings to fly.

The transit of Jupiter, the planet representing expansion and abundance, emphasizes your need to develop a security base and to strengthen your creative self-expression. From January through June, Jupiter's energy continues the cycle which began last summer, giving you more time to extend and improve your base of operations. You may feel unsettled, but you can diffuse these feelings by adding things to your life which satisfy your comfort and security. In July, Jupiter enters Cancer, and through the remainder of the year stimulates growth and outreach as you express your abilities in more favorable circumstances. Your ability to love grows, too, and whether you're adding more people to your circle or increasing products of your creativity, you're opening your heart.

Saturn's cycle in Taurus continues through April, bringing strength and consistency as you develop your skills and understanding. Then, from April, Saturn moves into Gemini, where it will remain for another two years. During this time you'll feel that you're being tested—and you are! The tests arrive to help you determine priorities and to challenge your ability to embrace responsibility for yourself, your thoughts, and your actions. While some challenges come from the outside, in reality they're originating from within. You're evaluating your needs and may find that you're more willing now to do whatever is necessary to assure that your deepest needs are fulfilled.

Pluto's cycle in Sagittarius takes a long time—it's just now at the halfway point (moving along in 2009!)—and it is this long cycle that's responsible for what feels like life transformation. The most significant changes will happen when Pluto is exactly square your Sun (check the listing below to see if this is your year), but through this entire transit of fifteen years you can see huge changes at work. Uranus and Neptune are also slow movers, but not quite as slow as

Pluto. Their influences continue to help you open to your inner self, awakening your ability to release the past and welcome dreams that open the way to your sense of personal renewal.

The eclipses of the Sun and Moon emphasize the balance between your personal and public lives, and you may feel that you have to deal with very personal issues before you experience true accomplishment. Each eclipse influence is described in the monthly sections which follow. However, the transit of the Moon's Nodes has significance for the entire year. This year the nodal transit signifies a time when you need to get in touch with how and where you experience love. Your ability to allow the flow of pure love into your life is challenged now. Not only are you exploring how you give love, but also how you receive it.

If you were born from February 19 to 24, you're experiencing a series of changes which challenge your ability to define your priorities and limitations, while you also develop the opportunities that will allow you to grow. From January through April, you're feeling the stimulus of Jupiter transiting in square aspect to your Sun, marking a time when there may be a lot of knocks at your door—but some of them bring empty promises. It's learning to say "no" to the distractions, and learning to say "yes" to the right offers that can be the big frustration of these four months. Then, during late April through June, Saturn moves into a square aspect to your Sun, putting on the brakes and testing the decisions you've made. If you've gotten in over your head due to the decisions made during the previous eleven months, it is now that you'll pay the price—or when you can begin to grow weary juggling burdens that have become too heavy. Is the phrase, "too much of a good thing" familiar? During Saturn's cycle, you will know precisely what that means! Finally, during July and August you have a chance to welcome more significant growth options which work with your life in more harmonious ways, and, past the testing of Saturn, will also be less inclined to make promises unless you're sure they can fit into your life and support your priorities.

If you were born from February 24 to March 1, you're experiencing new visions for yourself and your future while Neptune transits in semisextile to your Sun. Your momentum is likely to slow down a bit this year, taking the emphasis off the outside world and pulling your focus toward your inner life. This can be an exceptional time for developing creativity or getting in touch with your spirituality, and it's important that you find ways to integrate these needs into your daily life. While the temptation to withdraw from the world is strong, your best course of action may be to alter your perception of how the outside world and other people operate in relationship to your life and your actions. Creating positive personal boundaries is helpful now—learn when you need to let go and trust the universe to resolve things!

If you were born from March 1 to 8, you're feeling the brunt of Saturn transiting in square aspect to your Sun. This is a period of limitation and testing, but it can also be a time of great accomplishment if you are applying yourself to the things that promote personal growth. Nobody really enjoys Saturn squaring the Sun because it's so darn real—and this can be a special bother if you've been ignoring reality or denying your true needs. In addition, you become aware of your limitations and the passage of time. The things you want can seem very far away, and the things you don't like can seem to take forever to complete. Some of your support systems are also dwindling away or have become nonexistent. It's time to see what you can do on your own, or how effectively you're using your resources. Most find that they're more driven under this influence; some simply whine and accomplish nothing. This is where choice enters. If you are clueless about what you want and need, there's no time like the present to answer at least part of that dilemma. If you've been forging ahead, you're likely to run into resistance. You're being tested. Is this the path you want? Are you satisfied with yourself? If not, now you can see the steps necessary to help you move from point A to point B. Be aware of everything: your physical needs, your emotional drives, your external priorities. It's all being tested. While the test seems to be from the outside, remember it's really you testing yourself. Your higher self shines the light on your humanity, begging you to embrace all that you are and challenging you to make the most of yourself!

If you were born from March 4 to 9, you're experiencing the brunt of Pluto's transformational challenge to your Sun. You're probably saying, "But look at what I just read about Saturn!" Yes, you're feeling Saturn *and* Pluto. No small task, these cycles. But the results are likely to be the masterpiece you've dreamt of creating! Your first priority arises through the changes you're making regarding your physical health. Whatever limitations or weaknesses exist can become problems, but you're experiencing the kinds of cycles that allow you to uncover root causes and experience a powerful change in the way you deal with your physical needs. Pluto's square to your Sun will not happen again in your lifetime ("Thank heavens!"), and while there may be some losses, you're opening to amazing levels of self-expression and awareness. Think of the losses as the things that are no longer you, much like the polliwog becoming a frog or the caterpillar becoming a butterfly. As the old expressions of yourself transform, a new you is emerging. You may be more emotionally vulnerable as a result. For this reason, it's important to carefully evaluate the people who share your life, especially new relationships. In fact, some people will become the catalyst for your changes, and then may no longer be there. You're in a transition stage, and fortunately your innate adaptability can work to your advantage now. Learning to let go is one of your life lessons, and now you'll discover how adept you've become at going with the flow. Your creativity is also changing, and you may discover new forms of artistry or uncover talents that have lain dormant—much like the essence of your being. You are uncovering and integrating the power of your true self. It can take a while to get used to the way it feels, but, in the end, you're reborn!

If you were born from March 10 to 16, Uranus is transiting in semisextile to your Sun. This can be a year of serendipity—finding things in your life path you had not sought but which bring an awakening to fresh possibilities. It's time to experiment with options that were not previously available, including new ways of connecting your spiritual, emotional, and physical needs. Your impulse is to maintain a distance from others, but you may simply need more objectivity in your relationships and manner of relating. While sweeping changes are not the theme of this cycle, stepping onto a more exciting horizon is an element you're likely to enjoy. You're becoming more freely expressive of yourself and your needs. For those born from March 12-14, you're also feeling some confusion resulting from Neptune transiting in semisquare to your Sun. For this reason, you may sense that your timing is off, or that your circumstances are uncomfortable—like wearing wool in the summer. Trust can be difficult, since there's more uncertainty. Making slower, more deliberate changes can lead to healthier results, especially if you're in new situations. Physically, you can be more sensitive to effects of environment and food, and medications can have unusual results.

If you were born from March 16 to 20, Saturn is completing its cycle in supportive sextile aspect to your Sun. This influence ends in May 2001, but the effects of decisions and actions taken during this cycle can last for many years. Complete projects now, and use your accomplishments and responsibilities to help you step into a more rewarding future. Your commitments are important, and you're making promises you intend to keep.

Tools to Make a Difference

Staying healthy and strong during 2001 can require that you make alterations in your daily routine and lifestyle. The foundations you're creating are not only physical ones, but involve building a strong connection to your inner self. This is a year of becoming more familiar with the manner in which you nourish yourself at a soulful level, and by so doing, you're creating a quality of inner tranquility which sustains you amidst the clamor of daily life. You're more sensitive to vibrations than most people, and may need to make space and time to escape from the press of the outside world and reclaim your own truth. At home you'll benefit from creating a sacred space, whether you choose a garden, special room, or just a corner in your bedroom dedicated to quiet. Identifying a physical space which is kept vibrationally clear and where you can "tune in" gives you an anchor to build your connection to the soul, giving you a solid base to work with.

Alterations to your personal space, changing the flow of energy, can bring amazing changes in the way you feel—physically and emotionally. Apply techniques of feng shui, or consult with a feng shui master to help redirect the energy at home and at work. For yourself, working with vibrational tools like music, chimes, or tuning forks can produce amazing results, ranging from relaxation to revitalization. You may also be more responsive to bodywork—ranging from shiatsu to massage to acupuncture—as a means of balancing your energy. Chakra balancing, chi gung, and reiki can be effective tools.

You may feel that it's time to uncover or reclaim your past, and hypnotherapy, especially regression hypnosis, can provide illuminating results. If you feel that you need to return to a place, working with tools like astrocartography can help you pinpoint places on the earth that have a special tie to your soul history. Or you might be successful at following your heritage through genealogy. Revisiting the past can be a stepping stone to the future, and the goal is not to stay there, but to bring forward the elements of yourself which need to be integrated into your future evolutionary growth.

♓

Affirmation for the Year

I am embracing the essence of my soul
and I am at peace in the arms of Divine Love.

Pisces/January

In the Spotlight
Your enthusiasm shines through your artistry and special manner of expressing your heartfelt desires. A loving relationship blossoms, lifting you onto the higher plateaus of abundant joy; you can be healed through love.

Wellness and Keeping Fit
Your vitality is fueled by increased energy, and it's a marvelous time to become seriously committed to fitness. Work with a personal trainer can help you reach your goals more rapidly, and you'll benefit from disciplines that also strengthen your inner awareness.

Love and Life Connections
Let go and surrender to love. Venus and Mars add their shimmer to your manner of expression, and if you've ever wanted to show your most alluring qualities, now's the time! Love flows more easily during the lunar eclipse on January 9, and your actions and words can inspire trust and understanding, bringing you closer to one another. Old ideas about how to love can challenge what you feel, but it's up to you to decide what will serve your highest needs.

Finance and Success
Your talents and artistry need room for expression and can make all the difference in whether or not you're advancing in your field of endeavor. Convening with others in your vocation can bring remarkable results, although you may run into disputes arising from those who seem to want to unfairly use your resources to their own benefit from January 15-20.

Cosmic Insider Tip
You're attracting positive experiences and might feel a bit lazy. However, if you're putting your energy and effort behind your needs and desires, you'll see amazing and lasting rewards.

Rewarding Days: 4, 5, 8, 9, 17, 18, 22, 23, 27, 28

Challenging Days: 6, 7, 12, 13, 16, 19, 20

Affirmation for the Month
I deserve the love I need.

Pisces/February

In the Spotlight
Work on an existing project captures most of your attention; completing pressing obligations is necessary if you are to be able to move ahead in the months to come. Situations test your courage and priorities, but your vision is strong enough to see you through.

Wellness and Keeping Fit
Increasing your endurance and muscular strength adds momentum to your day, giving you the energy you need to deal with building tensions. Be alert to your limits after February 15, since you can exhaust yourself before you realize it.

Love and Life Connections
Practical considerations capture your attention, although you may feel that withdrawing from the scrutiny of others is necessary to allow you to nourish your spiritual needs during the Full Moon on February 8. Tensions within the family accelerate after February 15, and knowing when to become involved can be difficult during the Pisces New Moon on February 23. Using your sensitivity to gauge the volatility of the situation keeps you out of trouble.

Finance and Success
A situation can be misrepresented from February 1-5, and if you base your decisions on this information you may end up feeling frustrated and disappointed. During Mercury's retrograde from February 4-25 you'll benefit from taking a second look and comparing this situation to what you've experienced in the past. Power struggles after February 19 leave you sitting on a sharply pointed fence, since others may determine your advancement based on your loyalty.

Cosmic Insider Tip
Dealing with the status quo is the safe zone. Sudden changes after February 14 can lead to more problems than opportunities.

Rewarding Days: 1, 5, 6, 13, 14, 18, 23, 24, 28

Challenging Days: 3, 4, 9, 10, 15, 16, 17

Affirmation for the Month
I wisely use my time, money, and energy.

Pisces/March

In the Spotlight
Your drive and ambition can be strong, although it's necessary to watch for changes in the hierarchy to know how assertive you need to be. Gather support from others whose ideas and influence can stabilize your position.

Wellness and Keeping Fit
You're beginning a long cycle of increasing tensions, and while you may feel driven to accomplish your aims, you can easily overdo it and burn out before you reach your goals. Test your pace, remembering that time for rejuvenation keeps you alert and strong.

Love and Life Connections
Angry outbursts can be hurtful, and during the Full Moon on March 9 you are especially sensitive to criticism from others. While you may be eager to please, martyrdom is not necessarily your best option. You're reconsidering your involvements and commitments and may be seeking a way out of an unhealthy situation. However, you're eager to make amends if you know that love binds your hearts and you're both ready to work toward change.

Finance and Success
You may feel that you're being asked to do more than seems fair, although everyone could be in the same boat. Before you decide to stage a revolution (or follow one), compare the long range costs against potential rewards. Negotiations have some merit, and after March 17 you may even reach a reasonable consensus. Change is on the horizon, and short-term agreements may work to your benefit.

Cosmic Insider Tip
Power struggles seem to peak midmonth, although the fallout can last for a while. Fortunately, you're likely to reach a reasonable contract after the New Moon on March 25.

Rewarding Days: 4, 5, 12, 13, 17, 22, 23, 27, 31

Challenging Days: 2, 3, 8, 9, 14, 15, 16, 29, 30

Affirmation for the Month
I know what I hold precious in my heart.

Pisces/April

In the Spotlight
Review of your finances can reveal troubling information unless you've been keeping track. Fortunately, you're in a good position to regroup and initiate a plan of action that sets you on firmer footing before month's end.

Wellness and Keeping Fit
Since you're likely to be working extra hours you may fail to take good care of your body. Staying on track with your fitness routine adds energy at the time you need it most.

Love and Life Connections
While others posture in their arguments over family matters, you try to stay objective but can still feel hurt, especially if your illusions are shattered by selfish actions and attitudes. In some respects you may feel that you're distancing, while on another level, you're establishing a solid foundation on your own terms. Connections with siblings can be helpful reminders that you're not alone after the New Moon on April 23.

Finance and Success
Eliminating the items that are overstressing your budget can help bring a situation back into balance, and if cost overruns are the problem, take another look at the numbers from April 1-19, and then set up another plan of action from April 23-28. Questions over who's responsible arise during the Full Moon on April 8, when you may also decide that it's time to distance yourself from those who are misusing resources.

Cosmic Insider Tip
It's a new story after April 20, when Venus turns direct and Saturn changes signs. These cycles signal a time of changing values and indicate your need to establish strong priorities.

Rewarding Days: 1, 9, 10, 13, 14, 18, 19, 23, 24, 28

Challenging Days: 4, 5, 6, 11, 12, 20, 25, 26

Affirmation for the Month
I align my thoughts, words, and actions with truth and goodness.

Pisces/May

In the Spotlight
The actions and attitudes of others can be unsettling and disconcerting, especially if it seems like they're changing the rules in the middle of the game! It's time to look at your goals and determine what motivates you and whom you're trying to please.

Wellness and Keeping Fit
Your frustrations with career or family matters can begin to exhaust your vitality. Bringing your health into a top priority might require a change in attitude along with a change in your routine.

Love and Life Connections
Obligations at home require more time and energy than you anticipated, and you may feel that you're doing double duty. While some burdens are yours to carry, others are the result of another's lack of responsibility. Although it's difficult to say "no," that is the lesson to learn. However, those obligations which are yours are not going away, and it's time to find a way to satisfy them. This could be the reason to establish personal boundaries in the first place!

Finance and Success
While you may be experiencing career success, competition is arising and you may have to work harder to maintain your position than in the past. Evaluating your situation and determining what you need to do to stay up to date can put you on a firmer foundation. It's a good time to learn new skills or polish existing ones. You're also discovering what you need to do to get on track financially, although it may require more self-discipline.

Cosmic Insider Tip
Significant meetings on or near the Full Moon on May 7 can be the source of information and guidance you need to help turn around a baffling situation.

Rewarding Days: 6, 7, 11, 16, 17, 21, 25, 26

Challenging Days: 2, 3, 8, 9, 10, 23, 24, 29, 30

Affirmation for the Month
I am clearly aware of the best course of action.

Pisces/June

In the Spotlight
The pace quickens, and you sometimes feel that you're watching the world spin out of control. Your adaptability is tested at the same time that you're also proving your ability to maintain your focus. It's tapping into your creativity that finally turns the tide.

Wellness and Keeping Fit
All the things you've heard about doing to relieve stress are useful now: extra vitamin C, plenty of rest periods, adequate exercise. It's important now to get enough exercise to relieve tension.

Love and Life Connections
The good graces of siblings or trusted friends are a treasure-trove, and staying in contact or asking for help can bring you closer. It's also time to tell your sweetheart how you feel, since expressions of love strengthen your connection on every level. By the time of the solar eclipse on June 21, you're feeling a powerful need to make more room in your life to enjoy love's delights and to share celebrations with the ones dear to you.

Finance and Success
Misunderstandings, equipment breakdowns, and scheduling problems can all run rampant during Mercury's retrograde from June 4-28, since Mars and Jupiter add a "hurry up and wait" kind of energy to the picture. Finding constructive directions in which to focus your energy and attention can place you ahead of the game when this cycle finally ends. Look into investing after June 21, but wait until after careful research to determine if you'll buy.

Cosmic Insider Tip
You've probably heard that life is a circus, and now you have the evidence to prove it. Fortunately, the crazy things going on around you give rise to your creative inspiration.

Rewarding Days: 2, 3, 7, 12, 13, 18, 21, 22, 30

Challenging Days: 5, 6, 19, 20, 25, 26, 27

Affirmation for the Month
I am adaptable yet strong in the face of change.

Pisces/July

In the Spotlight
Your support and security systems gradually become more reliable, and standing on a firmer platform boosts your confidence in the future. Power plays in your career can be troublesome, but it's knowing when to step away that will save your reputation!

Wellness and Keeping Fit
Avoid situations for which you are unprepared or which are beyond your capabilities, since taking unusual risks now can place you in jeopardy. Concentrate, instead, on becoming more active in playful or amusing fitness activities as part of your regular routine.

Love and Life Connections
Spending more time at home or with family is thoroughly satisfying, and children are especially enjoyable. Invite friends to share your celebrations near the lunar eclipse on July 5, since getting back in touch with your buddies can be particularly heartwarming. Your romantic intentions may be high after the New Moon on July 20, but a family crisis or criticism from others about your love life can dampen your enthusiasm.

Finance and Success
You can be blindsided by those who insist on pushing their way to the top, and in order to safeguard your position you'll need to determine where and how your talents can be most constructively utilized. Careful attention to your professional associations aligns you with others who support your needs and position.

Cosmic Insider Tip
To take the edge off tension, exercise your artistry and playfulness when you have "free" time. However, a lax attitude will work against you on the job.

Rewarding Days: 4, 5, 9, 10, 14, 19, 20, 27, 28

Challenging Days: 2, 3, 7, 16, 17, 18, 23, 24, 29, 30

Affirmation for the Month
My true values guide my actions.

Pisces/August

In the Spotlight
Despite restructuring—or what may feel like a construction zone—in your career, there are better circumstances in which to exercise your talents and abilities. Relationships take a higher priority, and cooperative ventures become much more satisfying.

Wellness and Keeping Fit
Make an assessment of your health. It's a good time to see a health care professional for an objective point of view, and alterations in your diet or daily regimen can bring rapid improvements, too. Initiate changes after August 19.

Love and Life Connections
Your passion grows, and declarations of love made near the Full Moon on August 4 can awaken new aspirations for your future. You may still feel like keeping a distance on some levels, although your hesitation can lead your partner to wonder if you're actually committed. Talking about your concerns, fears, and doubts can serve to banish them, but if it's not true love, then these explorations can shed a different light on the picture!

Finance and Success
Since you understand that life does not come with guarantees you may be willing to ride through the storms of change if you know your company or career situation is based on reasonably sound principles. Alterations made after the New Moon on August 19 can open the way for increased productivity. Investments show the best results from August 1-26.

Cosmic Insider Tip
Empty promises will not work for you at all—which means that the illusions you've held are being exposed in favor of real choices. It's time to follow the dreams that work for your life.

Rewarding Days: 2, 5, 6, 7, 11, 15, 16, 23, 24

Challenging Days: 4, 13, 14, 19, 20, 21, 25, 26, 27

Affirmation for the Month
Abundant love fills my life!

Pisces/September

In the Spotlight
Balancing your needs with the demands of others works best when you identify your shared goals. Otherwise, you'll be more likely to become resentful if you feel that someone's taking advantage of you.

Wellness and Keeping Fit
Your physical energy is getting more vigorous. Building muscular strength through sports can be enjoyable, but you might also benefit from including more weight-bearing exercise in your routine.

Love and Life Connections
Feeling more sensitive to relationship issues, you're also aware of your own unanswered needs during the Pisces Full Moon on September 2. Old patterns in an existing partnership can become completely unbearable, but before you assume that an ending is the only solution, examine your attitudes. It's time to release past hurts in order to move on, and whether you stay together or not, communicating what's in your heart leads to a sense of inner strength.

Finance and Success
Professional associations and community activities provide an excellent opportunity to work in concert with others who share your aims. Setting goals which include interdependence is an important stepping stone toward establishing your professional reputation. Contracts and partnership agreements work to your benefit after the New Moon on September 17, but read the fine print regarding debt matters to avoid getting stuck with the short end of the stick.

Cosmic Insider Tip
Although it's not exactly that the cavalry has arrived, you are feeling relief since issues are on the table and you can see where you stand. Outside support is most reliable from September 21-30.

Rewarding Days: 2, 3, 7, 8, 11, 12, 20, 21, 29, 30

Challenging Days: 9, 10, 15, 16, 17, 22, 23

Affirmation for the Month
I always show my gratitude toward others.

Pisces/October

In the Spotlight
Money matters can be troublesome, especially if your plans are in stark contrast with those of your partner. You will not appreciate giving to others what you feel they do not deserve, but will definitely be obligated to pay your share of debts or costs!

Wellness and Keeping Fit
An old injury can become problematic if you're pushing beyond your limits or ignoring symptoms telling you to stop. It's easy to get into a rush, so watch your driving and be alert to others whose risk-taking can place you in peril.

Love and Life Connections
The stages of developing intimacy involve letting go of your barriers and addressing the inhibitions or concerns you each have about trust. These matters can be especially pressing during the Full Moon on October 2, and although you may want to work around them, you'll get past your fears more quickly if you simply talk about them. Arguments can result over money, but are likely to be driven by these deeper issues.

Finance and Success
While Mercury retrogrades from October 1-22 you may feel that you're stuck dealing with all those jobs which are the result of procrastination. Actually, it's a good time to go through those files gathering dust or to dig into projects that have gone unfinished for too long. Then, after October 24, you'll be free to pursue the things that will advance your career and lead to greater financial rewards.

Cosmic Insider Tip
There's room for vague misunderstandings to continue to create delays from October 26-31, although these matters can be resolved if you deal with them immediately.

Rewarding Days: 5, 9, 10, 17, 18, 22, 26, 27, 28

Challenging Days: 6, 7, 8, 13, 14, 19, 20

Affirmation for the Month
I understand my deeper motivations and embrace my true needs.

Pisces/November

In the Spotlight
Travel for business or pleasure inspires fresh visions for the future. However, if you're running away from problems, they're likely to pop up as soon as you unpack your bags.

Wellness and Keeping Fit
Taking time to connect with your inner self helps dispel a number of problems, but also provides a sense of tranquillity that's been eluding you for some time. Meditation or a time of retreat can be just what the doctor ordered to get physical problems under control.

Love and Life Connections
Suspending ongoing arguments or concerns from November 1-7 can give you the space you need to alter your perspective. To revitalize love, consider traveling to destinations that rouse your romantic spirit after November 8, but realize that your true search is for the spiritual connection your relationship needs in order to grow. An honest love takes wing during the New Moon on November 15, when you're ready to forgive hurts and move forward.

Finance and Success
Conferences and presentations from November 8-24 provide the perfect opportunity to showcase your talents and ideas, and you may meet others whose influence can play a role in your advancement. Follow through with communication after November 17 to clarify where everything stands. Finances are most fluid after November 14, but spending from November 8-17 needs to fit within your budget since it's not a good time to go into debt.

Cosmic Insider Tip
The Full Moon on November 1 can stimulate the break you've hoped for, but unless everyone involved is willing to be direct you may feel that you're being offered less than you deserve.

Rewarding Days: 1, 5, 6, 13, 14, 18, 19, 23, 24, 28

Challenging Days: 3, 4, 9, 10, 11, 15, 16, 17, 30

Affirmation for the Month
My ethical and moral values serve as a reliable guiding light.

Pisces/December

In the Spotlight
You're eager to enjoy the holidays, but still have to deal with obligations early in the month if you're going to feel free enough to let go after December 21. Forging a strong connection to your superiors puts you on track for advancement.

Wellness and Keeping Fit
After Mars enters your sign on December 8 you'll feel a stirring of vitality that's like awakening from a long sleep. The only problem is gauging the limits of your energy, since it's easy to overdo it after December 16 if you don't pace yourself.

Love and Life Connections
Family pressures can stretch your free time from December 1 through the solar eclipse on December 14, but after that you're eager to turn your attention to enjoying time with friends. Romance after December 9 can be heavenly, although sharing your fantasies with your lover will be most enjoyable after December 16. The lunar eclipse on December 30 inspires your creativity, and an enchanting getaway can be the perfect setting to share love.

Finance and Success
Clarify contractual agreements from December 1-7, when laying out details gives you a plan of action. Your enthusiasm goes a long way toward improving your career prospects, although you'll need to present a responsible attitude if you're going to stay on the good side of your superiors. After December 16 you're in an excellent position to set up a budget for a large scale project.

Cosmic Insider Tip
The Sun's eclipse on December 14 stimulates a careful look at your ambitions and the manner in which you deal with success and failure. Focus on accomplishments which light your path.

Rewarding Days: 2, 3, 11, 12, 15, 16, 20, 21, 26, 29, 30

Challenging Days: 1, 6, 7, 13, 14, 27, 28

Affirmation for the Month
My goals reflect my highest needs.

Pisces Action Table

These dates reflect the best—but not the only—times for success and ease in these activities, according to your Sun sign.

	JAN	FEB	MAR	APR	MAY	JUN	JUL	AUG	SEPT	OCT	NOV	DEC
Move					6-31	1, 2, 30	1-11					
Start a class				22-30	1-5						15	
Join a club	1-9											
Ask for a raise		23, 24										
Look for work							30, 31	1-13			27-30	1-15
Get pro advice	12, 13	9, 10	8, 9	4-6	2-3, 29-30	25, 26	23, 24	19, 20	15, 16	13, 14	9, 10	6, 7
Get a loan	14, 15	11, 12	10, 11	7, 8	4, 5, 31	1, 27, 28	25, 26	21, 22	17, 18	15, 16	11, 12	8, 9
See a doctor	10-31	26-28	1-16				30, 31	1-13				
Start a diet	10, 11	7, 8	6, 7	2, 3, 30	1, 27, 28	23, 24	21, 22	17, 18	13, 14	11, 12	7, 8	4, 5
End relationship			8, 9									
Buy clothes							13-29					
Get a makeover	3-31	1, 23, 24										
New romance						21, 22		1-26				
Vacation	16, 17	13, 14	12, 13	9, 10	6, 7	2, 3, 30	1, 27, 28	23, 24	19-21	17, 18	13, 14	11, 12

The Twelve Houses of the Zodiac

You may run across mention of the houses of the zodiac while reading certain articles in the *Sun Sign Book*. These houses are the twelve divisions of the horoscope wheel. Each house has a specific meaning assigned to it. Below are the descriptions attributed to each house.

First House: Self-interest, physical appearance, basic character.

Second House: Personal values, monies earned and spent, moveable possessions, self-worth and esteem, resources for fulfilling security needs.

Third House: Neighborhood, communications, siblings, schooling, buying and selling, busy activities, short trips.

Fourth House: Home, family, real estate, parent(s), one's private sector of life, childhood years, old age.

Fifth House: Creative endeavors, hobbies, pleasures, entertainments, children, speculative ventures, loved ones.

Sixth House: Health, working environment, coworkers, small pets, service to others, food, armed forces.

Seventh House: One-on-one encounters, business and personal partners, significant others, legal matters.

Eighth House: Values of others, joint finances, other people's money, death and rebirth, surgery, psychotherapy.

Ninth House: Higher education, religion, long trips, spirituality, languages, publishing.

Tenth House: Social status, reputation, career, public honors, parents, the limelight.

Eleventh House: Friends, social and community work, causes, surprises, luck, rewards from career, circumstances beyond your control.

Twelfth House: Hidden weaknesses and strengths, behind-the-scenes activities, institutions, confinement, government.

2001 Sun Sign Book Articles

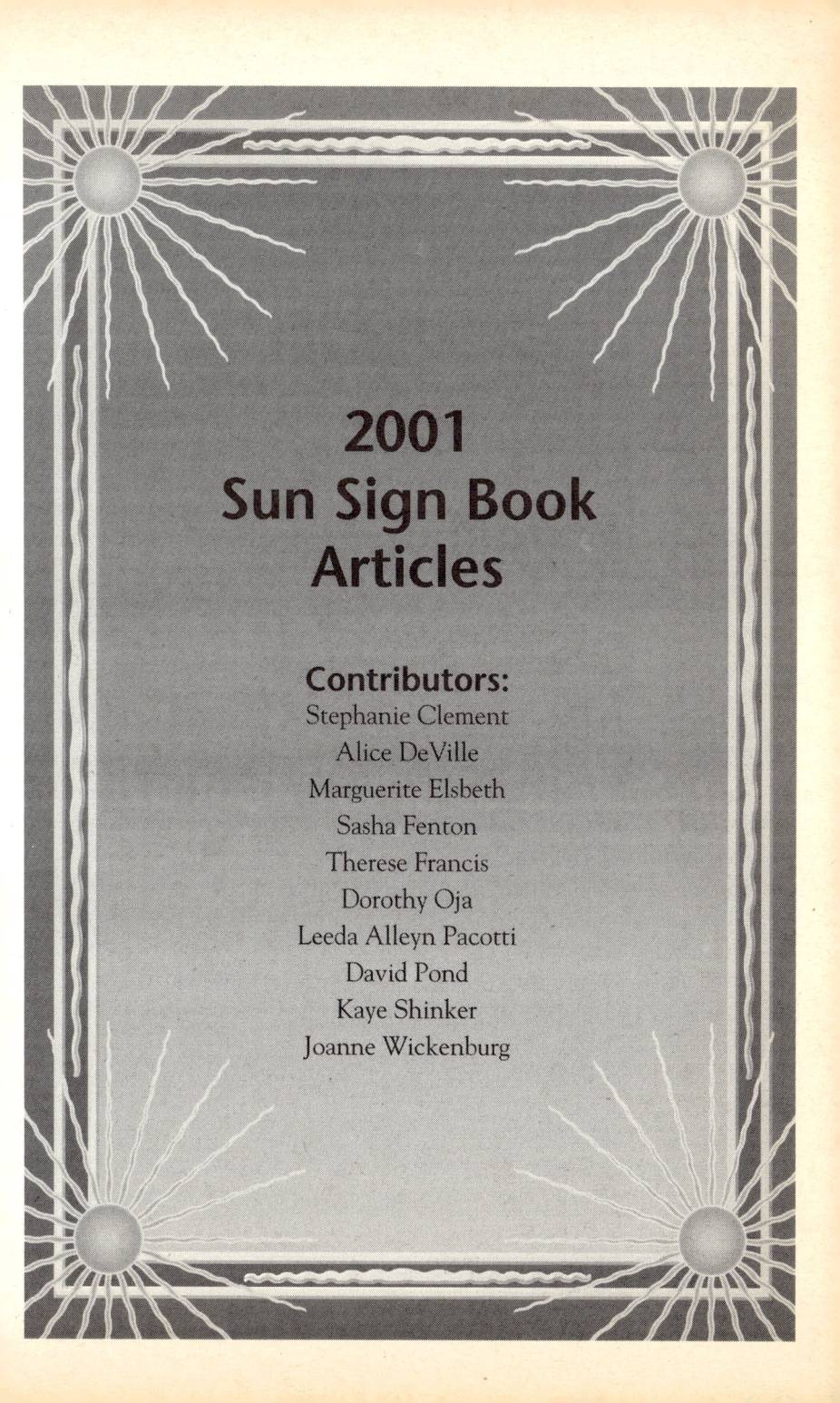

Contributors:
Stephanie Clement
Alice DeVille
Marguerite Elsbeth
Sasha Fenton
Therese Francis
Dorothy Oja
Leeda Alleyn Pacotti
David Pond
Kaye Shinker
Joanne Wickenburg

Rising Signs

by Sasha Fenton

If you are a regular reader of *Llewellyn's Sun Sign Book*, you will have noticed a table that shows you how to work out your rising sign, but you may not know what the rising sign is or what it represents. Your Sun sign depends upon the time of the year in which you were born, and the regularity of the Earth's orbit makes it easy for anyone to work out their Sun sign without the aid of special tables. The rising sign is different, and my explanation of how it is arrived at is a very basic one.

The rising sign is the constellation of stars up in the sky that was facing the place where day was breaking when you were born. The set of constellations that astrologers use make up the zodiac signs that we are all familiar with—Aries, Taurus, Gemini, Cancer, etc. For an astrologer to work this out, he or she needs to know the date, time, and place of your birth so that he or she can calculate the distance from this point to the place on the Earth where the Sun was rising. Your Sun sign and your rising sign are only likely to be the same if you were born around daybreak. If you were born at any other time of the day, your Sun sign and rising sign will be different from each other.

If you look at the table in the front of the book, and if you know your time of birth, you will easily be able to find your rising sign. This is a rough guide, and you will need to consult an astrologer or to buy a mail-order astrology chart if you want to ensure absolute accuracy. If, after consulting the table, you are unsure which of two possible rising signs is the right one, read the information for both and see which fits.

The following list is a very rough and ready guide. I have used the example of a person born under the sign of Scorpio as an example:

Dawn birth: Same sign rising (e.g. Scorpio/Scorpio)
Noon birth: Three signs along rising (e.g. Scorpio/Aquarius)
Sunset birth: Six signs along rising (e.g. Scorpio/Taurus)
Midnight birth: Nine signs along rising (e.g. Scorpio/Leo)

What is the Ascendant?

You may have heard astrologers using the word ascendant, and you may even know that it has something to do with the rising sign. Most astrologers say "rising sign" and "Ascendant" interchangeably, and that is perfectly normal and acceptable. For those who adore exactitude, bear in mind that each sign of the zodiac is divided into degrees and minutes, thus the true definition of the Ascendant is the exact point of a sign that is rising—for example, 17 degrees 45 minutes of Sagittarius.

The Rising Sign in your Horoscope

Many people project their rising sign personality far more than they do their Sun sign. It is probable that as many as half the world's population actually resemble their rising sign rather than their Sun sign. It is this phenomenon that makes it difficult for astrologers to guess someone's Sun sign in an off-the-cuff manner. Unfortunately, there are no hard and fast rules in astrology, so while many people do project their rising sign, others project their Sun sign, their Moon sign, or just about anything else that can be projected.

One of the reasons for the frequency in which the rising sign is so often projected outward is that it relates back to one's childhood circumstances and upbringing. Therefore, if a certain type of look, manner, and behavior was imposed upon a young person, it will still be there when he grows up—stuck like a mask over the real personality. The rising sign can also make quite a difference to the basic Sun sign personality. For instance, a member of the laid-back Sun sign of Libra who has the "chatterbox" sign of Gemini rising will be quite different from one who has the "keep your thoughts and feelings to yourself" sign of Scorpio rising.

In the interpretation section of this article, I have used the feminine "she," because, in my experience, it is mainly women who buy and read astrology books. I have used the third person, which makes it easier for you to check this out against your friends, relatives, colleagues, and even your enemies!

Aries Rising

A person with the Sun in Aries is open, friendly, noisy, and outwardly confident, but this isn't the case when Aries is the rising sign. The outer manner is quiet and reserved, and on first meeting the person may appear to be slightly hostile, with a don't-come-too-close manner that is more reminiscent of Scorpio than Aries. Once you have won the trust of this person, you will find her friendly, helpful, generous, and kind. This person is very active, and she enjoys sports and perhaps acting or gymnastics. She may also enjoy do-it-yourself jobs, heavy gardening, farming, or other outdoor pursuits, and there is a strong possibility that this person is an animal lover or perhaps a horse rider. She may be adventurous and unafraid of dangerous situations. She could be a good hand at electrical work, car maintenance, or engineering, and she has an instinctive feel for how things work.

Her childhood would probably have been quite unsettled, and there may have been many changes of home and school. This often leads to a cautious or reserved manner in new situations, as there would have been so many new places and new "pecking orders" to cope with during childhood. Another scenario is that the parents might have been rather unreliable or unconventional. An Aries-rising child would have had to think twice before inviting a friend to her home, because she couldn't be sure of the situation to be found there from one day to next. There may also have been friction between the Aries-rising child and her father: shouting matches might have been common during her teenage years, and her father may have been too much of a disciplinarian.

Taurus Rising

A person with Taurus rising has an outer manner that is pleasant, humorous, and fairly quiet. This person is very nice to chat with in a social situation or to enjoy a friendship with in a detached way. Living with this person can be a very different matter, as she can be rather mercenary and prone to argument. If the Taurus-rising subject can express herself through art, music, the creation of beauty, or even by running a catering business or a social organization, she may become so fulfilled that she becomes much easier to live with. She needs to relax and to learn to trust others before she can have good long-term relationships. This person needs lots of living space, as she would feel cramped and claustrophobic if she had to live in a very small apartment; she is best off with a spacious house, a good view, and a large garden.

In many cases, the Taurus-rising childhood was comfortable and probably of a fairly genteel middle-class nature. Her parents may have been social and outgoing. Material goods, money, and possessions would have been prized, and the child would have been given an education designed to fit her for a successful lifestyle. There may have been a family interest in the arts, which encouraged the child to explore her inner talents and abilities.

Another possible scenario, however, is that the family were very feckless types who never managed to provide a real home life with any sort of constancy or stability. If her childhood was impoverished in this way, the youngster may have been uncomfortably aware of this while growing up. This Taurus-rising child grows to adulthood with a burning desire to obtain the secure, stable, and impressive lifestyle that her parents couldn't, or wouldn't, aspire to. She also can feel a great reluctance to depend on anyone or anything but her own abilities.

Gemini Rising

This person is easy to talk to and even easier to listen to, as she has a large store of wise and funny stories to tell. This is the sign of the communicator, the broadcaster, writer, journalist, the talkative taxi-driver, and the comic. She is quick and clever, and she picks up difficult concepts in no time. Many Gemini-rising subjects teach or inform for a living. Some can be clever with their hands as well, and they may be the type of people who can fix any kind of broken gadget. This subject is good to her family and a loyal, generous, and kindhearted friend. Although not notably argumentative, when riled this subject becomes extremely cutting and sarcastic, and she won't hold back for the sake of others. Some Gemini-rising subjects are quick to tell the boss what they think of him and thus are frequently out of work.

Many Gemini-rising children are very independent. Intelligent and always in motion, a Gemini-rising child may be noisy, hyperactive, and easily bored, thus creating a lot of stress for her parents and school-teachers. Their constant need for attention sometimes leads these children to feel ignored, heavily criticized, or even insignificant. Another common scenario is that Gemini-rising children feel that a brother or sister is considered to be more clever, nicer, and more worthy of a higher status. Even if the home life is good, the child may find it difficult to fit in at school. One possible reason for this is that Gemini-rising children are often much brighter and faster than their schoolmates. Again, the child is set apart from others, feeling like a square peg in a round hole. The feeling never quite leaves, whatever happens later in life.

Cancer Rising

This person has considerable charm, and she can be quite charismatic. She has an excellent touch when dealing with the public, so a sales or PR career or some kind of agency work is a good choice. The Cancer-rising subject is a pleasant companion, but depending upon the rest of the chart, she can also be moody, tightfisted, and difficult to live with. This person is cautious by nature and careful with money most of the time, but she will spend freely on her children or sometimes on traveling—the Cancer-rising person loves to travel. She is quiet and gentle unless roused. The thing that is most likely to upset her is someone attacking her children or her family.

The Cancer-rising subject is likely to resemble her mother and the female side of her family. This is one of the luckier rising signs, as chances are she was a wanted child who grew up in a decent family with a reasonable amount of comfort and affection. She may be the eldest child or the one with the strongest sense of responsibility. She will save money from quite an early age and she is happy to leave school early and go out to work. This may be because she wants to help her family out, but often she simply feels happier and more purposeful when working than when studying. The parents are always a strong influence, the mother especially so. This child remains close to her family throughout life.

Leo Rising

This person has a confident exterior and sometimes a slightly superior manner, but this is offset by a friendly, open, and nonhostile approach. This subject has a lovely sense of humor and enjoys bringing fun and laughter to others. Many of these people are quite glamorous, and their lives always seem to include a touch of show-business pizazz. This person loves the company of children and young people and she may never quite grow up or grow old. There is always a bit of glamour about this subject, and she may become a top sports-woman, a show-business personality, a leading businesswoman, or the chair of the board. Nothing is out of her reach if she decides to aim for it.

The Leo-rising child usually is wanted and welcomed by her parents. Her childhood home is generally comfortable and the attitudes within it reasonable. There can sometimes be difficulties if one of the parents is a disciplinarian who expects more than the child can deliver. The Leo-rising child is often talented or "special" in some way, and parents may go to great lengths and make considerable sacrifices in order to give this child the specialized training or education that she seems to require. The Leo-rising child may be musical, a good dancer, singer, actor, or artist, or perhaps an excellent athlete. Whether the person keeps any of this up in adulthood or lets their talents slide away is a different story. Perserverance and discipline are required to nurture the innate Leo-rising abilities, and this does not always occur. The Leo-rising person is likely to resemble her father or his side of the family.

Virgo Rising

Virgo as a rising sign overlays the Sun sign character with a reserved and shy outer manner. She is modest and she dislikes making a fool of herself or showing off her talents in public, and in some cases this person can actually stand in the way of her own chances of success. Many Virgo-rising subjects would rather promote the talents of their children than those of themselves.

This person may wish to work in a field that helps humanity, and a career in medicine (either the established or the alternative kind) is a popular choice. Many Virgo-rising folk love to look after small animals. There is often a talent for research, writing, or detailed analytical work, but if it goes on for too long or becomes boring the Virgo-rising person can find herself losing interest and failing to finish what she starts. In some cases, it is her confidence that suddenly evaporates. She also may spend far too much energy on solving the problems of lame-duck friends and relatives when she should be concentrating on her own advancement.

Her parents did their duty by their Virgo-rising child, but there may not have been enough open affection. This child is self-disciplined and easily embarrassed, but the parents may ignore this and chastise or criticize her far too much. In some cases other children in the family seem to take precedence, while in others there is far too much emphasis on appearances, "what the neighbors think," scholastic success, or some other set of hurdles that is constantly set before the youngster. Luckier Virgo-rising subjects grow up in a comfortable home, filled with books and music, educational opportunities, and plenty of encouragement.

Libra Rising

This subject is blessed with charm, good looks, and an easy manner. This means that she makes friends easily and she gets through life without having to make much effort. This person needs a partner in life, and for this reason she may marry when quite young. The personal style is moderate, unruffled, and surprisingly capable, and as a result the Libra-rising subject is often quite successful in business, especially when dealing with the public or when working in a liaison capacity. She is likely to be a good homemaker and possibly a clever cook or gardener, and whatever she creates will be stylish and attractive. Some Libra-rising subjects can be argumentative; others may be too laid-back for that. These subjects can be more difficult to live with than their surface images would have us believe, but they are basically kindhearted.

Childhood can come in a variety of forms. Sometimes the father is absent, either due to divorce or because he is engrossed in his job, and sometimes neither parent pays enough attention to the child. In some cases, this is due to unavoidable circumstances, but in others it is due to absent parents. The child learns to be pleasant and to keep out of trouble, but she may still carry unexpressed resentment. Sometimes the child is overindulged, getting money and expensive goods tossed at her rather than being given the love and proper amount of discipline that she longs for.

Scorpio Rising

This rising sign is amazingly common among people who are interested in mind, body, and spirit subjects—especially the fields of alternative or psychic healing. The Scorpio-rising type searches for the essence behind everything that interests her, so she will delve deeply into her chosen subjects. She may be interested in medical matters, psychology, criminology, or some other important aspect of human behavior, and she simply loves to read, think, and investigate. These subjects are often amazingly generous and loving, and they only share their terribly intense feelings with those whom they truly trust. There is often a strong sense of duty, and considerable sacrifices will be made in order to keep a relationship going or to support a needy family.

The Scorpio-rising subject is physically strong and active throughout life, and she may be extremely keen on dancing or sports. An amazing amount of these folk take up sports that derive from killing, hunting, and self-defense—such as archery, swordfighting, karate, and even fishing!

Somewhere along the line, this child learns to keep her own counsel and not to spread her opinions around. Oddly enough, Sun-in-Scorpio subjects are often talkative and opinionated, and they quite like to live a dramatic life or to be center stage, but this is definitely not the case when Scorpio is rising. In a difficult childhood, a parent vanishes from the scene. In other cases, the child's bright and penetrating mind makes it difficult for her to fit in at school. The person eventually learns to appear to fit in with others while quietly pursuing her own interests. Many of these people become involved in slightly "different" religious or psychological organizations, but they are not easily influenced so they are not likely to be taken in by charlatans. She is thorough in all that she does, and her motto is, "If you are going to do something, do it properly."

Sagittarius Rising

This rising sign is very common among people who are interested in mind, body, and spirit subjects, and they can dive headlong into even the most weird and way-out philosophies. The Sagittarius-rising person is an idealist who has a strong desire to heal the world and its inhabitants. Often it is difficult for them to reconcile the demands of a normal job or family life with their search for a rich inner life.

This sign is characterized by an open, friendly manner and a wonderful sense of humor. This subject makes every person she talks with feel special, but there is a somewhat "skin-deep" element to this, as her real friends and those to whom she feels an abiding loyalty are actually few and far between. Even a formerly deep friendship can be forgotten quite quickly once she moves on. Freedom is the name of the game, and as long as she is free to come and go, to fill her home with waifs and strays, and to live her life as she wishes, she will stay around for ever. If not, then check the airlines to see where she has disappeared to! Travel will be a strong feature of her life, either in the form of physical journeys, or in the form of inner journeys of the mind and the soul.

The Sagittarius-rising childhood was probably not a particularly difficult one. The parents may have come from a different culture or a different part of the world than the one that either they or the subject later inhabits. Some subjects come from deeply religious backgrounds. In either case, the subject tends to reject her parent's culture or beliefs in favor of a more open-minded and universal view of the world. Whatever the childhood circumstances, the child found opportunities for a decent education, either because her parents were keen on this or due to her desire to overcome the limitations of her background. This subject's motto is, "Get on, in order to get out."

Capricorn Rising

This person is cautious and inclined to hang on to money or goods for a rainy day. She may be ambitious for herself or for her children, and she sees education and good qualifications as a way out of the poverty trap. Serious and determined, this apparently shy and unobtrusive person is often a force to be reckoned with. Even if this subject seems a bit unsteady when young, her solid nature and her tendency to take work seriously means that she does all right in the end. If she can't make it to the top herself, she does her best to ensure that her children do so. Some Capricorn-rising subjects feel most comfortable with older people, and only allow themselves to be young and frivolous when they are old. She is always loyal to her parents and other family members. This subject has a dry sense of humor, but she keeps her funny side hidden from outsiders, reserving it for her close friends and her beloved family. She has a soft, kind heart but it is often hidden under an austere exterior.

This subject learned early in life that nothing comes easily, and she may have grown up in a family where money was in very short supply. Surrounded by a strong family, she learned quickly that hard work, money in the bank, and a secure, self-made lifestyle ensure survival. The mother may be an absent figure, due to illness, death, or divorce. This can lead to emotional caution or even confusion later in life.

Aquarius Rising

Sun-sign Aquarians can be real oddballs, but those who have Aquarius rising are far more conventional. Somehow the Saturnian side of the personality is projected more forcefully than the Uranian one. Ambitious and hard working, this subject finds ways of ensuring a good lifestyle and making a comfortable home filled with enough possessions and gadgets to make her happy. She is devoted to her children, and she may blind herself to their faults or their problems. The Aquarius-rising subject can have passing interests in mind, body, and spirit subjects, or she may choose to live with others who do. This person can be quite fussy about any number of things and the list might include her appearance, her choice of diet, her choice of partner, and the slightly dignified lifestyle that she requires. Unlike the solar Aquarian, she is fairly ambitious.

The Aquarius-rising person usually has had loving parents and an excellent childhood. Something may have disrupted her childhood and made her aware that security is hard to come by. Sometimes it is poverty or a sudden fall in the quality of the family's status and lifestyle that brings these feelings of insecurity. It can also arise from witnessing sickness within the family or seeing losses arise through recklessness or weakness. Having experienced life's ups and downs at first hand, she develops a certain armor which may make her appear hard even towards those who love her. She isn't hard; she's just careful. The strong exterior covers a soft heart.

Pisces Rising

Sun-in-Pisces folk tend to be spiritual, chaotic, unusual, and somewhat "different," but when this sign is rising, the subject is far more conventional. This person may be quite ambitious and determined, and she can go far in her chosen career, but somewhere in her life there will be room for an interest in religious or mind, body, and spirit subjects. She may become a committed Christian, or she may delve into Eastern religions, astrology, or perhaps something a little more way-out, but she brings an unusually intellectual approach to her investigations. Whatever her personal lifestyle is, she discovers it early in life and tries to stick with it, but life inevitably forces her to face changes and to "go with the flow" from time to time. Her outer manner is often prickly and even quite hostile, and in some cases she can take offense over nothing. This defensive and self-protective mechanism is often displayed towards those who bear the subject no ill will whatsoever, and this can result in the alienation of those who would otherwise be friends. As a colleague, a friend, or a coworker she is amazingly reliable, and to her family she is the most caring and self-sacrificing person around.

The childhood was probably conventional and happy, but somewhere along the way lessons of loneliness were learned. She may have had reason to hesitate before bringing school friends back to her home. She may simply be a little different, a little otherworldly, and too unlike other children for them to engage easily with her. Oddly enough, many of these subjects compensate by becoming successful at athletics or dancing, and are very well-coordinated.

New Age Love
Romance and Your Sun Sign
by Marguerite Elsbeth

The solar attributes of will and energy, along with romantic love, are the most powerful forces of desire affecting the Western psyche. Contrary to Eastern cultures, where love is expressed as *agape*—stability, devotion, and loyalty to the cause of daily existence—our brand of "true love" here in the West is comprised of an idealistic package of romantic beliefs, attitudes, and expectations welling up from the subconscious depths of our souls. Thus we are often blindly dominated by our instinctual reactions and inherent primordial behavior patterns when seeking out a potential mate.

The idea of romantic love has appeared in many cultures throughout history. However, it would seem that the Western world has been most smitten with the concept, for few cultures base an intimate relationship solely upon eros (love) or infatuation the way we do.

We first became acquainted with the idea of romantic love through medieval archetypes such as Tristan and Iseult. The tale tells the story of Tristan, a noble hero who fell passionately in love with Queen Iseult. They ran away together, beautiful Iseult forsaking her husband King Mark, and Tristan deserting his liege, to whom he had pledged his fealty. They came to reside deep within the heart of a forest, where they became lost in love madness. However, star-crossed from the start, they had too many forces against them. Tristan and Iseult were eventually forced to leave the woods and return to the real world and their previous lives, and both died for love of one another in the end.

The Love Generations

During the Middle Ages, the troubadours perpetuated the myth of Tristan and Iseult with what was then called "courtly love." Brave knights admired fair ladies through love songs and poems, ecstatic in their adoration of the feminine symbol of beauty and perfection. The inspired knight was then moved to act in a noble, heroic, and high-minded manner (all solar attributes, by the way) due to the sublime qualities of another star seemingly more bright and shining than himself.

History tends to repeat itself. Indicative of the Westerner's continued fascination with romantic love is our most recent history, which links us to our culture and society through shared experience. We turned our attention from rational to romantic love around 1943, when the outer planet Neptune first entered into the sign of Libra. The troubadours were at it again, placing Frank Sinatra center stage. Sometime between 1956 and 1962, we made the auditory transition from Elvis to the Beatles. Elvis's gyrating pelvis set the stage for the dramatic entrance of Uranus into the sign of Leo, while the Beatles maintained a charming rock-and-roll tempo. As the tides of change silently converged upon the mindset of Western civilization, many popular figures emerged, becoming knights in shining armor to their many female admirers. They embodied that passions of the heart as they sang their songs of love and its enduring, though often painful and difficult, nature.

Throughout the sexual revolution of the 1960s, which transpired during Neptune's transit of Scorpio, "free love" became a prevalent theme, loosening the conventional standards of America's youth in the eyes of the moral majority. The sudden upheaval of the sexually ascetic standards engendered during the 1950s was insured by the transits of Uranus and Pluto through Virgo, sign of the Virgin, during the 1960s. The heightened spiritual approach toward what appeared to most as wild promiscuity actually satisfied Uranus's eccentric spiritual nature as well as Pluto's propensity for upheaval, transformation, and regenerative growth.

Toward the end of the '60s, when Uranus entered Libra, we were well on our way to embracing Peter Pan as our collective archetype; no one wanted to grow up, take responsibility, or commit themselves to a long-term relationship. Swinging singles predominated the dating genre, and divorce escalated among the married set. All this in the name of love and romance!

We did not begin to cool our ardor (or our heels) in our quest for the perfect mate until 1977, when the first AIDS case was discovered in Africa, even as Chiron, a planetoid orbiting between Saturn and Uranus, was discovered in the starry skies. Traditional concepts regarding home, family, and the modern, high-tech standards of conventional Western society then began to affect our soulmate search in earnest, as Saturn, Uranus, and Neptune entered into the sign of Capricorn in the late 1980s. Pluto's transit of Scorpio from the mid-1980s throughout much of the 1990s provided icing on the cake. What was in us came out for all the world to see, as per the nature of Pluto, and what appeared to be a collective emergence was actually an integral desire to attach ourselves to one another—mind, body, and soul—through absorption and codependent behavior.

A Synergy of Cause and Effect

Old habits die hard. Today's psychology intimates that because humankind is primarily motivated via innate reactions to the outer circumstances arising in daily life, it should stand to reason one's love interest would share a similar mechanism of automatic conscious response. This may be true at first glance and often extends into the early stages of a relationship, when all concerned are still in the idealistic throes of romantic love. However, these idyllic feelings begin to wear thin as negative behavior begins to manifest within the relationship and the primordial brain is activated.

The primordial brain is part and parcel of our memory banks. It is tied both to the collective unconscious and the personal subconscious, representing our survival instincts as well as all of our past memories and early conditioning. The outer planets—Uranus, Neptune, and Pluto—strongly affect both aspects for good or ill, especially when it comes to the old saw of codependence.

Uranus stimulates us to seek liberation from the confines of fear through independence, but this synergistic energy may also impel us to leap into the unknown, in rebellion of all we hold sacred and dear. The planet Neptune tends to dissolve old concepts surrounding our relationships; however, because we are creatures of habit resistant to change, many of us function according to past programming and experiences. Therefore, we may react to Neptune's energy by placing others on a pedestal and giving away our own higher power. Pluto opens the door to transformative deepening within ourselves and through our relationships, yet if we hold on to anger and resentments we may attempt to manipulate and control others, fix the world and the people we love for our own comfort, and punish others for our own immature actions.

Cosmic Reconditioning

It is far easier to accept solutions that place us in the role of victim over those which cause us to take some degree of personal responsibility for our actions. Most current scientific dogma contributes to the notion that almost all behavior is predetermined by genetic programming. While the genes comprising DNA do have a primary influence over our biological and behavioral expressions, we must face the fact that we are both collectively and individually responsible for our behavioral patterns, rather than blaming genes and nature. Genetics does not have precedence over consciousness, but promotes a predilection toward our physical, emotional, mental, and spiritual dispositions. Imagine the change in our collective and individual thoughts, words, and actions if we developed and heeded a new theory of evolution which proclaimed that our survival was dependent upon loving kindness, and the willing acceptance of the frailty and vulnerability of all creatures and things!

We are now living in a time when great Earth changes may or may not be physically cataclysmic in the global sense, but most definitely are synergistic in terms of our conscious awareness and biological evolutionary deepening. People from all walks of life sense that something is happening "out there" in the cosmos, something that is affecting our lives here on Earth both physically and spiritually. A possible theory for this change is based on current conditions just outside the Earth's atmosphere.

The intensity of the current cosmic vibrations suggests that the Earth is being bombarded with accelerated photons—the parts of electromagnetic energy that move in the form of cosmic rays. These cosmic rays could be gradually inducing evolutionary changes in our DNA, a basic material in the chromosomes of the cell nucleus which transmits our hereditary patterns, by altering our molecular structure, refining the sympathetic nervous system, and heightening our perceptions. Some highly receptive individuals would experience this influx of energy as a feeling of impending death. Indeed, this concept suggests that we are being encouraged to die to the old self, as we are living in a time when the universe is affording humankind the potential for rebirth to a progressed level of conscious existence.

Our receptivity to the current influx of accelerated photons and cosmic rays would awaken the latent potencies of human consciousness. By activating the motivation, energy, and inspiration necessary to lead us to transformation, our sensory abilities can be heightened. Again, these changes are both biological and spiritual. We may be experiencing a reawakening of consciousness to heal ourselves and our relationships with others. DNA itself does not institute a primary causation; the cause initiates from the cosmos. However, DNA in both the physical and spiritual sense serves as a mechanism which assists us in accessing the powers of nature through elevated thoughts and feelings, and enable us to make an evolutionary leap of heart and mind to awaken to the energy fields induced by the current transits of Uranus, Neptune, and Pluto.

The New Age

The New Age finds transiting Uranus and Neptune in Aquarius, with transiting Pluto slowly winding its way through Sagittarius. Uranus in Aquarius is in its own sign, and is therefore very powerful, indicating that we may develop a penetrating, intuitive insight regarding the mystical and religious concepts of love. Neptune in Aquarius serves to deepen the supersensory faculties of humanity.

Thus, we have at our disposal the innate potential to shift our romantic ideals from selfish competition to an enlightened humanitarian viewpoint based on selfless compassion. Pluto in Sagittarius may further enhance the potential for mass spiritual regeneration, wherein the love principle may reach a high point in evolutionary development—sympathy verging on spirituality, and a sense of unity with all of life.

Love in the New Age

How can we redefine our natures and relationships in order to act in accordance with the current influx of New Age love energy?

When looking for points of compatibility between two birth charts, an astrologer will examine the Sun for women and the Moon for men. We do this in order to determine what kind of personality would make for a suitable husband, wife, or romantic partner. However, while some astrological cookbooks say that the Sun in a woman's chart relates to the husband or male partner, and the Moon in a man's chart relates to the wife or female partner, time has considerably altered the status quo. The old formula still holds true in many cases, because we still hold on to traditional mental and emotional constructs regarding love and marriage. Yet people in general are becoming more complete.

Women now express the qualities of the Sun in their birth charts more fully; they no longer depend on the man in their life to fulfill their ego needs because they perceive and act upon their own individuality and desire for recognition. Likewise, although they tend to change at a slower pace, men are becoming more receptive and sensitive, and don't necessarily depend on the woman to provide a feeding ground for emotional self-expression, or relegate a woman to the traditional ideals associated with her "place" within the home or relationship.

This tells us that there is hope for mental and emotional equality between the sexes. Moreover, it indicates that we are now free to explore and perfect the lover within ourselves.

What is your New Age attitude?

Answer yes or no to the following questions to see if you need a New Age love attunement:

1. Are you afraid to be loving and affectionate in your personal relationships?
2. Do you enjoy the creative arts?
3. Do you negate your own needs and desires for the sake of maintaining relationships?
4. Are you are able to express your feelings clearly?
5. Do you allow others to dominate and control you?
6. Do people of the intimate sex find your company pleasing and nonthreatening?
7. Do you sometimes idealize your lovers, and are you often deceived as a result?
8. Are peace, harmony, and cooperation an essential way of life for you?
9. Are you compassionate, nurturing, and sympathetic, even when you are challenged or feel threatened by others?
10. Are your relationships intense, dramatic, and short-lived?
11. Do like leaving better than loving?
12. Are your lovers real people, or simply objects of your desires?
13. Do you have a close, personal relationship with outside spirit and nature?
14. Do your relationships end along with the flames of passion?
15. Are you are in love with love, rather than with anyone in particular, except maybe yourself?

If you answered yes to questions 2, 4, 6, 8, 9, 12, and 13, and no to questions 1, 3, 5, 7, 10, 11, 14, and 15, you are ready to flow with the exciting tides of spiritual transformation in the New Age love department. Otherwise, your ideas concerning love and romance may need some tweaking. Read on to determine how the cosmic energies will affect your love life or that of someone you love, and what you can do to shapeshift with the tides of romantic change.

Love in the Signs

Aries
Aries is more decisive than ever when it comes to making a permanent commitment to love, owing to an abundance of superphysical energy that will heighten your sensuality on all levels. You are also inclined to protect and defend your love interests with considerable force. Rely upon your pioneering spirit to stay on track, and exercise patience to curb your intrinsic need to get ahead of your overly competitive self.

Taurus
Taurus is drawn to experience love with an exhilarating, exotic edge. An overly active imagination inflames your passion, yet also increases your vulnerability, causing you to escape into a secret fantasy world, or possibly bestow your affections on the wrong person. You may also lose a lover due to cosmic circumstances beyond your control. Concentrate on your cautious nature, and be conservative when it comes to love.

Gemini
Gemini researches a variety of nontraditional relationship possibilities at this time. Psychic premonitions and mystical visions guide you to someone who complements your image of the perfect spiritual partner. Resist being too inquisitive, and keep your talkative, communicative self quiet when it comes to divulging shared confidences. Trust your quicksilver, mercurial instincts to guide you in the right direction.

Cancer
Cancer natives feel emotionally unstable, making it difficult to remain in an existing relationship for any length of time. A love may move too slowly to suit your need for emotional intensity. Your penchant for sentiment and nostalgia is currently outdated. A firm grip on reality helps you to overcome your unrealistic ambitions. Turn to intuition and introspection when seeking a new love.

Leo
Leo individuals are hypersensitive, willful, and rebelliously independent, with distorted illusions where love is concerned, thus creating problems in intimate relationships. You are inspired to take the lead in your connections by taking on a submissive partner who is willing to follow your dreams. Stop playing amateur therapist and forget the fan-club following. Use your executive abilities to overcome your own immature behavior, and have some fun.

Virgo
Virgo is more nervous than usual about romantic involvements, easily jumping to conclusions that simply aren't there. Concentrate on being more reliable and emotionally available if you wish to attract a lover with serious intentions regarding commitment. Refrain from telling your lover "like it is" according to your critical perceptions. Instead, let your innate virtues of modesty and practicality lead the way toward keeping your delicate self-esteem intact.

Libra
Libra looks for fun, surprises, and the brighter side of life. Love in the New Age is spontaneous and unusual, with a focus on aesthetic, emotional, and spiritual refinement. You may enter into a relationship with someone you feel you have known forever. Do not allow indecisiveness and procrastination to deter your dedication to the cause of love.

Scorpio
Scorpio natives find their love lives in a state of drastic upheaval due to overt willfulness and a penchant for radical behavior of a sexual nature. Use the strong energies at your disposal to heal old wounds in yourself and those you love. You are a natural nonconformist; don't be trapped and held by iconoclastic patterns when you are quite capable of emotional death and rebirth. Wield your power wisely.

Sagittarius
Sagittarius wishes to bestow a more philanthropic brand of love, choosing to help those who are less fortunate rather than focusing

on one individual. However, you may have difficulty holding on to your altruistic aspirations because your emotions are intensified at this time. Rely on internal spiritual guidance in your intimate relationships. Be expansive, versatile, and progressive when it comes to sharing love, and consider yourself lucky to have an abundance, with more than enough to go around.

Capricorn

Capricorn will be a loyal, dependable lover in the New Age, with a propensity for making solid plans for the future. Your romantic partner will take you more seriously now, making marriage or lifelong commitment an imminent possibility. Fight against your cautious dislike for risk-taking, and take the plunge with your usual confident air. This long-term relationship will be a winner that will soothe your soul.

Aquarius

Aquarius natives will develop a philosophical view of love that is attuned to the subtle forces of nature and the unfolding of spiritual potentials. You will have the ability to express yourself powerfully and effectively now, so don't hesitate to ask for what you want. Experiment by sharing your altruistic insights regarding New Age love with groups of like-minded individuals, and rise above the loneliness, shyness, and fear of intimacy you often feel when faced with a one-on-one relationship.

Pisces

Pisces has idealistic visions regarding relationships, and may desire unions that are more refined and spiritual. Beware of those who attempt to prey on your sympathetic nature, as the emotionally greedy and perpetually needy-beyond-repair are pulled to your healing and compassionate love-light. Sacrificing yourself for love can lead to your sensitive feelings getting easily hurt. Nurture yourself for a change, and depend on your strong psychic abilities when reading between the love lines.

The Sun in Relationships
Your Path to Vitality and Happiness in Love

by David Pond

With the dawn of new millennium, we are moving ever closer to the reality of a global community, and just the sheer number of people we will all interact with points to the fact that relationship skills are more important now than ever before. Knowing oneself and accepting the appropriateness of differences within relationships are the most important keys in learning to live in greater harmony with others. What better tool than astrology to help us understand our own uniqueness, and that of others as well?

So often we get hurt in relationships when we fail to acknowledge differences. We expect certain types of experiences in a relationship that are consistent with our values, but if we fail to allow for the differences of each of the signs, we make assumptions about others that come from our lens of looking at life, not theirs. One of the great benefits of astrology is that it gives you an opportunity to step outside of your own view and look at life directly through your partner's eyes. Reading through all the signs can help you develop an appreciation for the rich tapestry of the entire makeup of the human experience, but first let's explore the nature of the Sun itself, and its significance in relationships.

The Sun is the center of our solar system, and its warmth and light are the animating force of all life. Plants, animals, and humans all require the Sun to sustain their life. Could there be a more powerful statement concerning the importance of the Sun in astrology? Your Sun sign describes your connection to this central source of life: what you need to feel vital. It is also the single most important factor in your happiness. Ideally, you would be in a relationship that supported and encouraged this vital core of your being. Relationships magnify everything—they can bring out the best and the worst of who we are. Developing a strong, healthy identity is hard enough, but to balance that with the needs and pressures of a relationship requires real talent.

At the core of your being lies the animating fire of your self. Your Sun sign describes this core truth of who you are and what you need for happiness and a sense of personal involvement in life. To feel fulfilled in life, it is essential that: (1) You are in touch with these qualities within yourself, and (2) Your main relationships provide encouragement and support for these qualities. Being in a relationship that doesn't honor this part of your character can be simply awful! No Sun, no life. It is that simple. If you have to sacrifice your true nature to maintain the relationship, the price is too high. So choose wisely.

How do we find our happiness? Thich Nhat Hahn, the great Buddhist teacher and poet says, "There is no way to happiness, happiness is the way." (*The Art of Mindful Living*, recorded by Sounds True, 1992) This simple truth is incredibly powerful in its teaching. If you look for that perfect partner, the one who will bring out your hidden qualities of happiness, you put the experience outside of yourself, and make it something to grasp for, to attain. This puts the cart before the horse. Metaphysics teaches us that the outer world reflects the inner world, meaning that if you are searching for your path to happiness, you attract people into your life that reflect this same incompleteness.

To get the horse before the cart, take responsibility for your own happiness. Then you are bringing the fullness of your being, your heart, and your love into the relationship; you are not looking for it in the relationship, you are looking to share it there. Read the qualities of your Sun sign in relationships, and ask yourself, "Have I taken responsibility for creating a life that allows me to bring out the best of what I have to offer?" If you find your relationship lacking, ask yourself first if you are following the spark of your own inner spirit.

"Physician, heal thyself," goes the familiar quotation. It is so easy to fall prey to the trap of believing that a relationship would improve if only your partner would change. There is no power in this perspective. You have given away your power when you make your happiness dependent on how others treat you. To regain your power, get involved in everyday activities that resonate with your Sun sign. Read the descriptions of your sign and consider ways to get your Sun more involved in your life. Start with activities that you have control over. Then work on integrating more of your happiness into your relationship. The Sun is your joy; others aren't going to mind it if you become more joyous!

Of course, there is the high road and the low road of every sign. In this light, we will also explore the potential pitfalls of each sign in relationships. Every sign has its strengths and its weaknesses, and there is nothing in life like relationships to magnify the issues we need to work on. Read the Pitfalls section of your sign to get clues as to where you'll likely need to work on yourself to improve your relationships.

Never settle for less than the basic needs of your sign. You can't sidestep your Sun and discover your path to happiness. It *is* the path to happiness.

Aries

Aries is represented by the Ram, and with its strong horns it lowers its head down and charges into life. This is your style in relationships—jump in, go for it, experience life! You flourish in a relationship that allows for your abundant spirit and love of activity. As an Aries, you need to listen to your instincts and impulses to stay in touch with your vital spark. It would be ideal to be with a partner who allowed for your independence by not crowding too closely. When unrestrained, the Aries temperament is fiery and passionate, thus you need a partner who can stand up to you and not feel threatened by your intensity. Your "go for it" attitude requires a partner that is up for the adventure, or you end up feeling thwarted; when the Aries call to action is blocked, frustration results. You can't repress this fiery energy and find happiness; it needs an outlet. You thrive in relationships that allow for your spontaneity. You would love to be with a partner who planned surprises for you, just like you do for others.

Pitfalls

Impatience, impatience, impatience. In a word, impatience is the number-one issue for you to work on to improve your relationship skills. Of course, this is a test for an Aries in all areas of life, but in relationships others can feel pressured by you unless you give them space to operate at their own pace. As with all the fire signs, your defensiveness can also be a problem if you react badly towards any view different from yours. Obviously, this would be detrimental in relationships. Too much projection of self can create an imbalance, leaving no room for receiving. Knowing this, you can consciously choose to quiet your fire so as to better receive another.

Greatest Gift

Spirit. Life is never boring with Aries around! Your abundant enthusiasm for life can be pure inspiration for others.

Taurus

Taurus is the connoisseur of the zodiac, and your eye for quality is just as apparent in your relationships as it is with your possessions. You would love to build and enjoy a life of abundance and refinement with your partner. The softer side of Taurus comes out in an affectionate relationship. Taurus is the most sensual sign of all. You are naturally sexual as well, but simple human touch in an affectionate, nonsexual manner is delightful for you. Your core energy deciphers what is the best, what is realistic, what you really want from the myriad of choices available, and then brings it into an enjoyable form. You've got tenacity—and then some—and seem to know what it takes to make something real. These qualities promise a search for a strong commitment-based relationship that you can rely on. You simply can't tolerate mistrust. If you can't absolutely count on a person, forget it: this relationship is not going anywhere. Taurus is a straight-up sign; you prefer sincerity to flamboyance; you value the genuine in others. You are steadfast and loyal and would want these qualities in another, as you are seeking to build a secure, solid life with your partner.

Pitfalls

Stubbornness is the key issue here. Your ability to resist change is your strength when it helps you hold on to what you believe in, but this becomes your weakness when flexibility is required—and in relationships, flexibility is always required. Give some thought to the metaphysical saying, "That which you resist, persists." Your tenacity can be your fatal flaw when you can't back down from a stance, even when you know you're wrong! Overattachment, whether to possessions, opinions, or others, can be very divisive in relationships. The high road is learning how to have strong opinions rooted in your values, while simultaneously allowing others their different views.

Greatest Gift

Your capacity to fully enjoy the moment. When you focus your ability to fully appreciate life's experiences onto your relationship, it blossoms like a garden in full bloom.

Gemini

Your airy nature requires a life of mental stimulation, and this is nowhere more true than in your relationships. You need ideas and communication like other people need food. Obviously, you would thrive in an open-minded relationship with an easy flow of communication. You crave variety and would value a partner who was open to a constantly changing panorama of life opportunities. You don't easily settle down, preferring to keep your options open. A relationship that is too restrictive, too patterned and predictable, does not allow for your best to shine. At your best you are light-hearted and whimsical—if things don't work out in a particular direction, you are open to exploring alternatives. You like a partner who doesn't get bogged down with heavy issues—someone who lets go of the past and gets on with life. Your open and curious mind is naturally flirtatious in the most innocent of ways, and it would be best to be with a noncontrolling partner who gives you the freedom to interact with others. You're not a "dig in for the long haul" type of person, so relationships that become stale are on dangerous ground. Before you abandon ship, first make sure you are doing what you can to pursue a life that satisfies your appetite for new learning experiences and stimulates growth in relationships.

Pitfalls

Endlessly second-guessing life and fearing to make the wrong choice haunts many a Gemini. Your gift is your ability to consider both sides of any situation, but it can easily become your curse when you are trying to maintain a relationship. You can always come up with alternative options, and this can split your energy from your here-and-now reality, not allowing you to fully sink into the experience of the relationship in front of you. Yours is the most easily distracted of all the signs ("I've got just enough time to get one more activity in, and still make that appointment.") and this is likely to be a source of endless frustration for those who end up waiting for you!

Greatest Gift

Ideas. A relationship is always enriched by the abundant ideas that come from your avid curiosity about life.

Cancer

You are a nurturer, and your need to experience life fully with your emotions must have room for expression in your closest relationships. Up close and personal or not at all is your style. You need to feel involved with your partner's inner, emotional life. You are meant to feel your way through life, rather than think your way, so you get to know someone through your emotions and feelings. This is where your vitality and life-force are strongest, and it is essential in your relationships. Your emotional sensitivity doesn't let just anybody into your innermost circle—you first must trust that others won't trample on your sensitivities. But when you do allow others into your life, you are the most loyal of all the signs; once accepted, others become family and that's that. Although you attach slowly, the Crab's pincers hold on tenaciously to that which currently nurtures you—you are terrible with "goodbyes" and separations. Although gentle by nature, you are a protector, and your fierceness comes out if you feel that anyone you care for is threatened. Cancer is an affectionate sign, and you enjoy being with someone who likes to snuggle and hug.

Pitfalls
Cancer's protective crab shell can all too easily appear defensive to others. You are meant to experience life through your personal emotions, but this can inhibit the free flow of communication. "You take everything way too personally," is a common refrain in your life. Try placing your attention on the other person's feelings behind the words; this will help pull you out of your own feelings. Another issue can be over concern for safety, which can stifle growth in relationships. Others can feel hemmed in and cramped when you become overprotective. Allow others their room for growth; your rejuvenated partner will, in turn, nurture you.

Greatest Gift
Your emotions are your great gift—learn to create healthy, enriching activities for both "inward" and "outward" phases of your emotional cycles, and you'll help others also learn that it is safe to feel.

Leo

As in all areas of life, you conduct your relationships with a tremendous dramatic flair. The Sun is the ruling planet of Leo and functions as the center of the solar system. You, too, need to be the center of your world, especially in relationships. You don't play second fiddle or function well as one of the people your partner is dating—that's not special enough. You need to be front-and-center in your relationships. Yes, you are meant to be demanding, but you give as much as you demand, and therefore this is not arrogance—it is your standard. Truth be known, you shine in a relationship in which you are adored! After all, you pour your heart into your relationships and expect the same treatment. You can be a great deal of fun, as that is what Leo is here to teach the rest of the zodiac: life can be a celebration of the heart. You value a rich personal life and want to share in this aspect of your partner's life. You take great pride in all you do and this includes your relationships. You want to be in a relationship that you can be proud of, and loyalty is a must.

Pitfalls

Pride can be an issue. When your pride makes it impossible for you to hear any opinions that do not support your view, this will certainly be disruptive in your relationships. Petty power conflicts become the norm if you still are proving your power. Accept your power. Your power exists on its own: it does not need permission or approval; it just is. As you accept your natural power, your need to be competitive with others drops. Leos can be just awful when not getting their way. Relationships require a constant give-and-take attitude of sharing and accommodating each other's needs.

Greatest Gift

Your heart. Your love is born right out of your heart, not a mental concept. No one will feel more loved than your partner when this outpouring of your dynamic, dramatic, creative wellspring of love is focused upon him or her.

Virgo

Virgo is known for its discriminating taste and attention to detail like no other sign: nothing passes your eye unnoticed. The little things matter to you in relationships. You like to do things for people and try to help out wherever you can. It would be ideal to be with a partner who appreciates this. You tend to do more than your share anyway, so you certainly wouldn't want to be with someone who took advantage of that quality. Actually, you are more comfortable with appreciation than adoration. You are sincere and genuine yourself, and you value these qualities in others. If it is important to you, you'll likely screen out partners who have been intimate with many others—that is too indiscriminate for you, given all the diseases in the world. You would like to be with a partner who wants to build a life together and do the work to make it happen. Down to earth, practical, and realistic, you want a relationship that fits these characteristics. Virgo is a wonderfully sensual and affectionate sign, but again, with discrimination—right time, right place, right person are prerequisites for romance.

Pitfalls

Your task-oriented approach to life can fill your life with work, squeezing out needed time for relationship activities. Remember to schedule time for fun and romance, or they will get put off, and put off, and put off. Your hypercritical nature, with yourself and with others, can narrow your focus to problematic issues in your relationship. What needs to be fixed? What needs work? What isn't perfect? Although this comes with the territory of being a perfectionist, if you let this get carried away, it can make you seem more negative than you really are. You don't always have to focus on the problems. Virgo falls prey to what I call "preparer's consciousness." You're always getting everything ready to enjoy your life, but never finding the time to actually do it.

Greatest Gift

"A friend in need is a friend indeed," is a creed that you live by. You are always there to lend a hand and help out a friend. Your natural modesty rivals this helper theme as one of your great gifts—you can be so real, so natural, so present. This encourages others to drop their airs and just be real as well.

Libra

With your Sun in Libra, you are here to discover yourself though your relationships. We say in astrology that Libra rules relationships, so you, more than most, need to constantly stay attentive to your relationship skills. Venus rules Libra, and this influence brings a deep appreciation for beauty, charm, and grace—the aesthetics of life. Your vitality and happiness depend on a touch of style and elegance in your life. This influence spreads into relationships and you prefer a cooperative, harmonious involvement with others.

You are truly interested in your partner's point of view, and value feedback before you make important decisions. (Decisions are not Libra's strength.) Romance for you is not purely physical; the mental rapport is just as important—going out for an elegant cultural evening, or dancing, is very romantic for you. Early in life Libra engages in what I call the "empty wish syndrome"—wishing that you never have to deal with people who are unjust or unfair. It is empty because it is unrealistic. The active path for Libra is to get involved with the negotiation process; never settle for less, or more, than what is in your best interest. The high road is to bring honor and integrity into all of your interactions throughout the day.

Pitfalls

Libra has a tendency to avoid anything unpleasant as if it were the plague. This becomes a problem when your "peace at any cost" attitude leads to you sacrificing what is really in your best interests. You might have a tendency to confuse compromise with cooperation—always adapting to your partner's needs to create harmony. However, this path does not create harmony if your needs are compromised in the process. Fulfill the role of Libra: be the negotiator; be clever enough, diligent enough, and persevering enough to make agreements that honor everyone involved.

Greatest Gift

Sharing. At your best, you really understand the give-and-take necessary to sustain an ongoing relationship. Your ideals in partnerships are as high as they come, and are reachable if you are willing to go through the essential process of relationships: negotiation.

Scorpio

Scorpio is known for the deep currents of its emotional nature. "Still waters run deep," is an apt description of your personality. This is also the level of life that Scorpio would like to share with another: there is nothing superficial about you whatsoever. You steer clear of those who occupy themselves with trivial concerns, preferring passionate, intense relationships. You seem to be drawn to complex individuals, as you get bored with people who are too obvious and predictable. Scorpio has the reputation of being the "sex sign" of the zodiac, and it is true that your sexuality can be truly magical with a partner who appreciates your emotional intensity. However, sex is not just physical with Scorpio; the psychological, emotional, and even spiritual levels of intimacy are also important to you. Your vitality is enhanced when you feel attractive and desirable to your partner, and the softer side of your love blossoms when trust is impeccable in your relationship. You are much happier with private, one-to-one sharing than you are in large social gatherings.

Pitfalls

Scorpio has two main issues to work with, both stemming from mistrust: control and lack of forgiveness. The mistrust is there because Scorpios have had to confront some of the darker aspects of human relationships, such as abandonment and betrayal. If you become too guarded and protective of your vulnerability, you can also become manipulative and controlling, always afraid of losing the upper hand. But the cost is lack of intimacy—you can't experience intimacy without risking your vulnerability. The same problem can occur from a tendency to hold on to old hurts with the attitude of "Never forgive, never forget." The problem is that the jailor and the prisoner are both stuck in the same building, and by holding onto the old issue you are not free to experience the fullness of the moment. Instead of focusing on the other person and trying to find forgiveness, try looking into the hidden aspects of your own psyche and be willing to ask yourself what you needed to learn from the problematic issue.

Greatest Gift
Intimacy. At its best, Scorpio merges with its partner at such a total level that both individuals are transformed through the experience.

Sagittarius

Sagittarians are known for their fiery enthusiasm for life and adventurous attitude about everything. You are an explorer in life and want a partner who is up for adventure. You need your freedom in relationships to explore your many interests. Your ability to frame experiences in a positive light gives you an upbeat, fun-loving, and optimistic approach to life. Ideally, you would be with a partner who supports your dreams, but grounded in reality enough to know when you are being overly optimistic.

Most Sagittarians have a need to be out in nature to reconnect with their source of vitality, so hopefully you will choose a partner who likes to travel and get out and see life. You need a partner who can engage your higher mind; you get bored with mundane reality and prefer the loftier realms of philosophy, religion, the wisdom traditions, politics, and other academic interests. You tend to say it like you see it and prefer others to do the same with you.

Pitfalls
In your insistence on making every experience positive, others can experience you as judgmental, dogmatic, and out of touch with reality. In your search for the ideal, you're missing the real. Your homework is to expand your quest for truth beyond the teachings you assimilated from your family and culture. Look into the various religions, philosophies, and political views that are expressed on our planet. Then, when you attempt to help others expand their perspective, you will be coming from an expanded perspective yourself. Sagittarians tend to promise the Moon and then fail to deliver. This is not malicious or deceitful, just unrealistic. Jupiter-ruled Sagittarians tend to suffer from "Too much-itis"—you overdo everything, and expect too much too soon. A good partner for you appreciates your positive outlook, but also helps you see when your expectations are outreaching reality.

Greatest Gift
Enthusiasm. Your excitement about the possibilities in life is quite infectious, and others often draw inspiration from you.

Capricorn

Sincerity, loyalty, and commitment are Capricorn themes that will strongly affect your choices in relationships. Your "keep your feet on the ground" approach to all of life is just as true in your relationships. You have your standards. You are more willing to wait for the right relationship than get caught up in impetuous love. Fortunately, you do know when you have it good and know how to enjoy it when you do!

Your relationships have to fit with the overall structure of your life. You have high standards in all areas of life and it all must work together. You are at your best in commitment-based relationships that hold the promise of building a life together from the ground up—way up. Others can think of you as serious, but you prefer to think of yourself as sincere. Patience is certainly one of your virtues, and it will be rewarded in your relationships. The time spent cultivating your connection to the other person in your life will pay off again and again.

Pitfalls
Your organized, task-oriented approach is the key to your success, but when it starts taking over in relationships your love life gets reduced to one of the efficient cogs in the machinery of your life. The right partner could help pull you out of the "all work and no play" lifestyle that you too easily adopt. You can get too serious about keeping it all together and could definitely benefit from having a partner to get you out of your bouts of pessimism. Organize some time for spontaneity. Your gift of taking control of a situation pays off handsomely in career endeavors, but becomes a hindrance in your love life. If you are always in control, you never get to discover the magic of deep intimacy, which can only be experienced by surrendering to the moment and letting go.

Greatest Gift
Commitment. You are there for the long haul and don't get jumpy at the first sign of a challenge. At your best, you demonstrate the patience and perseverance that it takes to build a real relationship.

Aquarius

Your decidedly intellectual approach to life requires a relationship that stimulates and challenges your mind. Your natural talent is to rise up above the purely personal view and see things from a larger perspective; thus you lose interest in those who are immersed in their personal emotions. You are like an alarm clock helping others to wake up, challenging conventional thinking and pressing others for their original thoughts. You value originality, in yourself and others. With your genuine interest in people, you make friends easily. Yet the paradox of Aquarius is that you are at your best when you maintain your individuality and authenticity, so taking a relationship beyond friendship can feel like a threat to your freedom. Aquarius doesn't seem to fit into the mold that works for everybody else—conventional anything holds little interest for you. You need to experiment in life to find your way, and that includes experimenting with relationships. Aquarius is independent, and you need to be in a relationship that allows plenty of room for your needs for freedom. You want your lover to be your best friend.

Pitfalls
Your need for independence can feel threatened by any movement toward commitment as long as you consider freedom and commitment to be mutually exclusive. Yours is the challenge of learning how to maintain your independence within a commitment-based relationship. It's all in how you do it. You can be responsible, but do it in you own unique way, not sacrificing either way of life. Others can experience your detachment as insensitivity unless you cultivate your listening skills. Although talking about personal emotions and feelings might seem indulgent to you, your friends and partners need this periodically to feel personally connected to you. So for their sake, engage those you love at this most personal level.

Greatest Gift
Friendship and perspective. You want your lover to be your best friend, and this adds to the range of experiences you have to share with another. You also bring a fresh perspective and original insights into all that you do

Pisces

Pisces is the most emotionally sensitive of all the signs, and in relationships this can be both your greatest asset and your biggest downfall. Pisces can be the incurable romantic and, in the right relationship, this can come into beautiful expression. However, in the wrong relationship, you fall in love with qualities that you imagine your partner to have, but are not true in reality. So choose wisely. You are meant to feel everything, and with your sensitivity, you will also directly experience the joys and sorrows of your mate. You are the most forgiving of people, and you want to choose a partner who won't take advantage of this. You are quite able to adapt to another person's lifestyle, and as long as this is not sacrificial, this adds to harmony in your relationships. Your feelings run so deep it can be difficult to find words to express yourself. Therefore, it would be best to be with a partner who does not press you to put into words that which cannot be spoken. Your inner emotional world and your spiritual/religious beliefs are the source of your strength, and it is essential to be with a partner who honors this part of your life.

Pitfalls
All Pisces individuals are prone to various forms of self-sacrifice leading to self pity—the path of the martyr. This obviously would undermine happiness. Pisces is not a big ego sign, but when this humility goes too far and becomes self-denial, the inevitable "no one understands me" follows. This sabotaging of the self is the low road for Pisces and must be watched for. Another pitfall for compassionate, sympathetic Pisces people is that they carry the suffering of others as if it were their own. Learn to develop the skill of opening up to others, even feeling their pain; then bless it and lay it on the lap of the Divine.

Greatest Gift

Kindness and support for others is your natural gift. At your best, your love is nearly devotional in its all-accepting ways. When you regularly connect with the source of your faith, you have a never-exhausting well of affection to share with those you love.

House Hunting and Your Sun Sign

by Alice DeVille

Have you been contemplating a change of residence? Perhaps you are tired of renting and have saved the down payment for a nest of your own. Or maybe you're feeling cramped in your present quarters and could use more space to sprawl out and store your treasures. For some of you a job transfer to another city may be in the wings. If parenting is in your future, you may need the extra rooms and the security of a fenced-in yard when you welcome a new addition to the family. Maybe you're seriously contemplating spending inheritance or bonus money on a "move up" residence. In that case, your dream home could be just a set of blueprints away from reality. Wouldn't you like to know the best strategies to exercise your options for a move? Whatever your particular situation, there is no time like the present to begin your search.

Interest rates have been comfortably low in recent years whether the real-estate industry has favored a seller's or a buyer's market. New tax breaks for homeowners went into effect in the late '90s, making home ownership particularly attractive to a great number of people. Both couples and singles benefit from the reduced impact of capital gains taxes on resale housing. Creative legislation offers incentives to first-time buyers by offering low down payment loans. For would-be buyers with limited cash for a down payment, credit problems, or the uncertain income of the self-employed, financial institutions offer a variety of loans to suit your present needs and your pocketbook. If you are procrastinating about a move, this article may help you identify the accommodations you need and desire in a new home.

First, consider the help you may derive from using astrology to begin your search. If you have not had your natal chart constructed, by all means seek out a competent astrologer, or use the coupon in the back of this book to have Llewellyn's Computerized Services construct your chart. You'll have insight about your current financial picture, the type of home and amenities you might prefer, the best real-estate agent to work with, what to look for in the construction of your proposed residence to make sure it is safe and solid, and the timing and conditions for making a deposit and negotiating your contract.

The first thing you will want to do is get prequalified by a lending institution so that you know just how large a loan your current financial situation can support. That way you don't have to spend unnecessary time looking at homes that you can't afford. Your neighborhood bank may be the best place to start. If you need creative funding due to low cash flow, you may need to look for a mortgage banker—or even a mortgage broker—because they normally have access to more lending sources and types of loans than your local banker. You'll want to watch out for brokers who add lots of junk fees to the loan. Ask up front about the types of fees you might expect to pay. In other words, before you actually begin your housing search, you should have the peace of mind of knowing that you have a lender willing to do business with you at a price you can definitely afford.

If you enjoy surfing the net, you will find numerous real-estate web sites offering information about availability of homes, locations, asking prices, brokerages, appraisers, settlement agents, and financial sources. You may be able to take a look at the amenities, see actual pictures of the interior and exterior of homes that appeal to you, and learn about shopping, transportation, and schools—without leaving your home.

Next you'll want to find a competent sales agent. I recommend that you interview at least three agents before you make your decision. (I even suggest that my clients find out the agents' birth dates, if possible, for extra insight into compatibility. Many of them have no trouble getting at least the birthday, and an amazing number get the full date.) Let your agent know what you are looking for, and where, and how much you are prepared to spend. Then identify neighborhoods that appeal to you and ask your agent to run recent home-sale closing data so you can get a feel for how much you might pay. Remember these are *selling prices* you are looking for, not *asking* or *listing prices* which can be considerably higher than you might want to pay. After you have determined compatibility, sit down and discuss a schedule for looking at homes that interest you.

Some readers may feel that an agent is an unnecessary step in the process, especially if they are buying a new home or have completed these transactions in the past without the benefit of an agent. Buyers often think that if they deal directly with the seller, they will save fees and commissions. I could fill my back yard with people who have gone that route only to find out later about costly errors, clouded titles, vague wording, holdups at the settlement table, reneging on the part of the seller, or failure to cover their purchase with protective clauses in the purchase offer that leave them waiting for months on end for the sellers to vacate the premises. And then there are the horror stories over properties that have construction, plumbing, roofing, and electrical flaws or incurable defects—like the road that is about to go in behind your back yard and will lower the property's value. Several of these flaws go undetected because the purchaser has not paid for a home inspection prior to settlement.

Many of these setbacks may be avoided by choosing a competent agent—perhaps a buyer's agent who actually works for you and can provide additional insight into your home-buying transaction. Remember that unless you request a buyer's agent to help you in the transaction, the agent you phone actually works for the seller since the seller pays the commission, so you will not be told that you can bid much lower on the house than the asking price. And remember to have your attorney, financial advisor, or real-estate expert—who has no vested interest in the property—look over the contract before you sign it as well as the settlement papers when you are ready to close on your loan.

In case you are wondering how I know these details, I am a licensed real-estate agent in addition to holding credentials as an astrological and intuitive business consultant. Unlike most real-estate professionals, you won't find me showing listings, closing deals, or going to the settlement table. While I keep current through continuing education requirements on industry trends, policies, laws, and practices, I use my expertise along with the wonderful tool of astrology to educate clients in their housing transactions or coach agents toward a successful sales record. Agents often seek help in overcoming hurdles in their closing techniques, breaking the slump or slow sales periods, or working with challenging clients. Their natal charts reveal options for improving performance and increasing sales.

Clients want to know when, where, and how to buy a home. They may ask me to assess their choices, often through a site visit, before they offer a down payment. Since I am familiar with feng shui principles (the Chinese art of space and placement), I am able to pick up information on the home's energy and harmony. (In some parts of the country, the sales transaction includes a clause that says the sale is contingent upon a feng shui inspection.) Other clients like help in choosing an agent or a mortgage company. How about you? Are you ready to search for the perfect home? Well, grab your chart! Let's go house hunting through the signs.

Aries

Your taste ranges from the state-of-the-art Smart Home, with computerized technology monitoring activity at every level, to the well-appointed condominium offering maintenance-free living. You won't want to drag out the house-hunting adventure for weeks on end. You prefer to hit the ground running and see as many homes as possible in your price range in the shortest amount of time possible. You'll need an energetic, full-time sales agent who can keep up with your pace and has a clear calendar to show you available homes from dawn till dusk.

Real-estate agents who work with an Aries get clear signals about how the listed home impresses their client. Many an Aries opts out of a full-blown inspection. As soon as you cross the threshold, you have drawn conclusions about whether the house has any other charms you want to explore. Why waste time if you don't like the look? Besides, you want to look at at least seventeen more homes before dark.

Aries likes a home that makes a strong architectural statement. You may not want too many nooks and crannies—think of all that maintenance. While a good number of you are mechanically inclined and could do wonders with fixing up a neglected home, the majority of you want to channel that energy into creating private space, selecting comfortable furniture, and giving your hobbies and collections visibility in your new home. I have known a few Aries signs that wanted a home workshop, or at least the space to create one away from the main living quarters. Normally, you'll want a family room or recreation room that stimulates conversation and has the space to accommodate your stereo and home theater equipment. Once you find the perfect home, you'll celebrate with the people in your life and sign up a few recruits to help you pack.

Taurus

As a member of the esteemed earth-sign group, your house-hunting approach is practical and thorough. You do your homework regarding the neighborhood, property values, and the appreciation potential before you conduct your search. You care about getting a good return on your investment and will thoroughly assess the curb appeal of any prospective home. An impressive sales record appeals to you when you search for the right real-estate agent. You prefer a seasoned veteran and may well choose a buyer-broker to facilitate your home purchase, since you've already done your homework and know exacrly what you need. Canvassing a desirable neighborhood and checking the "For Sale" signs for evidence of a busy realty company appeal to you.

An impressive front door and impeccable, often formal, landscaping almost always catch your eye. Your green thumb needs a nice plot of land to plant those petunias, hollyhocks, and morning glories. Privacy is often a necessity for you—but stay away from homes that sit on a steep hill, or your prosperity may wash away with the spring rains. You normally prefer two-story homes rather than sprawling one-level contemporary styles because of the economical heating and cooling features. Many a Taurus complains about the high cost of home maintenance, yet few cut corners when it comes to comfort and style.

One home may not be enough for you, or you may buy and sell homes as investment properties. In that case, you upgrade just enough to realize a reasonable profit and reinvest the cash for the next venture. Some of you like to buy and manage apartment complexes or duplexes and live in one of the properties yourself. That way you can keep an eye on your tenants and your nest egg. No one has to tell you to get prequalified, Taurus. When you find your dream home, you'll have two or three bankers competing for your business. Then you'll hire the best moving company in town at a reduced rate to make sure your precious antiques arrive safely at their new residence.

Gemini

Although you enjoy the benefits and prestige of home ownership, many of you take your time in making that first house purchase. Your many interests keep you hopping, and you don't want the demand of lawn-mowing, painting, and plumbing repairs interfering with your social schedule. When you are ready to give up apartment living and the ease of having the maintenance supervisor change your light bulbs and fix those leaky faucets, you Geminis search for unique homes that cater to your lifestyle.

The residence that promises a smooth flow of chi energy and balance of yin and yang is the ideal choice for your sensitive nervous system. A perfect match is the patio home or a gated compound that includes caretaking, so you never have to pick up a rake or a paintbrush. If you are single or have a small family, you may prefer to own a condo in a savvy, elegant high rise with a breathtaking view and secured garage parking. Whether your chosen residence is large or compact, you'll want leading-edge storage and shelving options. A home library would appeal to you to display your extensive book, music, or hobby collection. And you'll probably want your computer located in this room to enhance communication opportunities on the Internet or chat with contacts on your favorite mailing lists. If you work from home, you may prefer built-in, modular furniture to store and display your high tech office equipment.

A compatible sales agent shows you homes that are light and airy. Pastel blues, greens, and yellows often attract you and dominate your color scheme. You dislike heavy window treatments and rooms without windows, preferring to let natural light in whenever possible. Screens are a necessity, and you probably like sliding glass doors that open to a deck or patio. Your home must be ready to move into with little or no work, and be close to shopping, bookstores, and transportation facilities. You often challenge sales professionals because at least *two* homes appeal to you and you have trouble making up your mind. After bearing with your inevitable procrastination, the lucky sales agent who closes your deal deserves every bit of the hard-earned commission. Why not offer to post the "Sold" sign so you get a chance to reaffirm your outstanding choice, and treat your exhausted agent to a gourmet dinner?

Cancer

In your often lengthy search for the perfect home, a well-appointed kitchen takes top priority. This room will get lots of living and loving. Who but the Queen of Comfort, Warmth, and Nurturing would be in tune with today's trend of putting big bucks into her kitchen? Open, spacious kitchens with granite counter tops, wall ovens, appliance garages, and huge work islands appeal to Moon children. While you lovingly create culinary masterpieces, you'll want a special gathering place with plenty of seating to carry on conversations with cherished guests. You opt for a floor plan that has an adjoining family room and breakfast nook with full view of your tantalizing kitchen. Remember to look for a layout where the stove faces the room's center to maximize chi energy and create prosperity in your new home. Your guests won't want to leave, but you probably have bedrooms to spare. You can put them up for a night and feed them blueberry pancakes and fresh-squeezed orange juice for breakfast.

Your sign favors buying new homes, and you'll want to look at several floor plans before you sign that contract. Look for a flexible builder who caters to your space requirements. Your sign rules the Fourth House of home and real-estate transactions, so you have a vested interest in the power of your purchase dollars. A contractor who is willing to pay closing costs and throw in a finished recreation room may get your business. You are not above reminding builders that they have competition for your hard-earned bucks.

Many housing styles appeal to you, Cancer, yet a more traditional look dominates when you actually furnish and decorate your nest. You may choose a color scheme and weave it artfully throughout the house. Wallpapered foyers and baths add drama, and you often use floral arrangements as the focal point of a room. You find the sound of water soothing and reflective. A preferred amenity is a water garden, whether you place a rippling fountain in your living room or install a pond beside your private terrace. When it comes to outdoor landscaping, you like a variety of shrubbery and blooms to dress up your velvety carpet of grass. A wise sales agent may discover the way to your checkbook by finding you a dreamy mansard roof cottage at the end of a curving flagstone path.

Leo

The astute real-estate professional should know that you like first impressions, and the threshold effect is definitely not lost on you when you open the door of a prospective purchase. Without a doubt you were meant to own a stately home with a breathtaking entry that has a parquet or imported marble floor. You like to make grand entrances and prefer a second-story foyer that has the feel of spaciousness and luxury. A sweeping staircase adds the perfect touch of opulence that sends you impulsive inner signals, urging *"Buy me, buy me."*

Many a Leo spends a considerable sum of money decorating the entrance hall. Your dramatic flair shows in the lion figurine that greets your guests, the custom brass umbrella stand, and the Ionic column that holds a Roman bust. Often a crystal chandelier sparkles high above a Palladian window and showers beams of welcoming light across the floor and gilt furnishings. One feature you normally won't find attracting a Leo is a bathroom placed near the front door. You are innately wise to the rule of feng shui that frowns on placing toilets anywhere near the entrance, which will clash with the home's sunny energy.

Leo is one of the signs most susceptible to buying a home based on love at first sight, before all the features have been studied. Let me encourage you to study the home from all angles lest you share the same fate as one of my clients who found the perfect home with "all the bells and whistles." Her choice had three decks that seemed to promise ravishing views from all three floors—when she faced the back of the home. Had she only turned around and faced the street she would have found a massive water tower as the scenic backdrop—clearly an obstruction that is called an incurable defect and can impede future resale of the property. So, be prepared to look at a variety of architecturally interesting home styles, get a thorough appraisal of the property, and find a seller willing to negotiate on settlement costs.

Virgo

For you, Virgo, a home search begins with your pocketbook. The idea that you first buy a modest little starter home and work your way up to an executive mansion over time has appeal, especially when you look at ways to turn over a large profit each time you sell. Advertisements that offer a home "as is" capture your bargaining interest, and you don't mind fixing up a home to meet your needs. In today's housing market, that tantalizing phrase often means "take it or leave it," as many sellers want to walk away from repairing the home before selling. If a home inspection reveals serious structural flaws, stay away. You've struck no bargain if all your hard-earned cash is spent on recurring problems in often unlivable homes.

Splurging for you might be adding garden windows in kitchens or baths, or finding a dream home with a plant-friendly sun room. Your green thumb fills entryways, corners, and empty spots with a variety of houseplants, tropical trees, and climbing vines. You may even have space for a greenhouse or a cutting room where you propagate your own seedlings. Kitchen wall treatments with herb or vine themes make a perfect backdrop for your copper collection and hanging pot rack. And pristine white ceramic tile baths with soaker tubs meet your requirements for the relaxation zone.

Prospective sales agents get your thorough scrutiny before you sign a contract to work with them. Since you don't like to take time off from work to go house hunting, you'll probably want a guarantee that your agent is available to show listings on weekends. You regularly request information about a home's monthly utility costs, and the age of appliances, the roof, heating, and air conditioning units. Unless you are buying a hobby farm or are self-employed, you'll want to know the location of the nearest fitness club, health food store, bus route, and park-and-ride lot. With your penchant for reducing stress in your life, you like to take public transportation to work and read in leisure, rather than fight the traffic jams. When you are sure that you have found the perfect location for your organized, efficient lifestyle, your grateful agent will celebrate the sale by sending you a set of pruning shears and a hearty ficus tree for your garden room.

Libra

As the ultimate host, entertainment-minded Librans select homes based on the possibilities for accommodating social gatherings. You prefer huge family or recreation rooms with inviting hearths and more than one seating option for group conversation. Space for game or pool tables, home entertainment centers, and children's toys need consideration. Your wish list includes wet bars, butler's pantries, china cupboards, generous food storage facilities, and ample counterspace for serving buffet dinners. Most of you own two or more refrigerators and a freezer to keep those canapés handy in case of drop-in visitors.

Storage and display mean a lot to Libras. Your sign requires harmony and balance in the home with no visible signs of clutter. Lots of walk-in closets, finished garages, and back-yard storage sheds for gardening equipment are often prerequisites. You like beautiful views from both inside and outside your windows. Your foyer or living room should have a fetching alcove for the decorative étagère that holds your porcelain eggs and one-of-a-kind china pieces.

Family size often dictates the square footage you desire in your home, but not necessarily the style of your preferred residence. Cramped quarters are much more painful to you than most signs. If your heart is set on finding a colonial and you run across a spacious, updated split-level with extra bedrooms and multilevel recreation options, you may be easily persuaded to part with your cash. Homes with bedrooms situated away from the bustling energy centers soothe your psyche. A savvy real-estate professional will find you an entertainer's delight complete with patio, deck, and hot tub to make your after-closing housewarming party the talk of the town. And with your charming Libra hospitality, you'll extend a lifetime of invitations to your annual summer barbecue.

Scorpio

Privacy-loving Scorpios often influence home builders' floor plans of the master bedroom suite. Designers have been known to change the layout based on a Scorpio's critical review of lack of amenities or wasted space. Every competent sales agent should know that the quickest route to a Scorpio's deposit check is to entice their client with a knockout bedroom. Both male and female Scorpios prefer spacious rooms with a sitting area, multiple closets, and dual sinks in the adjoining master bath. You like generous linen closets, eye-catching plant shelves, separate showers with a seat, and a Jacuzzi bath. Well-versed in feng shui, you are naturally attuned to what its principles suggest: you won't want to see the toilet from your luxurious, canopied, king size bed and will prefer that the "water closet" have its own separate door. Cathedral ceilings and chi-catching mirror treatments enhance the intimacy you want to capture in the bedroom suite of your dreams.

You may find compatibility in a multilevel town home or a tree-shaded single-family Tudor with a sheltered front entrance and a thick welcome mat. Your door will have a peephole so you can see who is calling before you open up. An entry porch appeals to you so callers stay dry in inclement weather while they wait for you to greet them. With most home styles, you prefer a brick or stone façade unless you reside in an earthquake zone. You prefer trees and boxwood varieties in your landscaping plan, yet low-maintenance flowering shrubs like azaleas, rhododendrons, and red border flowers add the drama you prefer to create an inviting refuge.

Resale homes with dramatic, strong colors normally attract you much more than subtle pastel decorating schemes. If you do buy a home with a monochromatic color scheme, such as tone-on-tone neutral beige, you will most likely use dramatic, contrasting prints, walls of artwork with various-sized frames, sweeping window treatments, and table-top sculptures to capture the essence of your decorating style. An ideal housewarming gift for you is a fertility garden for your bedroom or home office.

Sagittarius

Your fiery Sun sign likes warmth and comfort in key living quarters, especially the den, great room, and bedroom. A home with two or more fireplaces appeals to many Sagittarian home buyers. You like having them on every floor. For safety reasons, be sure they are lined and that the flues work properly. You enjoy homes that reflect favorite eras and have a sense of history. Since these homes generally sell in established neighborhoods, you will need to do a thorough job of home inspecting. Listings that appeal to you advertise homes as "quaint, cozy, rustic, or charming" which in layman's terms mean "needs work." Truth be told, you Sagittarians don't want to spend all your time on restorations and replacing furnaces, so select your pride and joy carefully. Ask your agent to request that the seller offer a one-year homeowner's warranty on major fixtures.

If you are a pet owner, you'll want accommodations for Fido and Fritzi, such as dog-runs in the back yard and interior mud rooms to hold pet bowls, beds, and grooming products. Some of you may prefer a home on several acres, complete with a stable and tack room to house your show horse. Or you'll buy a second home like a cabin in a rural or mountain community to get away from the urban bustle and enjoy favorite hobbies and pastimes. Tradable time-share properties hold appeal so you can enjoy exotic vacations without maintenance headaches.

You could use the advice of a real-estate professional with a working knowledge of feng shui. While you usually are drawn intuitively to homes that offer all five elements—metal, earth, water, fire, and wood—to balance your energy, you often settle on properties with inadequate storage that neutralize the positive flow and clutter corners with all your collectibles and flea market finds. Or you flip over one of those ornate Victorians which has a few too many windowless rooms. But when you find a treasure, nothing gives you more pleasure than wrapping up a solid deal. As one of the zodiac's true optimists, you bring your checkbook along when you go house hunting. Be sure you don't pay an inflated price for your find. Instead, spend the leftover cash on a Tiffany lamp for your inviting front parlor and silvery wind chimes for the charming and spacious master suite balcony.

Capricorn

Ambitious Capricorn envisions a stately manor home framed by exotic hollies, majestic oaks, and shapely junipers. Impressive landscaping is a must for home buyers under the sign of the Goat. If you're buying a new home, you look for lots based on the potential array of life-affirming gardening options that are available. Your eyes like to travel over high and low plantings, and you savor the impact of pathways that are sculpted with ground cover like pachysandra, liriope, or English ivy. The rear balcony or deck of your home should overlook your carefully designed Power Garden so that you may appreciate its form, design, and order—qualities dear to your Capricorn heart.

Most Capricorns follow the rule of thumb that says "buy as much home as you can afford," and don't want to move unless upward mobility and a substantial promotion pay off. Home improvement of your investment is a continuing process. You want every room to look its best and probably have a plan to update your castle one room at a time. You like fine furnishings and custom touches like shadow panels, murals, and covered light switches. Decorative wall and window treatments, chair rails, and crown molding attract you, since you tend to prefer a formal decor.

Although you like to exercise your bargaining power in negotiating the price during your home purchase experience, you put quality and impeccable maintenance high on the list of preferences for available properties. Woe betide the real-estate agent who shows you run-down, dirty, or garishly decorated homes when you undertake your search. You may not step a foot over the threshold before saying, "Not interested," if the appearance is seedy. You tend to settle on a property you like almost immediately and mentally compare it to other listings. Yet you keep your preference to yourself and go through the exercise of looking at numerous homes before revealing your choice. Your practical business sense dictates that you visit the home at all hours of the day and weekends to see what goes on in the neighborhood. When you successfully seal the deal, mark your sacred passage by planting a fragrant blue spruce or Japanese maple in the heart area of your Power Garden.

Aquarius

The prospect of home ownership appeals to your investor's mindset and fondness for competing for choice properties. Before you venture out into the frenzied real-estate market, you'll grab your trusty calculator and crunch some real-world numbers to see how much house you can buy. You are one of the signs who prefers to plunk down large down payments or pay cash for your purchase. You won't want any of your hard earned cash going toward monthly PMI (Private Mortgage Insurance) payments that a down payment of less than 20 percent requires. Using online listings as a major source of identifying the market offerings, you pinpoint neighborhoods of primary interest. After you have seen detailed street maps, you'll drive by the sale properties and give them the once-over before you contact the listing agent.

Aquarian tastes in homes and furnishings tend to be eclectic. Exteriors with decking in recycled materials that resemble wood appeal to your environmentally sensitive conscience. You may prefer a thoroughly modern home with walls of glass and terraced gardens; a private, one level loft with exposed beams and a sprawling open look; or an imposing center hall colonial with a turreted wing. In some cases, you tend to mix furniture and accessory styles and create your own unique look. If your Moon is conjunct Venus or Jupiter, your preference is often for rich wood furnishings with burl accents. A sleigh bed in the square-shaped master suite balanced by functional night tables, crystal lamps, and round mirrors on adjoining walls gives you the sense of security you need to get a good night's sleep. Many of you keep a computer in your bedroom. If you do, be sure you isolate it from the sleep area with an attractive screen or an overstuffed chaise.

Homes with hardwood floors attract your sign. You'll complement them with luxurious imported carpets that unite conversation areas, or round dhurrie rugs that bring flow to long hallways. You tend to select square or rectangular furniture and need to break up the lines with round or oval pieces. Add tropical floor plants and lofty trees to dress up corners and buffer sharp angles. A well-placed skylight or two may be the deciding point when you narrow down your choices. Be sure you don't procrastinate though, or your dream home will go to the next bidder! When you find a home that matches most of the preferences on your wish list, notify your e-mail network that you'll be logging on at a new address. Let them know that you're recruiting a moving team and will honor all the volunteers at your Open House celebration. And be sure to tell them you have hired a body worker to help them relax their aching joints.

Pisces

One of the most romantic homeowners on the planet is Pisces. You know how to create ambiance and flow with your choice of beautiful furnishings and your talent for accessorizing. In record time after move-in, you have the knack for giving your new home a completely ravishing look using dried flower arrangements, colorful candles, fragrant potpourri scents, and privacy screens to enhance each room's comfort and elegance.

A variety of home styles appeal to Pisces. Whether you choose a roomy town house with a garage, a rambling rancher, or a gracious Georgian, you look for unique structural features like built-in window seats, curved arches, stained glass windows, and hideaway laundry facilities. You'll turn an extra bedroom into a hobby or exercise room, and relish the thought of extra closets for your clothing and shoe collection. High on your list is an inspiring water view to attract prosperity, but if that is not possible you will create one. Inside, you like desk-top water gardens with natural stones and plants that accent your favorite color scheme and soothe you into relaxing moods. Your outdoor landscaping may include a meditation garden, complete with rippling seafoam pond and water lilies.

Your real-estate agent should know that you give prospective properties the white glove test—especially when it comes to bathrooms and kitchens. If they are not pristine, you seldom leave a deposit. True to the sensitivity of your sign, you get strong energy vibes when you enter homes. Your ESP speaks loudly when something is amiss. Wisely, you should avoid jutting corners that cut rooms in half, or very long hallways that disrupt chi energy. Strong pet odors, mustiness, and mold often trigger an allergic reaction or sinus problems. Be sure to check the interior ventilation system, basement, and plumbing area of properties under consideration for moisture, leaks, and fumes. When the home of your dreams appears, you'll wave your magic checkbook and visualize an early settlement date. Long before moving day, you'll place an order with a closet design firm for custom racks to hold your extravagant collection of shoes. Then you'll dance till dawn with your soul mate to celebrate your outstanding find.

How Your Sun Sign Affects Your Career

by Stephanie Clement

The Sun in your horoscope indicates your deepest character traits and the direction of your ambition. Just as the Sun is the source of energy for physical life, it reflects your thoughts and desires concerning your career or mission. The Sun sign reveals the direction of your ambition, how you express your will power, and where you can take a leadership role.

The Sun sign element is indicative of the primary psychological type. The Sun signs belong to one of four elements:

Element	Sun Signs	Type
Fire	Aries, Leo, Sagittarius	Intuition
Earth	Taurus, Virgo, Capricorn	Sensation
Air	Gemini, Libra, Aquarius	Thinking
Water	Cancer, Scorpio, Pisces	Feeling

The three fire signs share many qualities, as do the earth, air, and water signs. They each have qualities specific to the sign as well. So

Cancers, Scorpios, and Pisces all think somewhat alike in terms of broad psychological process, but each sign also has its own focus.

Individuals do not necessarily conform to their psychological type. If you were raised by air-sign people, your water-sign Sun may have learned to conform to their ideas. Practical earth-sign parents may not have encouraged your fire-sign type of creativity. Nevertheless, your primary approach to life is through your Sun sign and its corresponding element.

Fire – Intuition

If your Sun is in Aries, Leo, or Sagittarius, then you are the intuitive type. Intuitive types listen to inner, less conscious sources of information. These people are inventors, artists, and forward thinkers because they can see the possibilities of an idea long before development is possible. Therefore they pursue what they know the world is not yet prepared for. Fire types jump to conclusions, yes, but not necessarily without the intermediate steps. They may go through those steps at light speed by sizing up an underlying principle. They also may simply recognize on a less conscious level the inevitable match between an idea and their own desires.

The intuitive fits into the educational system rather well, as many high school and college courses make use of the deductive skills intuitives share with the thinking type. They respond well to the timed testing that is prevalent today. They master the complexities of mathematics because they can grasp the results without having to ground their learning in a physical way.

Intuitives contribute through their inventiveness. They are willing to sacrifice the pleasure of the moment in the hope of greater future achievement. They are often restless and crave inspiration. Because they thrive in situations where getting to the answer is important, they are good at problem-solving and tasks that require ingenuity. Careers in the creative arts, religious inspiration, and scientific discovery all suit the intuitive type. They make inspired leaders and promoters. For them, the problem is more exciting than the solution, the game is more important than winning, the chase more interesting than the end result.

Mata Hari's Leo Sun casts her as an intuitive type. She demonstrated her intuitive ability throughout her extended career as a spy, constantly figuring out what to do regarding her less than certain future: she knew other people's next moves intuitively.

Aries

Creativity revolves around the moment of inspiration. Like a small child, you thrill to the moment of discovery, the inception of a new plan, the desire to forge ahead, and have a passion for all that is new. Your creative process may not be evident to others at first, but there is action nonetheless. Like a brooding hen, you warm and protect your initial ideas with the assurance that they will produce a worthwhile result. It is this initial stage of creation that most pleases you, and you like to be the idea person.

Your creative process is complemented by the energy of assertiveness. You can take the initiative when it is necessary, and you have a penetrating mind. You bring enthusiasm and energy to your work and can be spontaneous. Yet you also sometimes seem too forceful to others. The direction of your career will present opportunities for you to be reckless and daring, and you may be successful using these tactics. However, you will find that it takes courage to moderate your own behavior to suit the corporate situation. Unless you own it, you probably can't get your own way all the time, and even then you will want to encourage others to do their best work by allowing them the chance to be bold and enterprising.

Traits not to display in the workplace include excessive displays of impatience, anger, resentment, and selfishness. Instead, strive for spontaneity, constructive criticism, ambition, and audacity.

Leo

You have the will to create and the stamina to see a process through to completion. You are self-reliant. Your urge for offspring can focus on children, or it can be directed toward some other manifestation in the material world. You thrive on the process of bringing ideas to fulfillment, on the heat of production, if you will. You want assurance that your works will survive you in some way. Your creative heat is like the oven that bakes the bread or hardens the pottery, and you recognize that creativity takes a certain amount of time and cannot be rushed. You take the greatest pleasure from the pregnant process of development, whatever the line of work you pursue.

While the approval of others is nice, it is self-approval that you ultimately need. You are able to carry off the dignity required in stressful situations. Your fearlessness can get you into tight situations, but is a valuable career asset most of the time. You act honorably and expect the same from your peers. Your leadership skills include enough impulsiveness to keep the work interesting, enough ambition to get others moving in a positive direction, and enough faith to allow them to do their work without interference. Once given a task, you are determined to see it through.

Traits not to bring to work in the morning include vanity, arrogance, contempt, cruelty, stubbornness, and selfishness. Replace them with magnanimity, strong leadership, a courageous attitude in the face of difficulties, fearlessness, determination, and an authoritative posture when it is appropriate.

Sagittarius

Creativity for you involves the spiritual side of life. You find pleasure in being inspired and in inspiring others to fulfill their greatest potential. Yours is a quiet creativity, immersed in thought. You seek to blend your experience of the physical world, your educational process, and your intuition into a creative admixture where nature and art comingle to produce something spiritually pleasing. You are the individual who can see beyond the initial idea, through the building process, and yes, past the completion of a project. You are able to envision the effect of your work on the world and to transform creative energy into a spiritual tool.

You bring a philosophical attitude to your work and you are able to adapt to rather unusual circumstances. You thrive in situations that require an open-minded look at the facts. You probably have profound religious or spiritual values, but you do not inflict them on others or require others to follow your path. You perceive the apparent duality in the world and aspire to recognize oneness in it. Thus you can resolve dilemmas more easily than most people. Generally optimistic, you can lift the spirits of your coworkers with funny stories that show how to resolve difficulties. You are able to apply the rules uniformly and bend when the time is right.

Traits not to bring to work include impractical planning, a dogmatic attitude, gullibility, the urge to gamble, lack of restraint, self-righteousness, a spendthrift attitude, and indulgence. You will find that these qualities work better: idealism, a philosophical outlook, benevolent open-mindedness, moderate risk-taking capacity, and emotional generosity.

Earth – Sensation

You are a sensation type if your Sun sign is Taurus, Virgo, or Capricorn. Sensation types are primarily interested in practical considerations of the world. They look at the facts and depend on their five normal senses for perception. They prefer to have the experience, not hear about it. They learn by doing, so the learning process may be slower. To be satisfied, they need to go over things carefully. They are not less intelligent because they go slower—they are more careful. When given the time to assimilate information, the sensation type may remember it longer and understand the practical applications more fully.

The earth personality demands satisfaction along the way. They do not select occupations that lack concrete feedback. They are healthy consumers, loving life and what it has to offer on the material level, and they are best in careers involving real "stuff." They make good real-estate people, interior decorators, and chefs. Earth signs enjoy working with their hands and can make this a vocation, or at least an avocation. They make good doctors and health-care professionals. Any career that requires attention to and intimate understanding of the details is suited to the sensation type.

Sigmund Freud had the Sun in Taurus. His psychology was built on the principle that a root cause for a problem could be found, and that the finding itself would produce some kind of cure. This theory is actually very simple and to the point. The reductionist psychological theory is, at its heart, based on the sensation function. He gave us a framework for understanding mental illness in a practical and material way.

Taurus

You invigorate the creative process by sensing the form a project may take and fostering the development of that form. You strengthen the creative ambiance by consolidating the resources needed, providing creative structure to the growth process, and persevering when others may falter. You thrive on the comfortable knowledge that growth continues even though not much can be seen on the surface. You take the greatest pleasure in surpassing the painful moments of doubt and seeing activities through to a more comfortable outcome. "We did it," can become your mantra.

You like to focus on the practical considerations and leave the daydreams to others where work is concerned. You measure success in terms of results. Results for you include completion, harmony, and dependability, all managed in a timely manner. Thorough effort should be rewarded, in your view, and you consider every angle as you move toward your goal. Patience is a quality you can easily master, and you can successfully teach it to others. You are happiest in an environment of steady progress and growth, and dislike disruptions that take you away from a task.

Traits not to display in the work environment include excessive stubbornness, indulgence of your own appetites or the foibles of subordinates, vanity, rigidity, and laziness. Instead try these: persistence, creativity, industriousness, firm resolve, and reserve.

Virgo

Your creative strength lies in your ability to analyze situations and see beyond the obvious. You are able to accumulate data from sources that others may overlook, digging deep into a problem. You are the ultimate systems analyst, whatever the system may be. You can test the end product, finding pleasure in discovering its best qualities as well as its correctable faults. Others may have had the idea to produce diamonds from coal; you are the one who can see and measure the results of the process in detail, thriving on the final process of refinement into true gems.

You bring diligence and orderly procedures to your creative work, giving it a logical balance. You are capable of being overly critical, and you recognize that quality in others. Your methodical approach solves many problems without undue stress. When offered a new direction, you study the possibilities, both before you accept the position and after you are into the new tasks. You are able to go through massive quantities of text and data, sifting out the few points that pertain to your immediate problem. This capacity for discrimination saves you a lot of time and effort. Your moral judgment is generally right on target. You are unwilling to take the low road when the high road will do just as well.

Traits that are inappropriate in the workplace include fault-finding and blaming, skepticism, a mental superiority or inferiority complex, nosiness, and indecision. Alternative qualities to develop include discrimination, dexterity, good research technique, precision, attention to facts, and a considered decision-making strategy.

Capricorn

Your creativity lies in the ability to focus on yourself and your personal process. Your serious attitude toward life, the planning and striving for success, form a large part of your creativity. You thrive in the midst of change because you are able to keep one eye on the job and the other on the larger goal. You take the greatest pleasure from using the materials at hand and producing concrete results from them. Never one to wait until all the optimum conditions exist, you make conditions change to suit you. Your self-control is not the result of lack of emotion, but rather emerges from your self-examination and understanding.

You can achieve more than most people because of your sheer determination. It is imperative that you have creative outlets in your work environment, so watch out if your responsibilities begin to seem like drudgery. You are systematic in the development and completion of complex tasks. Because you are less demonstrative than many people, you will need to practice telling others when they have done well, and you need to tell others when you are happy. Your sense of duty may not make you popular among your peers, but they will admire the results you obtain, and your superiors will reward your diligence.

Capricorn traits that don't fly in the workplace include fear, secretiveness, resentment, selfishness, a lack of sympathy, rigidity, and pessimism. Instead, you can cultivate prudent security measures, focusing on what is important, honoring the achievements of others, efficient distribution of resources, conscientious attention to the feelings and needs of others, patience, and a practical "is it working" attitude.

Air – Thinking

If your Sun sign is Gemini, Libra, or Aquarius, then you are a thinking type. Thinking types tend to be less personal in their approach to the world. They are focused on objective truth and not on the people in their path. They choose to be logical. They choose to be argumentative—after all, they argue with themselves enough! They are usually able to go through a thought process once and stop, without needing to re-evaluate. Air types benefit from an education that includes logical training, but they remain one-sided if they skip over the opportunities to appreciate the people and things around them. They judge the world through a logical process that puts feelings on the back burner, or at least in second place.

Thinking types are good in careers where it is important to organize and assess quantities of information. They tend to be somewhat more businesslike, able to "cut to the chase" in planning as well as performance. They contribute to society through intellectual criticism, through the exposure of wrongdoing, and through scientific research. They perform well in executive positions partly because such positions are more impersonal. They are willing to tell the truth, even when it is not convenient.

Charles Darwin and Abraham Lincoln were born within hours of each other and had the Sun in Aquarius. They were both deep thinkers, applying logical processes to the understanding of their fields. They also each had a practical strategy for supporting that logic with concrete action. They both ended up giving to history ideas that radically changed our thinking.

Gemini
Your creativity lies in the ability to diversify an idea. You could have been the original fractal designer, taking one idea and working it into many. You thrive on sharing the creative process with others, and brainstorming is your forte. You have the capacity to

take a broad view of things, not becoming overly attached to details. When you come back down to earth, you bring with you the sense of space in which to implement your ideas. Your greatest pleasure lies in sharing your experience, and you work well in situations where teamwork is encouraged.

Your mental creativity is a definite career asset. Generally open-minded, you are also able to speak your mind. You can be a valuable mediator in difficult situations. You can develop the capacity to study a question thoroughly before beginning a project. Take a lesson from computer programmers: about ninety percent of their effort goes into planning and designing a program before they write a single line of code. The same general approach applies to most job-related tasks, in that thinking them through saves a lot of duplication and wasted effort. On the other hand, you also have the capacity to change direction when the task requires it, moving on to a new line of attack. This ability makes you a strong asset to any work team. You are a natural mediator, able to see both sides—even multiple sides—of a question. And you can communicate with the people in various positions and encourage them to work together.

Traits not to demonstrate on the job include superficiality in work or speech, excessive worry, nervousness, impatience, and experimentation. Instead you may want to develop openness to the ideas of others, creative concern, effective outlets for physical energy, and practical resourcefulness.

Libra

Your creative eye focuses on refinement and elegance, both in the process itself and in the result. For you, means do not justify the ends if the means are messy and undignified. The ends are satisfying only when they have the stamp of quality that elegance suggests. You thrive on the creation of glamour around your work, but not if it detracts from its meaningfulness. You take the greatest pleasure in partnerships, and therefore work best in situations where you have someone with whom to share projects. You are able to balance the objective and subjective perspectives in your creative work.

Your sociability contributes to your creative efforts in the work environment. While you desire a position of importance, you are able to work well with others in positions at, above, or beneath yours. Manners are a strong asset. Generally you are appreciative of the efforts of others, and can cultivate an appreciation of yourself as well. You enjoy the romance of your work, and will do best in jobs where there is a sense of value and meaning, because, at heart, you are an idealist. You find that the emotional energy of others affects your attitude, so you may want to learn how to perceive feelings in others without soaking them all in and losing your objectivity.

Traits that won't work on the job include depending on others to do your work, extravagance, indecisiveness, impatience, aloofness, exacting so-called justice, and tending toward extremes. Better qualities to demonstrate include a cooperative attitude, impartiality, creative management of resources, sympathetic exploration of possibilities, honest assessment of what needs to be accomplished, adaptability, and balance.

Aquarius

You are a master planner, able to wait for just the right moment to take action. Your creative talent lies in acting decisively when that moment arrives. You are a good observer of human nature, yet you can maintain a suitable distance when that is required. You thrive in situations where you can remain detached enough to see the overall picture, and you desire a certain freedom at work. If you are able to analyze your inner feelings and thoughts, your creativity is unlimited. You find pleasure in your ability to convince others of your viewpoint.

Your creativity is aided by strong powers of observation and the willingness to participate in a group effort. You understand human nature in general, but it may not be quite as clear when it comes to individual differences. You have a sixth sense about other people that is based on perceiving their energy fields. On an individual basis you may seem aloof, but this is because you try not to become engulfed in that energy. On a global level you have strong opinions about what progress is needed. Your style of cooperation incorporates inventive solutions to problems. You are not afraid to dig into the work.

Aquarian traits that can create friction at work include following every fad, exploitation of others, crankiness, impetuousness, eccentric habits, reclusiveness, and inhibitions. Instead, substitute openness to new ideas, cooperation, humanitarianism, detachment, self-sufficient lifestyle, progressive yet moderate sharing of your beliefs, participation in work-related activities, and persistent personal effort.

Water – Feeling

With the Sun in Cancer, Scorpio, or Pisces, you are a feeling type. If the earth types say, "Just the facts, ma'am," the water types say, "And how does it feel when that happens?" Water types evaluate situations on the basis of sentiment and may feel that logical processes are ineffective or unsatisfying.

Feeling types are successful in careers that call for sensitivity in relating to others. They have the ability to bridge the gap between people, and therefore make good counselors, sales people, heads of families, members of the clergy—any job where interpersonal relationships are at the core of productive work.

Elizabeth Taylor is a Pisces. Her stock in trade is her ability to evoke feelings in her audience. She also allowed feelings to periodically engulf her own life, and is renowned for her many marriages and divorces. Her Academy Awards and career of stunning performances show that she understood the role of the feeling function, even if she didn't always control it.

Cancer

Your creative power lies in the ability to rest with thoughts and feelings, to allow them to run their course without interference. Your fertile mind is able to soak up the facts; you thrive in situations where you can apply that knowledge to problem solving. You tend to immerse yourself in projects, and may need to take a moment out for yourself to enjoy the process. You take pleasure in the fact that you can manifest a stillness in the midst of the turmoil of intense work effort. You are at your best creatively when you work with the natural direction of life, not fighting the currents around you.

You bring a decided dramatic touch to your work, and this keeps you interested and interesting. Often your impressions of situations are right on the mark, so don't discount them. You can add an artistic touch to the final product. When others are at a loss for an intriguing idea, you let your imagination run with a task, developing numerous possibilities, some good and some not so good, knowing that one will develop into a good result. At the same time you are cautious enough to evaluate your ideas for practicality. You may like to work late into the night: swing shift may be just the ticket for you.

Traits not to display at work include self-indulgence, possessiveness, touchiness, a tendency to live in the past, and procrastination. Instead work toward a sympathetic demeanor, the capacity to preserve the work environment and the work itself, a dramatic flair, patience, prudence, and the steady effort of water flowing downhill.

Scorpio

You are often at your creative best when others cannot see anywhere to go. You have a somewhat ruthless ability to hang on and survive, and in fact you thrive on crises. You understand the cycle of birth and death, and can see past the end of a project to the next gig. Your creative work demands steady attention to achieve complete transformation. Your greatest pleasure is found in work that achieves the birth of something new and wonderful out of something old and dead, and your feelings are always an integral part of the creative process.

You are able to sacrifice the desires of the moment in order to achieve something far greater in the future. The course of your career should embody a steady forward and upward development. You may find that you have to change jobs or move great distances in order to take steps up the ladder. This is because others become so dependent on your reliability that they cannot see how they can manage without you in that position. You tend to devote yourself to the task at hand, and can be depended on to complete whatever you are given. Be aware that because you understand the nature of sexuality so deeply, it is best to avoid its expression in the work place.

Scorpio traits that should be kept out of the work environment include jealousy, rebelliousness, suspicion, cruelty, distrust, and sarcasm. Leave them at home and instead try assertiveness, a practical level of trust, keen perception and cooperative expression of your opinions, and frank statements based on facts.

Pisces

Your creativity grows from a place of serenity where you can see the goal and the path as part of a seamless unity. Because you do not approach life piecemeal, career considerations must be part of the seamlessness or you will not be happy. You thrive in situations where you are participating in the larger vision of the future and not isolated to contend with the details. Your intuition is a vital part of the creative process. Your greatest pleasure comes in situations where you can demonstrate the compassionate and generous side of your nature creatively.

Your receptivity puts you in a position of being in on the creative pulse of most situations. You are able to keep a secret, however, and this is a valuable asset in the work environment. You need to maintain a positive outlook, or create one. Your modesty can be a limitation, as you seem never to sing your own praises. You may want to develop an inner "press agent" who can be mobilized when it is time for your annual review. It may help to write about yourself in the third person to get some distance and perspective. You absorb knowledge and feelings easily, yet you need to focus on what you are studying and shut out the feelings that drift by your doorway. You have the capacity to be the emotional barometer of the work environment, and others may look to you for leadership where management of feelings is concerned.

Pisces traits that are better left outside the office include hypersensitivity, moodiness, the tendency to merely imitate the style of others, indolence, secretiveness, and susceptibility to psychic negativity. What you can joyfully bring along is your inspirational attitude, a sympathetic ear, the capacity to give feedback to others in a nonaggressive way, patience, reserve, and active intuition.

The Current Mode of Thinking

As the Sun moves into new signs, by slow progression or annual transit, the balance of the elements will change. You then get a chance to experience each of the elements and to develop skills associated with them. No one goes through life with only one psychological function. The periodic shifts provide the learning experiences we need to achieve balance within an otherwise lopsided personality, if we take advantage of the learning opportunities as they are presented. You can probably recall times when you acted or felt very different from your typical self—the Sun was very likely in a different element, or at least a different sign at the time.

See the pages at the end of this book for information about how to obtain a complete interpretation of your career potential using astrology, or for a forecast of the coming year.

The Sun, the Moon, and Compatibility

by Dorothy Oja

We are engaged in relationships at every moment of our lives. It's just that the people or things we relate to vary. We relate to ourselves and our bodies and who we think we are as human beings. We relate to our health, spirituality, ethnicity, family of origin, family traditions, parents, siblings, environment, our learning and experience, our community, religious beliefs, our friends, coworkers, life and people in general, political and life views, the world, the universe, the meaning of it all, and our role within it. But of course, when we come right down to it, what we're most interested in is the intimate relationship we seek to establish with other human beings. We can't learn enough about what makes our relationship-life work. Everything we are or experience in the course of life, as well as our belief about what is possible, combine and play a role in the drama of our personal and intimate relationships.

Getting along with another human being is among the most difficult and frustrating, and the most rewarding and fulfilling, conditions we deal with on an everyday basis. We will discuss some of the basic principles involved in the dynamic of relationships, which contribute to and create either compatibility or conflict. Then we'll speak about the Sun and Moon positions in your chart as keys to your relationship comfort.

What creates the biggest problems in relationships is the balance between being independent, self-regulated, self-motivated, and self-fulfilled with personal responsibility, versus being dependent on another person to fulfill us and do things for us or with us. The reason for this is not that we need one more than the other, but that we come together in relationships with often vastly different expectations and definitions of what these differences are.

Relationships hinge on the interconnected and highly complex understandings between dependence and independence, and also on our ability to be fulfilled so that we don't look to someone else to complete us. This translates simply into the ability to be happy in and of oneself. The wisdom is that if you are capable of making yourself happy, then the chances are better that you can create happiness and cooperation in a relationship with another person.

The Sun

The position of your Sun describes, in part, your ability to have an equal relationship with another person. The Sun rules Leo, which is half of the planetary pair Leo/Aquarius (Uranus rules Aquarius). This sign pair, in particular, describes the ability to grow into an independent and authentic person, with a distinct and uniquely expressive personality. A person who is self-fulfilled and independent is a person who will be most successful in relationships with another human being.

Since life does not give us perfection at all times, we know that there are often factors in our personal charts and in our lives that prevent easy compatibility in relationships. Look to the Moon as part of a pair (along with Saturn) that rules the Cancer/Capricorn axis in the chart. This axis is most responsible for the conditioning factors of your early life, and the framework and habits which you were required to absorb through the foundation of your family—your mother, father, and siblings.

The potential and opportunity to be blissfully independent and self-fulfilled, or simply happy with yourself, is easily seen in the character of the Sun. What does your Sun say about these abilities for you?

Aries

Sun in Aries is a doer. Fiery Aries likes to have a plan or goal to pursue and this includes you, if you're the object of affection! Aries is often perceived as being very independent, but true to its fire element, it wants to have someone around to watch it achieve goals. In other words, Aries needs to be noticed and applauded, and to receive accolades in its attempt to win first prize. The downside of Aries is selfishness. The Aries person does not always ask others what he or she can, will, or should do. Aries is more than capable of making decisions alone and taking action. This part of the Aries personality obviously creates friction in partnerships, where it is necessary to confer with another and negotiate plans. A positive in the Aries arsenal is the ability to feel a zest for life and, therefore, to want to participate in many offerings. This increases the independence of Aries and contributes to a certain amount of fulfillment. Aries will not wait to proceed or to act. If an Aries wants to participate, he or she does so, no problem, with or without a partner. Aries the pioneer will walk miles, forge new pathways, and reach the unreachable all to bask in your adoration when he or she gets back to you. This brings up another Aries issue: impatience. In the impulse to pursue life in all its delight, Aries doesn't like to be stopped or tied down by lengthy negotiation with a partner. A simple solution would be to formulate common goals that you could pursue together and others that can be undertaken individually, to give you the free rein you need.

Taurus

Sun in Taurus holds down the fort. This earth sign wants things to be very comfortable, above all else. And this impulse extends to all areas of life, including financial security. Taureans have a natural sense of their own value, as well as the value of available goods and services. They tend to gravitate to the very best-made products and the most sensually pleasing people. So, if you want to snag a Taurus, make sure that your voice is velvety, that you smell wonderful, that you're neat and tidy, and that you enjoy fine food. Once a Taurus has found a good thing, he or she doesn't want to let go, or give up. This can apply to you, too. Taurus is not at all keen on too much change. According to the Taurean sensibility, why give up the pleasure life has to offer? Isn't life tough enough? Taureans are typically generous with time and usually with money, although they want to make sure that they have an abundant supply of both. Pushing Taurus is an exercise in futility. Taurus moves according to a rhythm that is personal and mostly internally dictated. Nothing you can say will sway the Taurus in the moment. There is the key. If you suggest something, be sure that you give enough lead-time for a final answer. Taurus will usually say no first, mull it over, and then typically give in to your request later. Remember, Taurus is a pleaser. As for relationships, most Taureans don't like to be alone and will seek out the physical pleasure of a warm body and lots of hugs until they've found a main squeeze they can stick with and depend on. This is a sign that requires lots of physical proximity (cuddling) and gains ultimate pleasure from closeness with another.

Gemini

Sun in Gemini gathers and disperses information, and sometimes people too. These air signs love to talk, so please don't tell them any major secrets that you don't want the world to know about. This is not meant to disparage Gemini. It's just that Gemini somehow experiences all information, once on the airwaves, as free for all. A Gemini is likely to have oodles of friends and even more acquaintances, and so is rarely lonely. These folks are very people-oriented and have some difficulty being alone with only themselves for company, though some have been known to talk to themselves and amuse themselves quite well. Geminis are highly alert and in the know. If you're hankering for the affections of this Sun sign, you must be witty and have an opinion on thousands of subjects. You'd better also like to talk on the phone, because if you're not running hither and yon with Gemini, you'll most certainly be having lengthy phone sessions. Geminis are naturally relationship-oriented, but they do have a tendency to flirt (they love to play with words). If you're set on a Gemini, make sure that you understand this personality tendency and that you can live with it. Geminis are very visual and are constantly distracted by moving objects or people in their peripheral vision. Like a warm breeze, Geminis need to feel the freedom to come and go as they please and (even more importantly) to change their minds often. When involved in a relationship, these characteristics can make them appear indecisive or flaky. If you're in a partnership with a Gemini, you can counteract these tendencies by appealing to their desire to make logical deductions and reach reasoned conclusions. Mostly independent, Geminis can have nervous breakdowns when their juggling act of too many projects comes crashing down. Then they'll really need your support to set things in motion again.

Cancer

Sun in Cancer's basic instinct is to nurture. Cancer is always looking for someone to feed—and not just with food. These watery types can care for you by listening to your problems, lending emotional support, and, in general, supporting whatever emotion you're going through or whatever need you are expressing. Cancer is naturally nurturing, sympathetic, and helpful. In fact, Cancers will rarely say no, if they feel you really need their help. This Moon-ruled sign is so sensitive it internalizes your sharp tone or your cross-eyed look deeply. If you're impatient with tears and a certain amount of complaining or whining, this Sun sign may not be compatible with yours, yet Cancers are among the kindest people you will ever know. Unfortunately, one of their weaknesses is a certain insecurity, which leads them to compromise—sometimes in the wrong ways and for the wrong reasons. Cancers need the support of a group, a family or clan, a club, or a social organization. Cancers are big on community and often find themselves with a job within the public sector or working as champions of social causes. Wherever they are and wherever they go, Cancers will seek to create a comforting and nurturing environment, so that safe growth can take place and development is assured. A Cancer is most independent when he or she feels safe, has a cozy nest, is financially secure, and feels emotionally understood and protected. This sign also needs emotional closeness, someone to care for, and someone to care for and about them. These characteristics do incline Cancerians to seek out intimate relationships. Because Cancers have a tendency to need to be needed, they often base their self-esteem on whether or not they can be of assistance to someone. Cancers flourish with kindness, caring, and understanding. They become most insecure when separated too long from the people they love.

Leo

Sun in Leo is creative, spontaneous, and loving. Leos are by nature worldly, generous folks and like to participate actively in the good things of life. This fire sign is sunny, lively, laughs easily, and usually smiles often and beautifully. An independent breed, these cats are identified by their proud bearing and their expectation of being treated well. Others sometimes see Leos as arrogant, but often it is only Leo's clear sense of what they want from life. One of Leo's greatest assets is the ability to maintain a youthful joyfulness that keeps them young at heart well past middle age. These proud lions do not like being told what to do by anyone. They seek and need love but will not compromise their dignity for very long. Mistreating a Leo is tantamount to treason, and you'll soon be banished from their royal kingdom as persona non grata. They want nothing more than to love and be in love, yet this overriding need brings them into difficult love relationships—often with the wrong people. Although needing independence, these lions are also very loyal once they've chosen a partner to hang out with. If you're interested in a Leo be prepared to put on the ritz at least some of the time. These cats want to be seen about town, since most of them enjoy dressing in full regalia and strutting their stuff. If going out gets to be too expensive, you can always throw a party and watch your Leo light up. Be sure to acknowledge where she or he excels and compliment her or his good points. In other words, be sure to stroke and cuddle frequently, and you'll have a play-pal for a long time.

Virgo

Sun in Virgo is attentive and careful by nature—even in relationships. Virgo, as an earth sign, is first and foremost practical. These natives take responsibility for themselves and their lives in stride. Because they tend to be meticulous in at least one specific area of their life, they notice details. If your heart is set on being with a

Virgo, make sure your shoes are polished and you've brushed the cat or dog hairs off your coat. Virgos are finely tuned and often experience stress about one thing or another. Their careers in particular are areas of great concern. Virgos want more than anything to be skilled, to make a difference, and to play their part in the larger scheme of things. Their place in the work arena is vital to them, and when they cease to be useful their self-esteem plummets. Because these natives are somewhat picky, they may wait for Mr. or Ms. Right for quite a while, or go through many candidates before selecting one to stay with. Because they are practical, they won't have much trouble figuring out how best to take care of themselves. Virgos know what they want. Although, if they don't have a partner, they may fuss too much at work or drive their friends crazy with their nitpicking. Virgos enjoy a certain amount of order and can really get used to sharing life with someone, as long as they get to do much of the planning—especially regarding the mundane elements of your life together. One of Virgo's greatest skills lies in taking care of chores or unpleasant tasks with dispatch, so as to have more time to participate in hobbies or learning situations. Typically quite bright, these people are fact-gatherers, and the longer you know them, the more you realize just how many skills and how much knowledge they possess.

Libra

Sun in Libra is cooperative. Libras are air signs, and their natural proclivity is to socialize, share life's passages, and gossip about other people they may know. Somewhere along the way, these folks learned to tune in to others. Because of this, they have exceptionally honed people skills and can easily understand and place themselves in the shoes of another. Gracious and charming by nature, if a Libra is interested in you, he or she will compliment you from dawn to dusk. Because of their natural gifts of charm and fair dealings, Libras usually have many wonderful people contacts. Equipped with the best social graces, you can take a Libra anywhere and you can expect diplomacy, tact, and ease in conversation from them. Libras also are very interested in the character and accomplishments of others. Because of this they carefully choose the people with whom they wish to be associated. If you want the affections of a certain Libra, you had better have something to show for yourself and be able to handle regular social gatherings. Knowing how to entertain in your own home would also be a plus. Libras want to be liked and will work diligently to be complimented and accepted into a group of their choosing. This air sign wants partnership and, in fact, really doesn't like the idea of going it alone. Not that they can't, mind you, but sharing and working together to make the most of life's opportunities is definitely more appealing to them. Incessant matchmakers, they enjoy keeping mental notes on their single friends and are always on the lookout for potential partners for them. They like to get to the bottom of issues, and they pride themselves on understanding others. This last skill in particular tends to make Libras fair and cooperative partners, willing to compromise for the sake of harmony in relationships.

Scorpio

Sun in Scorpio is intense and powerful. A water sign, Scorpio is not to be trifled with. These people have a memory that's a mile long, and they won't soon forget when they've been wronged. Exceptionally analytical, Scorpios want to know everything that they don't know. Please have no secrets from your Scorpio partner. First of all, it will drive them crazy; second, they'll find out anyway; and third, they'll wonder why you wanted to keep it from them in the first place. Scorpios struggle with the deeper mysteries of life and are always brooding about or processing one thing or another. Not only do they want to know why something happened, they want to know the psychological reasons and the hidden motives behind it. If you're serious about a Scorpio, make sure you are on the up and up. If you cross these folks, that will be the end of the relationship. They will be unable to trust you ever again. And once their trust is breached, they simply won't allow you to be as close as you once were. With Scorpio it's simply a survival thing. They will not be fooled twice. Scorpios spend their waking moments (and probably also their dream time) trying to figure out how to get the most out of life. To some that means accumulating money or power, to others it means getting a grip on the mysteries of life and living wisely in empowerment by having developed their talents to the max. Scorpio is resourceful and, in that way, can channel energy into all kinds of projects that pique their interest. They can remain single for a time but eventually get lonely for physical closeness. They make great partners because they have an instinct for knowing who they want, and if the situation is right they are willing to invest enormously in a partnership. They will remain loyal as long as their most important needs are met, but they do not like to feel that they've made a bad investment, which includes a partnership. They are willing to work through difficulties and complex emotional times, but if you deceive them they may forgive, but they simply can't forget.

Sagittarius

Sun in Sagittarius is the adventurer, the gambler. This fire sign loves to be footloose and fancy-free. Often called the bachelor sign of the zodiac, you'll have to run to keep up with a Sagittarius. It would also be great if you can be versatile, meaning that you'd be equally comfortable in jeans or black-tie threads. Sagittarius will make you laugh and promise you everything, but in the final analysis may not come through. Ever enthusiastic, Sagittarius, like other mutable signs (Gemini, Virgo, and Pisces), easily gets distracted from the goal in order to explore the side roads and detours of life. This inclination gives Sagittarius lots of adventures and stories to bring home and tell. Sagittarians are funny, wise, and wonderful. They are also generous and philosophical, but it's not in their make-up to stay in one place for too long. If you have your heart set on a Sagittarius, be prepared to continually plan the next adventure in tandem and be sure that you're willing to take new risks and go exploring with them. If things become too predictable or boring, your Sagittarius will be tempted to see what's beyond the next hill. Flexibility is a key part of their lifestyle. This sign is one that never seems to mind being alone. Sagittarians make friends with everyone they meet and easily fit into any environment. Their unselfconscious communication is refreshing to most and blunt to others. But by and large Sagittarians means well even though they often say things that seem to simply pop out of their mouths unbidden. Exaggeration is one of a Sagittarian's biggest pitfalls and it seems to crop up in every area of their lives. They love to do things in a big way, which can mean overspending. They like to live in the moment, which can be utterly charming but at the same time, applied to daily living, can be trying. Sagittarius is a very lucky sign and, with some application, can do quite well, because people love the contagious enthusiasm, generosity of spirit, and the truisms that flow constantly through Sagittarian communication.

Capricorn

Sun in Capricorn is the planner and organizer. Worlds apart from Sagittarius is this earthy sign, which seems to be born knowing how to accept responsibility and shoulder burdens and challenges. Capricorns often have difficulties, especially early in life. Like a fine wine, they age well, and seem to mellow and lose their excess seriousness and uptightness with maturity. Once Capricorns make a commitment, they will do their best to uphold their end of the bargain. And they will make sure that you do the same. Capricorn wants to belong, and often chooses the traditional path, which includes marriage and family. These people need a firm foundation from which to go out and achieve. They are strong and reliable, and seek to improve their circumstances and those of their loved ones. But if Capricorns won't compromise, they may find themselves alone until they come around. They can get stuck on the "right" and "wrong" way to do something, and this can make them unyielding and somewhat rigid. They are, however, the keepers of tradition and time, and they yearn to create and perpetuate traditions with their own family. If you want a Capricorn, you will find he or she has very sharply defined values and will want to know that your values blend with theirs. They need to respect you for who you are and feel that you're pulling your own weight. Integrity and self-sufficency are vital to a Capricorn. If those kinds of things are in place and the chemistry is there too, you may find that you have a relationship made in heaven. With Capricorn as your partner, you are likely to be striving for the best in whatever direction the two of you choose, because Capricorn is geared for excellence. Capricorn does even better within the security of partnership and community. With that kind of support, there's no telling where your Capricorn will go—and you, of course, will go along, too.

Aquarius

Sun in Aquarius is the eccentric and the truth seeker. Your Aquarian freedom-fighter may seem somewhat aloof, but surer than sure they need love too. This air sign is super-cognizant of the prevailing social condition and social evolution. Aquarians will stand up for abuses of human and animal rights. Fiercely independent, the natives of this sign will tell you quite readily when you're stepping on their toes or invading their space. But if they invite you into their space . . . well, that's another matter. Aquarians certainly can seem otherworldly, maybe even alien, to the rest of us. But they are kind and quite often brilliant in their applications of talent and perspective to life here on Earth. There will be no double standard in relationships with an Aquarius. Whatever freedoms you decide you need for yourself, make sure you don't deny them to your Aquarian partner. You can be sure they won't stand for it. Another thing: you must always tell them the truth, because if they find you've lied to them, it will be a breach of one of their most important life standards. Aquarians generally have many friends but few close bosom buddies. They can often find intense emotions too wearing and cloying for their taste. It's not that they don't love you, it's just that they prefer to love you at a distance so that they can take in the sum total of who you are. They do not like to be crowded because it obscures their peripheral vision, and that just doesn't work for an Aquarius. Aquarians can make loyal mates, but they're looking for a best friend first, so if you want to make things work with an Aquarius make sure you brush up on your friendship skills. Communication, sympathy, and understanding are key components in the attempt to win the heart of an Aquarius. They're really not interested unless they can converse easily with you and make a special mental connection.

Pisces

Sun in Pisces is dreamy and romantic. Pisces will tear up at corny movies and surprise you with flowers, cards, and other romantic gestures for no apparent reason. It simply happens when the mood strikes them, or they're remembering a particularly wonderful moment you've shared together. If you can catch a water sign fish with your bait, you've got a slippery personality on your hands.

Pisces is not known for constancy, but rather for unifying and blending the disparities of life, and enduring or redeeming the gray emotional conundrums of relationships. These people are highly sensitive, artistic, musical, and most certainly finely tuned. They get hurt much too easily and require delicate handling. Most of them find life disappointing and difficult. Some even seek to escape, which is not too problematic unless the medium of escape is a negative addictor like alcohol, drugs, or even excessive sex. There are other and necessary escapes that don't destroy bodies or souls, and Pisces must find them as sources of inspiration. Your Pisces love can be utterly devoted and mystifying. They are precious souls and offer much in the way of enjoying life and in inspiring others to creative expression. They have difficulty with those who are too black and white or too rigid in their ways. You may find your Pisces has trouble with authority figures. Pisces can succumb to playing the victim but, hopefully, not for too long. Although born somewhat trusting and naive, Pisces soon learns that one must be alert and wary. Their kind and compassionate nature is often taken advantage of by opportunistic others. If you're in love with a Pisces, expect some chaos as part of the deal. These folks just don't swim in the same direction as everyone else. In fact, they will often change course with no warning at all.

The Moon

Your Moon sign characteristics, in combination with your Sun sign's attributes, will give you excellent information about basic traits, natural needs, and learned disposition, as well as how you are likely to apply these in relationships. However, there is certainly more to assessing your relationship needs and potentials. The geometric angular relationship between your birth planets and their placement in the horoscope wheel are vital in determining more detail and influence. Other planets such as Venus and Mars play into the pattern of fulfillment in relationships. Each of the twelve houses in a natal chart also plays a part in relationship connections. If you want a complete interpretation of your relationship potential, consult with a competent astrologer in a professional personal session.

Aries
Moon in Aries gives a fiery early life, which could have meant a busy household with a variety of overt emotional expressions, including anger or impatience, but it also results in a great vitality. Family life was probably spontaneous, and favored activity and goal setting. Habits were formed concerning movement or progress. The learned issues affecting adult relationships could be: anger when you don't get what you want, impatience, or selfishness with your time and energy. The positives include warmth, ardor, quickness, energy, and humor.

Taurus
Moon in Taurus learns early about the value of material things in either a positive or negative way. Practical lessons around money and its meaning in life are easily absorbed. A desire for pleasures and pleasurable experiences is cultivated. For the most part, home life maintained a certain consistency—even if that consistency was not always positive. The conditions of early life affect adult relationships by producing great desire for constancy, harmony, and security. These issues include money and material goods—how it is made and spent. Sensuousness is strong, and physical and emotional closeness are vital for overall relationship harmony.

Gemini
Moon in Gemini learns to be communicative and flexible. The home is likely to be rather unstructured, a bit distracted, and very verbal. There could be particular issues with siblings to deal with. Friendliness, interaction with others, and schooling is emphasized in the early learning environment. In an adult relationship, quick wit and easy sociability are natural skills. Learned inconstancy could breed flirtatiousness and certainly lots of word play. Issues around communicating with one's partner are paramount to the success of the relationship. Stress associated with juggling too many projects, making choices, and scattering energies can interfere with harmony. Variety and mental stimulation are necessities.

Cancer

Moon in Cancer's conditioning can be a bit more traditional and centered around an extended family. Issues of nurturing and food may take precedence over everything else. The emotional atmosphere, especially the connection with the mother, would set the tone for emotional availability later on. Feelings in the home lie close to the surface for good or ill, and in adult relationships this early conditioning can result in easily hurt feelings or misunderstandings. The greatest gifts are the ability to empathize and care for loved ones, and a domestic sensibility, often generously expressed by someone in childhood.

Leo

Moon in Leo learns about the power of love given and received. Early in life, someone gives deeply to the child and a strong bond is established. Pride and ego can play a big role in the household. Conditions prevail in which the child becomes the center of attention for one reason or another. This could be to make up for a lack elsewhere in the family system. Family conditions encourage the child to excel and shine. In adult relationships, the Moon in Leo wants to continue to be the center of attention and can have trouble sharing the limelight. Relationship issues stem from a stubborn pride, willfulness, and a desire to be loved immensely, as well as the ability to give steady and loyal love to another.

Virgo

Moon in Virgo's early learned habits include preoccupation with chores, work, and order. This Moon sign discovers the necessity of practical skill development and can sometimes be deprived of the simple joys of playing. Later in life, relationship issues often center around the need to work long hours, since that's where most of the learned satisfaction lies. Pickiness or excessive neatness can burden a love relationship. Order and reliability are a source of comfort to this Moon sign. On the positive side, Moon in Virgo is conscientious and concerned enough about the smooth functioning of daily life to stay on top of the endless chores and minutiae of living, leaving time for togetherness.

Libra

Moon in Libra's early conditioning revolves around tact, diplomacy, and good relationships with other people. Those born with a Libra Moon quickly discover that charm and grace are ways of getting what one wants from others. This Moon sign involves a childhood filled with observing the habits and ways of others and noting the responses received. In adult life, this native learns to adapt more easily to the eccentricities of a partner, and understands and accepts compromise. Sometimes the willingness to give in is simply a deep desire to be free from conflict, since confrontation was so unpleasant in early life. Unhappiness can result if Moon in Libra fails to become aware of its own needs or depends too much on a partner for happiness.

Scorpio

Moon in Scorpio experiences the unspoken tensions or inherited legacy of the family. There are often unresolved life and death struggles for which the Scorpio Moon somehow feels responsible. Emotional pressures from early on can result in feelings of suspicion, guilt, rejection, or betrayal. Moon in Scorpio is born deeply sensitive, with an enormous capacity for healing and powerful intervention. Its ability to use these gifts depends largely on whether it has healed its own wounds. The Scorpio Moon is typically very loyal in relationships but may struggle with intimacy issues. Still, these natives are willing to probe their issues much more deeply, deliberately, and thoroughly than most, and are willing to tolerate the psychological complexity of others.

Sagittarius

Moon in Sagittarius learns early on to adapt to changes in circumstance and to take advantage of opportunities. Moving frequently, foreign influences, or household upsets are common. There are concurrent messages that instill a positive, optimistic spirit. The capacity for joyous expression and a sense of adventure are great. This Moon sign may have experienced big promises that led to disappointment, so in adult relationships it has difficulty with exaggeration and expectations. Their desire for new experiences can cloud judgment. This wandering Moon sign needs to freely participate and seek greater wisdom amidst many choices and projects. Moon in Sagittarius is generous of spirit, but avoids commitment unless there is freedom and variety.

Capricorn

Moon in Capricorn learns the values of responsibility and discipline early on. Children with this placement mature earlier because of their particular family circumstance. They learn to make themselves useful, and are sometimes shortchanged on simply being carefree and playful. In adult life these Moon signs feel the need to be competent, productive, and respected members of society. They will do whatever is necessary to be recognized as such. Once they commit themselves in personal relationships, they are very reliable, and motivated toward building a relationship system. Closeness, trust, and warmth can be struggles for them, since they were often used to getting only the minimum and not much extra in the way of nurturing. It takes time, but the effort is worth it.

Aquarius

Moon in Aquarius comes from a home life that was unique, different, or unusual in some way. They are often advanced in their thinking, creative interests, and certainly in their perceptions. The fact that their upbringing was unconventional can make them feel ill at ease with others who had more "normal" lives. It is important for these Moon signs to find their "clan." In adult relationships, Moon in Aquarius subjects can feel distant or separate emotionally and have difficulty making true intimate contact. The natives of this sign are loyal to their many friends and associates. They are really looking for a best friend in an intimate relationship, who can accept their eccentricities and their offbeat humor. They remain loyal unless lied to.

Pisces

Moon in Pisces is sensitive in the extreme. The feelings of natives with this sign are finely tuned and, in childhood, may often feel misunderstood. The arts are saving graces for them, since the solace they need may not have been available to them as children. In adult life, this can indicate a certain irresponsibility or victim attitude. If they've resolved their issues, found a home for their most important sensitivities, feel heard and seen, they are exceptionally loving and romantic. These folks retain magic sensibilities and seek souls to commune with on a deep spiritual level, to create an oasis from the harshness of living. They can give, but they also need inspiration.

Solar Returns

by Joanne Wickenburg

The Sun is the great giver of life; without it, nothing would exist on our planet. In fact, without the Sun, our great Mother Earth never would have been born. The Sun is the nucleus of our solar system; all planets revolve around it and are held in orbit by its incredible power. Likewise, in astrology, the Sun represents the very core of our lives. It portrays the essence of who we are. It is the glue that holds us together.

In the astrological chart, the Sun sign describes how we make sense out of life—how we come to understand and synthesize the various experiences we encounter on our pathways through life. Its mission is to help us grow and evolve; to understand the importance of life. If it weren't for the Sun, all other "parts" of our personalities (planets) would function haphazardly with no direction, without the ability to work together cohesively as a team.

As an example, consider the planet Mercury, whose job in your life is to gather information. If the bits and pieces of data acquired by Mercury were never illuminated by the Sun, you would be unable to weave the many fragmented facts together in a manner that made any sense. The Sun operates like a neon sign going off in your head that says, "I get it now! I finally see the light." Without the Sun, we could never make these connections.

As another example, reflect on the planet Venus. It represents your values. Its sign, house, and the aspects it makes to other planets in the chart show what you want for yourself—what will make you happy. If the Sun never touched Venus in your chart, you would never come to understand or appreciate your individual value, nor would you fully appreciate the fragrant aroma of a field of flowers, the feel of a newborn's skin, or the pleasure of a lover's kiss.

Throughout the course of each year, the Sun moves through each sign of the zodiac and highlights, by transit, every planet in the chart. In other words, it moves through the degrees of the zodiac that held planets when you were born. As it does so, it brings new life, vitality, and purpose to the various planetary energies. On or near your birthday every year, the Sun returns to the same sign, degree, and minute of space that it occupied at the exact moment of your birth. When it reaches this point, you are infused with new solar energy that will sustain you for another solar year.

The Sun's return can be likened to replacing worn-out batteries in a beautifully crafted clock. The clock, no matter how elaborate its design, serves no real purpose without its energy source.

The Sun's annual return to the position it occupied at the time of your birth sets the stage for the year to come. A horoscope can be constructed for the precise moment of this yearly event. This chart describes the overall conditions in your life between one birthday and the next. The Sun's position in the Solar Return chart defines the kinds of experiences you need throughout the year to keep your batteries charged, to keep you on your path, and to help you find enlightenment.

An experienced astrologer will look at not just the Sun, but all of the planets in the signs and houses of the Solar Return chart and make certain conclusions, based on their positions, regarding the way in which the coming year will unfold. However, you don't need to be a seasoned astrologer to glean useful information from the Solar Return chart. You will, on the other hand, need to have a Solar Return chart constructed for you. If you don't own astrological computer software, your Solar Return chart can be ordered from a company that offers such services. You will need to provide your birth date, time of birth, location of birth, and also note the age for which you would like the Solar Return chart calculated.

The exact moment at which the Sun returns to the precise degree it occupied when you were born determines which house it will occupy in the Solar Return chart. If this celestial event occurs during the daylight hours, the Sun will be in the top half of the chart (Houses Seven through Twelve), highlighting areas of life involving other people, therefore requiring a certain level of objectivity on your part. Likewise, if it occurs after sunset, the Sun will be in one of the lower sectors of the horoscope (Houses One through Six), encouraging you to focus on personal development and subjective growth.

The actual sector or house containing the Solar Return Sun shows a specific area of your life where the "lights" will be turned on for the duration of the year. It describes where experiences will be met that encourage you to learn, to grow, and to become more conscious of your basic needs and the effects of your behaviors. Because the Sun illuminates, something that has been hidden in the past will likely "come to the light."

Solar Returns in the Houses

First House

This is your year to shine; the lights will be on you. Pay attention to how others see you. The first impression you make on them is a reflection of your self-image. If you are confident, your persona will be radiant and others will be warmed by your solar glow. If not, this year brings opportunity to work on self improvement.

This year will bring opportunities to grow as an individual. It's your year to be "self-centered" in the most positive sense of the term. Ask yourself, "What do I need for me?" Take advantage of available resources this year to help you find a new source of strength and confidence in your ability to meet life's challenges independently and with strength.

This is a year to tell the world that "what you see is what you get." Your dress, your mannerisms, and your overall presentation to the world makes a loud, if unspoken, statement about who you are. Pay attention to your body language: what is it saying to others? This is a year to learn about you.

Second House
Can you survive independently without relying on others to sustain you? Perhaps the survival strategies you have used until now have become a bit obsolete. This is a year to focus on your value as an individual. What are you doing with your life that has real worth?

In today's world, personal worth is sometimes only measured by what people own in the material world. But your Second House "assets" include something much more complex than mere money. Yes, this sector of the chart rules your financial well-being; that's a vital part of survival. It is important to realize, however, that the Second House rules physical, emotional, and spiritual strengths and survival skills as well.

The experiences you encounter throughout the year will challenge you to define what your worth really is. What are your natural talents? Are you using them in your daily life? Do you have the strength and fortitude to maintain your life independently? You will meet opportunities to explore, understand, and utilize your assets in a new "light."

Third House
This area of the chart deals with your relationship with your community. The Solar Return Sun here promises that there is new information available to you within your immediate environment, and it encourages you to take advantage of new learning opportunities. By connecting with those around you, you will grow. There's no need to travel to faraway places to find answers to important questions. What you need is close at hand if you just look around.

Communication is important this year. Try your hand at writing; spend time reading; ask lots of questions and learn something new. Get in touch with your intellect. Get involved with your community and take advantage of the facilities available within it. Take time to get to know your neighbors. Because this is the house ruling siblings, it is a good year to examine your relationship with them as well.

Fourth House

This is an important year for you. Old beliefs about emotional safety will be highlighted; you will meet opportunities that encourage you to redefine what security really is. This is a good year to look back in your life, to examine your past in order to see your future in a new light. Perhaps you will want to explore your family genealogy. How have early family dynamics colored the way you feel about yourself? This is your year to examine your roots and start building new personal foundations that will hold you up in the future.

Does the physical home where you now reside provide a safe haven for you? Does it still fulfill its original purpose? Is it where you want to be? If not, this is a year you might consider relocating in order to find a home that reflects not just who you are, but who you are becoming.

Fifth House

What kind of legacy will you leave for the future? Your children? Your works of art? Hopefully it's a piece of your heart. Explore your passion and create something that truly reflects the essence of you.

The Fifth House is where your heart is; it describes what and who you love—what gives you pleasure, what brings you joy. This is the house of recreation, procreation, and the process of creation itself. Thus, it rules your children, and issues surrounding children may be important to look at this year.

The Sun will highlight your creative potential. While the Second House rules your innate talents, this house provides the outlet for their physical manifestation. Create something this year that carries your "signature" and says to the world, "I was here."

Sixth House

There are certain things in life that require daily attention—basic responsibilities that must be met. The focus of this year involves basic work obligations that may not bring recognition, but must nevertheless be acknowledged and dealt with. Are you fulfilling a useful purpose in the routine hours of your life? Examine your habits and make changes if changes are needed.

How do you handle the daily responsibilities that your job requires? Do you get along with coworkers? Is the work that you do important? You need to shine in the workplace, but not at the expense of production. Don't worry about standing out—take care of your work, and it will speak for you.

And what about your health? Do you take good care of yourself on a routine daily level? This is an outstanding period to design new health routines.

Seventh House

The Sun in the Seventh House sheds light on your relationships and how you interact with others. Cooperation and sharing will be highlighted this year. Do you know how to function in a partnership with others? Can you stand in another person's shoes without losing yourself in the process? Can you both give and receive? Are you in a relationship that encourages both? While the First House Sun shines on you personally, this position of the Sun requires you to share the limelight with others.

There's an old expression that goes, "Like attracts like." You will have an opportunity to see yourself through the eyes of others; they will be your mirror, showing you a truer reflection of who you are than what you may believe yourself to be.

The opposite of cooperation is competition, also ruled by the Seventh House of a chart. For this reason, you need to be aware of the things going on in the lives of your competitors.

Eighth House

While the Seventh House deals with cooperation and sharing, the Eighth House deals with intimacy and the personal transformation that occurs as a result of the merging of life energies. Ego-centered patterns must be curbed in order to maintain relationships over time. Trust must be established.

This will be a year that will challenge you to deal with issues of trust. If trust cannot be attained, this might be the time to let go and move on with your life. This is your time for "house cleaning," a year challenging you to get rid of superficial people or ideas in your life in order to make room for relationships that have value.

This is also the house of financial investments—merging your resources with those of others in order to create a new source of income that you could not create alone.

Ninth House

This is your year to look beyond the immediate to find answers. Explore what has previously seemed "foreign" and unavailable to you within your environment. Broaden your horizons through travel or extended learning.

This House rules not only philosophy, but also intolerance and bigotry. If ideas or people who are different in some way have been intimidating to you in the past, now is a great time to open your mind and be more inclusive. It's also a good time to return to college, to travel, to search for a larger meaning to your life. Don't be limited by your surroundings. Dare to look beyond.

Tenth House

This year promotes recognition and highlights career and success. You will be recognized for your accomplishments, or, if not motivated, your lack of them. Your public image—the "professional" you—will be highlighted in an important way.

Does your career support your sense of purpose? Can you see importance in what you do? Are you recognized and appreciated for what you bring to the world? You need to be. You need to shine, take pride in your accomplishments, and feel good about your social role. You've reached an important apex this year and you deserve the limelight for awhile. Be the boss; be the pilot of your own ship. Experience being a leader.

Eleventh House

This is your year to get out and socialize with others; come to know yourself as a part of a larger group. If you tend to be a private or timid person, this year will give you more confidence to move into the world and mingle. There are things to learn through group encounters. There are opportunities to be gained from the networking that occurs within a group dynamic.

If you are professional person, this is a year to reach out and meet others who share your professional expertise. New opportunities, new ideas, and new inspiration will be the result. Goals for the future will be defined, especially if they include some social "cause." If you are drawn to a humanitarian objective, the Sun will light the path to a doorway that will welcome your admission.

Twelfth House

This is a year to explore your past and come to terms with old patterns that could inhibit future progress. You'll be learning lessons in humility as you are reminded by life events that you are only one cell in the body of mankind, and while your role is important, there is more to life than just you.

This is a great year for spiritual development. Be sure to put aside more time than normal for meditation and quiet contemplation. You are completing a cycle and preparing to begin anew. This requires faith in an unknown future and a strong belief in yourself. Your physical vitality may be at low ebb; the solar rays are focusing on spiritual and psychological revelation.

The Twelfth House rules the "hidden" you, the quiet you that others can never fully know. It rules your secrets, and it also rules your innermost strengths. If there are skeletons in your closet, they might very well come to the light. The Sun's illumination into the Twelfth House of privacy is sometimes uncomfortable, but always brings opportunity to commune with your higher self.

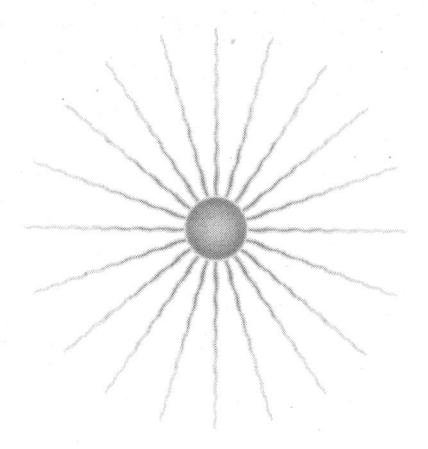

When the Atman Meets the Dragon

How the Sun and Lunar Nodes Interact

by Therese Francis

As the Earth moves around the Sun, it seems to us that the Sun is the one moving and the Earth is still. The path that the Sun makes as it appears to circle the Earth is called the ecliptic.

Planets and the Moon move in a much broader range, appearing to move "up" and "down" in their orbits from our point of view, crossing over the ecliptic plane. This adds a third dimension of movement (a z-coordinate for you math folks) to all the planets and the Moon. So, in addition to appearing in a location around the 360-degree zodiac, a planet can be north or south of the ecliptic.

The point at which a planet crosses the ecliptic is called a Node. As the planet travels from north of the ecliptic to south of the ecliptic the intersection is called the South Node, and where the planet crosses the ecliptic when traveling from south to north is the North Node. Hence the South Node is sometimes referred to as the

Moon's orbit

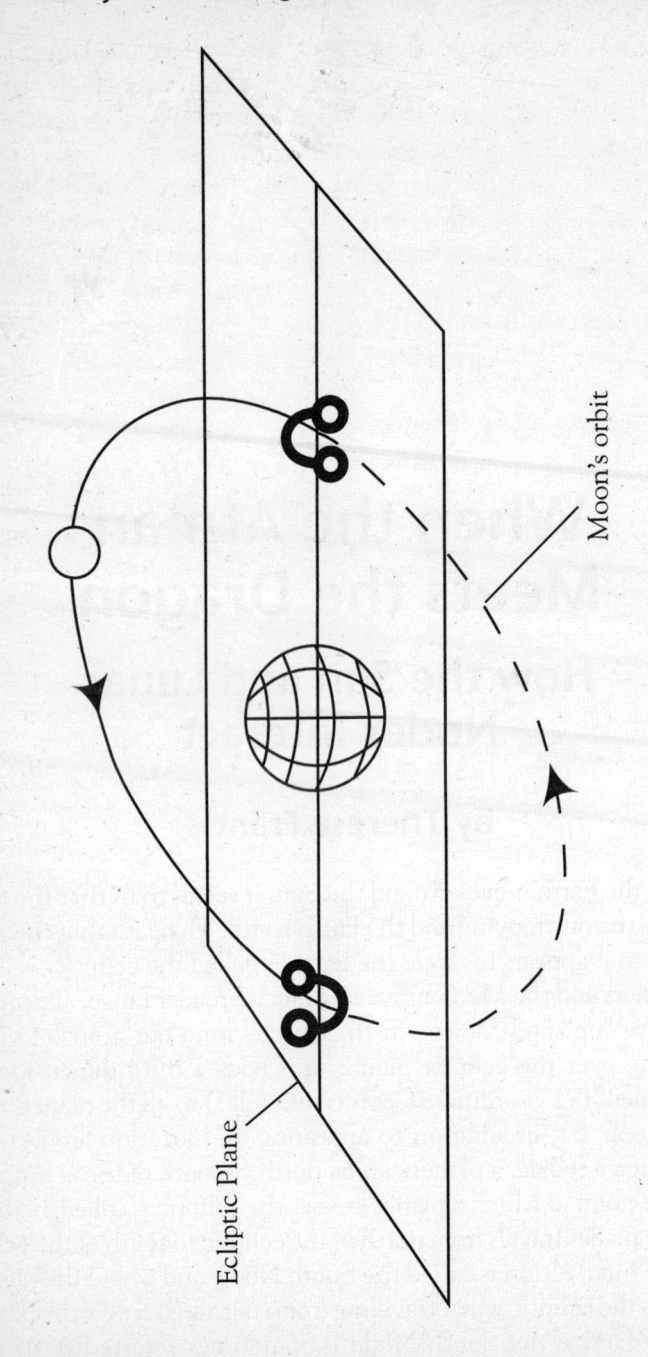

Ecliptic Plane

Descending Node and the North as the Ascending Node (the name of the Node indicates the direction toward which the planet is traveling). All the planets and the Moon have Nodes, but generally only the Moon's Nodes are considered in an astrology reading, and only lunar Nodes are listed in a standard ephemeris.

The North and South Nodes are always in exact opposition. For example, if the North Node is at 3 degrees 27 minutes Virgo, then the South Node is 3 degrees 27 minutes Pisces. An ephemeris will only list the lunar North Node, assuming that the reader knows that the lunar South Node is always the North Node's opposite.

The Atman and the Dragon

At the center of each of us is the soul, called the Atman by the ancients. This is symbolized by the Sun in our natal charts. The Sun is our central core, our essence, our purpose, what motivates us, and how we see ourselves. The Sun is our inherent potential: it represents the materials and essences available for us to work with in the here and now.

At death, the ancient Egyptians believed that Ma'at, a goddess of the afterlife, measured how well a soul used its essence and the resources available to it during its lifetime. An Atman or soul that used what was available to the best of its ability would be lighter than a feather, and thus be eligible to pass into the next world. But a heavy Atman would lead to pain and the need to work off the weight—the karmic debt accrued during the soul's lifetime.

Ancient legends also say that a mighty dragon eats the Sun at the time of an eclipse. Eclipses occur when two conditions are met: first, the Moon must be conjunct or opposite the Sun within five degrees (in other words, a New or Full Moon); and second, the Moon must be within eighteen-and-a-half degrees of crossing the ecliptic—which marks a lunar Node. It is this connection between eclipses and lunar Nodes that gives the North Node its name of Caput Draconis, the dragon's head, while the South Node is called Cauda Draconis, the dragon's tail.

Western astrology, in the spirit of the ancient beliefs, considers the Nodes to be karmic indicators. They represent the lessons we are here to learn in this life, and the habits we must overcome in order to progress. The Nodes, the ancient dragon spread across the

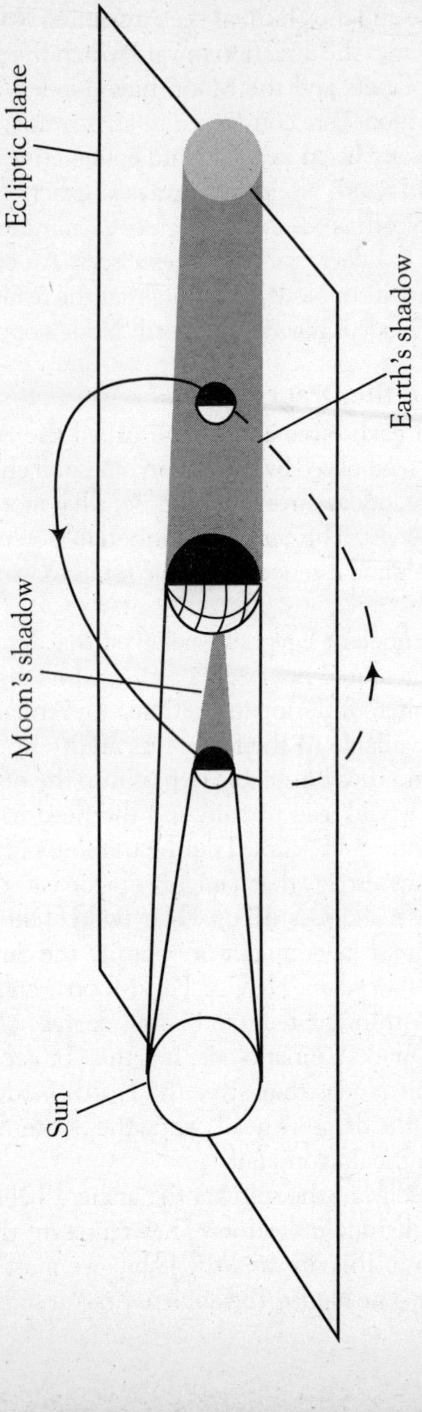
Ecliptic plane
Earth's shadow
Moon's shadow
Sun

sky, work with the Sun, the ancient Atman, to bring about our karmic destiny.

The Modern Dragon

The North Node is the symbol of spiritual power and integration. It depicts the future and represents the ways in which new learning experiences can lead to personal growth. The North Node represents the direction the soul wants to go, but the personality/ego often resists this direction because it is not the comfortable, familiar way of doing things. That is exactly the point of the North Node: to break us out of our old patterns and allow us room to grow. Although learning to incorporate the behaviors, attitudes, and concepts of the North Node into our lives can be difficult at first, there are great rewards.

The South Node, on the other hand, is a symbol of the past. It is the path of least resistance and is made up of familiar (even if painful) patterns. The South Node represents deeply ingrained behaviors and habits that may limit development. If we stay in the familiar, we stagnate.

The solution is to balance the behaviors represented by the North and South Nodes, and satisfy our Sun/Atman by using the known (South Node) to develop the desired/unknown (North Node). The Nodes point the way to the history and development of the soul.

Nodes in the Signs

Throughout the year, as the Moon travels around the Earth and crosses the ecliptic, the point of its intersection gradually moves through the signs of the zodiac. The position of lunar Nodes in the signs and houses of a natal astrological chart tell us a great deal about lessons and trials in this life. Each sign and house in the chart lends its own influence to the energies of the Nodes, and we can combine these influences to create the full picture of the karmic lesson we are here to learn.

North Node Aries
Our tendency is to depend too much on others, and to live vicariously through friends and family members. We need to learn to depend on ourselves and be individuals.

North Node Taurus
Our tendency is to seek gratification of our desires through relationships that may become self-destructive. We need to learn self-sufficiency and build a healthy set of values.

North Node Gemini
Our tendency is to be self-righteous and to shrink from responsibility. We need to learn to communicate clearly, focus our attention, and be open to others' views.

North Node Cancer
Our tendency is to pursue power at the expense of everything. We need to learn that vulnerability is the only path to love, and that emotions have value. We need to learn how to give and receive nurturing, toward ourselves and others.

North Node Leo
Our tendency is to be too erratic, inconsistent, and unpredictable. We are detached. We need to develop confidence, personal will, and belief in ourselves.

North Node Virgo
Our tendency is to escape through daydreams and fantasies. We are not known for touching the ground or for having healthy boundaries. We need to learn discrimination, clarity, and the ability to screen out unwanted energies.

North Node Libra
Our tendency is to be selfish in an unhealthy manner. We need to learn to cooperate with and respect others.

North Node Scorpio
Our tendency is to be selfish due to insecurity. We need to learn to "let go" to the mysteries of life and to transform negative energies into positive ones.

North Node Sagittarius
Our tendency is to be indecisive and superficial. We fear commitment. We need to learn to expand our awareness and find universal truths.

North Node Capricorn
Our tendency is to be insecure and dependent on others. We either cling or climb into our shells, refusing to deal with situations. We need to learn to be organized, disciplined, and to accept responsibility for ourselves.

North Node Aquarius
Our tendency is to be self-involved, proud, elitist, and superior. We need to learn to develop impersonal humanitarian attitudes and to be able to put aside our own needs.

North Node Pisces
Our tendency is to be excessively skeptical, critical, and analytical. We worry too much. We need to learn to have faith, understanding, and compassion.

Nodes in the Houses

North Node in the First House
Our tendency is to be other-directed and to sacrifice until there is nothing left. We need to learn to develop a sense of self and to become independent.

North Node in the Second House
Our tendency is to lose ourselves in other people. We need to learn our own sense of values and the ability to provide for ourselves.

North Node in the Third House
Our tendency is to wander and to gather trivia. We need to learn to relate, communicate, and share knowledge with others.

North Node in the Fourth House
Our tendency is to neglect family and home responsibilities through too much emphasis on worldly achievements. We need to learn to value home life equally to work, to develop personal foundations and emotional strengths.

North Node in the Fifth House
Our tendency is to indulge in fantasy, placing too much emphasis on potential and possibilities. We can let group involvements take away from personal development. We need to learn about the creative process and how to materialize the creative impulse. We need to focus on children.

North Node in the Sixth House
Our tendency is to be withdrawn, isolated, paranoid, and self-pitying. We need to learn the value of work and service to others. We need to balance our lives, eat good food, and develop healthy physical habits.

North Node in the Seventh House
Our tendency is to be self-centered and self-oriented. We need to learn to cooperate with others and develop compassion.

North Node in the Eighth House
Our tendency is to be too materialistic and to identify with material objects and possessions. We need to distinguish between real desire and just wanting to accumulate things. We need to learn to share possessions and feelings with others.

North Node in the Ninth House
Our tendency is to become lost in facts, details, and gossip. We need to learn to broaden our interests and focus on higher ideas.

North Node in the Tenth House
Our tendency is to allow insecurities, fears, and family to block our potential. We need to develop a selfhood and social respect through professional achievements.

North Node in the Eleventh House
Our tendency is to be overly involved in our egos, especially through love affairs and conquests. We need to learn impersonal service and the value of friendship.

North Node in the Twelfth House
Our tendency is to obsess with detail, imperfections, and pettiness. We can be workaholics. We need to learn to feel part of a larger whole. We need alone-time to meditate.

Dragon Meets Atman

Just as the meaning of a node is clarified through its position in the chart, another level of understanding is added when we consider a node's position relative to the Sun. This can tell us a great deal about the difficulties we may experience as we try to employ the lessons the lunar Nodes suggest. It is here that the Dragon and the Atman come together to reveal a true picture of karmic intent.

Sun Conjunct North Node
Conjunctions are a mixed blessing and curse. If we choose to be aware of the lessons represented by our North Node, then the lessons are easy. Our soul provides simple, safe opportunities to practice the lessons of the North Node.

But if we choose to deny the lessons, they become like a beach ball being pushed underwater—the more effort used to push the ball into the water, the stronger the resistance and the higher the ball bounces out of the water when it is let go. This can lead to "scary" situations. A person with North Node conjunct Sun, after one or two such experiences, may decide that the beach ball (the lesson of the North Node) is too dangerous, and go into complete resistance to North Node lessons. This only aggravates everything in the long run, causing the person to expend more and more energy in keeping the ball underwater. When the ball finally gets out from under the native's hands, it explodes into the air, confirming the native's fear that if he lets go, even for one second, everything will explode out of control. Often the result is that more energy is used to keep the ball down than would be used to learn the lessons the North Node has to teach.

The person needs to recognize that the beach ball is not dangerous; what is causing the trouble is the native's resistance. To get out of this spiral, the person needs to slowly release his resistance to the lessons of the North Node. He needs to accept that his resistance has blown the lessons out of proportion. He needs to allow the power of his Sun sign (the Atman or soul) to give him ideas for pursuing the lessons of the North Node, instead of expending tremendous amounts of energy in resisting and denying those lessons.

Many famous people have North Node conjunct the Sun. H.P. Blavatsky (born August 12, 1831, at 7:02 am, Sverdlovsk, Russia), Theosophist, occultist, spiritualist, and medium, had a North Node/Sun conjunction in Leo in the Second House. She needed to learn (and did learn) to value her own abilities as equal to those of others, and to express them in ways that benefited individuals close to her, and not just humanity at a distance.

Eleanor Roosevelt (born October 11, 1884, at 11:00 am, New York City), U.S. first lady, social reformer, and U.S. delegate to the United Nations (1945-53), had Sun and North Node conjunct in Libra in the Tenth House. Mrs. Roosevelt is a good example of someone who, at first, resisted the lessons of the North Node. Her Sun was square her Moon, which probably made it very difficult for her to trust herself. With age and experience, she discovered, "No one can make you feel inferior without your consent."

Sun Opposite North Node

Oppositions indicate areas where we need to focus our attention. These are not areas of our lives that just fall into place without effort. Frequently we project our issues onto others, and fall into the belief that our troubles are due to other people's problems interfering with our lives. When we realize that the people around us are mirrors of our souls, we can own up to our projected and denied parts and incorporate the power that comes from learning and accepting the new lessons.

Whenever the North Node opposes the Sun, the South Node conjuncts it. In terms of karma, when the South Node conjuncts the Sun, the person is repeating the karmic lesson. Possibly she did not achieve as much of the North Node lessons as she could have, or ignored the lessons entirely, relying on the placement of the South Node. With the South Node representing familiar ways of approaching life, it is easy to "fall" back to the tried-and-true patterns, and avoid learning the new lessons. However, it is our soul's joy to grow and expand. With this placement, the person has given herself another opportunity to address the issue, situation, lesson, or relationship (or any combination) that was not fully addressed in the past.

Aleister Crowley (born October 12, 1875, at 11:00 pm, Leamington, England), magician and occultist, had Sun opposed North Node. His Sun was in the Fourth House in Libra, with the North Node in the Tenth House in Aries. His lessons were based around the need to learn to rely on himself, and to express himself through his work.

Paul Newman (born January 26, 1925, at 6:30 am, Cleveland, Ohio), actor and businessman, has Sun in Aquarius in the First House, opposed to North Node in Leo in the Seventh House. He finds it easy to identify himself by the groups he belongs to, and not necessarily as an individual. His lesson is to bring his strength as an individual into group situations—something I believe he has accomplished with his business. In addition, he has expressed his Atman (the Sun) by focusing the business on generating money for causes he believes in (a very Aquarian way to run a business).

Sun Sextile North Node

Sextiles represent areas that harmonize well. When the North Node and the Sun are sextile, there are no hindrances to creatively using both types of energy. Since the North and South Nodes are always exact opposites, if the North Node sextiles the Sun, then the South Node trines the Sun.

Mohandas Gandhi (born October 2, 1869, at 2:29 am, Porbander, India), lawyer, activist, and mystic, had a Libra Sun in the

Twelfth House sextile a Leo North Node in the Tenth House (and trine an Aquarian South Node in the Fourth House). Gandhi took his philosophy that all people are one family (South Node), and combined it with wanting diversity and balance in government and culture (Sun in Libra). As a young man, he had attempted to force the South African government to treat Indians better. But it wasn't until he returned to India and started his nonviolence campaign to get Great Britain to recognize India as a sovereign nation that he met with success. In India, he expressed his concepts through his work in new, creative methods (North Node) of nonviolence.

Franklin D. Roosevelt (born January 31, 1882, at 1:40 am, Hyde Park), president, had his Sun in the Fifth House in Aquarius, sextile the North Node in the Third House in Sagittarius. This meant the lesson he was to repeat related to the fact that his Sun was trine the South Node in the Ninth House in Gemini. President Roosevelt's lessons revolved around communicating high ideals to many people; something he accomplished through his fireside chats and his sweeping economic and social reforms.

Sun Square North Node

Squares represent areas where we get in our own way. The energy of two planets speak different languages; one may say "act" while the other says "feel." The challenge comes when we believe that only one is correct. We need a common focus so the two energies can "stand back-to-back" instead of "squaring off against each other."

Since the purpose of the Nodes is to allow our souls to experience new ways of approaching life, squares between the Sun and the nodes are not very logical or helpful. That might explain why there seem to be very few people with Sun-Node squares. (Remember, with North and South Node always being exact opposites, if the Sun squares one Node it also squares the other.)

One famous person with this aspect is Jack Nicklaus (born January 21, 1940, at 3:10 am, Columbus, Ohio), golfer. He has a Second House Aquarius Sun squared against a Libra North Node in the Eleventh House and an Aries South Node in the Fifth House. The South Node is in the house of activity, in the individualistic sign of Aries. Golf is certainly an individualistic game. With North Node in Libra in the Eleventh House of team sports and groups, I suspect that one of his lessons is to move away from individualistic pursuits and to put more energy into groups. However, with the Sun squared against the Nodes, he may believe that there is no money in group situations for him, and so he may have trouble letting go of a sure source of money to pursue more socially interactive activities. A possible solution would be to start a Little League equivalent for children to learn golf, or to work with the Special Olympics to design golf courses for their events.

Sun Trine North Node

Trines represent areas that speak the same language. When the North Node and the Sun are trine, their energies combine to create a bigger energy.

Martin Luther King, Jr. (born January 15, 1929, at noon, Atlanta, Georgia), activist and minister, had Sun in Capricorn, trine the North Node in the First House in Taurus. Dr. King did not intend to be active at a national level; he focused on local situations and participated in local nonviolent demonstrations, which, in turn, propelled him into the nation's awareness. His work is a great example of how the energies between trined planets combine to make something much larger without needing a lot of extra effort on the part of the native.

Other people with North Node sextile Sun (and South Node trine Sun) are William Blake (poet, philosopher), Robert Redford (actor), Nicholas Culpepper (herbalist, writer), Natalie Wood (actress), and Dwight D. Eisenhower (president).

Solar Eclipse

Eclipse births are rare, since eclipses come so seldom in the year. But two famous examples are Pope John Paul II and Karl Marx. Pope John Paul II (born May 18, 1920, at midnight, Wadowice, Poland) has Moon conjunct Sun in Taurus. The South Node is also in Taurus. Karl Marx (born May 5, 1818, at 2:00 am, Treves, Prussia) has Moon conjunct Sun in Taurus, and the North Node also in Taurus.

Pope John Paul II has the New Moon in the Fourth house, conjunct the South Node. Remember, when the South Node and Sun are conjunct, it is generally an indicator that the native is getting a second chance around on the issues he or she is to learn. One possible interpretation is the Pope John Paul II needs to bring family values (the theme of the Fourth House) to his work situation.

Karl Marx's chart shows the New Moon/North Node conjunction in the Second House. His karmic lesson was to take the information he knew about other peoples' resources and money (South Node in the Eighth House) and learn to value his own resources and money (North Node in the Second House).

Another solar eclipse baby is Elizabeth Kubler-Ross (born July 8, 1926, at 10:45 pm, Zurich, Germany), grief researcher, psychologist, and activist. Her Moon, Sun, and North Node are in Cancer, with the Moon in the Fourth House and the Sun and North Node in the Fifth House. Her lessons have been based around bringing dignity to death and understanding of the grief process. She has made great strides in issues involving hospice and the right-to-die in a home environment (very Cancerian concepts).

Born On a Lunar Eclipse

Lunar eclipse births appear to be even more rare than solar eclipse births. A lunar eclipse birth combines the intensity of a Full Moon birth with the intensity of an eclipse. In Vedic astrology, a Full Moon birth is believed to indicate the birth of an old soul—one with enough experience to be able to use the intense energy of such an alignment.

To give you an idea of how rare a lunar eclipse birth is, out of 1,300 charts in *The Circle Book of Charts* (listing famous and semi-famous people from all walks of life), I found ten Full Moon births (compared to almost four times that many New Moon births). Out of the ten, only three were lunar eclipses.

Christopher Isherwood (August 26, 1904, Cheshire, England, time unknown) has a Sun conjunct North Node in Virgo, opposing the Moon conjunct South Node in Pisces. Mr. Isherwood was a novelist and translator. His most famous book is *Goodbye to Berlin* (1932), which was made into the musical *Cabaret* in 1966. Since the time of birth is unknown, we can't make any interpretation by house. But with North Node in Virgo, we can draw the conclusion that his lesson was to learn to be more critical and discerning in life.

Raymond Chandler (born July 23, 1888, time and location unknown), mystery writer, had Sun and North Node in Leo, opposing the Moon and South Node in Aquarius. Again, without the birth time, we can only look at the North Node sign. Mr. Chandler's lessons revolved around being creative, expressive, and generous to individuals (Leo).

Nodes can be looked at as karmic indicators or simply as new behaviors, concepts, and attitudes that our essences (represented by the Sun) wish to experience. By looking at the placement of the Nodes in relation to any aspects to the Sun, we can gain new insight into our lives.

Economic Forecasts for 2001

by Kaye Shinker

Since ancient times, astrologers have looked at a select number of charts set for the capital of their country to determine the future economic picture. Financial astrologers look at the same charts, studying the position of the Sun, Jupiter, and Saturn, specifically. First they look at the position of these planets in the solstice and equinox charts, when the Sun reaches the zero degree points of the cardinal signs Capricorn, Aries, Cancer, and Libra. Next, they look at the solar eclipses. There will be two eclipses of the Sun in 2001. However, there is also an eclipse on December 25, 2000, right after the Winter Solstice. This eclipse is close enough to the natural cycle and energies of the New Year that we will include in this forecast. So, in total, there are three solar eclipses between December 21, 2000 and December 21, 2001.

The year 2001 promises to be extremely busy. One theme will be full employment with wage inflation. Consumer spending on durable goods will continue to push up the earnings of most corporations. Throughout the year there is a trine between Jupiter and

Uranus, and then a trine between Saturn and Neptune. These two aspects will expose deceptions and accounting irregularities. As a result, publicly held corporations will require astute public relations personnel for damage control.

Jupiter in Gemini and Cancer

Vehicles Multiply Like Rabbits

Jupiter starts the year retrograde in Gemini. It goes direct on January 25, quickly transiting through Gemini until it reaches Cancer on July 13. Jupiter will remain in Cancer until August 2, 2002.

The inauguration of the new president is the first major event of the new year. Who's who in the computer industry will be in conspicuous attendance. The dealmakers will wear tuxedos with jogging shoes, and pocket protectors instead of handkerchiefs. The ladies will opt for denim.

The financial markets will be very quiet until the inauguration festivities are complete. Then the Bull will shove the markets up. Business writers call it the "honeymoon" of the new president, and the astrologers say "Jupiter direct."

The sign through which Jupiter moves indicates the commodities that are in abundance. A bountiful supply means a lower price. Items in short supply tend to be expensive, due to the effects of a supply-and-demand economy. For example, Gemini rules automobiles and Cancer rules houses. Jupiter will transit Gemini this year, so cars are relatively cheap until August 2001. In August, when generous Jupiter moves into Cancer, the supply of houses will be large, and therefore buying a home could be less expensive.

Jupiter's transit of Gemini indicates plenty of cars, trucks, cabs, and bikes. The highways will be jammed. Gemini also rules communication and thought, so cellular phones, calculators, and computing devices will be stuffed in briefcases or even hang off of the now-fashionable telephone line-worker's belt. Begging for a corner in your home will be a supply of all kinds of telecommunications devices. For example, satellite dishes, cable boxes, VCRs, radios, and skinny television sets will all be plentiful. Office supply stores will be overwhelmed with merchandise. Expect price wars.

There will be a flood of books, newspapers, and magazines. These will fill the mail box, creating an annoying oversupply of paper for the recycling bin. Recycling junked televisions, computers, telephones, and other electronic gadgets will become a start-up business for entrepreneurial types. Imaginative folks will find many creative ways to use the resulting material.

Inexpensive vehicles suggest all sorts of new business opportunities for self-starters. At-home workers need supplies delivered to their doors. Local package services will jam their trucks with merchandise ordered on the Internet.

Industries that produce chemicals, drugs, perfume, and plastics will find their raw materials rather hard to find. Oil and fish will be expensive. Food processors will find their supply lines difficult and their labor very expensive. These industries are not shy about increasing their prices and profit margins.

On July 13, Jupiter moves into Cancer, the ruler of the home, and the whole economic environment changes. Suddenly there are too many houses on the market. Home builders have outdone themselves. Real-estate brokers blame higher interest rates for the unsold houses. There is also a glut of appliances, furniture, and building materials.

The sprawl of houses away from the city centers demanded a corresponding sprawl of shopping malls. The builders constructed too many fast food joints, restaurants, grocery stores, and bakeries in their enthusiasm. In great supply are beauty shops, cleaners, barbers, gas stations, and junk-food shops. Competitive discounting means that eventually quite a few of these businesses will fail to pay the rent, and have to fold.

The large shopping malls have quickly evolved into an array of clothing and shoe shops. But they are beginning to lose their customers as people shift their purchasing styles. Instant relics, many malls become the ghost towns of the twentieth century. Local authorities will have some new headaches trying to keep these places from becoming the new "playgrounds" for mischief makers.

A point to remember is that there will very likely be shortages in gems, handcrafted fine furniture, and designer clothing. There also will be shortages of eyeglasses, dental supplies, and other kinds of medical equipment. Newer medical equipment, utilizing new technologies, will be in demand, and will be correspondingly hard to find. Other areas to watch for shortages are entertainment, recreational vehicles, casinos, software games, and toys.

The Baby Boomlet of the '80s is providing some minimum-wage employees during the summer holidays. However, many are employed by their parents in home businesses, and a good percentage have jobs training their grandparents how to shop online.

Hotels, restaurants, and cruise ship holidays, also related to the home and comfort sign of Cancer, are in oversupply, and they are cheap. Airline tickets may be a little more difficult, but still relatively easy to get. Those who schedule a vacation for August and September will be able to purchase excellent values with their vacation dollar.

The focus of Jupiter's transit through Cancer will be adjusting the family to new technology. In the nineteenth century, genteel ladies gave their friends calling cards that stated which day they would be home and available to entertain visitors. The twenty-first century version will be communicated via e-mail to plumbers, carpenters, electricians, repair folks, and delivery services.

In the first part of the twentieth century, groceries, merchandise, and services were delivered to homes because shoppers lacked transportation. Twenty-first century shoppers are time-starved and working erratic hours. The labor shortage continues to demand that the traditional working hours of nine-to-five disappear.

Movies and television have created a pent-up demand worldwide for North American products. The order-fulfillment capabilities of the Internet make it possible for international customers to purchase anything. Internet auctions will add to the flow of goods. The world economy is booming.

Saturn in Taurus

The Business of Business is the Customer

Saturn finishes his long transit of Taurus on April 20, 2001, whereupon he enters Gemini to stay until June 2003.

Banks have made too many acquisitions. It's a Catch-22: every time they achieve organization, their personnel quit or retire. Even the best-organized financial institutions are dealing with personnel problems. The larger banks have so many services that none are done well. The financial news headlines criticize banks, complaining that these financial warehouses have too many irons in the fire. Around April 15, at the tail end of the Saturn-Taurus transit, the largest banks complete some strategic divestitures. This helps them focus their attention on the banking business. There is plenty of restructuring, and a few more strategic mergers. Their shareholders finally get a good return on their investments.

Rising interest rates are advantageous to the boutique-style banks. These neighborhood banks realize that there is no such thing as a small account. Their mini-accounts offered to young customers will begin to pay off. For the average consumer this is a bull market as the various financial institutions beg for business.

Speaking of April, the other problem as the new administration takes office is that the IRS, with its penchant for paperwork, continues to frustrate the public. The federal government has collected plenty of tax money, but it hasn't spent it, or for that matter reduced taxes. The new president promised to cut taxes—but so did his opponent. The public wants action and they want to see it in their paychecks. Congress, on the other hand, doesn't know how to stop spending—and continues fighting along party lines. They finally get the chore done around the first of May.

The mood changes when Saturn returns to Gemini. He made a brief appearance in Gemini during the late summer of 2000—remember the tiny pre-election tax cut? Fortunately, wages increased and everyone spent the extra dollars getting organized and buying two of everything.

Gemini is still working its transportation and communication angles, and the major topic of conversation will be traffic and how to avoid it. Metropolitan areas are finding the freeways jammed twenty-four hours a day. Some folks are moving away from it, creating a housing glut in the most congested areas. Others are arranging flex hours or computer commuting. Truckers and delivery people simply have to deal with the problem. Public transportation is the issue on the agenda of every local government.

Qualified commercial drivers are scarce. Vehicle repair folks have their appointment books filled. Repair technicians for communications equipment are nonexistent. Skilled labor is undereducated. Senior citizens are finding themselves teaching basic mechanics at night school.

The Baby Boom generation has begun to retire from the work force. Rich and healthy, many have looked forward to playing. Employers offer consulting fees, stock options, and travel perks. The labor shortage is acute.

Immigration is not an option. The world economy has now developed a middle class. The Internet and other communications devices have empowered second- and third-world citizens to stay home and work for Yankee wages. Retired U.S. citizens with a sense of adventure or teaching skills have found employment abroad. Retired teachers or civil servants are in demand in every emerging economy. English is the language of technology.

Basic education has a very real shortage of teachers. This is especially true in grammar schools. Private as well as public schools have huge retirement woes. Neither pay enough to encourage recent college graduates to seek employment. Parents who demand a quality education are finding that they have to do it themselves. Publishers of educational software and books need to develop new selling strategies. Targeting the parent as well as the child may be a useful tactic.

The Baby Boomlet (eighteen and under) loves research. The Internet was designed just for them. They can find anything they want, and busy parents are very frustrated with their little geniuses. Computers are cheap enough for each child to have his or her own, and content-blocking software is in great demand.

Corporate America is spending too much money on public relations, in the opinion of their shareholders. Too many products are winding up in court. Quality control has slid by lower-level management, and enough products have slipped through to cause some major public relations difficulties. This is especially true of vehicles and various communication devices. Litigation seems to be fashionable. The Internet has made researching liability-law a new game for the ordinary citizen.

Earned income continues to fuel the markets. Investor's portfolios are moving away from mutual funds, and teams of investors are having fun doing their own research. Technology gives them equal footing with the brokers, and they manage their portfolios with online trading. There are a lot of millionaires making very creative use of their electronic gadgets.

Uranus in Aquarius

Efficiency Begins at Home

Uranus entered Aquarius on January 13, 1996, and will depart December 31, 2003. Aquarius, the sign of invention, is ruled by Uranus—the planet that travels through space upside down and backwards. As a result, the electronics industry is busy changing anything and everything.

Mall owners find they need to be creative with live entertainment, events, and demonstrations, similar to a state fair. Kiosks proliferate with sampling booths and customers ordering online. Customers with notebook computers will enter their own ordering data. Retailers who relied on their giant warehouse buildings to attract customers will convert them into shipping centers. Commercial drivers will earn good money.

Remember when nine-to-five used to mean business hours? Since 1996, casual Fridays have taken over the entire week. Office hours are when the professional's converted bus shows up in your neighborhood. The stock exchanges and other financial venues have redesigned their business time periods to include all twenty-four hours. The twenty-four-hour clock set for Greenwich Mean Time will be a favorite gift. "Work time" will be when you happen to be doing it, and yet another business tradition dissolves.

Education is in the midst of a revolution. Parents need their older children at home and are willing to take time to instruct the younger ones. Public schools will offer local tax-credits for various home-school classes.

Control of personal environment is a big theme during this time, stimulated by the Uranus-Aquarius emphasis on innovation. Fuel cells that fit in the garage are almost possible. Farmers and ranchers are already checking the possibility of using them on their operations. Outdoor sporting events have found them invaluable. Homemade electricity should be common before Uranus leaves

Aquarius. Innovation is truly taking off!

Jupiter will be trine Neptune and Uranus throughout 2001. This means that the news media will have lots of fun. There were some interesting shenanigans during late 1999 and 2000, and these will be exposed. Financial institutions are the most vulnerable, since their employees are followed by trails of paperwork. Deceptions by various market makers will also be exposed. Recently deregulated utilities and transportation systems are vulnerable to scandals, since they've been taking advantage of their new freedoms.

The whole Internet information system is sneaking into our lives through the telephone and cable wires. Every once in a while we've been taking a peek, buying a few things, and sending jokes on e-mail. By 2001, the Internet is part of our lives and we run to the little machine every morning to check the e-mail and the weather.

Neptune in Aquarius

Time is Money

Usually every invention has a number of applications other than its original purpose. An incredible number of inventions have appeared since November 28, 1998, when Neptune entered Aquarius. New applications will appear throughout the Aquarius transit, which ends February 4, 2012. Creativity with electronics is the major objective.

Imagine a journalist sharing an interesting story with several thousand folks via an e-zine that pays by percentage of subscriber hits. Could be a good deal. As a consumer, imagine an empty magazine rack or fewer trips to the recycling bin. That sounds like an even better deal. Business will be desperate for bright young students to work with their various electronic venues. Creative management techniques will be the answer. One possibility is to divide work into take-home projects, as "telecommuting" becomes the wave of the employment future. Businesses will take advantage of their bright young employees, and be able to offer post-high school education via the Internet as an employment perk.

Time is a precious commodity, and students are anxious to use what they have efficiently. Technical students and writers with communications and technology skills are the first choice of employment recruiters. Their skills will be highly flexible during the twists and turns of the new economy.

The traditional ivy-covered university will need to recreate itself. For example, English and philosophy classes could be best taught online. Accounting and Sociology are also easy to translate to the electronic medium. Lab classes in the sciences, however, might require several weeks on campus. No matter how far "virtual" technologies progress, they are still no substitute for hands-on learning.

Alumni associations and supporters of brick-and-mortar universities just don't know what to think. The traditional university is slowly dwindling, and it sometimes seems that the only students on campus are the football team. Students and their parents will have found creative ways to make use of their time and money. They are going to school via the computer and only showing up for class when hands-on learning is required. Time periods for student classes will change the university structure.

Neptune's thoughtful and rather eccentric influence on Aquarius will start changing the arts. Fashion, drama, music, painting, and literature will make a quantum leap. If it is outrageous, it will sell. Three-dimensional art is favored—especially if light and shadow change the painting. In drama, expect a definitive philosophy expressed in the story line. Commercial music will combine electronic and acoustic instruments to create preposterous sounds.

The new art does not appeal to the usual establishment agencies for distribution. All of these innovations in the arts will require expensive risk-taking by the artists. This suggests that penny stocks will be available to investors willing to back entertainers.

Pluto in Sagittarius

Travel is Broadening

Pluto has been in Sagittarius since November 11, 1995, and will leave the sign Thanksgiving 2008. In the middle degrees of Sagittarius, all people can think about is travel and having fun. Trains, planes, and automobiles will be full of passengers seeking beautiful views and exciting adventures.

Tourism will become a bread-and-butter issue for countries with exotic parks and attractions. Safety of visitors will be a local issue. Making sure the visitors have a unique experience with all the local cultural entertainment will provide third-world entrepreneurs with plenty of extra dollars to spend shopping on the Internet. The world is slowly becoming a true globalized market.

Imaginative outfitters with interesting tours will add even more tourist dollars to rural economies. Festivals as well as local sporting events will find their venues crowded. Local restaurants and craftsmen will have a new audience.

While business travelers have cut back on overnight stays, they have been replaced by the extended-stay visitor. The hospitality industry finds they must revise their marketing strategy to attract a new breed of clientele. Leisure travelers spend more time occupying their vacation properties, and they make extensive use of the inviting facilities.

The result of all this is that economic opportunities are plentiful. The new administration has promised to make international trade and travel simple. They have also decided to cancel regulations they can't enforce. Technology has made whole sections of international law useless or silly. It has simply become too easy to bypass trade regulations.

A new invention worthy of huge accolades: a special booth to quietly check a cell phone before entering a restaurant, train, plane, museum, or concert. The solstice and equinox charts add further details as to the specific areas of the economy the transiting outer planets have exposed.

Winter Solstice

Capricorn Ingress

The Capricorn ingress for 2001 is December 21, 2000, at 8:37 am EST. This predicts the year ahead for government and business. Time to celebrate the official beginning of the twenty-first century. The elections are over and corporate America has won. Now they are planing parties in Washington, D.C. Country casual seems to be in vogue.

Never have Americans had so many new toys. Whether they're members of the Baby Boom (forty to sixty years old), Baby Bust (eighteen to forty), or Baby Boomlet (less than eighteen), each generation loves toys with wheels, batteries, and dialogue. The holiday season isn't long enough to try all of them. We'll want to play with these gadgets all year long.

The buzzword on Wall Street is fuel cells. Energy from fuel cells has made the "might want to buy one for the garage" list. In fact, every business is trying to decide whether to buy now or wait until the price goes down. This will probably be the dilemma for the year—similar to 1990, when buying a home computer was the issue. Just as that problem is now fading due to dwindling prices, this, too, shall pass.

If it is small, it is good. Capricorn's responsible and pragmatic energies are encouraging efficiency, and the theme of this year is to downsize every mechanical gadget we possess. The miniaturization that puts the laptop on the nightstand is moving into everyday life. This is a whole new economy, and start-up companies dot the landscape. It's as though everything is being reinvented.

The focus for the year ahead will be on institutions and the government in particular. Treaties will present all sorts of opportunities, with the power of the Internet, and its capacity for international communication, forcing new agreements between nations. Fluctuating international currency is increasingly a problem.

Intellectual property is a huge issue. Lots of protective measures are proposed, as well as ways to compensate authors and inventors. North Americans hold most of the patents and copyrights that keep the World Wide Web up and running. They have a lot of control and probably are not willing to give it away. Protecting their intellectual property is a priority.

So the new administration will have some interesting challenges, but keeping the economy rolling is not one of them. Once again there just is not enough labor to get the work done. The Mexican and Canadian borders must allow free-flowing immigration no matter what organized labor proclaims as unfair.

During 1999-2000 there was a lot of chicanery, and various financial institutions were deceived by their customers or employees. These boring scandals will make headlines.

"Zero year" elections are difficult for vice-presidents. Somehow the new V.P. will need to take over the job. But for now the new president is quietly handling his new power. He is arranging to cut taxes, eliminate red tape, and figure out what to do about the huge number of civil service employees who have chosen to retire. "Help Wanted" ads litter the Washington, D.C., newspapers.

December Eclipse

The Christmas Eclipse December 25 at 12:22 pm EST

The eclipse will be visible in North America. And yes, it happens on Christmas Day. Probably every doomsday prophet will have an opinion on its effect. If you have time, run out to take a look—just be sure to take your eclipse glasses.

The significance of this eclipse is in international trade and the expansion of telecommunications. The crisis centering on intellectual property is just one of the many issues. Exchanging currencies will be another. There is talk that a currency similar to the Euro is being negotiated by international banks.

This eclipse is full of promise for international business. Communications are overcoming language and cultural barriers. International commerce is the big deal, and no one wants to miss the opportunity to invest. The world is opening up in a big new way. The whole change in international commerce is fated, and little can be done to alter the trend.

Throughout the holiday season various religious groups will find young people joining their celebrations. Yes, it is a form of rebellion. Their parents have avoided church and young folks need the social activity. Parents are suspicious, but the inherent sterility of the computer forces people to seek out social activities, and religious groups can offer a good way to provide them.

Throughout January 2001 money will pour into the stock exchanges. February will see new highs for all exchanges. The climb is steady with an emphasis on various international funds and durable goods manufacturers.

Spring Equinox

Aries Ingress

The first day of spring occurs on March 20 at 8:31 am EST, and predicts the year ahead for agriculture. It will be a beautiful spring, with a wide variety of crops planted by farmers and gardeners. The more the better, since times are picking up.

The economy is terrific. Farmers foresee fair prices for their products. Organic farmers have more orders than they can handle. Trucks are hauling all sorts of machinery to their rural customers.

The word is out: "Generation X" is willing to pay for good food. In fact, they insist on eating only the highest quality calories. Organically grown produce and meat will continue to reward the upscale grocers with higher profits. Of course, organically grown products require intense labor, and a new type of sharecropping will find rural land owners visiting their contract lawyers.

Agriculture interests are creating new partnership opportunities. Corporate operations are downsizing for lack of labor. Still, there will be abundant supplies of food. There is a demand for new harvesting equipment and marketing techniques. Unhappy past experience with government controls finds the agriculture community seeking new ways to share their surplus.

The markets have already anticipated that the new president will get everything he asks from Congress. During the political conventions candidates determined what the country really wanted from its government. The winner will be the most sincere candidate, who promised to reduce government and taxes. Corporate America is sick of red tape. Entrepreneurial America is sick of paperwork. Everyone else is sick of paying civil service employees for programs that are useless.

Summer Solstice

Cancer Ingress and the June Eclipse

The second eclipse of 2001 occurs roughly four hours after the Cancer ingress on June 21. The Cancer ingress is June 21 at 2:38 am EDT, and the eclipse is June 21 at 6:58 am EDT. The Summer Solstice is about home and family, and the eclipse quickly alters the seasonal forecast.

The housing boom is coming to a conclusion. Prices have made their final push upwards. The new group of buyers is willing to avoid spending half their income on shelter. They consider their money better spent on the kids' education, entertainment, and recreation. Also, it is almost impossible to find someone to clean those big suburban barns. As a result, real-estate prices are on hold and some are actually going down.

Labor is so tight that fast-food restaurants are offering double the minimum wage just to flip hamburgers. Wage inflation is very real and this will force the Federal Reserve to push up interest rates.

Family income is the issue of the Summer Solstice, and the whole family is working. Mom and Pop's home computer business is keeping everyone in the family employed. Mom will certainly make sure these extra dollars find their way into special savings accounts as banks begin to make special offers to attract new customers.

Families have adjusted to managing their money online, and banking with their credit and debit cards. The cashless society is becoming a reality. Very few people are willing to spend one Saturday a month on bills.

The government will try once again to tax the Internet. The excuse is that children have access to pornography. Of course the kids are giggling over the debate, since Mom has held a monopoly on Internet access since she started her business. The kids are also too busy for such foolishness—they've been working in the family business since last summer.

The real concern of government is fielding the complaints about aggressive offshore gambling. International law is designed for the regulation of fishing, drug-shipping, and wars—not casinos. Taxing would provide some controls. Congressional committees determine that enforcement is impossible.

A great deal of aggressive male energy is concentrated on uncovering international money scams. In 1999 and 2000, a lot of people were deprived of their hard-won savings by con artists. Summer 2001 will find all sorts of news headlines exposing these swindlers.

In summer sports the struggle between talent and the team owners makes headlines. The bottom line is that earned income from the media just can't match the salary expectations of the talented employees. This is not necessarily a strike—it is just a power struggle with lots of public controversy.

Various software companies are finally able to manufacture encryption devices that are cheap enough for the artistic community to purchase. Hackers on the Internet are getting more numerous, and their reach is becoming even greater. The June eclipse shows that the encryption software is finally sophisticated enough to solve some of those problems.

The Fall Equinox

Libra Ingress

The Fall Equinox is September 22 at 6:04 pm EDT. It describes both national and international trade. This is the time of year we weigh in the crops, count the money, and go shopping. It is also the time of year when folks weigh and measure their holdings in the stock market. Usually they sell a few of their winning purchases to pay the bills left over from summer. Stockholders are promised dividend increases as the market falls into its October doldrums. Movement in price by year's end will be minimal, so little money is made. Equity shares are still in short supply but prices have remained lackluster. The Dow has taken to hovering around 15,000 and the S&P at about 2,200 with the NASDAQ around 4,000.

However, near November 12 there is volatility in REITs. The problem is the auto market. No one needs a new car. Easy maintenance and fewer miles means that there aren't many reasons to trade the old one. Auto stocks have been the least-favored equities most of the year because the new models are ugly and the sturdy SUVs and light trucks are still running very nicely.

Labor is again winning and being wooed with hiring bonuses, stock options, and higher hourly wages. Many skilled employees are demanding $35–$50 per hour and guaranteed overtime. Eagerly anticipated is the high school graduation of the class of 2002. The Baby Boomlet will begin feeding into the labor pool. There are enough of them to fill minimum wage jobs, and they have enough "I wants" to keep them on the job. Many will be prize employees since they have been trained to work by their self-employed parents. This group works relentlessly on any task assigned. They need very little management.

The Internet is completing its consolidation phase. Popular sites collect a lot of revenue from advertising and also a lot of criticism from subscribers. Cultural misspeaks bring floods of e-mail, and the international quality of the net gives providers some real headaches.

Shareholders meetings are starting to appear on the integrated versions of the net, where it is possible to vote in real time as the corporate officers bring up the pros and cons of various issues. These meetings can be as interesting as sitcoms.

Local and state governments have finally adjusted to their new computers. They might decide that elections will be possible through the Internet. However you look at it, the computer hardware companies will find a way for all of us to have a computer in every room of the house (color coordinated) and one for each vehicle in the garage. They'll soon be working on one for jogging around the park.

December Eclipse

The December 14 Eclipse 3:27 pm EST

Everyone is getting married. You wonder how they managed to find a reception hall. Online gift registration works, thankfully.

Corporate weddings are also in. Merger mania is all the rage, and international unions are common. Again corporations are trying to succeed with old leadership. Marketing and sales are intertwined and difficult to distinguish.

Presenting a sales pitch is very difficult without voice and follow-through. Price has to be everything. Public relations writers are in demand—they're the only ones who are still suited for the medium of cyberspace. Those who can write with flair are the new darlings of the Internet business craze.

Earned income is fairly high and folks are saving for special events. Luxury travel is the most favored way to spend this discretionary income. Time and money are both becoming more accessible to everyone.

Health issues are making headlines. Drug stores and vitamin companies will have extra profits. This winter season brings some pretty irascible flu germs. A healthy lifestyle, exercise, and a good diet will help keep the sniffles away.

Selling partnerships is happening via the malls and the computer. Your favorite retail store is now a different place. Malls are becoming something like a continuous state fair. If you like something, you put your card in a terminal and it's delivered to your house or office. A market will open up for returned merchandise.

Creative advertising will be required to realize sales. Media outlets will include all public transport. There will be www.coms on all those give-away coffee cups, ballpoint pens, and key chains.

International sales will be the focus of managers as the world economy finishes its Internet connections. The emerging middle class abroad will focus on purchases for their homes. The demand from customers abroad will be for beautiful furniture and electronic gadgets for their homes and offices.

Winter Solstice

Capricorn Ingress

The Winter Solstice begins at 2:21 pm EST on December 21, 2001. The household budget for 2002 includes that new fuel cell. The commercials equate it to the invention of the internal combustion engine. The fuel cell promises to revolutionize the way we get around. Farmers and small businessmen are particularly enchanted with its possibilities. The rest of us are trying to picture it in the garage providing electricity for all of the gadgets in our homes. Most of us are waiting for the price to diminish.

Change is the key word for 2002, especially in the corporate offices of publicly held companies. The new economy has created splendid partnership opportunities for management-type folks. There is a plethora of new businesses. Large corporations where mentoring has been neglected will find new managers impossible to hire or retain.

Congress has given up trying to please the public with tax policy. Now they are asking businesses. Every news program and chat network during the year ahead will have taxes as its topic. We are amazed at the how the new administration that promised to simplify and rewrite the tax code has managed to make it more complicated. The public begins to wonder if their home computer is smart enough to sort out all of the complicated rules.

The twenty-first century is about partnerships. Equality is the major theme. The new economy will force management and their operations staff into a new style of leadership that will use two people with equal powers and responsibilities. The paradigm has changed and everywhere management is forced to try new ideas.

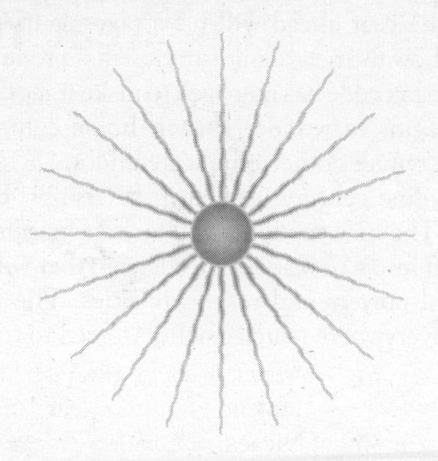

Coming of Age
World Predictions for 2001

by Leeda Alleyn Pacotti

Welcome to the twenty-first century! Now a historical reference, the twentieth century lies behind us, waiting to be evaluated and judged for its significance. A shattering realization overwhelms everyone with a birth year beginning "19": we are the relics of a misty century, unfathomable to our successor generations.

Wide-eyed with wonder, we ponder what magnificent insights will advance science and art, and what fine contributions will alleviate humanity's needs. We are no different from those who went before us at the beginning of each new century, playing god with our prospects. Daily concerns for survival and private dreams will converge on us soon enough, but for the moment we let our thoughts turn to the ensuing 100 years and the unimaginable wealth of changes a new century brings.

There is another cycle of time, however, that is nearing a new beginning. This cycle, measured not in centuries but in millenia, contains as much promise and hope as the thought of the new century to come.

Turning of the Great Year

The Great Year, the astrological precession of the ages, lasting 25,868 years, is ready to turn from the Great Month or Age of Pisces to the succeeding 2,156-year Great Month of Aquarius.

Easily encompassing two millennia, the Age of Pisces is popularly thought to have begun with the birth of Christ, leaving the worrisome prospect that it will continue for another 156 years. A limited focus on charismatic religious matters, attributable to Pisces, precluded speculative thinking from other possibilities. Other historical events, however, indicate the Piscean Age was in full swing well before the heralded Nativity. Near 140 BC, a Greek astronomer, Hipparchus of Nicaea, discovered the underlying principle of the precession of the ages when he observed changes in the movement of the stars behind the Sun during the vernal equinox. This astronomical feat strongly resonates with a keynote of Pisces: connection with the universe or universal.

The empire of Rome, congratulated for its land armies, tightened its hold on nations surrounding the Mediterranean by expanding seafaring trade into naval armadas. Gaius Julius Caesar incorporated naval strategies to secure his expanding conquests, with planning maneuvers present on his campaign tables at the time of his assassination in 44 BC. Throughout the Piscean Age, a pinnacle determiner of military power for any nation was its naval strength.

Taking the extraordinary discovery by Hipparchus as the birth of the Piscean Age, the senatorial acclamation in 27 BC of Augustus—the first of the imperial Caesars, who later exemplified a squalid, indolent decadence—confirmed the bursting blossom of Piscean influence. Despite careful day-reckoning in sequestered monasteries, agitated calendaring through papal one-upmanship, and frenzied time-sequencing with leap days and universal seconds, historical momentum permits the beginning of the Age of Aquarius at about the year 2016.

Great Months, near their cusp, have a commingled influence, stretching 180 years on either side of the subtle change from one Age to another. Penetrating the veil of Pisces, Aquarius began stirring social, military, and scientific changes in the 1830s, leaving behind the bloody, decimating revolutions of the 1700s. Altered social structures, and factors contributing to those alterations, fall directly to Aquarius.

Steam-powered railways, first introduced in 1802, eventually permitted mass troop movements, enabling continental and global wars and mass immigrations, which altered national genetic integrity and created diverse genetic pools, dubbed melting pots. The deluge of labor-saving inventions which poured into domestic life and industrial trade alleviated the wearisome, life-shortening toil of a disregarded humanity. Born in 1833, literary giant Charles Dickens became the progenitor of Aquarian social consciousness, exemplified in his classic, *A Christmas Carol*, portraying the significant interaction between individual expression and society's consciousness. Finally, the triumph of the Wright brothers at Kitty Hawk fulfilled rulership over the air, shifting the primary focus for long-distance travel away from the oceans.

From the waning influence of Pisces come the last ballyhoos of an ending world-without-end, the creaking groans of a rickety, hierarchically bound Church, and the indolent, self-indulgent couch potato, that consequence of twentieth-century convenience.

Erecting an equal-house chart for the departing Age, the last thirteen minutes of Pisces remain, with zero-degree cusps on all houses. This chart for the last breath of the Age of Pisces strongly foretells the major transitions which will take place over the next fifteen years. During the coming year, the transits of Jupiter conjunct Saturn, opposing Pluto and Chiron, hold the greatest sway.

The Continents Drift

The global demand for preferred trade alliances, which began its influence last year, necessarily commits one nation on each continent to assume leadership and spokesmanship for its neighbors. Pressure to make alignments without sacrificing economic standing is a powerful incentive. The failure to take a strong stance opens less stable or organized countries to plunder.

While young psychics sense tremendous ruptures in continental masses over the next fifty years, the real upheaval lies in altered governmental structures, precipitated by expanded group consciousnesses of continental populations. Countries are forced to carefully examine the basis for their presumed status on the global stage. Reflecting an Aquarian theme that the identity of the group culminates from the identities of individuals, continental populations recognize that their national identities must be based on knowledge of their special needs, rather than dictated pronouncements by foreign trade partners.

In the Age of Pisces chart, both Jupiter and Saturn transit from the Fourth House cusp, with Jupiter continuing into the Fifth. Confusion reigns over available land. Everyone believes there is a shortage, but plenty to purchase. Housing construction still booms throughout the world, but people are less inclined to buy, feeling there isn't enough money for all domestic needs.

Opposing the Fourth House, Pluto and Chiron transit the Tenth House. Monarchies, dictatorships, presidencies, and other leaderships experience upheaval. In many cases, aloof executives of long standing are eliminated in favor of those with greater sympathy and recognition of the common man.

The opposition between Chiron-Pluto and Jupiter-Saturn demolishes the medieval precept that the land and king are one. The entire Earth is the staging ground for a clash between the god of heaven, Jupiter, representing magnanimity toward others, and the god of the underworld, Pluto, indicating advantage through abuse of power. Every country senses that woes, arising from the past, will heal if the old leadership is destroyed. Hereditary leaders and groomed successors are surprised to find that their expected thrones or seats of power are denied.

In the Twelfth House, Uranus and Neptune transit through Aquarius, sounding a mutual chord for brotherhood. Uranus is in its own sign with Neptune in its natural house. Together, ideals and desires meld to resurrect archetypal images of kindness and humanitarianism, which burst the global subconscious, overwhelmingly surfacing in dreams, visions, and meditations.

Uranus understands the story of siblings and the conflicts of sibling rivalry. During suppressed conflict, each sibling views the other as competition, failing to recognize that they contribute to each other's expression and well-being. Open conflict creates insight, urging people to treat neighbors and strangers as cordially as cherished brothers and sisters. Under the secondary influence of the forthcoming Libran decanate of Aquarius, confrontations arising from feelings of alienation and disaffection lead to compromise, even if it is an agreement to disagree. Live and let live is the goal; disenfranchisement is no longer safe.

The Centenarian Scare

Accepting each other in brotherhood finds its first test as the young confront the issues of the old. Wealthy nations are the hardest hit, because of life-prolonging developments which explode their elderly populations. Programs meant to ease conditions at the end of life drain already burdened funding—a situation foretold by the striking transit of Saturn in the Fourth House. The world no longer knows what to do with its seniors, fearing they will usurp other limited resources, spending the remainder of their increasing life spans in idle pursuits or in degenerative health.

During 2001, as nations recover from plummeted market values, working classes everywhere have faced their worst fears. Curtailed productivity, shrunken earnings, and hurried bankruptcies demolished presumptions about personal security, forcing people to relinquish savings, retirement holdings, and the old homestead. The foundations for a secure future have crumbled, while the social and physical ills of an aging population have consumed public awareness and energies.

The idea of living 100 years or longer produces a backlash from the younger generations. The powerful undercurrent of 2001 is the centenarian scare, in which the young and strong feel they are made beasts of burden for dallying or barely cognizant seniors. This fear has its roots in the mid-twentieth century, sprouting as a dark reminder of the generation gap of the 1960s. The old rallying cry, "Trust no one over thirty," sparks hateful ideas of justified euthanasia pogroms directed at the old.

Although Saturn screams that there is not enough to go around, Jupiter says to look again. The planetary monarch, helped by advance shocks from lunar and solar eclipses falling in the Fifth House, demands that a higher consciousness prevail. Overtaking

Saturn's influence, Jupiter puts a fresh face on the possibilities of senior life. Untenable notions of languished retirement disintegrate with Chiron's opposition to the Fourth House, exposing these ideas as the pipe dreams they are and ushering in healing for distraught families and communities.

As Jupiter moves toward the Fifth House of individual expression, suggestions for reeducation, rehabilitation, and reemployment of the aging foreshadow a flowering of individual creativity, firing the imaginations of all generations to recognize that agedness has incredibly special freedoms. Reinvigorated to become valuable contributors to society, retirees demonstrate inspired inventiveness accumulated from a rich variety of interests and life experiences. Among their ideas to satisfy the needs of their age group are geriatric game stores, emphasizing improved mental acuity and agility; senior fashion design, developing clothing styles to promote flexibility and movement; and hybrid health approaches, cultivated from traditions throughout the world, especially the shamanic. As they come to recognize that their needs are mirrored by all ages, many seniors promote small businesses based on these ideas, tailored to reduce stress and increase enjoyment of life in every age group. Eventually, society learns that agedness is not synonymous with frailty or decline.

Focus on Nations

As the continents separate into isolated power bases, the nations within them which have either historical power or organization jockey for positions of leadership. Specific nations, discussed below, have the greatest likelihood of leading the continental masses.

Argentina

Emerging as the leader of South America, Argentina underwent constitutional reforms in 1994. Although military factions are in balance, she faces internal turmoil from covert operations by other nations, which covet Argentina as an asset, refusing to accept her as an equal on the world stage. As Argentina goes, these nations know, so goes the rest of South America. Now in her seventh year, this newly reformed Virgo nation seeks to establish internal economic self-reliance, with development going well throughout this year. Attempts at international trade flounder, as do anticipated foreign alliances and treaties. A religious upset in early January shakes dogmatic faith, forcing her increasingly educated population to question religious precepts and restrictions. Through August 22, Argentina works on her identity, especially the way that identity is perceived by foreign powers, which view her as an up- start. Her efforts need to be directed on the domestic front through increased interaction among her social groups, rather than defining herself through each elected leadership. To united her diverse groups, she is helped by teachers, widows, and women in holy orders, who directly experience society's problems. After August 22, Argentina recognizes the need for universal education. She makes this outreach through health programs, in which women physicians have an expanded role. Again, outside covert groups attempt to thwart any stabilization that leads to a mentally and physically strong population.

China

Beginning January 9, eclipses rock this populous nation, which seeks control of Asia. China considers greater restrictions, in the tradition of Mao's reforms. She has lost her sense of domestic identity and believes it can be regained by revisiting the past. In late June, her legislative body attempts to enact more stringent laws to curtail population growth, and may even exact physical penalties of castration and mass sterilization. By early July, a domestic propaganda campaign is launched, claiming that less-than-zero population growth will cure China's social ills. A secret rebellion begins among educated groups, which spread word of unsavory human rights violations over the Internet. Throughout the year, China's international status declines as she inhibits overflowing expression of individual creativity, recognized as liberating, but dangerous. Through September 18, China focuses on creating a self-sustaining economic trade among her various provinces. The actions and legislation to restrict the population result in a growing underground rebellion and secret communications with foreign correspondents. After September 18, China exerts her efforts in still more restrictive

Worry over declining educational measurements takes center stage. Everyone now recognizes that illiteracy of future generations will topple the U.S. posture in foreign relationships. Higher education takes a new turn, as the government devises imaginative tax breaks, education loans, and tuition offsets for participation in study programs, conducted exclusively by computer over a proposed secondary Internet. However, this educational assistance robs coffers earmarked for expanded health research funding. Many are confused over relinquishing the conditioned idea of achieving an education within ivy-covered walls, but the outpouring for attendance in study chatrooms and on-demand class and lecture participation are irresistible incentives. Domestic commerce has a shot in the arm from sales of computers, peripherals, and furnishings. A demand for professional services to remodel home and business interiors is on the upswing, as family rooms and meeting rooms are converted into educational centers. Many businesses begin extending hours of operation around the clock to meet the educational preferences of their employees by providing flexible shifts and on-site study halls.

African United States

The African countries, diverse in every direction, recognize the need to pull together as a single nation, a united effort postulated for more than fifty years. Power bases massing on other continents create alarm for eclectic Africa. From Muslims in the north to Christians in the south, wealthy states to the east and poor nations of the west, each heeds the call for summits to develop and enact an encompassing declaration of continental sovereignty. Without unification, Africa knows it will fall plunder to outside continental powers, as they seek increased resources to fuel their economies or recolonize land to feed their populations. African heritages are in harm's way.

Gateway of Greece and Turkey

While we often consider Greece to be European and Turkey as Asian, these two countries share cultural history. Hellenistic Greece maintained sway over the Mideast through Alexander's conquests. Developments in arts, sports, and mathematical inquiry flourished throughout the later Arab and Palestinian nations, returned to

Europe through Moorish invasions in the Dark Ages. Although the Ottoman Empire reacquired the bulk of the Mid-East, basic cultural attitudes remain. The differences lie in religious preferences—differences which still lay waste to these populations through rebellion and revolution. Any armed conflict, whether internal or external, energizes not only these two nations but also the shaky Balkan states to the north and the conspicuously militant Arab countries to the south. As Jordan teeters under new leadership, a plunge into Turkey's heart, through covert Arab groups, raises the specter of a bloody, devastating, and protracted war. To preserve the integrity of Europe and the Orient, should the war come to pass, four continents will suffer unspeakable human losses.

Mundane Natalogy

Republic of Argentina
August 24, 1994, 12:00 am BZD, Buenos Aires.

People's Republic of China
September 20, 1954, 12:00 am CCT, Beijing.

Great Britain
December 25, 1066, 12:00 pm GMT, London (Julian Calendar).

Republic of France
October 4, 1958, 12:00 am CET, Paris.

United States of America
March 4, 1789, 12:13:12 am LMT, New York City.

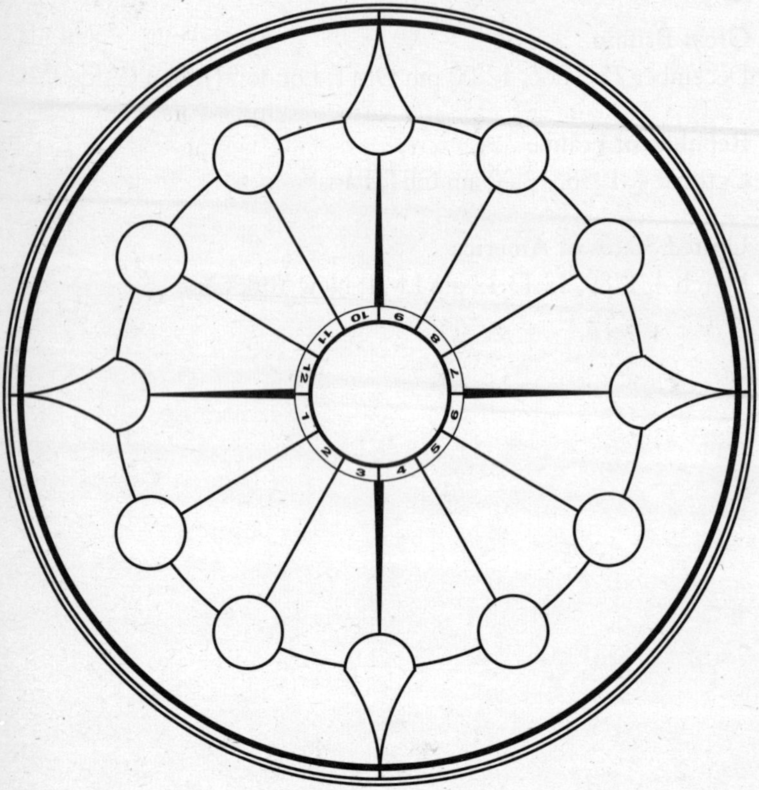
1
2
3
4
5
6
7
8
9
10
11
12

Activities Ruled by the Planets

To check aspects for the activity you have in mind, find the planet that rules it.

Sun: Advertising, buying, selling, speculating, short trips, meeting people, anything involving groups or showmanship, putting up exhibits, running fairs and raffles, growing crops, health matters.

Moon: Any small change in routine, asking favors, borrowing or lending money, household activities such as baking, canning, cooking, washing, ironing, cleaning, and taking care of small children.

Mercury: Bargaining, bookkeeping, dealing with literary agents, publishing, filing, hiring employees, learning languages, literary work, placing ads, preparing accounts, studying, telephoning, visiting friends.

Venus: Amusement, beauty care, courtship, dating, decorating homes, designing, getting together with friends, household improvements, planning parties, shopping.

Mars: Good for all business matters, mechanical affairs, buying or selling animals, dealing with contractors, hunting, studying.

Jupiter: Activities involving charity, education, or science, correspondence courses, self-improvement, reading, researching, studying.

Saturn: Anything involving family ties or legal matters such as wills and estates, taking care of debts, dealing with lawyers, financing, joint money matters, real estate, relations with older people.

Uranus: Air travel, all partnerships, changes and adjustment, civil rights, new contacts, new ideas, new rules, patenting inventions, progress, social action, starting journeys.

Neptune: Advertising, dealing with psychological upsets, health foods and resorts, large social affairs, nightclubs, psychic healing, travel by water, restaurants, visits, welfare, working with institutions.

Pluto: Anything dealing with energy and enthusiasm, skill and alertness, personal relationships, original thought.

Planetary Business Guide

Collections: Try to make collections on days when your Sun is well aspected. Avoid days when Mars or Saturn are aspected. If possible, the Moon should be in a cardinal sign: Aries, Cancer, Libra, or Capricorn. It is more difficult to collect when the Moon is in Taurus or Scorpio.

Employment, Promotion: Choose a day when your Sun is favorably aspected or the Moon is in your Tenth House. Good aspects of Venus or Jupiter to your Tenth House are also beneficial.

Loans: Moon in the first and second quarters favors the lender; Moon in the third and fourth quarters favors the borrower. Good aspects of Jupiter or Venus to the Moon are favorable to both, as is Moon in Leo, Sagittarius, Aquarius, or Pisces.

New Ventures: Things usually get off to a better start during the increase of the Moon. If there is impatience, anxiety, or deadlock, it can often be broken at the Full Moon. Agreements can be reached then.

Partnerships: Agreements and partnerships should be made on a day that is favorable to both parties. Mars, Neptune, Pluto, and Saturn should not be square or opposite the Moon. It is best to make an agreement or partnership when the Moon is in a mutable sign, especially Gemini or Virgo. The other signs are not favorable, with the possible exception of Leo or Capricorn. Begin partnerships when the Moon is increasing in light, as this is a favorable time for starting new ventures.

Public Relations: The Moon rules the public, so this must be well-aspected, particularly by the Sun, Mercury, Uranus, or Neptune.

Selling: In general, selling is favored by good aspects of Venus, Jupiter, or Mercury to the Moon. Afflictions of Saturn retard. If you know the planetary ruler of your product, try to get this well-aspected by Venus, Jupiter, or the Moon. Your product will be more highly valued then.

Signing Important Papers: Sign contracts or agreements when the Moon is increasing in a fruitful sign. Avoid days when Mars, Saturn, Neptune, or Pluto are afflicting the Moon. Don't sign anything if your Sun is badly afflicted.

Planetary Associations

Sun: Authority figures, favors, advancement, health, success, display, drama, promotion, fun, matters related to Leo and the Fifth House.

Moon: Short trips, women, children, the public, domestic concerns, emotions, fluids, matters related to Cancer and the Fourth House.

Mercury: Communications, correspondence, phone calls, computers, messages, education, students, travel, merchants, editing, writing, advertising, signing contracts, siblings, neighbors, kin, matters related to Gemini, Virgo, and the Third and Sixth Houses.

Venus: Affection, relationships, partnerships, alliances, grace, beauty, harmony, luxury, love, art, music, social activity, marriage, decorating, cosmetics, gifts, income, matters related to Taurus, Libra, and the Second and Seventh Houses.

Mars: Strife, aggression, sex, physical energy, muscular activity, guns, tools, metals, cutting, surgery, police, soldiers, combat, confrontation, matters related to Aries, Scorpio, and the First and Eighth Houses.

Jupiter: Publishing, college education, long-distance travel, foreign interests, religion, philosophy, forecasting, broadcasting, publicity, expansion, luck, growth, sports, horses, the law, matters related to Sagittarius, Pisces, and the Ninth and Twelfth Houses.

Saturn: Structure, reality, the laws of society, limits, obstacles, tests, hard work, endurance, real estate, dentists, bones, teeth, matters related to Capricorn, Aquarius, and the Tenth and Eleventh Houses.

Uranus: Astrology, the New Age, technology, computers, modern gadgets, lecturing, advising, counseling, inventions, reforms, electricity, new methods, originality, sudden events, matters related to Aquarius and the Eleventh House.

Neptune: Mysticism, music, creative imagination, dance, illusion, sacrifice, service oil, chemicals, paint, drugs, anesthesia, sleep, religious experience, matters related to Pisces and the Twelfth House.

Pluto: Probing, penetration, goods of the dead, investigation, insurance, taxes, other people's money, loans, the masses, the underworld, transformation, death, matters related to Scorpio and the Eighth House.

About the Authors

Stephanie Clement, Ph.D., is an accomplished astrologer with twenty-five years of professional experience. She has written numerous magazine articles and several books, most recently, *Charting Your Career* (Llewellyn, 1999).

Alice DeVille has been a consulting astrologer, metaphysician, and writer for more than 25 years. Alice develops and conducts workshops, seminars, and lectures on a variety of subjects. You may reach Alice via e-mail at DeVilleAA@aol.com.

Marguerite Elsbeth is a professional tarot and astrology reader, and a practitioner of Nativism (American Indian healing) as well as European healing methods. Elsbeth is the author of *Crystal Medicine*, and coauthor of *The Silver Wheel: Women's Myths and Mysteries in the Celtic Tradition*, with Kenneth Johnson.

Sasha Fenton has been reading hands, cards, and horoscopes since childhood, and she eventually teamed her talents with her writing ability to become the author of 23 books and 5 years worth of annual horoscope guides (total sales of over 5 million copies worldwide)—with more in the pipeline!

Therese Francis, Ph.D., is the author of *Age of Aquarius Astrology Game & Divination System*, *20 Herbs to Take Outdoors*, and *The Mercury Retrograde Book*. Dr. Francis teaches astrology, numerology, and shamanic techniques throughout the country. She has a private astrology practice in Santa Fe, New Mexico.

Dorothy Oja is a career astrologer with twenty-eight years of experience, offering full-spectrum astrological counseling through her practice MINDWORKS Her specialties include timing/electional work and composite/Davison relationship analysis. Contact her by e-mail at DOja96@aol.com.

Leeda Alleyn Pacotti embarked on metaphysical self-studies at the age of fourteen. Her career encompassed antitrust law, international treaties, and governmental management. She now plies a gentle practice as a naturopathic physician, master herbalist, and certified nutritional counselor.

David Pond is a national speaker and has been a full-time professional astrologer since 1976. He is the author of *Chakras for Beginners* (Llewellyn, 1999) and *The Art of Relationships* (ACS, 2000). He can be reached at his website: www.Reflectingpond.com.

Kaye Shinker, C.A.-NCGR, teaches financial astrology at the Online College of Astrology, www.astrocollege.com. She serves on the NCGR Board of Examiners. A former teacher, she and her husband own race horses and travel around the United States in an RV.

Joanne Wickenburg is the author of several books on astrology and has designed the internationally distributed Correspondence Course in Astrology. She is the chair of Kepler College, the first degree-granting college of astrology. She can be reached at her website: web3.foxinternet.net/jwickenburg.